Culture, Thought, and Social Action

Culture, Thought, and Social Action

An Anthropological Perspective

Stanley Jeyaraja Tambiah

Harvard University Press
Cambridge, Massachusetts, and London, England   1985

This book is printed on acid-free paper, and its binding
materials have been chosen for strength and durability.

Library of Congress Cataloging in Publication Data

Tambiah, Stanley Jeyaraja, 1929–
  Culture, thought, and social action.

  Bibliography: p.
  Includes index.
  1.   Rites and ceremonies.   2.   Folk
classification.   3.   Ethnophilosophy.   I.   Title.
GN473.T36   1985   306   84-27927
ISBN 0-674-17969-2 (alk. paper)

For Mary Wynne, Jonathan, and Matthew

Acknowledgments

I would like to thank the following people for their constructive comments and editorial help: Dan Rosenberg in the preparation of the introduction; Monique Djokic, Dan Rosenberg, and Michael Rhum in the preparation of Chapter 9; and Mitzi Goheen and Dan Rosenberg in the preparation of the conclusion. I am also indebted to Karl Lamberg-Karlovsky, director of the Peabody Museum at Harvard, for placing at my disposal the professional services of the museum's Illustration Department. Last but not least, I gratefully acknowledge the invaluable typing and secretarial assistance provided by Jane Trahan and Susan Rosenburg.

Contents

Culture, Thought, and Social Action

Introduction

From the General to the Particular and the Construction of Totalities

This book contains a selection of essays that I wrote between 1967 and 1984, a period of seventeen years. I chose these particular essays because they represent a sustained and developing discussion over time of a set of interrelated themes and issues.

The essays devoted to the interpretation of ritual are united in that they address these themes in both reiterated and variant ways. A great deal of anthropological writing has been concerned with elaborating the classical tripartite scheme set out by van Gennep (in terms of the phases of separation, liminality, and reaggregation); the foremost contributor in this vein in modern times was Victor Turner. My own preoccupations have led me to elaborate the implications of rituals as amalgams or totalities constituted of both word and deed, of speech interlaced with the manipulation of objects, of a simultaneous and sequential use of multiple media of communication (auditory, tactile, visual, and olfactory) and of presentational modes (song, dance, music, recitations, and so on). Another entailment of this approach was the openness to and search for patterns and rules of combination, sequencing, recursiveness, and redundancy that make up the totality, and that cannot be discovered by a too formulaic addiction to the tripartite scheme (which may be illuminating in some but not all cases).

A second and more encompassing aspiration has been to unite semantic and pragmatic, inner and outer frames of meaning, to wed "structural" analysis of the kind stemming from Saussurean structural linguistics to the implications of "performative" speech acts as developed by Austin, and of "indexical" signs as dissected by Peirce.

Another way of phrasing the idea of semantic and pragmatic features riding on the same forms and components of ritual is as follows: if rituals, wherever enacted, tend to have certain recognizable paradigmatic structural features and syntagmatic arrangements of form, to what extent can these be attributed, on the one side, to their being integrally linked to a culture's or society's central collective valuations and preferences (that is, its "cosmological" constructs and a priori) and, on the other side, to their being task-oriented and power/prestige-conferring enactments in human situations and contexts (that is, their "uses" within a "form of life" in the Wittgensteinian sense)? Perhaps the phrase "performative blueprints"—to coin still another label—conveys the conjunction of semantic and pragmatic features, and of thought and action, that occurs in rituals.

The interpretive forays also brought into focus for me a tangle that has puzzled me—namely, how to understand the "efficacy" of ritual acts. I have become increasingly hostile to attempts that place ritual acts, including that problematical entity which writers have (loosely) labeled "magic," solely or mainly within the framework of "causality." Such an approach entails declaring something "true" or "false" in terms of verification rules as postulated in positivist science—or even in terms of Popper's criterion of "falsifiability," and his conventionalist thesis that universal statements "are never derivable from singular statements, but can be contradicted by singular statements" (Popper, 1968: 41). A Popper-influenced notion of "rationality" and scientific vigilance has been happily embraced by anthropologists of a neo-Tylorian persuasion—such as Robin Horton—who view belief systems as the primary feature of religious life, and subject these beliefs to tests of logical coherence and testability in a causal mode, to the exclusion of understanding the performative logic of ritual action in its own terms. I have myself progressively moved away from such a science-inspired monolithic notion of "rationality," which as a mode of thought—most explicitly developed and explored in the West—is a "dominant" dogma at this time of our world history. Instead I have been attracted by the idea that human beings anywhere and everywhere are simultaneously in their actions involved in two modalities, the modality of causality and the modality of performative acts. The efficacy or validity of the latter rests on social conventions different from those accepted by the scientific community practicing the natural sciences and accepted on trust by the laity in general. Of course the degree of explicitness and self-consciousness of these modalities, their relative weighting, centrality, and hierarchical ordering, may differ from culture to culture, or between social segments within the same society, and within the same civilization at different points in time. Although modern science as a self-conscious and reflexive method of making knowledge has been, since the Enlightenment, a European achievement, we cannot deny the premoderns who have practiced systematic agriculture, sophisticated arts and crafts, and sailed the seas an awareness of causal relations. Can we unambiguously separate human acts into one or the other type? And are there "mixed" acts which are "technical-causal" in their objective but "performative" in their communicative patterning and vice versa? If so, how are we to interpret their dual patterning and the nature of their efficacy? Such questions are better dealt with once we accept "technical" acts and "ritual" acts as different kinds of conventional acts, and once we renounce the imperial claim that the best way to understand all congeries of ideas or beliefs is by testing how far they constitute logically coherent systems whose purpose is the explanation of events in the "causal" mode of predictions and empirical proof.

The essays pertaining to ritual show how cosmologies are embodied in ritual action. In the second part of the book I deal with classifications and cosmologies in their own right. Classifications and cosmologies have been, as is well known, a central anthropological interest, the foremost exponents being members of the *Année Sociologique* school, particularly Durkheim and Mauss, and their successors.

In a general sense, I mean by "classification" some kind of structured system of categories, most of them verbalized, constructing and labeling some universe of things, beings, events, or actions.

Cosmologies (and I include cosmogonies under this rubric) are the classifications of the most encompassing scope. They are frameworks of concepts and relations which treat the universe or cosmos as an ordered system, describing it in terms of space, time, matter, and motion, and peopling it with gods, humans, animals, spirits, demons, and the like. Cosmogonies consist usually of accounts of the creation and generation of the existing order of phenomena, explaining their character and their place and function in the scheme.

Cosmologies (and cosmogonies) nearly always, and classifications frequently, tend to be viewed as enduring arrangements of things and persons, their underlying premises and initial ordering seen either as having an existence outside the flux of ordinary and everyday changing events and expectations, or as motivating and generating to some degree the surface everyday phenomena of the present time. There could be, as Max Weber pointed out, different answers of variable logical and explanatory adequacy to the problems of theodicy and suffering and other existential worries.

Be that as it may, what I want particularly to emphasize is that a classification as a system of categories in the first place *describes* the world, and that this description usually also implies and entails evaluations and moral premises and emotional attitudes, translated into taboos, preferences, prescriptions, and proscriptions. Imperatives are thus related to indicatives, and the actors who subscribe to particular classifications and cosmologies ordinarily (unless they are comparativists such as anthropologists, moral philosophers, or some other intellectual breed) accept them as given in "nature," and as the "natural" way the world is ordered.[1]

Thus, I chose the words "thought and action" to signal the thesis that the cosmologies and classificatory schemes I am dealing with are thought as well as lived. They are not only contemplated but also translated into practices. They are designs for living.

And in employing and living them, the actors—who are after all distinguished by name, status, gender, and expectations—always act in situational contexts. In doing so, they face and work through certain anomalies and contingencies of a semantic and pragmatic nature. Classifications and cosmologies—to adapt Kuhn to my purposes—are after all "paradigms," in that they are frequently schemes that provide "model problems and solutions to the community of practitioners" (Kuhn, 1968: x).

The encoding and enactment of classifications and cosmologies as performative blueprints and exemplars inevitably generate puzzles, anomalies, liminal categories, vacant and fuzzy spaces, which may be seen as requiring correctives and avoidances or as enabling creative constructions and transformations. Since this issue crops up in the individual essays on Thai animal categories, Hindu caste segments, and Trobriand sex and gender divisions, let me make a synthesizing statement to cover these and other cases.

In disaggregating the issue, I will make use of Frege's distinction between "sense" and "reference." By the "sense" of a term in a classificatory scheme I mean its place in a system of relationships with other component terms. In Saussurean fashion, I will say that these terms or components of classification derive their meaning and value from contrastive, overlapping, and hierarchical relationships within a lexical universe. It is an empirical question as to how and to what degree these particular contrastive sets are closed or fuzzy, and intersect with other sets, but here I will stick to the ideal case of a classification that enjoys closure in certain well defined contexts of application.

By "reference" I mean the things in the world out there that the terms of classification or cosmology "name" or "designate." According to the classical Saussurean formulation, each language imposes a specific *form* on the a priori undifferentiated *substance* of the content plane. This way of looking at the matter necessarily sets up a dialectic between the sense and referential axes of a classification scheme, and gives rise to problems which are difficult to sort out and relate. On the one hand it is held that the semantic distinctions that are made in different languages and cultures concerning a problem area are not necessarily isomorphic—that indeed, different languages and cultures may cut up the substance of the content plane quite differently. But this "relativity" becomes possible to contemplate by virtue of a comparison that accepts a commensurability. This commensurability is that the lexical items of classifications are taken to refer to *fields* or *domains* that are labeled "kinship," "colors," "plants," "animals," "status orders," and so on.

As is well known, some of the most contentious debates in recent anthropology have raged around the issue of what is signified by such named fields or domains. Is it meaningful or realistic or defensible to talk of semantic structure as the imposition of form upon an underlying substance common to all languages and cultures?

The domain of color is relatively uncomplicated for purposes of explication. It is generally thought that the "color" words of any language subdivide the color spectrum into segments. At the level of a physiology of vision, no doubt, modern science can claim that all (normal) human beings are capable of seeing and discriminating between the same colors on the basis of hue, luminosity, and saturation. In a narrow experimental way, Munsell color chips can be presented to a cross-cultural sample of subjects who can, or can be taught to, make roughly similar sequential segmental discriminations.[2] But we well know not only that different cultures produce dissimilar color vocabularies, but also that the uses and meaning of colors differ in cultures and societies (and internally within them if they are differentiated complexes). Portions of the color code—such as black, white, and red, which are related in basic oppositions at the level of the physiology of vision—could be used by cultures to signal quite different meanings (Sahlins, 1976). Or to put it differently, certain structures of thought —binary, triadic, pentadic, and so forth—that employ an ensemble of colors can be used to convey complex messages at the substantive level. As Peirce taught us, an interpretant could become the basis for another superimposed on it, and thus progressively meanings are piled up and their networks extended in an open-ended and creative way. Moreover, single colors such as purple, the royal color in a Western setting, and ocher, the renouncer's color in Asia, may enjoy a special focal status and be instantly recognized and saluted by different actors. In short, cultures will differ in their use of color coding in dress, ceremonials, and public life, in order to express and motivate varieties of polyvalent meanings. Thus, the meaning of color for the members of a culture or society is equivalent to discovering, tracing, interpreting the cognitive-affective-evaluative salience of their color schemata for their statuses, roles, actions, and collective representations. In the way in which I have spelled out the issue, human universals at the level of physiology of color vision, and cultural diversity at the level of meaning and use of color, are not contradictory but quite consistent and interrelated. And this vast space between the deterministic role of physiological and genetic coding and the open-ended pole of diverse cultural creativity and patterning could be divided among disciplines and specialties with their different objects of study. For me, the anthropological task *par excellence* is to constitute the totality of meaning at the collective cultural and sociological planes, and therefore I find the passage from the general (of human universals) to the particular (of sociocultural totalities) all-absorbing.

Anthropologists of our time—such as Conklin, Berlin, Bulmer, and their predecessors—have made important contributions to the careful study of ethnoclassifications of flora and fauna. Lévi-Strauss celebrated such achievements with scintillating theorizing in *The Savage Mind*. Others like Leach and Douglas have extended and embellished this theorizing. It is clear from the documentation that native classifications frequently take the form of levels of taxa arranged hierarchically. It is therefore tempting to compare these schemes with the species (and subspecies), genus, family, and other labeled levels pertaining to Western Linnaean-type taxonomies. Using the concepts of sense and reference, one can say that a folk taxonomy comprises an interrelated and more or less hierarchically ordered sense system, and that it also simultaneously refers to a domain or domains in the world of living things.

Let us now limit ourselves to zoological schemes. Since animals are at some level "other" than that of humans, whose connections with them are conceived in varying degrees and intensities of separation and affinity, it is relevant to ask to what extent folk taxonomies reflect the "objective" features of size, color, form, motion, habitat, and so forth in the animal domain that are potentially recognizable by all humans, and therefore capable of being reflected in all taxonomies as their universal substratum.

In this regard it is interesting that students of taxonomy such as Bulmer (for purposes of explication he will serve as my exemplar here) have boldly claimed that in New Guinea, people like the Karam show in their lower-level taxa an awareness of certain "natural" attributes and of "discontinuities" between groups that are objectively coded in the natural world. They therefore see these taxa as equivalent to the "species" in Western scientific classification. Thus, Bulmer has surmised: "One generalization that has to be considered is that species-like units which contrast in multiple dimensions of morphology and behavior are basic to zoological folk-taxonomies," and that this observation tallies with the observations of Simpson and Lévi-Strauss that folk taxonomies can be highly rational or rationalized systems which reflect "the objectivity and obviousness of discontinuities between very many species in a particular geographical region" (Bulmer and Menzies, 1972: 472–473).

Be this as it may, what is marvelously interesting and triggers the anthropologist's detective impulses is the fact that all folk taxonomies of animals become more and more distinctive and nonisomorphic as the taxonomic classes ascend to higher levels. For at the higher level of primary taxa the division into classes bears the imprint and the influence of a community's other orders of valuation—sexual, dietary, religious, or other—as indeed these orders themselves, in reciprocal action, use the "sensory" and "objective" properties of the animals to image and mediate that community's existential puzzles and contingencies.

My essay on Thai animal classification, "Animals Are Good to Think and Good to Prohibit," is concerned with certain issues relating to the higher levels of taxa. It is by now part of conventional anthropological wisdom that animal classifications are intimately associated with rules of eating (whether they concern preferred ceremonial festive diet or tabooed or fast-restricted food), and that in many cultures eating and dietary rules are associated with sexual intercourse and rules regarding mating. As a matter of fact, systematic studies usually show that even other orders or domains of categorization—such as physical cum social space (closely related to social intimacy and distance, formality and informality)—are also dialectically involved.

This is what Bulmer confirms: "Classification being a human activity, all classification starts with man. His perceptions of discontinuities in nature and of the relationships between the groups of phenomena he discerns in nature, and himself, are not only governed by his sensory capacities, but in part conditioned by the way he sees his own body, its products, and his most significant social relationships" (1975: 303).[3] Thus, Bulmer's richest exegeses concern, among other things, the implications of the three primary taxa of the Karam—*kmn* ("game animals," whose most important signification is "the ritual status these enjoy as food"), *kopyak* (applied to all rats "found in or near homesteads, graves, latrines, and other unclean places") and *as* (which includes frogs and "applies to the residue of marsupials and rodents . . . with ritual and culinary status intermediate between *kmn* and *kopyak*"). The "mystical" notions, totemic links, fears, hatreds, and efficacies attached to various animals in the taxonomy are indicative of its cognitive salience, affective charge, and intellectual relevance in the life of the Karam people.

Let me by way of summation make three central points regarding such animal classifications as blueprints that are thought and lived. The schemes per se as relational paradigmatic systems, and in their actual application or reference to the animal creatures in situational contexts, inevitably give rise to anomalies in the form of overlaps, composite forms, unclear identities, and residues. But how a particular set of actors will consider these puzzles cannot be deduced from the scheme per se—or rather cannot be deduced except insofar as the moral and social valuations that are embedded in the seemingly "zoological" classes are taken into account. Whether the product of a particular "mixed" union is regarded as eminently "with the hair" or disastrously "against the hair," as in the Indian caste system, or whether a "liminal" animal is to be repudiated as inauspicious (as in the case of the Thai otter) or acclaimed as supra-auspicious (as in the case of the Lele pangolin) or peculiarly multivalent (the Karam cassowary's not being a "bird" comes to mind), is mainly a function of the cultural valuation of their sensory properties as these are linked to the larger context of total cultural design. Three essays in this collection—those on Thai animal classification, on Indian caste categories, and on Trobriand cosmology—explicate the logic of different modes of handling anomalies and liminal entities.

A second feature of animal classification which I emphasize as part of its significance as performative blueprint is the actual use of both the verbal phonic and metaphorical resonances of names in ritual speech, and the culturally coded physical and sensory properties of whole animals, or their body parts and their body products,[4] in ritual action in order to remedy the breaking of taboos, or to intensify the bonds of marriage, or to bind together parties to a gift exchange, or to reconcile disputants and enemies. In this way classificatory ideas are translated into practices, and social ethics are implemented as disciplined commitments.

Finally, the question "What is the meaning of animals in a particular culture or society?" cannot be answered without a completed total analysis—of how a particular classification dialectically relates to other such schemes, of how they are inflected by the total institutional structure and the contours of the entire system of collective representations, and of how animals enter into the social practices and cultural concerns of a people in their lives, in both everyday and extraordinary events.

It is difficult to stretch a semantic net for the vexed subject of kinship in the same way as I have done for the topic of color categories and animal classification, from the pole of human universals to the terminus of cultural and social diversity. It seems to me that the "componential" theorists' assumption of an invariant language and culture-independent "genealogical" grid onto which any society's basic kin terms are mapped is untenable. In fact it grants privileged status to a European "biological" episteme. The "sociobiological" tenets of atomistic, individualistic "maximizing of reproductive success" and of "inclusive fitness" as the keys to mating strategies have scarcely decoded and illuminated the logic of diverse kinship classifications, marriage preferences and prescriptions, and so forth that make up the data base for the cultural or social anthropologist.

The path which componential analysts of kinship terms have taken and the destination they have reached are instructive. On the one hand these analysts have first tried to disaggregate the ultimate or elementary semantic components of kinship terms, and then taken the fateful and unproved step of linking them to a "genealogical" framework that is considered, despite its folk dressing, to be ultimately language- and culture-independent, and therefore universal to all humans as an a priori. But when they have confronted the issue of the logic by which the elementary terms have been "extended" to larger classes and ranges, and the issue of the very marked differences between classification terminologies across cultures, they have been forced to appeal to sociological and cultural factors—that is, to the contours and emphases and patterning of the historically constructed and open-ended sociocultural system or totality, in which the kinship terminology and the kinship system are embedded. This is why the work of the componential theorists, even if it has formally extracted certain linguistic rules and elicited certain transformational and reductive strings embedded in terms, has run into a cul-de-sac, not only because these rules and strings may have no cognitive validity for the actors but also—and more importantly—because they have their *raison d'être* not in a genealogical underpinning, but in the larger institutional and cultural totality which encompasses them.

The journey embarked upon by those cultural anthropologists who have criticized the componentialists is initially more attractive and sympathetic to anthropologists who emphasize the cultural construction of reality, and see the semantic maps and categorical systems devised by each culture as conventional and potentially incommensurable. But from this position, two options are open to the cultural relativists. One is to argue rigorously to a conclusion that may be anarchistic and solipsistic. In insisting that different cultures may construct their kinship universes differently, and that therefore no cross-cultural comparisons of, say, particular descent structures or marriages are admissible or feasible because the phenomena can be semantically incommensurable, they will also have thrown out kinship itself as a meaningful subject of general study. Thus, the issue of kinship would have been raised, nursed, and worried over only in order to be dissolved. A radical relativist would hold that no *translation* between cultures or societies is possible, for there might exist no comparable entities at all.

But, happily, many of the "cultural" symbolic practitioners do spend much time mapping and glossing one culture's categories and structures onto another's, in terms of a third (usually Western) language. This very process of translation and matching necessarily implies some assumed common bridgehead, some sharing of space, without which the interpretive project and translation of cultures is impossible. This circumstance inevitably suggests that we cannot prematurely throw away the idea of certain domains as universally shared spaces which individual cultures may plough, cultivate, and delimit differently. But these virgin spaces themselves may play a minor and restricted role in the total meaning and significance that kinship classifications and cosmologies may have for the life of the people who raised them as their man-made gardens upon those virgin grounds.

At the present stage of the debate about kinship, it is salutary to begin with a few general empirical observations which might point to some basic existential constraints, needs, and requirements that affect all humans as *social* beings. There is no pristine biology of man untouched and uninflected by cultural codes and social existence. It is therefore true of every society about which we have adequate information that it has created sociocultural arrangements pertaining to mating patterns, to householding and coresidence, to infant care and socialization of the young, and so on. Such evidence suggests that the "initial" situation of kinship, its substance planes, and its initial constraints are located in this space, though of course mankind had already, as far back as we know, devised nonuniform culture- or society-specific patterns to meet these existential tasks. We know full well that although constraints cannot be flouted, and although they set certain restrictions, they do not dictate the final outcomes. What is more important, these outcomes do much more than the minimum requirements set by the constraints. Hence the richness of culture and the complexity of our social lives. We may label the foregoing existential tasks and constraints, and responses to them, as the sociological grounding for kinship as a sociocultural (not an innate "biological") phenomenon. If we cannot logically grant some such domain of existential tasks and solutions as the *initial point of reference* for kinship, we shall have to resign ourselves to dissolving kinship altogether as an object of general anthropological study.

The general aspect of kinship systems anywhere is their resort to certain elementary contrastive and complementary structures—dyadic, triadic, quadratic, pentradic—for arranging and relating persons who are, as the case may be, "blood" kin, or who share "substance," or who "give and take women," and so on, as each culture may formulate its ideology of connections and relations. Kin concepts distribute "kin" in a field of structured relations, and this distribution is in terms of a culture-specific design, a design which both as a conceptual system at the level of "sense," and in application to empirical persons at the level of "reference," will generate its own anomalies, overlappings, and manipulations.

But once again, the uses and meaning of kinship are exhausted only when we have recognized its patterned ramifications for the larger society's political economic and religious structures, its relative weight and centrality within these configurations, and the nature of its assimilation to the entire social formation and cultural totality. Moreover, we are unlikely to recognize why certain anomalies, puzzles, manipulations, taboos, and avoidances occur in "kinship" structures, unless we are able to see how the larger sociocultural totality and its value emphases and weighted interests inflect, intervene in, and leave their imprint on the classificatory logic.

The explication of these ramifications is the essential constructive task of the anthropologists of kinship: here among the Tallensi how lineage and clan structure fan out to fill the political-jural arena; there among the Kachin how asymmetrical matrilateral cross-cousin marriage aligns alliance relations between wife givers and wife takers, and how these kinship features fuse with the hierarchy of chiefship, land tenure, ancestral spirit cults, and so on to constitute a distinctive and dynamic social formation; and still again, there in another place in north India how notions of descent, residence, and correct marriage via hypergamous strategies and conceptions of purity and impurity, auspiciousness and inauspiciousness, participate in a system of caste dominance and subordination in a region.

My advocacy of these procedures and objectives of study at the present time carries this entailment: that although anthropologists may provisionally identify classificatory systems or conceptual systems in a number of societies that are focused on an ostensive domain or field, it is more rewarding, in the light of the discipline's previous problem-ridden and low-yielding comparisons of partial structures between societies, to engage in a total analysis than in fragmentary formalism. This involves the dialectical and recursive interrelating of particular classifications—of color, flora and fauna, kin terms, gender attributions, and social ranks—with one another and with the total social formation and its collective representatives. Some of the essays in this collection exemplify this interweaving of parts and the whole.

Partial analyses across societies in the mode of fragmentary formalism are fraught with problems for two reasons. Take kinship as an example. One reason is that general "analytical" concepts such as "descent," "marriage," "filiation," "exogamy," "bridewealth," and so on cannot be taken to be neutral, abstract, nontendentious concepts that can be easily employed in the translation of cultures. These concepts, which have become the tool kit of anthropology over the decades, are useful only insofar as we can demonstrate two things: first, that they represent nodes for cultural structuring of relations and interconnections regarding procreation, householding, coresidence, which serve as the "referential" substance plane of kinship; second, that the anthropologist has imaged each culture's own formulations, constructs, and emphases from within, and only thereafter mapped them onto these general nodes. Each portrait of a society therefore will be a palimpsest, and comparison ought to consist of looking at the overlapping and distinctive spreads of a number of such palimpsests of different societies that are superimposed on one another.

Partial cross-cultural analyses are also problematic because the phenomena that are usually chosen for comparison—whether "descent groups" or "marriage patterns" or "polygamy" or "polyandry"—do not constitute bounded or self-contained systems. Artificially imposed boundaries also result in privileging restricted meanings. Similar caveats and cautions apply to other partial comparisons. For example, in the case of flora and fauna, one must be vigilant about the cavalier use of comparative hierarchical taxonomic concepts—such as species, genus, family, and so on—derived from Linnaean precedents.

My proposal also turns away from any attempt to formulate a universalistic and deterministic scheme of evolution of culture and society. I prefer "cultures" and "societies" and "forms of life" to "Culture" and "Society" in the singular, and therefore seek to constitute historical configurations and historical totalities as open-ended crystallizations over time. In recent anthropology it is the "neo-Marxists" or "structural Marxists" who have emphatically held fast to the ambition of describing such total social formations. I applaud them, while rejecting their version of an invariant universal determinism that assigns to the system of "production" as infrastructure a privileged and nonnegotiable ultimate status. Like proverbial sectarians, they exhibit virtuoso sophistry and polemical infighting in trying to fit the contours of noncapitalist and preindustrial societies to their molds. And not even revisionist concessions such as the possibility of multilinear evolutionary chains, or of kinship functioning as both infrastructure and superstructure are of avail, for such ploys are neither economical nor objective solutions to the problem of cultural and social diversity. In this collection I offer the essays "The Galactic Polity" and "The Theater State in Southeast Asia" as attempts at totalization in which I have tried to steer clear of the Scylla of dialectical materialism and the Charydbis of symbolic transcendentalism.

The systematic and imaginative assembling of total sociocultural formations according to their emphases and valuations would open up for anthropology a kind of comparative study that so far has been indifferently or inadequately accomplished—namely, the comparison of the profiles, centers of gravity, and hierarchical orderings of total formations, and the substantive sites which they choose for their greatest elaborations and richest embellishments. This proposal derives from the implications and results of the essays in this book, which demonstrate that rituals, cosmologies, and classifications entail both thought and action, and that to fully understand their ramifications—their multivalent meanings and multiple uses, the puzzles they pose and the mode of their overcoming, the extent to which they are grounded in human universals and the extent to which they are culturally diverse historical outcomes—they must be dialectically and recursively related to one another and to the larger sociocultural whole.

I

Ritual as Thought and Action

1

The Magical Power of Words

Anthropologists have in recent years become aware of the relevance of linguistics to their theoretical work, and it is remarkable that Malinowski, perhaps more far-sighted than many of his successors, not only saw this relevance but also put forward an ethnographic theory of language which sprang directly from his fieldwork, particularly from his immersion in Trobriand magic.[1]

Malinowski argued that the potency of Trobriand magic was felt by the Trobrianders to lie in words (spells). In many of his works, particularly in volume 2 of *Coral Gardens and Their Magic,* he provided an unusual amount of supporting linguistic data. This evidence has had some influence on linguists, notably J. R. Firth, but it has never been critically examined by anthropologists. Can an anthropologist get more out of the evidence than Malinowski himself managed to, either by resort to comparative material from other cultures or by closer attention to Malinowski's own material?

Although Malinowski's immediate successors who worked in the same or nearby regions confirmed that the verbal component in ritual was important (Fortune, 1963; R. Firth, 1967), the orthodox anthropological approach devalued the role of words in ritual, which was seen as stereotyped behavior consisting of a sequence of nonverbal acts and manipulation of objects. However, recent literature has again shown appreciation of the role of words,[2] and no one today I think will dispute this statement by Leach (1966: 407): "Ritual as one observes it in primitive communities is a complex of words and actions . . . It is not the case that words are one thing and the rite another. The uttering of the words itself is a ritual."

One virtue at least of defining ritual as consisting of the word and the deed is that this formula solves the dilemma posed by Goethe's Faust—whether in the beginning there was the word or the deed. Freud concluded his *Totem and Taboo* with the rhetorical statement that in the beginning was the deed. According to Gellner (1959: 22), linguistic philosophy has unsuccessfully tried to solve the puzzle by saying that "the word *is* a deed." What I find interesting about Faust is that he progressed from the *word* to *thought*, then to the notion of *power*, and ended with the *deed*. These four terms are in fact the ingredients of most ritual systems in which there is a reciprocal relation between the word and the deed, with the other two terms intervening. The formula raises one question that is quantitative in nature: the ratio of words to actions may vary between rituals in the same society (or between societies). At one extreme is the case of rituals performed with words alone, and at the other the case where actions dominate though perhaps words are not excluded. Most rituals fall in between, yet may show distinct differences in the proportion of words to acts. Thus, a healing ritual or an initiation rite may emphasize words whereas a collective rite in which there is mass participation may rely less on auditory communication and more on the display of conspicuous visible material symbols.

In most cases it would appear that ritual words are at least as important as other kinds of ritual act; but besides that, and this is an intriguing point, very often (but not always) if the ethnographer questions his informants, "Why is this ritual effective?" the reply takes the form of a formally expressed belief that the power is in the "words" even though the words become effective only if uttered in a very special context of other action.

In attempting to solve this puzzle, the first point I want to make is that ritual words cannot be treated as an undifferentiated category. Rituals exploit a number of verbal forms which we loosely refer to as prayers, songs, spells, addresses, blessings, and so forth. It is necessary to study whether a ritual is composed of such recognized categories and to analyze their distinctive features in terms of their internal form and their sequence. The fact that such a battery of verbal devices may appear in a single rite should not only give us insights into the art of ritual but also dispel any lingering traces of a Frazerian hangover. Some anthropologists have operated with the concept of "magic" as something different from "religion"; they have thought of "spell" as acting mechanically and as being intrinsically associated with magic; they have opposed "spell" to "prayer," which was thought to connote a different kind of communication with the divine. Frazer carried this thinking to an extreme by asserting that magic was thoroughly opposed to religion, and in the interest of preserving this distinction dismissed half the globe as victims of the "confusion of magic with religion."

It is possible to question the general validity of this dichotomy by demonstrating that in a single class of rituals practiced in Sri Lanka a variety of verbal forms in a particular sequence are used, and that the very logic of the ritual depends on this order and distinction. A Sinhalese healing ritual or exorcism ceremony exploits three main kinds of verbal form[3] which accompany other ritual acts (such as dance, mime, food offerings, and manipulation of objects). They are called *mantra, kannalavva,* and *kaviya,* and they are arranged in a progression of four sequences beginning and ending with the *mantra.*[4] The *mantra* corresponds to the stereotype notion of "spell." It is in prose, it has no poetic structure, it has a characteristic opening and ending (for example, *"ōm namō"* and *"hring").* The *mantra* is muttered by the exorcist and it is not meant to be heard, for it constitutes secret knowledge. The ceremony begins with the recitation of *mantra* which summon the demons responsible for the disease. This summoning is phrased in Sinhalese as "hitting with sound" (*anda gahanavā*), but the language of command is also accompanied by the language of entreaty and persuasion. These spells contain abbreviated allusions to myths and thus prepare the ground for the next sequence.

This sequence is the *kannalavva,* which is chanted aloud in rhythmic prose composed of ordinary intelligible language and is meant to be heard and understood by the participants. The ritual as a public ceremony may be said to begin with the *kannalavva.* It states why the ceremony is being held, describes the nature of the patient's affliction, and makes a plea to the gods to come and bless the ceremony and to the demons to act benevolently and remove the disease. Typically the pleas are accompanied by food offerings.

The next in sequence are the *kaviya* (verses), which take up the major part of the ceremony. *Kaviya* are composed in quatrains with end (and sometimes also beginning) rhymes. Sinhalese *kaviya* are highly lyrical and framed in literary Sinhalese (of the sixteenth to eighteenth centuries), perfectly intelligible yet distinct from contemporary everyday language. They are normally recorded in texts. From the point of view of the dramatic presentation of the ritual, it is important that they be sung loudly to the accompaniment of music and mime. The semantic content of the verses is a long and highly redundant recital of the origin myths of gods and demons and their encounters, in which the demons finally subject themselves to the practice of conditional evil, sanctioned by the deities (*varam*), provided that humans reciprocate by appropriate gift giving. In the rite the myths are sung in order that evil and disease can be defined, objectified, or personified and are presented realistically on the stage so that the appropriate action of changing the undesirable to the desirable—in other words, the act of transfer which changes the condition of the patient, with his unequivocal participation—can take place. The redundancy, lengthy recital, and staging are contrived to achieve that crucial understanding by the patient of his illness which is a necessary prelude to and a condition of the cure.

The ceremony, logically enough, concludes with a *mantra* which enacts the expulsion of the demon itself. Typically this spell concludes: "Just as god so and so by a certain action subdued such and such a demon, by that power may the patient overcome the disease and the demon be subdued." The lexical and semantic contents of the spells present a special problem when compared to the other two forms (invocation and praise songs), which are readily intelligible and heard by the audience. Indologists will be familiar with the literature on the long history of charms and spells—*mantra, dhāranī,* and *parittā*—in Hinduism and Buddhism. Here I will limit myself to the Sinhalese situation.

A prevailing misconception is that Sinhalese *mantra* are unintelligible or even nonsensical.[5] Credibility is lent to this notion by the fact that *mantra* are referred to as the "language of the demons" (*yaksā bāsāva*), as opposed to human language. A linguistic analysis of some recorded and published Sinhalese *mantra* made by Wimal Dissanayake of King's College, Cambridge, shows that they embody a subtle design which uses the notion of a hierarchy of languages. When Hindu gods are invoked and their origin myths referred to, the spells contain Sanskrit expressions—no doubt distorted, from the point of view of the purist. When the Buddha and Buddhist mythological events are alluded to, Pali words are employed, once again portraying syntactical infelicities. When, however, the spell actually narrates an origin myth, the language used is that of the classical Sinhalese literary forms prevalent in the sixteenth and seventeenth centuries. Finally, when demons are directly addressed and commanded, the words are a polyglot mixture and therefore unintelligible, being compounded of Sinhalese, Tamil, Pali, Sanskrit, Malayalam, Telegu, Bengali, and even Persian. This exotic and powerful mixture is the "demon language." Some points can be briefly made concerning the design of these spells. The language stratification is indicative of the hierarchical positions of gods and demons. The "demon language" is consciously constructed to connote power, and though largely unintelligible is nevertheless based on the theory of language that the demons can understand. Thus, far from being nonsensical and indiscriminately concocted, the spells show a sophisticated logic. The logic of construction must of course be separated from the problem of whether the exorcist actually understands all the words contained in the spell. From his, as well as the audience's, point of view, the spells have power by virtue of their secrecy and their capacity to communicate with demons and thereby influence their actions. However, *mantra* do not fall outside the requirements of language as a system of communication, and their literal intelligibility to humans is not the critical factor in understanding their logic.

What I have indicated in this example is that a single Sinhalese ritual progresses from spells which summon the demons to invocation and supplication of the gods and demons, proceeds to myths in verse form which are sung and dramatized, and concludes with a spell which uses the language of command and exorcism. Each type has a characteristic form and content (though this shows redundancy), and this structured sequence is fundamental to the logic which has dictated the construction of the ritual. The verbal forms and their sequence have at least two dimensions. On the one hand they directly correspond to the pantheon, the theology it embodies, including man's interaction with the gods and spirits; and on the other they suggest another logic which relates to the craft of communication whereby patient and participants successfully experience the passage from illness to the promised cure. Furthermore, in this example, it is difficult to see where magic ends and religion begins.

I am of course not suggesting that this Sinhalese example provides a cross-cultural representative scheme, but I am certain that exploitation of different verbal forms arranged in ordered sequence can be found in many complex rituals. Following are some examples. The Stratherns report (personal communication) that the Mount Hageners distinguish between prayer (*atenga*) and spell (*møn*); both may on occasion be combined in different patterns, as for example when a spell may be said to remove a sickness, and then a prayer is made to the ancestral ghosts, accompanied by a sacrifice. Whereas a prayer is an audible invocation and a supplication, the spells are muttered, use the language of command, and employ a series of metaphorical images (see Strathern and Strathern, 1968, for details). Audrey Richards (personal communication) states that Bemba rituals combine prayers and spells which are distinguished as are praise songs and other formal uses of language. Victor Turner reports (1964) that in the Ndembu *ihamba* performance there is mass participation in hunters' cult songs which are sung to "please *ihamba*," followed by a spate of confessions and the airing of grievances, then by the reverent or hortatory prayers made by the doctor and the elders. He comments that all these elements constitute a dialectical and dialogical pattern of activity, but he does not focus his attention on this particular problem of alternating verbal forms and their structured progression. It thus seems to me that there is scope for using this frame of analysis to provide additional illumination in the study of ritual.

Sacred and Profane Language

I would like now to pursue further the question of the intelligibility of sacred words to both officiant and congregation. If sacred words are thought to possess a special kind of power not normally associated with ordinary language, to what extent is this due to the fact that the sacred language as such may be exclusive and different from the secular or profane language?

The role of language in ritual immediately confronts problems if placed in relation to a primary function of language—namely, its function as a vehicle of communication between persons. By definition, the persons in communication must understand one another. In ritual, language appears to be used in ways that violate the communication function. For instance, it is possible to distinguish three different uses of language in the rituals of a village in northeast Thailand.

First, there are rituals conducted by Buddhist monks in which the sacred words are chanted aloud—that is, they are meant to be heard, but paradoxically they are not understood by the majority of the congregation (and by some of the monks themselves) because the sacred language is the dead Pali language. In this case the words are broadcast but not understood.

There is a second set of rituals where again the major feature is the loud recitation of texts, but here the words are understood because the local Lao language is used. The rituals in question are called *sūkhwan*, or "calling the spirit essence." They are used by village elders when installing members of the junior generation in village statuses, or as inaugural or threshold rites before individuals start new enterprises. In this instance, words are broadcast and understood.

In a third set of rites, relating to the exorcism of demons which possess and cause mental disorders, the interrogation of the patient is in the local language but spells are secretly muttered by the exorcist over substances like water which are used to cleanse and purify the patient. Here the virtue of the spells resides in the fact that it is secret knowledge similar to the Sinhalese *mantra*. The language is private and is not meant to be heard. The spells, which are called *gāthā* (verses), are said to be portions of Buddhist *sūtra* (sacred texts) which are in this context used in a special manner, and there is some evidence for saying that the exorcist is an inversion of the Buddhist monk.

The second and third types of ritual represent forms well known to anthropologists. The spirit essence rite shares the character of that class of healing rituals which are constructed on the therapeutic theory that messages are to be transmitted to and understood by the celebrant or patient. The words recited invoke and invite the divine angels (*thewada*), paint the ritual situation as a grand mythological event in which the participants become gods themselves, define status requirements, bind a person to his new role commitments, evoke past experience (especially of early childhood and dependence on parents), and anticipate future events. By contrast, the exorcism ritual uses shock therapy in which the patient is made to confront, formulate, and give objective form to his illness in terms of a demonic agent which is culturally defined. Here the exorcist as protagonist must appear more terrible and powerful than the demon inside the patient, and the secretly muttered spells not only constitute the language the demons can understand, but, more important, contribute to the image of the exorcist's own power.

The first set, the Buddhist rituals, represents a general but baffling situation. The majority of village monks in northeast Thailand (as in many other parts of the country) are young men who only temporarily occupy the status of monk. Their most important role is to conduct calendrical temple rituals for the community as a whole, and mortuary rites and certain other threshold and protection-giving ceremonies for individual families and groups of kin. There are some conspicuous paradoxes in the communication system of Buddhist ritual. The view is emphatic that the Pali chants should be recited aloud and that through listening to them the congregation gains merit, blessings, and protection. Yet the sacred Pali words as such are not understood.[6] The chants are of course not nonsensical—they expound matters of Buddhist doctrine, the noble truths of detachment and conquest of life, and victorious episodes in the Buddha's life, which have no direct relation to the everyday concerns of village life. Yet at the conclusion of the chants, especially those designated as *parittā* (chants of blessing and protection), the blessings transferred by the monk to the layman are long life, good health, and fair complexion. The intriguing paradox is that the conquests of the Buddha which relate to the withdrawal from life are, in the process of transference, transmuted to an affirmation of life. Between the recitation of the sacred words (*sūtra*) and the final "payoff" to the layman intervenes a mechanism of transfer which is not far removed from that implied in the Sinhalese *mantra*. For instance, the *chayamangalagāthā*, the victory blessing so often heard in Buddhist rites, states in each of the stanzas a victory won by the Buddha and concludes, "By this power, may you be endowed with conquests and blessings." The mechanism of transfer depends not only on the semantic structure of the words and the ritual acts that accompany them (for example, transmission of grace through a sacred cord or by sprinkling lustral water) but also on a particular social relation between monk and layman, which connotes an intergenerational reciprocity. Village sons temporarily renounce their virility and sexuality and transfer to elderly householders long life and ethical merit; the latter in turn sponsor the young men's ordination, maintain them in the temple, and, afterward, when they themselves give up their robes, install the young men as their successors (Tambiah, 1968).

The fact that the Buddhist chants are couched in Pali is representative of a more general feature of most of the so-called world religions, which also show the same remarkable disjunction between religious and profane language: Latin in the occidental Catholic Church, Hebrew for Jews, Vedic Sanskrit for Hindus, and Arabic for Muslims are sacred languages that are different from the language of ordinary use. But the nature of the authority attached to the sacred language and its range of exclusiveness show complex variations. The Muslims take up the extreme position that the Koran is efficacious only in its original Arabic and that it will cease to be the Book by being translated. The Jewish attitude to the Biblical texts is the same—the word of God is in Hebrew. On the other hand the Catholics have never maintained that any part of the Bible was originally written in Latin, but it is the case that the official version, the Vulgate, was authorized by the pope as Vicar of God in 1546 at the Council of Trent. This text went through certain revisions in the second half of the sixteenth century to reach a definitive version. But more interestingly, Latin had by A.D. 250 supplanted Greek and become the language of church government and worship in Rome and for the entire Western world, and was explicitly considered the holy language of the occidental church.

In Islam, Hinduism, Buddhism, and Judaism the view has been strictly held that in religious ceremonies the sacred words recited should be in the language of the authorized sacred texts. The problem whether their congregations understood the words or not was not a major consideration affecting either the efficacy of the ritual or the change in the moral condition of the worshippers. The Catholic Church maintained the same view with respect to the Latin liturgy until 1967. It is interesting that many reformist movements which attacked the extreme formalism and ritualism of the established church attempted to destroy the exclusiveness of the sacred language in an attempt to increase accessibility and understanding among the faithful; Lutherans, Calvinists, Waldensians are cases in point. But note that they also attacked the Latin Bible on the grounds that there were older and more genuine Greek versions. There is an important lesson to be learned here. English-speaking evangelical Protestants are often passionately committed to the precise wording of the Biblical text, as it appears in the English of the authorized version of 1611, even though it was authorized, illogically perhaps, by the king. The Buddha used a local dialect in contrast to the Sanskrit of the Brahmans to preach his message, but Pali itself was later to become the enshrined language of Theravada Buddhism. And breakaway churches in turn come to have their true versions and first editions of doctrine around which problems of orthodoxy center and which generate the familiar activities of textual criticism and commentary that provide the bread and butter for theologians and scholars. Thus, in all these cases it could be said that texts tend to acquire authority because they are ancient, but that it is authority that matters more than antiquity.

The question then is: How important is it in unraveling the problem of the power of sacred words that the sacred language be different from the ordinary language? Is there a vital difference in the fact that the Koran is in Arabic and the Trobriand sacred words are in Trobriand? I think the distinction is not absolute but only relative. It is true that in many of these higher religions the sacred language is thought to be that language in which the savior or prophet or saint first revealed the message (or, in the case of Catholicism, to be the language authorized by the papacy). But this argument in terms of revelation or authority is just as applicable to the Trobrianders, who believed that their spells came with their first ancestors, and it therefore provides no distinguishing criterion between higher and primitive religion. Tylor's distinction between revealed and natural religion is false.

A more convincing reason may be that the sacred words of Islam, Buddhism, and the Jewish and Christian faiths at some point came to be written down, and that writing is a revolutionary technology that fixes and freezes religious dogma in a manner that is different from the dogma of oral tradition, which is inevitably flexible and adaptive, even though it believes in an unchanging tradition. But again, is this a fundamental or a relative difference? For the problem that I am dealing with—whence the magical power of sacred words—this distinction again is by itself insufficient. The sharp disjunction between the case of a written holy language and a secular language in higher religion is paralleled in the Trobriands by a weaker disjunction, nevertheless of the same kind, between the elements of archaic or esoteric language in the orally transmitted spells and the language of ordinary use. Many "primitive" peoples who recite their religious mythology in saga form do so in an "archaic" form of speech which is only barely comprehensible to contemporary speakers; this is the case among the Kachin. The point is that as long as religion both in literate or preliterate societies harks back to a period of revelation and insists on the authority of properly transmitted true texts either orally or in written form, its sacred language will contain an archiac component, whether this be represented by a totally different language or older elements of the same language.

It is perhaps relevant to note, whenever we meet such formalized oral or written texts, that their "archaicness" may also be related to the fact that they are composed in a special style, which uses highly symbolic devices, specially coined words, and words without meaning to fill in gaps (Vansina, 1965). Furthermore writing per se, made possible by the alphabet, by giving a physical existence to words, may lend added veneration to written texts. Thus, it is not at all accidental that the present-day term for the major alphabet in India is *Dēvanāgari* ("the abode of the Gods").

Another criterion—that of the degree of specialization and training and differentiation of religious personnel—is again of little value in accounting for the belief in the power of sacred words. It is frequently true that the societies in which the higher religions exist are stratified, that literacy itself is specialized and the vast bulk of the population depends on specially trained intermediaries, and that the professional priesthood is separated from lay occupations and modes of life. But specialized skills, subjection to taboos, and exclusive knowledge of sacred lore are in varying degree characteristic of the religious experts of simpler nonliterate societies as well.

Finally the fact that the Pali chants of Buddhism are normally not strictly understood by the laity but that the language of Trobriand spells is largely intelligible to the Trobrianders has not produced any significant difference in the attitude toward sacred words. This is so because for the Buddhist layman the fact that he does not understand does not mean for him that the chants are mumbo-jumbo. He believes quite rightly that for those who know Pali the words contain great wisdom and sense; his ignorance is a reflection of his unworthiness and involvement in an inferior mode of life compared with that of the monk. I have thus come to the negative conclusion that the remarkable disjunction between sacred and profane language which exists as a general fact is not necessarily linked to the need to embody sacred words in an exclusive language[7] or in writing and, second, that both higher and lower religions portray no qualitative differences with respect to their beliefs in revelation and true knowledge, specialization of religious office, and attitudes to sacred languages whether those languages be understood or not.

It therefore appears necessary to try to formulate a general statement about the widespread belief in the magical power of sacred words. No book on religion or the origins of language fails to refer to this ancient belief in the creative power of the word. It would be possible to confirm this belief in the classical literature. The Vedic hymns speculated on *vāc* ("the word") and asserted that the gods ruled the world through magical formulas; the Parsi religion states that in the battle between good and evil it was through the spoken word that chaos was transformed into cosmos; ancient Egypt believed in a God of the Word; the Semites and the Sumerians have held that the world and its objects were created by the word of God; and the Greek doctrine of *logos* postulated that the soul or essence of things resided in their names. But commentators have entangled themselves in the somewhat barren debate about whether such ideas asserted that the word in its own right was powerful, or whether it acted through the participation of the supernatural or through the agency of the Lord's anointed. What has not been seen is that within any single religious system, multiple values are given to the character and role of the sacred language, and that these values taken together form a set of three postulates in mutual tension.

The Bible illustrates this trinity of ideas:

The first idea is that God created the world by assigning names. "And God called the light Day, and the darkness he called Night" (Genesis 1.5). (Together with this goes the idea in certain religions that the Creator God created himself by uttering his own name.)

Second, the Bible asserts the directly opposite idea that after God had created heaven and earth, man assumed the naming function through speech. "And out of the ground the Lord God formed every beast of the field, and every fowl of the air; and brought them unto the man to see what he would call them: and whatsoever the man called every living creature, that was the name thereof" (Genesis 2.19–20).

There is yet a third character assigned to the word: it is an entity which is able to act and produce effects in its own right. Thus, we read in Isaiah (55.11): "So shall my word be that goeth forth out of my mouth: it shall not return unto me void, but it shall accomplish that which I please, and it shall prosper in the thing whereto I sent it."

These Biblical notions express Hebrew concepts and I think come together in the first lines of the Gospel according to Saint John, which also explicitly refers to the Greek notion of *logos:* the word was in the beginning with God, the word was made flesh in Jesus Christ, and those who received Christ became the sons of God and the word dwelt with them.

It is these three notions that are also reflected in Buddhism, which constantly affirms its three gems: the Buddha, the all-enlightened one, was the source of the sacred words; the Dhamma, the doctrines preached by the Buddha and inscribed in the texts, are themselves holy objects in their own right and can transmit virtue and dispel evil; and the Sangha, the monastic order whose ordained members practice good conduct, is the most appropriate agent for a recital of the sacred words.

These notions are also represented in Trobriand thought. Consider the following Trobriand propositions:

1. Magic appeared with the first ancestors and culture heroes, together with the gardens and natural phenomena they created. "Magic is a thing never invented and never tampered with, by man or any other agency" (Malinowski, 1960: 402). It was handed over to man, whose descendants have inherited it in unbroken succession.

2. At the same time, the Trobriands conceived of magic as an essentially human possession, especially of the accredited magicians. Malinowski asserted that, for the native, magic was "not a force of nature, captured by man . . . and put to his service; it is essentially the assertion of man's intrinsic power over nature." It was the human belly that was the tabernacle of magical knowledge; the force of magic resided in man and could "escape only through his voice" (1960: 409).

3. The Trobrianders also had the notion that magical formulas, once voiced, influenced the course of events. Hence their insistence that the spell was the most important component of magic, a view also held firmly by the Dobuans (Fortune, 1963: 101).

It is clear that we are dealing with three notions which form an interrelated set: deities or first ancestors or their equivalents instituted speech and the classifying activity; man himself is the creator and user of this propensity; language as such has an independent existence and has the power to influence reality.

I suggest that it is the perception of these characteristics of language that has perhaps brought about the elevation of the word as supremely endowed with mystical power. Let me explain. There is a sense in which it is true to say that language is outside us and given to us as a part of our cultural and historical heritage. At the same time language is within us; it moves us, and we generate it as active agents. Since words exist and are in a sense agents in themselves which establish connections and relations between both man and man, and man and the world, and are capable of "acting" upon them, they are one of the most realistic representations we have of the concept of force which is either not directly observable or is a metaphysical notion which we find necessary to use.

With respect to religion and ritual, the three notions in their widest extension correspond to the following levels of behavior, which we meet time and again in many societies:

1. the domain of myth, which relates stories about the doings of saviors or prophets or ancestors and the arrival of the message, be it doctrine or magic;
2. the ritual or magical system itself—that is, the linguistic structure of the sacred words and the grammar of the nonverbal acts that go with them;
3. the present-day human priests or magicians, their sacred status, their links with the saviors or ancestors, and their special behavior and preparations which make their ritual practices effective.

Any exhaustive study of religion and ritual needs to examine not only those levels but also the functional relations between them. And there is again another major relationship to be unraveled, a relationship that is difficult to establish in a meaningful sense, and is least well established in anthropology. This is the link between religion and ritual and the domains of social and practical activities into which it penetrates, and which it influences but is also at the same time separated from in some fashion.[8]

To return to my major theme, which is the basis for the belief in the magical power of words: I have taken the inquiry up to a certain point, but the hardest part of the exercise is yet to come. If ritual is defined as a complex of words and actions (including the manipulation of objects), then it remains to be shown what precisely is the *interconnection between the words and the actions*. This I shall attempt to show with respect to the Trobriand magical system, paying particular attention to the verbal component. Before I can do this, it is necessary to clear the decks by critically reviewing the theory of language which Malinowski himself propounded to explain Trobriand magic, and also certain other attempts by philosophers and linguists to account for the belief in verbal magic.

Theories of Magical Language

Malinowski's views on language can be roughly divided into two related theories, one pertaining to what he called an "ethnographic theory of language" in general, and the other to the language of magic in particular.

The chief feature of his general theory was the pragmatic character of language. He viewed language as a vehicle not so much for expressing ideas, concepts, or categories as for achieving practical effects. We recognize in this stand a self-conscious attack on the mentalistic theories of language current in his time, such as those held by Sweet and Sapir (1921). Malinowski's approach to language corresponded with his approach to myth and magic: he saw them as anti-intellectualistic and nonexplanatory—they were simply hard-worked tools for practical living.

Malinowski made no distinction between "langue" and "parole," language and speech. His analysis was specifically related to the speech context. Speech was a part of concerted activity, like gesture and motion, "an adjunct to bodily activities." Words were a part of action and were equivalents to actions (1965b: 9). It is from this perspective that he developed his "contextual theory of meaning" and the notion of the "pragmatic setting of utterances." The role of language could be understood only in relation to other activities; language regulated concerted work, transmitted knowledge, and set in motion a series of tribal activities, and "the effective force of such verbal acts lies in directly reproducing their consequences" (1965b: 49).

Malinowski's definition of "meaning" was a logical derivative from his pragmatic perspective: "Meaning is the effect of words on human minds and bodies and through these on the environmental reality as created or conceived in a given culture" (1965b: 53). Compare this formulation with that of structural linguistics, for which the speaker and the listener are contingent and belong to "la parole," whereas meaning is the relation between sign and the thing signified, between "signifiant" and "signifié," which belong to the engraphic system of "la langue."[9]

Linguists have criticized Malinowski for confusing the context of situation with other levels of analysis pertaining to language qua language (J. R. Firth, 1957). It was his passion for viewing words as a part of action that made Malinowski argue with excessive flourish that words had no existence and that texts divorced from context were meaningless. These arguments were directly contravened by him because his exposition in *Coral Gardens and Their Magic* was in terms of a word-for-word translation and a commentary on recorded texts. It was the same histrionic talent that led him to dwell on the problem of meaningless words and the "coefficient of weirdness" in magical language. In fact his translation was excellent, and he concluded that the "coefficient of intelligibility" in the spells was high. His strategy of teasing the credulous reader and taking him on a circuitous and repetitious route, strewn with his sins of commission and omission, was adopted so that in the end a dramatic answer could be produced, which was that magical language was eminently intelligible. And he graciously conceded that the untranslatable words were untranslatable because he failed to get the services of a "competent commentator."

Malinowski chose not to follow the perspectives offered by this finding and maintained that magical language worked differently from ordinary speech. The difference was that magical utterances were believed by the natives to produce supernatural effects which they did not expect ordinary speech to produce. The very basis of verbal magic was the "creative metaphor of magic"—a suggestive phrase that he interpreted as "the belief that the repetitive statement of certain words is believed to produce the reality stated" (1965b: 238). This belief again, that the knowledge of a name or the correct repetition of a formula produced mystical effects, Malinowski traced to mythological associations or, as he put it, "some other aspect of Frazer's principle of sympathy" (1965b: 232). The implication is that the laws of association that apply to ordinary speech do not hold for magical speech, an inference that inevitably led Malinowski to the barren conclusion that magical language is objectively a delusion and "irrational in nature." "The essence of verbal magic, then, consists in a statement which is untrue and which stands in direct opposition to the context of reality" (1965b: 235). He thus searched for another kind of rational reason grounded in individual psychology for the objectively false use of magical language.

There was however another strand in Malinowski's thought which led him to posit a rather different relation between magical and ordinary language. The question was, how did man come to believe in the first place in the mystical power of words? He argued from his pragmatist and behaviorist premises that there was a real basis to the human belief in the mystical and binding power of words. Language gave man a sense of power over his environment. "The belief that to know the name of a thing is to get a hold on it is thus empirically true" (1965b: 233). Thus, although he saw in magical language obvious distortions of ordinary language in the direction of mysticism, both types of language engendered the belief in the creative force and pragmatic power of words, which he traced to childhood experience. A baby reacts to bodily discomfort with cries which attract the mother's attention, and later the child learns that the utterance is the essence of welfare and that he can act upon the environment to satisfy his needs. Here lies the early magical attitude to words, that a name repeated sufficiently often can materialize the thing.

This biographical theory is subject to the same criticisms which have been directed against Malinowski's attempt to account for the classificatory categories of kinship in terms of ego-centered extensions. Furthermore, this theory is question-begging because the notion of language precedes a child's comprehension of language. It is because adults respond to the cries as meaningful, and direct a child's efforts at communication, that a child learns the concept and use of language. Finally, the random acts of a baby are susceptible of diametrically opposed interpretations: Malinowski saw the child's physical grasping movements as the beginnings of its belief in the power to control the environment, whereas Cassirer (1966: 181) saw the displacement of the grasp to a pointing or indicative gesture as the genesis of symbolic behavior.

I turn now to certain other theorists of language who have tried to account for the primitive's "magical attitude to words." I shall briefly mention the ideas of Ogden and Richards (1923), Izutsu (1956), and Cassirer (1953). Happily, Ogden and Richards's linguistic and philosophical arguments in *The Meaning of Meaning* (for which Malinowski wrote his classic supplement) converged with Malinowski's arguments based on anthropological field experience. Unlike those theorists of today who hold the elevated view of language—that it is the basis of categorical knowledge—Ogden and Richards were impressed with the delusions produced in man by language, "a medium developed to meet the needs of arboreal man" and therefore a cumbersome instrument for contemporary needs. They saw the roots of the mistaken belief in the magical powers of words in the superstition that there was a direct, even causal, relation between the word and the thing it referred to, between a symbol and its referent. The denotative fallacy explained man's logophobia.

There is one simple retort to this theory. It is perfectly conceivable that speakers of a language, especially those who are unaware that there are other languages in existence, may think that words are not arbitrary and conventional but truly represent the objects they stand for. But surely, if many contemporary Westerners who may be victims of this fallacy do not thereby think that by saying a word they can conjure up a thing into existence, it is amazing that we can contemplate attributing this magical outlook to the primitive. This cavalier attitude of investing the savage with linguistic pathology is portrayed by another writer who has advanced a connotative theory of the origins of verbal magic. Izutsu (1956) describes with great perceptiveness the capacity of words as symbols to evoke in our minds references and images. Extraverbally, words enable us to reexperience past events; intraverbally, they evoke the associative networks between words within the language system. All this is impeccable, but what warrant is there to speculate that primitive man believes that words produce images as concrete reality?

Cassirer (1953) propounded a philosophical cum linguistic theory to account for the basis and origin of the word veneration reflected widely in religious thought. He opposed mythic thought to theoretical, discursive, logical thought—the two poles in an evolutionary continuum—and directly linked the evolution of religious ideas to the evolution of linguistic notions. Since it was language which actually produced the organization of reality and shaped the forms of predication, the contrasting characters of mythic thought and logical thought, he argued, would be reflected in man's attitude to language. Cassirer related the phenomenon of the hypostatization of the word (which implied the notion that the name of a thing and its essence bear a necessary and internal relation to each other) to the mythic consciousness and imagination of early man, who first grasped his experience of the world through *separate* mythical images. Mythic imagination "tends towards concentration, telescoping, separate characterization" of images. In the sphere of language it results in the belief in word magic, in attributing a physico-magical power to the word, and in a relation of identity and substantial unity between name and thing. Logical thought, a later development in man, has an entirely different attitude to the word, which is seen as a symbol and vehicle which mediates between the immediate data of sense impressions and ideation. Being theoretical and discursive, logical thought "tends towards expansion, implication and systematic connection," and toward the establishment of *relations* between phenomena which are "alike" according to some coordinating law.

Cassirer's theory, which appeals to shaky ethnography, is in fact an imaginary and speculative evolutionary scheme of religious ideas and language. Insofar as Lévi-Strauss has demonstrated the logical and relational character of mythic thought, Cassirer's basic dichotomy of modes of thought disappears. And if it can be demonstrated that primitive magic is based on true relational metaphorical thinking, we shall explode the classical theory which postulates that magic is based on the belief in a real identity between word and thing. The basic fallacy of linguists and philosophers who search for the origins of the magical attitude to words is their prior assumption and acceptance that the primitive has in fact such an attitude. This axiom they have derived principally from Frazer, and indeed from Malinowski, who had affirmed the truth of this classical assertion on the basis of his fieldwork. It would perhaps have been safer for the linguists to have held fast to their knowledge of how language works and to have questioned whether anthropologists had correctly reported primitive thought.

Before I conclude this survey I should refer to another feature of the theory of language formulated by Ogden and Richards—a feature that did not appeal to man's evolution but to a synchronic scheme which fitted beautifully with Malinowski's assertions. They postulated two uses of speech: the scientific use, in which words symbolized a reference which could be verified in relation to external reality; and the evocative or emotive use, in which words simply became signs for emotions or attitudes, their referential power being secondary. I. A. Richards (1938) argued that poetry made its impact through the emotive use of language. Malinowski, too, asserted that magical language was an emotive use of language, that magic was born of the emotional tension of particular situations and that the spells, ritual acts, and gestures expressed a spontaneous flow of emotions. When carried away by his own emotive use of language, he even argued that the paraphernalia and ritual substances of Trobriand magic were used as they happened to bear on the purpose of the act through emotional association (Malinowski, 1948: 53). These statements do not do justice to the highly formalized nature of Trobriand rituals. And as for emotive use of words, Richards's views find their match and corrective in Leach (1964), who has demonstrated that even the most emotive words of abuse have a referential and structural basis.

A Reanalysis of Trobriand Ritual

If I am critical of these theories, I should try and provide an alternative view of how the language of ritual works. I shall attempt a brief reanalysis of some aspects of Trobriand magic in order to demonstrate my point of view. But first I should outline the scheme and assumptions that guide my analysis.

Trobriand magical language is intelligible language, not mumbo-jumbo shot through with mystical ideas resistant to rational examination. It is not qualitatively "different" from ordinary language, but is a heightened use of it. The same laws of association that apply to ordinary language apply to magical language.

Trobriand magic is a clear case of a system that combines, more often than not, word and deed, language and action. Therefore, rather than analyze the words separately from the actions, we should find a way of linking them.

This difficult inquiry I call the "inner frame" of Trobriand magic, and it deals with the technique of transfer, the manner in which spells are constructed, the logic of choice of the substances used, and the mode of synchronization of linguistic devices with those of nonverbal action in a structured sequence. I call this perspective the "semantics" of Trobriand ritual.

I use the term "outer frame" to refer to another level of meaning. Here the ritual complex as a whole is regarded as an activity engaged in by individuals or groups in pursuit of their institutional aims. This perspective we may call "pragmatics," and it corresponds in some ways to what Malinowski called the "context of situation." It investigates how ritual relates to other activities, in what contexts and situations it is practiced, and what consequences it may produce for various segments of the society.

At the cost of oversimplifying, one could say that there are two perspectives for viewing this relationship between ritual and other activities. Ritual can be seen as a stimulus or signal for activities that follow in time—for example, in the case of prospective magic exemplified by Trobriand agricultural and canoe magic. It can also be seen as a response to preceding events, as in the case of "retrospective" ritual, a good example of which is witchcraft.

In investigating how language and action are synchronized in Trobriand magic, I have found it useful to elaborate a suggestion made by Jakobson (1956). Having discussed two devices or operations in language, the metaphoric and metonymic, which are based on the principles of similarity and contiguity, he indicated a formal correspondence between them and Frazer's division of magic into "imitative" and "contagious" kinds, also based on the principles of similarity and contiguity. Frazer used these principles not in relation to the words but to the objects used and actions enacted in magical rites.

With respect to linguistic operations, the concept of metaphor presents no problem. The dictionary defines "metaphor" as a figure of speech in which a name or descriptive term is transferred to some object to which it is not properly applicable. The implications of metaphor (which is a shorthand expression I use to include simile and analogy) are that it is a surrogate which has a dual reference to the original object and to the object for which it now stands. Every metaphor or symbol contains both truth and fiction: if it is taken literally it misrepresents, but it is more than a conventional sign because it highlights a resemblance. The metaphor is a mode of reflection and enables abstract thought on the basis of analogical predication (Urban, 1939). In terms of Jakobson's formulation, the metaphoric use of language exploits the procedures of selection and substitution by which words or ideas replace one another in terms of semantic similarity.

This device may have profound implications for ritual, which has for its aim the actual transfer of an attribute to the recipient. The spell can exploit the metaphorical use of language, which verbally and in thought makes the transfer. There is no trick here; it is a normal use of language. The verbal transfer is an example of what was called in traditional theology the analogy of attribution.

The dictionary meaning of "metonymy" is "a figure of speech which consists in substituting for the name of a thing the name of an attribute or part of it"—for example, when "scepter" stands for "authority." This is a case of the part standing for the whole based on the contiguity principle. If a metaphor is a substitute, a metonym is a complement; both involve verbal transfer. Jakobson expands the notion of metonymy to discuss linguistic operations, based on the principles of contiguity and contexture, which make it possible to formulate complex forms of linguistic units according to syntactic rules—the rules by which words are combined and strung together to form sentences and sentences combined to form utterances.

Metonymy as traditionally understood and expanded by Jakobson sheds light on the structure of Trobriand spells. Frequently the various parts or constituent units of the recipient of the magic, whether it be a canoe or a human being, are enumerated and the magical transfer made to each of them. Thus, we get a realistic picture of the whole built up from the parts, and this metonymic technique has several implications for lending realism to the rite, for transmitting a message through redundancy, for storing vital technological knowledge in an oral culture, and for the construction of the spell itself as a lengthy verbal form.

Both linguistic procedures, metaphoric (through substitution permitting abstractions) and metonymic (through building an organic whole through details), are accompanied in Trobriand magic by action.

Objects and substances are used as agents and vehicles of transfer through contagious action. In these vehicles of transfer we find expressed Frazer's substitution (or similarity) and contiguity principles, imitative and contagious magic, but never in an exclusive manner. A close analysis of Trobriand ritual shows that it actively exploits the expressive properties of language, the sensory qualities of objects, and the instrumental properties of action simultaneously in a number of ways. The semantics of ritual are more complex than suggested by Frazer's principles, which lead to absurd inferences about the logic of magic.

Now we are in a position to see how these propositions hold in detail in the Trobriand case.

Malinowski considered the spell (*yopa*) as the most important constituent of Trobriand magic. The magical rites took two forms. In one, spells were uttered without a concomitant rite (that is, without manipulation of objects), but this abbreviated form was not practiced in the major rituals. In the other, which was the more important, the spells were accompanied by simple rites of "impregnation" or "transference," which shared a common grammar.[10] Typically, certain substances (for example, leaves) were brought into contact with an object such as an adze, or a lashing creeper, or a pregnancy cloak, and spells were uttered close to them so that they became charged; these objects in turn transferred their virtue to the final recipient of the magic. Thus the *wayugo* creeper, which was used for lashing together the parts, imparted speed to the finished canoe, and the charmed medications of *kula* beauty magic conveyed beauty and attractiveness to the voyager.

The most elaborate Trobriand spells had three consecutive parts: the *u'ula*, the *tapwana*, and the *dogina*. The meanings associated with *u'ula* are "foundation," "cause," "beginning," "first possessor," "reason." The *tapwana* had a similar coherent range of meanings: "surface," "skin," "body," "trunk," "middle part," and "main part." The *dogina* meant "tip," "end," "tail," or "final part." The three parts appear to present the following progression. The *u'ula*, which is brief, states the basis on which the spell is constructed: first, the major theme or metaphorical idea which is elaborated in the spell and, second, the mythical heroes and ancestors who wielded the magical powers in question and with whom the magician himself becomes identified. This second feature is the portion of the spell that relates the magic to myth, which I will not discuss here. The *tapwana* is the longest and main part, and is essential to an understanding of how the spell is constructed and of the logic and technique of the rite. The *dogina,* which is also brief, is a statement that the intended effect has been achieved. It is clear that the Trobriand spell is constructed as an ordered progression.

Malinowski described the *tapwana* as a "continuous stream of utterance" and, what is important for my argument here, he stated that this main part of the formula was easier to translate than the *u'ula* because it was expressed in a less condensed form and in words approximating ordinary language. It thus consisted of descriptive referential language rather than untranslatable language.

In the simpler kind of spell, a list of words is repeated in sequence with changes in key expressions. The list is an enumeration of the constituent parts of a canoe or a yam house, or the anatomy of the performer. These words I loosely call "substance words." The key expression is an action word or a verb. The logic of the recitation is that each part enumerated undergoes an event or process by which it acquires the desired attribute or quality (Examples 2 and 3 in Exhibit 1 illustrate this construction). Alternatively, a single substance word or noun may be attached in succession to a series of verbs which represent a range of related states or processes (see Example 1a in Exhibit 1).

A more complex structure consists of the use of two series of key expressions, one consisting of the body parts of the recipient, to each of which are transferred energies represented by another series of verbs (see Example 1b).

Exhibit 1. The structure of Trobriand spells (with special reference to the *tapwana*).

Example 1. The striking of the soil. Formula 2 in *Coral Gardens and Their Magic.*

    a. The belly of my garden ⟶ leavens
                                    rises
                                    reclines
                                    grows to the size of a bush hen's nest
                                    grows like an anthill
                                    rises and is bowed down
                                    rises like the ironwood palm
                                    lies down
                                    swells
                                    swells as with a child

b. List 1 (garden pests)   List 2

the grubs ─────────────────────────────→ I sweep away

the insects   I blow

the beetle with the sharp tooth   I drive off

the beetle that bores   I send off

the beetle that destroys the taro underground   I chase away

the white blight on taro leaves

the marking blight

the blight that shines

Example 2. Anchoring the garden (after planting and erecting posts). Formula 10 in *Coral Gardens and Their Magic*.

Parts of the garden named:

soil ───────────────────────────→ "shall be anchored"

magical prism (*kamkokola*)

yam pole (*kavatam*)

branching pole (*kaysalu*)

stem saved from the cutting (*kamtuya*)

training stick (*kaybudi*)

uncharmed prism (*kaynutatala*)

partition stock (*tula*)

slender support (*yeye'i*)

boundary line (*tuklumwala*)

boundary triangle (*karivisi*)

light yam pole (*tamkwaluma*)

tabooing stick (*kayluvalova*)

great yam pole (*kayvaliluwa*)

Example 3. Post-harvest magic of prosperity—the second act of *vilamalia* magic (anchoring the yam house and village). Formula 29 in *Coral Gardens and Their Magic*.

Parts of the yam house named:

corner stone (*ulilaguva*) ──────────────→ "shall be anchored"

floor (*bubukwa*)

log house (*liku*)

compartments (*kabisivisi*)

young sprout of taytu yam (*sobula*)

sticks that divide the log cabin (*teta*)

decorated front board (*bisiya'i*)

gable boards (*kavalapu*)

supports of thatch (*kiluma*)

roof batten (*kavala*)

rafters (*kaliguvasi*)

thatch battens (*kivi*)

lower ridgepole (*kakulumwala*)

thatch (*katuva*)
upper ridgepole (*vataulo*)
ornamented end of ridgepole (*mwamwala*)

Other examples which show the same regularity of structure are:

1. The *kayikuna sulumwoya* spell in *kula* beauty (*mwasila*) magic (1960: 439). In this spell first a man's *kula* objects are enumerated and each is said to "boil"; next the performer's own head parts are enumerated and each in turn "boils" ("to boil," "to foam," "to stir" are frequently used to represent activation). *Inventory of kula objects:* my mint plant (boils); my herb ornament, my lime spatula, my lime pot, my comb, my mat, my presentation goods, my personal blanket, my magical bundle. *Head parts enumerated:* my head (boils); my nose, my occiput, my tongue, my larynx, my speaking organ, my mouth.

2. The renowned *wayugo* (lashing creeper) spell used in canoe building magic transfers speed to the canoe under construction (1960: 431). Technically the lashing creeper maintains the cohesion of the various parts of the canoe. Here is an enumeration of the constituents of the canoe, each of which is followed by the verb "might heel over" (that is, overtake). *Inventory of canoe parts:* I (might heel over); my keel, my canoe bottom, my prow, my rib, my threading stick, my prowboard, my transverse board, my canoe side.

There are some readily comprehensible features in the spells constructed on such simple principles.[11] Such permutations with words allow for a great deal of repetitiveness, which Malinowski referred to as the prosaic pedantry of Trobriand magic. Today in the light of communication theory we would say that the redundancy is a device used in ritual to transmit its message (Cherry, 1961), a point that has already been argued by Leach (1966).

Another implication of the repetitive pattern, which in contemporary jargon we would call "store of information" or "memory bank" in the absence of written language, was noted casually by Malinowski. Commenting upon the Kudayuri canoe myth, which contained a detailed account of canoe parts and their building sequence, Malinowski wrote: "He [the native] is quite used to recite one after the other the various stages of customary proceedings in his own narratives, and he does it with an almost pedantic accuracy and completeness, and it is an easy task for him to transfer these qualities to the accounts which he is called upon to make in the service of ethnography" (1960: 318). It is clear that the spells and myths contain information which is not the remains of archaic beliefs but a living knowledge related to technological and social activities.

Furthermore, and this I emphasize, the spells I have cited portray a metonymic use of language—that is, linguistic operations in terms of combination and context, based on contiguity principles. All the parts of a canoe, or a human head or a yam house, make up a configuration or a set by virtue of contiguous association which when systematically varied with action words creates a long utterance. Metonymy so used lends a "realistic" coloring to the description.

Each utterance sounds as if it states an imperative transference— for example, "The belly of my garden swells" or "The floor of my yam house shall be anchored." It is a common view, also shared by Malinowski, that a magical spell is identifiable by its insistent use of imperatives and that this provides the evidence for saying that primitives believe that words create their effects by their very utterance. This, however, is not the case. The verbal assertion is mediated by a middle term which is the substance (or *materia medica*) into which the spells are uttered; and these substances in turn convey the attribute to the final recipient. It is therefore necessary to investigate the role of these mediating substances.

Let us take as our example the substances used in two contrasting rites in the gardening cycle. The inaugural rite of the first cutting of the soil, the first in the cycle, has for its purpose the conferring of fertility on the soil; the *vilamalia* which comes at the end is enacted after the storing of the yams, and seeks to confer durability and permanence on the yam stocks.

Exhibit 2. The metaphorical associations of substances used in two rites in Omarakana garden magic. (Compiled from *Coral Gardens and Their Magic*, vols. 1 and 2, and *The Sexual Life of Savages*.)

Substances used in the inaugural rite (first cutting of the soil):
A. Leaves, plants and creepers.
1. *Yoyu:* coconut leaves. "They are of the dark green color which the *taytu* (small yam) leaves should have if they are to be strong and healthy."
2. Arecanut leaves: same association as substance 1.
3. *Ubwara:* wild plant with long tubers which are white and beautiful. Used so that "the *taytu* in the garden will also produce beautiful white tubers." (The white color is associated with fertility and purity in the pregnancy ritual.)
4. *Kaybwibwi:* white petals of the fragrant pandanus. Used so that the "*taytu* should have a pleasant smell." (Here again the symbolism of "whiteness" used in pregnancy ritual is relevant.)
5. *Kubila:* a plant with scented flowers. Same association as substance 4.
6. *Sasoka:* tree with big round bulky fruit. Used to influence the size of the *taytu* yam.

7. *Wakaya:* largest variety of banana. It has a massive trunk swelling out near the ground; same association as substance 6.
8. *Youla'ula:* creeper with white flowers and luxuriant foliage resembling *taytu* foliage. Used so that the *taytu* will have the same luxuriant foliage. Also "whiteness" is associated with "pregnancy."
9a. *Ipikwanada:* creeper with luxuriant foliage. Same association as substance 8.
   b. *Yokunukwānada:* creeper with luxuriant foliage. Same association as substance 8.

B. Earthy substances.
10. *Ge'u:* enormous mounds scraped together by the bush hen for breeding purposes. "Used so that the *taytu* may grow and swell up, like one of these mounds."
11. *Kaybu'a:* chalk from large boulders. Same association as substance 10. Also note the symbolism of "whiteness."
12. *Kabwabu:* large round nests which hornets make in the ground. "The *taytu* should be as bulging and large as one of these nests."

Substances used in *vilamalia* (prosperity of the village magic):
A. Trees and plants. The materials 1–5 figure in the two acts of *vilamalia* magic which "anchor" the yam house and the village. The metaphorical association of the objects as regards "anchoring" is clear.
1. *Kakema:* dwarf tree with powerful roots used in the first act of *vilamalia.*
2. *Lewo:* stunted tree reaching to very old age, used in the second act.
3. *Setagava:* tough weed with strong roots used in the first act.
4. *Kayaulo:* an extremely tough tree whose wood cannot be broken but can be cut with an axe or knife.
5. *Leya:* wild ginger used in the second act. Associated with fierceness and toughness.

B. Other substances.
Binabina: stone or volcanic rock imported from the south. It is heavier, hardier, and less brittle than the local dead coral. The two stones used in the ritual are called "the pressers of the floor" which impart their qualities to the stored food.

The contrast in the meanings of the material symbols used is clearcut in this exhibit. In the inaugural rite the substances brought into contact with an adze or ritually planted while the spell is recited are luxuriant green leaves, wild plants which produce large tubers, plants which produce scented white flowers and tubers (the white connoting fertility and sexual purity), soil scraped from the enormous mounds made by the bush hen, and so forth. In the *vilamalia* the substances used connote hardness and durability: tough weeds with strong roots, wood of stunted long-lived trees, hard volcanic rock. The logic guiding the selection of these articles is not some mysterious magical force that inheres in them; they are selected on the basis of their spatiotemporal characteristics such as size and shape and their sensible properties like color and hardness, which are abstract concepts and which are given metaphorical values in the Trobriand scheme of symbolic classification.

What then is the garden magician up to when he scrapes some soil from a bush hen's nest, brings it into contact with an adze, and recites, "The belly of my garden grows to the size of a bush hen's nest"? Is this a case of mystical contagion between bush hen mound and the size of the yam, or is it simply a metaphorical equivalence set up verbally between the property of size portrayed by the bush hen's nest and the desired same property in the yam, and lending the mental comparison an air of operational reality by using the soil of the bush hen's nest as a medium of transfer? The rite of transfer portrays a metaphorical use of language (verbal substitution) whereby an attribute is transferred to the recipient via a material symbol which is used metonymically as a transformer. Frazer would simply have described the procedure as contagious magic. The technique gains its realism by clothing a metaphorical procedure in the operational or manipulative mode of practical action; it unites both concept and action, word and deed.

Confirmation is lent to this argument when we scrutinize the spells used without the mediation of material substances, spells which the Trobrianders call "mouth magic" (*o wadola*). A good example of this category is the magic of growth performed in the middle phase of gardening. The natives are aware that nature must do its work and that the crops have to sprout and grow by themselves. The magician's function is described by Malinowski thus: "In a rapid succession of rites, he has to anticipate each stage in the growth of the gardens, and stimulate the various crucial phases in the development of the plant" (1965a: 139).

In the following examples, taken from formulas 13, 17, and 18 in Malinowski's "The Magic of Growth" (1965a: ch. 4), I state some suggestive lines and then in parenthesis the native commentary upon them.

Formula 13. "O *dadeda* tree that sprouts again and again." (The native commentary is that the *"dadeda* is a plant of extremely rank growth; we cut it, already it has sprouted.") The same formula contains other metaphors suggesting speed of growth: "Thy shoots are as quick as the eyes of the *kapapita,* the quick bird, / Thy shoots are as quick as the *kababasi'a,* the quick black ants."

Formula 17. "Thy head, O *taytu,* shoots along as the millipede shoots along." (The natives say that the millipede is noted for its rapidity of movement.)

Formula 18. "Thy open space, the open space between thy branches, O *taytu,* the spider covers up." ("The natives told me," reports Malinowski, "that as the spider spins his web, so should the *taytu* plant produce many branches.")

It is obvious that the mouth magic depends entirely on suggestive metaphors and similes which the Trobrianders themselves recognize as such. It is puzzling indeed why Malinowski, who compiled notes on native exegesis, should have insisted on the "pragmatic function of words" and in the same breath "the mystical associations" of magic. Thus, when in the wind-blown gardens the Trobrianders invoke the image of a dolphin playing in the water, Malinowski interprets the act as portraying "the mystical association between the undulating movements of the dolphin and the windings and weavings of the vine" (1965a: 170).[12]

Because of his commitment to his emotional and pragmatic view of language, Malinowski failed to connect the symbolism of the inaugural garden magic with the pregnancy ritual, which he described in *The Sexual Life of Savages* (1929). The gardening magic constantly refers to "the belly of my garden." Malinowski denied that this implied any metaphorical allusion to animal or human fertility, but he disarmingly went on to say: "My informants, as a matter of fact, commented on it in this sense . . . 'taytu is the child of the garden' " (1965b: 262–263).

Let me consider the pregnancy ritual, for it succinctly illuminates the inner form of Trobriand magic and also some of the behavior of the garden magician.

When a woman achieves her first conception, the *tabugu* (women of the father's matrilineage, chief of whom is the father's own sister) are charged with the conduct of the pregnancy ritual. They prepare two fiber skirts and two mantles, white in color; one set is worn by the pregnant woman at the celebration of her first pregnancy (about the fifth month) and the second set after childbirth when she emerges from seclusion and returns to her conjugal household. The mantles are the garments of special importance on which the *saykeulo* magic is performed. They are placed on a mat, the fleshy lower parts of the creamy white leaves of the lily plant (which bears a snowy white flower) are cut and strewn over them, and the *tabugu* thrust their faces close and say spells.

The symbolism of these objects and operations, as well as those of the subsequent rituals, cannot be understood without paying close attention to the words of the spell (see 1929: 181). The *u'ula*, the stem of the spell, refers to the *bwaytuva*, a bird of white plumage (similar to the reef heron) which is invited to hover over the bathing place and the principal locations of water in the village. The white bird is the major symbol and there is no doubt that the pregnancy cloak stands for the bird's plumage. The *tapwana*, the main part of the spell, shows the following pattern: the white bird is said to make resplendent the different parts of the robe (the top, fringe, and so forth), which are named in turn; next the bird makes resplendent the various parts of the body of the pregnant woman from head to foot (head, nose, cheeks, chest, belly, groin, buttocks, thighs, knees, calves, and feet). The *dogina*, the conclusion of the spell, states that the pregnant woman has been whitened; a metaphorical equivalence is stated between the head of the woman and the pallor before dawn, between her face and the white sprouts of the areca plant (1929: 182).

It is clear that the robe (which materially represents the bird) and its charming have for their objective the transference of "whiteness" to the pregnant woman. This is also the emphasis in the ceremony at which a woman is actually invested by the *tabugu* with the robe after five months of pregnancy. She is carried into the water on a "queen's chair" formed of human arms, cleansed and bathed, isolated from the earth and made to stand on a mat, subjected to an elaborate toilet which smoothes out and whitens her body, dressed in a robe, lifted up, carried and deposited on a small platform in her father's or mother's brother's house. There she remains elevated, sacred, and separated: she should not speak, she is fed by her *tabugu* because she cannot touch food, and she washes frequently to become white, and keeps indoors away from the sun.

Thus the "whiteness" which is conveyed to the woman itself stands for the attributes of elevation, sexual purity (by whitening "she does not think about adultery" and she must also henceforth refrain from sexual intercourse with her husband), and beauty of motherhood. The bathing ceremony, apart from ritually cleansing her, loosens the child in the womb.

The pregnant woman is subjected to certain food taboos: she avoids delicacies, mainly fruit (*kavaylu'a*), for if she eats fruit the child will have a big belly; it will be full of excrement and die. She also avoids fish that live in submarine holes, and fish with sharp-pointed and poisonous fins. The logic of these taboos is a metaphorical *similarity and difference principle* which is the first rule of Trobriand food taboos. For example, normally edible things that suggest an analogy to the condition of the mother in some respect (fruit of the tree, and fish in holes are like the child in the womb) but are also antagonistic in certain other respects (fruit rots, and fish in submarine holes do not easily emerge, but a child must be delivered easily and whole) are tabooed.

One more set of facts requires to be brought into focus before we return to the garden magician. In the pregnancy ritual, the concept of "whiteness" is opposed to the concept of "blackness" of black magic. The father of the pregnant woman has to give part of the *sagali* distribution to women who possess black magic, to appease them, "for by addressing the *mwanita* [black millipede—the symbol opposite to the white bird], the sorceress is able to make a pregnant woman's skin black, as black as the worm itself" (1929: 190). If a woman's skin is black, she has men on her mind.

The customs of mourning after death, especially those imposed on a widow, show a precise reversal of those associated with pregnancy. The color of mourning is black and the widow's mourning behavior is concordant with the idea of ugliness. The widow's hair is shaved, she wears soiled clothes, she cannot wear ornaments, her body is thickly smeared with soot and grease which will not be washed off for a long time. Her body blackness is associated with the blackness of witchcraft, which she and her matrikin must publicly disavow. She is confined in a small cage and relegated to darkness inside the house. But her ritual uncleanliness resulting in her separateness also shares some aspects of the sacred state of the pregnant woman, in that the widow too should not speak and cannot touch food and therefore has to be fed.

Some of the symbolism of the inaugural gardening rite and the food taboos imposed on the garden magician become intelligible in the light of these facts. Both the garden and the magician are considered "pregnant." It is the garden that is impregnated and activated (as indicated by the word *vatuvi,* the first word of the magic formula, which means "to make rise"), and the white scented vegetable substance and coral chalk used in the rite have the same value as the white substances in the pregnancy ritual. But it is the magician who simulates the woman and practices her food taboos. Thus, in the act of "striking the soil," as he inserts a sapling into the ground, he assumes a female sitting position which no male would normally adopt, for men squat and women sit with their buttocks touching the ground (1965a: 101).

The food taboos he observes are the following. He cannot eat immature or imperfect *taytu* taken from the soil during the thinning process, for they imply imperfect children; and the *sina* bird with black plumage, cuttlefish which squirt black fluid, and other black fish which live among coral rocks (all associated with the inauspiciousness of black) are forbidden. He also avoids the flesh of the ordinary bush hen and its eggs, *wakaya* bananas, and tubers of the *ubwara* creeper, all of which are either mentioned in the spell or used as substance in the inaugural rite. The logic of these taboos belongs to a second rule elucidated below.

One last example will help round off my discussion, for it introduces the third primary color of red and also brings out other dimensions of the logic of the food taboos. The aim of the "beauty magic" of *kula* (*mwasila*) is to make each man attractive and irresistible to his *kula* partner, and the magic harks back to the myth in which an ugly old man is transformed into a radiant, charming youth. All the voyagers wash in sea water, rub themselves with medicated leaves, apply coconut grease on their bodies, tease out their hair with combs, paint ornamental designs on their faces in red and black, and insert in their white armlets mint plants preserved in coconut oil. In the spells recited (for example, *kaykakaya* and *talo* spells; see 1960: 338–339) the major reference is to red color as represented by certain kinds of red fish (for example, "Red paint, red paint of the *udawada* fish"), which are the "foundation" of the spell. With characteristic regularity the spell says that the various *kula* appurtenances and the parts of the head of each man will "flare up" and "flash."

It is clear that this magic does not say that the men become red fish or that there is a substantial identity between them. It simply postulates a comparison between the redness of the fish and the red painting on the human face, redness itself standing for flashing and irresistible attractiveness. At the same time the fact that red fish are tabooed food on the expedition ("We eat bad fish and we are ugly") leaves no doubt that the identification with red fish by physical ingestion is repudiated, that the comparison is strictly metaphorical, and that the "transfer" made is that of abstract qualities and not physical resemblance. Thus, we can infer the second law of Trobriand food taboos: objects invoked as metaphors whose abstract attributes are to be transferred to the recipient of the ritual must be avoided as food; any physical identification with them is thereby unambiguously rejected.

My elucidation of Trobriand magical symbolism, its inner semantic frame, is thus quite different from that of Malinowski, who attributed to this beauty magic "an exceedingly obscure and confused concatenation of ideas" and said that it expressed "one of the typical forms of magic thought, the contagion of ideas" as propounded by Frazer. There is much more that can be said about Trobriand color symbolism (see appendix), which again shows a systematic organization not appreciated by Malinowski. It would appear that Malinowski misunderstood the "semantics" of the magic he described, but that he had a keen appreciation of another feature of that magic, its outer frame.

The Relation between Magic and Technical Activity

The final question I will deal with is the outer frame of Trobriand magic, its pragmatics. What is the relation between Trobriand magic and practical activity? I must emphasize that I am dealing here with Trobriand prospective magic, and I shall argue that the examination of the functional relationship between magic and technical activity reveals a refraction of the magical prism that has not yet been fully appreciated.

A rite is never conducted in a vacuum, but in the context of other activities or events which precede it and follow it. Malinowski insisted that the Trobrianders did not confuse magic with practical work; for them the road of magic (*megwa la keda*) was distinct from the road of garden work (*bagula la keda*). Yet at the same time, magic and practical work were, in native ideas, inseparable from each other, though they were not confused.

From the evidence (linguistic and behavioral) Malinowski provided, there is little doubt that the whole cycle of gardening or of canoe building must be seen as one long series of activities which form a regular pattern of M $\rightarrow$ T, $\rightarrow$ M $\rightarrow$ T, $\rightarrow$ M $\rightarrow$ T, M $\rightarrow$ T, where M stands for the magical rite and T for the technical operation that succeeds it. (We could substitute S for T where a social activity is involved.) Malinowski's descriptions clearly show that there is a long chain in which two distinguishable kinds of activities were united in an alternating sequence. It is only when we see in canoe building, for example, that first the sequences of technical construction are punctuated by magical rites which precede them, and second that for the Trobriander the building of the seagoing canoe is inextricably bound up with the general proceedings of the *kula* (that in fact the construction of the canoe is the first link in the chain of the *kula* exchanges), that we can appreciate the semantic content of the magical spells and the functional relation of the rites to their extraritual context.

Exhibit 3 is a summary of the sequences of magical rites and technical activities in canoe building which together form a single chain. I shall select three sequences in canoe building for particular comment.

The *ligogu* spell is uttered in theory to impart magical virtue to the adze; it is followed by the technical activity of scooping out the canoe hull and making the canoe parts; the spell as such evokes images of the fantastic speed of the canoe about to be built. Another operation is the fixing of the ornamental prow boards; it is immediately preceded by the recitation of *kula* beauty (*mwasila*) magic, which will make the canoe owner irresistibly attractive to his *kula* partner. One of the most important spells, the *wayugo* (lashing creeper), in its verbal content imparts great speed to the canoe while the technical operation that follows is the fixing of gunwale planks and ribs, and the lashing together of the parts with the lashing creeper.

Exhibit 3. The interrelation of magical (M) and technical (T) sequences in canoe building.

1. *First phase.* All ritual sequences except the first are performed by the *canoe-building expert.*

M1   Rite of offering to wood spirits and their expulsion before the tree,
↓   which in anticipation is referred to as "canoe" (*waga*), is cut.
T1   Felling of the tree and cutting of the log into the rough shape of the
         canoe.
M2   Rite for dispelling the heaviness of the log and for giving it lightness;
↓   the spell also evokes the image of a fast canoe.
T2   Carrying of the log to the beach.
M3   Chanting of the *ligogu* spell to impart magical virtue to the adze; the
         spell in fact evokes images of the fantastic speed of the canoe and its
↓   parts (which are enumerated and charged with speed).
T3   Scooping out of the canoe and making of the canoe parts.
M4   Rite of "final determination"; the canoe makes up its mind to run
         quickly.

2. *Second phase.* All ritual sequences are performed by the *owner of the canoe* (*toliwaga*).

M5   *Kula* beauty (*mwasila*) magic is performed by the owner to influence
↓   his *kula* partner.

T5   Fixing of ornamental prow boards.
M6   Chanting of *wayugo* (lashing creeper) spell to give speed to the
↓   canoe.

T6   Fixing of gunwale planks and ribs and lashing of the parts with the
         creeper.
M7   Rites of smoking and fumigating to cleanse the canoe and to impart
↓   speed; chanting spells over the paints.
T7   Painting of the canoe with black (primary color), red, and white
         colors.

M8   *Kula* (*mwasila*) magic and "staining of the red mouth" (ocher spots
↓   on bow and stern) performed.
T8   Launching of the canoe.
S   Proceedings concluded with the ceremonial and social activity of *sagali* (ceremonial distribution of food by the canoe owner to the
builders and helpers).

It is clear that the chief focus of the canoe magic as judged by the
words said is the subsequent *kula* activities in which reputation is
gained through the speed and seaworthiness of the canoe which give
renown to the owner, and through the personal success of each man
in his dealings with his partner. But there appears to be a discrepancy
in that these words are said immediately before scooping out the log,
or lashing the canoe, or fixing the prowboards, and are indeed addressed to the implements and parts used in these operations. Hence,
we may well wonder how the dramatic description of feats of sailing
can give magical virtue to an adze, or what relation the fixing of the
prowboards has to the beauty of the owner. Since explanations in
terms of irrational mystical associations seem to me to be the refuge of
the literal-minded, I must seek a different answer.

Surely there must be another way forward. We can ask whether
there is not an expansion and overflow of meaning from the mechanics of the rite to the human participants themselves, who, let us
not forget, are always part of the scene. I shall presently examine this
suggestion more rigorously, but let me here pose the question of
whether a sharp adze is not an extension and part of the canoe
builder, and the ornamental prowboard not an apt representation of
the painted face and plumed head of the canoe owner leading an expedition. More important, is not the expanded meaning of the magical
ritual an imaginative, prospective, and creative understanding of the
very technological operations and social activities the Trobrianders are
preparing to enact?

It was precisely because he viewed Trobriand magic in terms of the
"context of situation" that Malinowski illuminatingly argued that
magic signals, inaugurates, and regulates systematic work. But he
subjected this positive sociological functional statement to a negative
psychological function which was in direct contradiction to the first.
He argued narrowly that magic is a product of man's limitations of
thought, of gaps in his empirical knowledge, that it is objectively absurd but has a subjective pragmatic rationale as an anxiety queller. He
thus reduced a highly formalized and structured system to the spontaneous expression of emotion with no intellectual content. It would be
more in line with his evidence to say that Trobriand magic is a testi-

mony to the creativity of thought, that its logic is an anticipatory effect. I am not merely stating that the magic provides incentives to work—though that is a part of the matter. More important, it is a blueprint and a self-fulfilling prophecy and embodies for the Trobriander an understanding of the technical, aesthetic, and evaluative properties of his activities, in a manner denied to us in our segmented civilization. The point about gardening is not that it is uncertain but that it is a regularized activity repeated year after year and with which is associated the pride of matrilineal values reflected in generous *urigubu* payments; the point about the *kula* is not so much the dangers it carries but that expeditions are regularly made to prove individual success through competitive transactions with neighbors cast in the role of stereotyped fierce foreigners. In a sense, Trobriand magical rituals produce what they predict, not in ideal or fantastic terms as painted in myths but in terms that are in accordance with reality. The Trobrianders regularly enjoy good harvests and *kula* successes.

Perhaps I can make my point obliquely through the words of Wittgenstein, who wrote: "An intention is embedded in its situation, in human customs and institutions. If the technique of the game of chess did not exist, I could not intend to play a game of chess. In so far as I do intend the construction of a sentence in advance, that is made possible by the fact that I can speak the language in question" (1953: 108). The Trobrianders practice prospective magic because they have engaged in systematically conceived activities in the past and because they intend to engage in them in the future. But when fate does withhold the regularity of events—when pigs run away into the bush, when drought strikes or when canoes prove unseaworthy—they resort to a retrospective system of evil magic (*bulubwalata*) with which to reorder their experience and come to terms with failure. As with all classic types of witchcraft, the Trobriand system deals with misfortunes *ex post*, not in terms of "laws of nature" but in terms of deviation from an ideal order of social relations.

We can now return to the question: To whom are rituals addressed and what kinds of effects do they seek to produce? This question is not problematic when the rituals in question are directly addressed to human beings, as in healing rituals, initiation rites, beauty magic, and the like (see, for example, Lévi-Strauss, 1963: ch. 10; Turner, 1964). But what about agricultural and canoe-building rites? Descriptions by anthropologists of these almost persuade us that it is immaterial objects such as the adze and the canoe or the soil that are addressed and that the spells and magical substances are used as causal agents in direct contravention of known physical laws.

The Trobrianders provide us with a revealing case which mystified

Malinowski and which throws light on the problem I am discussing. Before and after the filling of the ceremonial yam houses (*bwayma*), they perform the *vilamalia* magic: the ritual words anchor the yam house, and hard *binabina* stones and tough substances are placed on the floor to impart qualities of durability. Malinowski phrased his incomprehension thus: "Whereas the objective facts reveal to us that the whole performance is directed at the yam-house, at the food accumulated there, the comments of the native make the human organism the real subject-matter of magic influence" (1965a: 226). While the rite says that the yam house, yams, and the village should endure, the Trobrianders have not the slightest doubt that it does not directly act on the food but on the human organism, specifically the human belly. If the *vilamalia* were not performed, man and woman would want to eat all the time, but after its performance hunger would be reduced, and the yams would rot in the storehouse.

Malinowski found this explanation astonishing and wrote an unnecessary harangue on the Trobrianders' misunderstanding of the process of nutrition and metabolism (matched by their misapprehension of the fundamentals of human procreation).

What are the facts? The natives have postulated a homology between the yam house and the human belly. A man's ceremonial storehouse is filled with the *urigubu* gifts—the yams are used primarily for ceremonial distributions or for *wasi* (ceremonial barter). The yams are the foundation of wealth, and a Trobriander gloats over his full storehouse. One never returns a yam to the storehouse or adds to its contents. It is better to let the yam rot than to deplete the stock.

While the yam house should be "full," the human stomach which diminishes the stock of yams should be "empty." The Trobriand ideology in the midst of plenty is that abstention from food is a virtue, and to have little food or to show hunger is shameful. There is no greater insult than "no food thine" or "thy hunger." In Trobriand thought, the belly is not only the receptacle of food; it is also the seat of *emotions and understanding* (1965a: 10). It is the storehouse of magical formulas and traditions—that is, it is the seat of *memory* (1960: 409). Since the belly is the tabernacle of magical force, food taboos and restrictions are intimately connected with the preparations of the magician to achieve a sacred state before performing magic.

The Trobriand logic is that a rite conducted realistically to make the storehouse endure is really a metaphorical analogy urging the human belly to restrain its hunger and greed for food. It is the belly that "hears" and "understands" the rite which is externally performed on an inanimate object. The Trobrianders carry the metaphor further to its exacting conclusion. There is a Trobriand taboo on cooking imposed on any dwelling that stands in the inner ring of the village near the yam houses. In fact, only the bachelor house and the chief's dwelling stand there, and cooking is prohibited in them. The Trobriand phrasing of the taboo is in terms of the "sensibility of the *taytu* (yam) to the smell of cooking." Is it so difficult to understand that it is the human belly that is sensitive to cooking in the vicinity of the yam houses?

Thus, it is possible to argue that all ritual, whatever the idiom, is addressed to the human participants and uses a technique which attempts to restructure and integrate the minds and emotions of the actors. The technique combines verbal and nonverbal behavior and exploits their special properties. Language is an artificial construct and its strength is that its form owes nothing to external reality; it thus enjoys the power to invoke images and comparisons, refer to time past and future, and relate events which cannot be represented in action. Nonverbal action, on the other hand, excels in what words cannot easily do—it can codify analogically by imitating real events, reproduce technical acts, and express multiple implications simultaneously. Words excel in expressive enlargement, physical actions in realistic presentation.

It is a truer tribute to the savage mind to say that, rather than being confused by verbal fallacies or acting in defiance of known physical laws, it ingeniously conjoins the expressive and metaphorical properties of language with the operational and empirical properties of technical activity. It is this which gives magical operations a "realistic" coloring and allows them to achieve their expressiveness through verbal substitution and transfer combined with an instrumental technique that imitates practical action. Lévi-Strauss (1963: 221) aptly said that magic treats certain human actions as if they are part of physical determinism. Let me emphasize that there is only a simulation involved here, and that the mechanics are also accompanied by a "humanization of natural laws" which implies not only that material objects and sensory dates are given symbolic meanings but also that supernatural entities are postulated and impersonated by human actors. Language figures importantly in this double relation of ritual to myth on the one hand and to instrumental action on the other.

This perspective allows us not only to retrieve ourselves from the Frazerian absurdity but also to see certain problems in Mauss's formulation. Mauss (1902–3) was surely right in his view that magical ideas are a category of collective thought. He was not sensitive to the role of words in magic and concentrated primarily on the manual act.

Taking the notion of *mana* as his point of reference, he located the concept of spiritual force as the essence of magic, comparable to our concept of "mechanical force," and was thus able to assimilate magic to the more general theme of causality. Magic was described as a "gigantic variation on the principle of causality." But this theoretical step also led him to assert that magic was "absurd from the standpoint of pure reason." While perhaps Mauss understood some aspects of the inner frame of magical action, especially the technique of transfer, he missed its expanded meanings and refractions.

Lévi-Strauss applauded Mauss's views and was therefore unable to extricate himself from the difficulties contained in them. In *The Savage Mind* (1966: ch. 1) Lévi-Strauss engages in a series of equivocations when he first argues, on the lines of Mauss, that magic postulates an all-embracing determinism, an "unconscious apprehension of the truth of determinism," "an act of faith in a science yet to be born"—that is, magic is like science; then shifts his ground in the face of magic's sometimes illusory results to say that to order is better than not to order and that therefore "taxonomy" as represented in magical ideas has eminent aesthetic value—that is, magic is like art; and finally says that the analogy between magic and science is merely formal, and that therefore instead of contrasting magic and science, it would be better "to compare them as two parallel modes of acquiring knowledge." These vacillations indicate at least that the primitive has with incomparable wit and imagination posed for anthropology an ingenious puzzle. Malinowski was by comparison more consistent and less equivocal and in some ways remarkably close to Evans-Pritchard.[13] Malinowski was quite clear in his mind that Trobriand magical ideas should not be confused with ideas of determinism implied in their practical activities; and he was equally clear that magic and practical activity were joined in complementarity in one total series. This view commends itself to serious consideration.

APPENDIX
Trobriand Color Symbolism

The Trobrianders appear to have three primary colors—white, red, and black—which are of aesthetic, symbolic, and ceremonial importance. White and red have relatively unambiguous meanings; black has positive and negative aspects shifting with context, although it too has a dominant meaning. Perhaps more important than their single values is their configurational significance when all three colors are combined—as, for example, in face and canoe painting. I summarize below first the connotations of each color separately and then of all three in combination.

Primary Colors

White. A set of rituals in which white appears as the dominant color is that associated with pregnancy. The dominant symbol for the spell and the rite is the white bird *bwaytuva,* or the white pigeon. The fiber or banana leaf cloaks and skirts which the pregnant woman dons are white in color. In the rite for charming the cloak, creamy white leaves and white flowers of the lily are used. During her toilette the face and body of the woman are stroked with the mother of pearl shell and she is decked with white shell ornaments. Note that the *kula* valuables are red (necklaces) and white (armlets). In the pregnancy ritual the white symbolism is expressed in terms of whitening and smoothing of the skin and body. Washing and cleansing also achieve this objective. Whiteness here stands for beauty of body, but not of an erotic kind; fertility or conception; sexual purity, in that the pregnant woman must not indulge in adultery or even intercourse with her husband; elevated status like that of the chief, expressed by sitting on a platform and being "off the ground." In the inaugural agricultural rite, which also connotes impregnating of the soil and the rising of the belly of the garden, white vegetable and chalky substances are used. Whiteness has also certain peripheral negative connotations, as in the case of the white blight that attacks the yam leaves and albinism in human beings.

    Black. Witchcraft and sorcery are associated with black, one of their dominant symbols being *mwanita,* the black millipede. Blackness of skin is considered ugly and unattractive; with black skin (as opposed to whitened skin) go patchy skin, boils, ulcers, baldness, deformity, and defective speech. Blackness also connotes adultery in women: if a woman's skin is black she has men on her mind. Blackness gets its unambiguous emphatic expression in mourning customs, when the widow wears dirty clothes, her body is blackened with grease and charcoal, she does not wash, and she is prohibited from wearing festive clothes, ornaments, and scent. Thus, black is associated with physical and ritual dirt. Paradoxically, by shaving her head hair and by being blackened, the widow (and the affines) show that they are innocent of witchcraft which may have caused the death. Shaving of hair will become more comprehensible when we examine Trobriand conceptions of beauty and head decoration.

The garden magician's food taboos include the avoidance of black fish. Blackness, however, has in certain contexts positive virtue. A child's head is smeared with charcoal and coconut oil to make the head strong. A black head of hair is positively beautiful. Also, black color has the power to dispel the very thing it is associated with—sorcery, witchcraft, and evil intentions. When black is used in combination with other colors it has positive connotations.

Red. *Kula* beauty magic for attracting the *kula* partner puts emphasis on red. Red paint is called *talo,* which is also the name of one of the *mwasila* magic spells (see Malinowski, 1960: 337, 339). The major symbol in this magic is the red fish. Red fish is also the proper food for ancestors, presumably in order to "animate" them or their power. Redness on the whole connotes radiance, animation, irresistible physical charm and beauty. The main words associated with *talo* are *ikata* ("flares up") and *inamila* ("flashes") (1960: 449). In the beauty ritual performed for ceremonial dancing and courtship, redness has erotic value. Chewing of betel nut (which produces red liquid) is associated with "excitement." Lovers chew betel nut together. In the *kula,* betel nut is given to the partner after charming it with a seducing spell.

Red appears to have no special association with blood, except that the Trobriand theory of conception says that the mother contributes flesh and blood to the child. Nor does it appear to stand conspicuously for matrilineal values as among the Ndembu. The Trobrianders have no menstruation taboos, nor special ablutions at first menstruation, and there is "no pronounced dislike or dread of menstruous blood" (Malinowski, 1929: 144–145).

Face Painting (*Soba*) and Head Ornamentation

All the colors come together in this activity. Malinowski at several points notes that all three colors are used for painting the face with graceful scrolls and designs, but he does not bother to document the intricacies, primarily because he views the matter as simply ornamental and nothing more. But he shows a lively appreciation of Trobriand ornamentation and ceremonial display, and provides enough evidence for us to compile the symbolic basis.

The Trobrianders rarely paint their bodies, but anoint them with aromatic oil. The wished-for state of the body and its skin is "whiteness." The shape of the ideally beautiful face is that of the full moon (Malinowski, 1929: 249), in which image roundness and whiteness are expressed. The main erotic interest of the Trobriander is focused on the head and face, while the seat of emotions is located in the lower part of the body, in the breasts and belly. Face painting and head ornamentation are an important feature of beauty magic in general associated with pregnancy rituals, *kula,* and ceremonial dancing. Both men and women appear to practice the same toilette.

The three paints are manufactured thus. Red (*talo*) paint is obtained from a compound of crushed betel nut and lime; red ocher is also used. White paint was traditionally made from certain kinds of clay mixed with crushed coral, but imported white lead is also used. There are two kinds of black paint—aromatic paint (*sayyaku*) made from charred coconut fiber or charcoal mixed with scented coconut oil, and *nowa* which is the ordinary charcoal blacking.

The individual parts of the face and head, decorated with paints and ornaments, are given complex aesthetic values. The eyes are considered the "gateways of erotic desire," "the seat of desire and lust," the cause (*u'ula*) of sexual passion (1929: 141), with communicating ducts to the lower parts of the body. (The eyes, we may note, are a combination of black and white.) However, black hair on the face is not appreciated, and the eyebrows are shaved. (The biting off of the eyelashes is indulged in in sexual play.) Next to the eyes it is the mouth that is the focus of attention. The magic of *talo* (the red paint made of betel nut) is used to redden the lips. The vermilion lips are set off against the teeth, which are blackened by contact with a special mangrove root. The earlobes are pierced and the holes enlarged and ornamented, normally with earrings of turtle shell and other ornaments made especially with red spondylus shell discs. The proper place for hair is the head (and not on any other part of the body). Black, thick, moppy hair is highly appreciated, gray or white hair and baldness being considered ugly. The Trobrianders have elaborate modes of hairdressing and hairstyles, such as the favorite mop (*gugwapo'u*) or the elongated cylindrical form (*bobobu*); there are separate mourning styles, including full shaving of the head to convey withdrawal from normal life and obligatory assumption of a dirty state (1929: 253). In ceremonial attire the black head of hair is crowned with flaming (red) hibiscus flowers. The ornaments worn on the body are red necklaces and white arm shells.

We have little information about facial designs: white, though used, appears to have secondary emphasis, and red and black paint are the dominant colors. One could guess that red stands for animation and erotic charm, black for power to dispel the evil forces and intentions stemming from other human beings. On the whole, the face and head decorations emphasize red and black, with white showing in the armlets and being given its value mainly in relation to the body and skin.

Festive dress for women is described as a "radiant combination of crimson, purple, and golden skirts" (with black probably excluded?). Normal dress is the yellow-white or golden color of fiber or banana leaf skirts.

Canoe Painting

The canoe (*waga*) is also painted in the three primary colors, of which the most important is black (Malinowski, 1960: 140). It is clear that the dominance of black is expressive of the canoe's speed, and the power of dispelling or withstanding the dangers of sailing. When the canoe has been constructed, three magical rites of exorcism are conducted, to smoke and cleanse it and to impart speed and lightness. This sequence is followed by the painting of the canoe. Rites are performed for each paint: the *kaykoulo* for black paint, the *malakava* for red paint, and the *pwaka* for white paint (1960: 416). The first is compulsory (the others being optional), and the substances used are the wings of the bat, the nest of a small bird called *posisiku*, and dried bracken leaves (all black but here connoting, in addition to dispelling power, lightness and therefore speed), which are charred with coconut husk. The first ceremonial strokes of black are made with this mixture, followed by a watery mixture of charred coconut.

It is clear that the magic of black paint and the symbolism of the color is related to the Trobriand notion of female flying witches (*mulukwausi*), who in the night take the form of flying foxes or nightbirds or other creatures and attack corpses and shipwrecked sailors. But by an inversion, this same image of the witch becomes the image of the much desired "flying canoe" (see "Myth of Kayaduri," in Malinowski, 1960), which has great speed and power to dispel dangers. The substances used in the magic are a "witch's brew."

The next painting sequence is the "staining of the red mouth" of the canoe: a cowrie shell attached to the prowboard (*tabuyo*) is stained at each end (bow and stern). The rite is a component of *kula* magic, and the red may be said to symbolize the animation and flashing beauty of the canoe. Unfortunately, Malinowski provides no data on the designs on the prowboards and how they were painted (however, see plates 26 and 27 in Malinowski, 1960).

The reader may wish to relate the significance of Trobriand color symbolism to the assertions and hypothesis made by Turner (1966). There is confirmation of his thesis of a basic color triad. Each color may be emphasized separately in particular rituals (white in pregnancy rites, red in *kula mwasila* or beauty magic, black in mortuary rites), but they also come together as a configuration in face painting and canoe painting. But, unlike for the Ndembu, red for the Trobrianders does not appear to be an ambivalent color. They do not hunt, and they do not fear menstrual blood. White is positive, and black dominantly negative, but it too in its proper place and context can be inverted to produce positive virtues.

2

Form and Meaning of Magical Acts

Like one of the proverbial blind men who probed different parts of the elephant's body, I shall investigate merely a fragmentary portion of the gigantic question: Is there a basic difference in the modes of thought of "traditional prescientific" and "modern science-oriented" societies? This was implicitly the theme of Evans-Pritchard's justly famous "dialogue" with Lévy-Bruhl. I shall attempt here only a mini-dialogue with Evans-Pritchard concerning the theoretical implications of his Zande data on magic.

My general thesis will be as follows. The *analogical* mode of thought has always been exploited by man generally. While both "magic" and "science" are characterized by analogical thought and action, they comprise differentiated varieties whose validity it would be inappropriate to measure and verify by the same standards. Magical acts, usually compounded of verbal utterance and object manipulation, constitute "performative" acts by which a property is imperatively transferred to a recipient object or person on an analogical basis. Magical acts are ritual acts, and ritual acts are in turn performative acts whose positive and creative meaning is missed and whose persuasive validity is misjudged if they are subjected to that kind of empirical verification associated with scientific activity. Neither magic nor ritual constitutes applied science in the narrow sense.

In contrast, the exploitation of analogical thought in science consists in making the known or apprehended instance serve as a model for the incompletely known in the phenomenon to be explained. The model serves to generate a prediction concerning the *explicandum,* which is then subjected to observation and verification tests to ascertain the prediction's truth value.

"Performative" acts of a persuasive kind are by no means confined to the primitive; modern industrial societies also have their rites and ceremonies which achieve their effects by virtue of conventional normative understandings. However, science (strictly defined) is an achievement perhaps only of certain complex and literate civilizations. In the West at least, where it has attained its fullest development, science probably developed and differentiated out of certain forms of traditional and magical thought and activity; but this should not automatically serve as a universal linear scheme, nor should there be a retrospective and backward thrust by which the "rationality" of magic is pitted against the "rationality" of science, to the former's inevitable and foregone detriment. Indeed it is precisely because many Western anthropologists have approached the ritual performances of other societies from the perspective of their own historical experience and intellectual categories that they have misunderstood the semantic basis of magical acts.

I shall try to give flesh to these programmatic assertions by working through a body of concrete ethnographic data.

The Observer's Problem: The Example of the Azande

Although Evans-Pritchard in his book on the Azande (1937) and in an earlier article written in 1929 admitted that the spell was nearly always a part of and indeed essential to Zande magical rites, he emphasized over and over again (perhaps to drive home the difference between Zande and Trobriand magical systems) that it was "medicines" which played the major part. Mystical power, producing the desired end, resided in the material substance used, whereas spells, having no specific virtue by themselves, were merely words of direction uttered to the "medicines" linking them to the desired ends.

A major concern of Evans-Pritchard was to investigate the attributes and logic of selection of Zande "medicines," and their role in effecting the end sought by the rite. It is my view that in most of Evans-Pritchard's discussion of the potency of Zande "medicines" he was troubled by a theoretical framework whereby "magic" stood for effects automatically ensuing from the ritual operations alone (particularly the manipulation of material substances), and also whereby the efficacy of the ritual acts was sought to be seen within an observer's empirical "cause-effect" scheme.

At several points in his book Evans-Pritchard (1937) tried to apply the observer's distinction *ritual* (or *mystical*) versus *empirical* to the rites he was examining and found them difficult to apply consistently. This question of whether Zande medicines were mystical or empirical plagued him with recurring insistence in his final chapter, entitled "Leechcraft." It is instructive to summarize the findings of this chapter, for here at least where the subject matter was the etiology and cure of disease and the efficacy of Zande "drugs" and "pharmaco-poeia" we might expect the discussion to be more concrete than that pertaining to the more elusive magical rites and witchcraft attacks. A-propos his use of concepts which I have put in quotation marks above, Evans-Pritchard disarmingly states: "We can later decide to what ex-tent their leechcraft is magic, their leeches magicians, and their drugs mere *materia medica* of magical ritual." I shall be concerned here with the implications of that postponed decision.

In the chapter under discussion Evans-Pritchard makes the follow-ing seemingly contradictory points in the space of a few successive pages:

1a. The object or animal chosen as "resembling" the disease may not only constitute the medicine but also the cause of the disease (for example, fowls' excrement is the cause and cure of ringworm).[1]

1b. In seeming contradiction to the above, Evans-Pritchard, agreeing with De Graer, asserts that a Zande, if he feels the need to do so, will attribute sickness to "some mystical entity like witchcraft or magic." The thing or animal that appears in the name of the disease may be a participant in the genesis or a tool of magic, *but is never the object of therapeutic treatment.* The implication of this assertion is that the cause of disease is a "mystical" entity, that there is no direct "causal" relationship between symptom and object resembling it. What then is the logic of using the object as a "cure" in treatment?

2a. The Azande show discerning powers of observation and commonsense inference—as seen by their naming of dis-eases by symptoms, by their perceptive diagnosis and cure of some diseases by the "logico-experimental" use of drugs, and by the employment in a few instances of "em-pirical therapeutics" (p. 495)—for example, treatment of headache, use of massage or emetics, and so forth.

2b. But the true answer to the question of whether Zande

leechcraft "is in any degree empirically sound, or . . . pure magic" is this:

"The enormous number of drugs which Azande employ and the variety of herbal products they bring to bear on a single disease at once demonstrate their lack of therapeutic value when we reflect what scientific pharmacology really implies" (p. 494). Evans-Pritchard's final verdict is unambiguous: "In spite of . . . empirical elements in Zande treatment of minor ailments, my own experience has been that Zande remedies are of an almost completely magical order" (p. 499). And Evans-Pritchard concludes that the "drugs" of Zande leechcraft are no different in their preparation from the "medicines" of Zande magic (p. 499), that most cases of prophylactic and therapeutic treatment have little or no objective value. The performances of leeches are similar to the magical performances: "drugs of leeches are boiled and spells are uttered over them in the same manner as medicines of magicians" (p. 504).

Evans-Pritchard's final attempt at sorting the data, in answer to the query: "To what extent are Zande medical practices 'empirical' as opposed to 'ritual'?" ran something like this. In acute and sudden illnesses the attribution of genesis may be to "mystical" causes like sorcery and witchcraft alone; in chronic and prolonged illnesses recourse is to a theory of *dual causation* in that there is the disease itself *plus* witchcraft, which conditions its occurrence and continuance. (This dual theory is paralleled by Evans-Pritchard's earlier elucidation of witchcraft: while the Zande are aware of the physical circumstances of accidents and disease, witchcraft explains why a particular sufferer and no other was the victim. "Witchcraft explains why events are harmful to man and not how they happen"—p. 72.) In both acute and chronic illness, in which mystical forces are at play, the drugs used are appropriately thought to have "mystical" efficacy, as seen in the notion of *mbisimo ngua*, "the soul of medicine" (corresponding to the notion "soul of witchcraft").

Mild illnesses, in contrast, bring to the fore, so Evans-Pritchard says, "natural" or organic causation, with the witchcraft allegation sinking into the background. But even here "the treatment may be just as useless in a slight as in a serious illness" (p. 505). It is not surprising then that Evans-Pritchard admits with a touch of bafflement: "There are many varieties of behaviour and opinion which defy rigid classification because they shade into one another in a complicated pattern of interconnexions" (p. 506).

Despite this confession, it is evident that Evans-Pritchard did sort things out after a fashion. With the benefit of hindsight it might seem that a greater attention to folk classification of disease and "medicines" and the native exegesis about them might have provided additional clarification. My thesis is that this lack itself is the concomitant of a certain theoretical perspective. Evans-Pritchard had clear clues that much of Zande magic was based on analogical thought and action, but rather than investigate its semantics deeply, he, being at this stage of his thought unable to liberate himself from the influence of the observer's distinction between things empirical and things mystical (and the like), simply subjected Zande magic and leechcraft to the Westerner's criteria of induction and verification. The unstated assumption of such an intellectual exercise is that Zande practices had the same empirical purposes and objectives as those of Western science and that they, like science, were concerned with "causal" relations. This chapter is largely concerned with the consequences of (erroneously) submitting Zande analogical thought and action to Western scientific standards of induction and verification.

The Uses of Analogy

Evans-Pritchard's originality could not, of course, be confined for long within the bounds of limiting frameworks. Consequently, fresh insights break through here and there in the Zande book. One such is contained in the passing phrase "imitative symbolism," and another in the idea of "homeopathy," discussed briefly in two pages (pp. 449–450). Here we find the seeds of an approach to Zande magic (and indeed other magical systems) which I shall call "analogical action."

Apparently the Azande themselves recognized the analogical and metaphorical basis for the use of material substances in their rites—a revelation which is also embedded in Malinowski's account (see Chapter 1). Evans-Pritchard (1937) writes: "They [the Azande] say, 'We use such-and-such a plant because it is like such-and-such a thing,' naming the object towards which the rite is directed. Likewise they say, 'We do so-and-so in order that so-and-so may happen,' naming the action which they wish to follow. Often the similarity between medicine and desired happening is indicated in the spell" (p. 449). Evans-Pritchard proceeds to give the example (which he also gave in 1929) of the tall *bingba* grass, which is profuse in growth and has featherlike branches, being used by verbal direction and by direct action to make the oil-bearing melon (*kpagu*) flourish.

There are many examples of analogical action in word and deed scattered throughout the book. A systematic assembling and examination of these examples may provide an alternative interpretation to the one proposed by Evans-Pritchard.

Scrutinize these preliminary examples with this objective in view:

1. When the Azande prick the stalks of bananas with crocodiles' teeth they say, "Teeth of crocodile are you, I prick bananas with them, may bananas be prolific like crocodiles' teeth" (p. 450).

2. Azande tie *gbaga* (the fruit of a palm tree) to their girdles as a medicine of masculinity and to secure sexual potency. When tying they say: "You are *gbaga*. May I be very potent sexually. May I not become sexually weak" (p. 455).

3. Here is an expressive example that could equally well come from Sri Lanka or Thailand. If a man is a victim of *menzere* (sorcery) medicine, he goes to a much-frequented crossroads, kneels there, and verbally disperses it: "If it is *menzere,* may it follow all paths and not return" (p. 394).

4. Finally, there is the celebrated case of the stone placed in the fork of a tree to retard the sun: "You stone, may the sun not be quick to fall today. You, stone, retard the sun on high so that I can arrive first at that homestead to which I journey; then the sun may set" (p. 469).

Note here that the Azande refer to the stone used as *ngua uru,* which Evans-Pritchard translates as "sun-medicine."

It is my submission that, had Evans-Pritchard followed leads of this sort, he could have thrown more light on why within the range of plant life and arboreal substances (which form the major category of "medicines") used by the Azande, certain woods or roots or leaves rather than others were chosen to represent specialized ideas. Furthermore, the utterances and spells are in fact, as we have seen in these examples, critical for telling us which feature of an object-symbol is the focus of attention on an analogical basis. A shift of theoretical interest from "inherent potency" of medicines to "analogical transfer of their qualities" might have made the botanical enumeration of Zande medicines less tedious and unnecessary than Evans-Pritchard feared.

Here is a critical passage which I shall take as the text for my discussion. It encapsulates the "closed" system of Zande thought, a central theme of this book (and grist for the Popperian mill):

> I do not know whether more than a verbal analogy is implied in the Zande name for mumps (the affected parts are massaged with an unguent): *imawirianzoro*, sickness of the little (*wiri*) *anzoro* birds (finches) which have lumps on their necks. But it may well be so, for we know that in primitive patterns of thought objects which have a superficial resemblance are often linked up by nomenclature and ritual and are connected in mystical patterns of thought. In Zande therapeutics this mystical connexion is found in notions about cause and cure. Ringworm resembles in appearance fowls' excrement, and fowls' excrement is at the same time both cause and cure of ringworm. Blepharoptosis resembles a hen's egg, and a hen's egg is its cure. Generally the logic of therapeutic treatment consists in the selection of the most prominent external symptoms, the naming of the disease after some object in nature which it resembles, and the utilization of the object as the principal ingredient in the drug administered to cure the disease. The circle may even be completed by belief that the symptoms not only yield to treatment by the object which resembles them but are caused by it as well. (1937: 486–487)

A number of words appear in this commentary that are worthy of "practical criticism." "Superficial resemblance" can get its meaning only by unstated comparison with the notion of deeper identity from a scientific causal viewpoint; "mystical connexion" can only mean unobservable and unknown connection by comparison with empirically observable connection. The backdrop then is the standards of verification of science.

A classicist who was exploring the use of analogy by early Greek philosophers and who consulted Evans-Pritchard on Zande magic inferred certain principles from the extract quoted above. He wrote:

> This passage illustrates very clearly three quite distinct functions which an analogy may serve.
>
>   1. First, an object may be named or described by referring to another object which it resembles. (Here it *need* not be implied that there is a causal connection between the two objects, though it is often the case that some causal connection is, in fact, assumed to exist.)

2. Secondly, the recognition of a resemblance between two objects may serve as the basis for an explanation of one of them, that is, an account of its cause.

3. Thirdly, the resemblances between things may be thought to form magical links between them and attempts may be made to control or influence certain objects by manipulating other objects which resemble them: the Azande hope to effect cures by using the natural object which resembles the particular disease, and such "homoeopathic" magical practices are, of course, common in all parts of the world. (Lloyd, 1966: 178)

I consider the last inference the most important (it includes the other two as well), for it is the basis on which philosophers and historians of science see the similarity and difference between magic and science, as well as the ground on which they postulate linear evolution from magic to science. Lloyd (1966) thus takes the next interpretive step:

> We can see from these examples how analogy fulfills two roles in what is now for us largely, though not exclusively, the province of science, namely to provide explanations, and to control reality. As regards the second function, the most important difference between science and magic may be simply their relative effectiveness. Magic fails in practice. Yet its general aim is similar to that of applied science, to control events, and one of the means whereby it hopes to achieve this is *using the links which it believes may be formed between things by their similarities.* (pp. 178–179; italics added)

Most historians of science begin with the Greeks, and one of the principles of thought attributed to early Greek natural philosophy is that "like attracts like," which in its application meant "that a relationship of similarity may sometimes constitute a magical bond between two things, so that what happens to one of them may influence what happens to the other" (Lloyd, 1966:180). Thus, Hesse (1961) explains that one of the commonest analogies in "primitive" Greek thought was "the analogy of attraction": men apparently, having experienced sympathy and antipathy, attraction and repulsion, between themselves and other men, and between themselves and nature, therefore see these as forces which can produce effects in nature. Popular maxims based on ideas of attraction and repulsion provided, we are told, concepts of *motion* and *change*—thus, "like attracts like" was supplemented by other maxims such as "like nourishes like,"

"like affects like," "like perceives like." The doctrine of attraction explained why animals flock together with their kind, seeds of the same size seek each other when shaken in a sieve, and pebbles of like size are grouped on the seashore. In Plutarch is found the example of treating jaundice with the yellow eye of a stone curlew.

For the historian and philosopher of science, the analogy of attraction is principally of interest because the early Greek philosophers used it to explain the phenomenon of *action at a distance,* a perennial problem in scientific explanation. The Greek breakthrough from primitive analogy to "scientific" thinking, we are told, began to occur when two things happened: first, when a firm distinction was made between the animate and inanimate, and when it was recognized that phenomena of gravity and radiation were different in kind from the behavior of animals; second, when thereby a certain amount of "mechanization" of physics took place, with Aristotle and with the atomists. Indeed "action at a distance" became intellectually problematic only when this stage had been reached. "Part of the history of the problem of action at a distance is therefore that of the growth of a mechanical conception of matter, and the use of mechanical analogies in explaining natural processes" (Hesse, 1961:30). Thus, for example, it was the "atomists," we are told, who by virtue of their notion of atoms in motion introduced a purely mechanical theory of motion and change through contact.

Readers of the Azande book will have noticed that Evans-Pritchard was very concerned with this classical problem of "action at a distance," which was spelled out in terms of "mystical" ties, the "soul" of witchcraft or of "medicine" affecting a victim, and the like, all of which are adduced in an attempt to solve an "intellectual" problem which is not necessarily the Azande's.

How relevant are classical Greek scholarship and the writings of historians of science for illuminating the thought patterns of the Azande, Trobrianders, and other "prescientific" peoples? I cannot go into this matter at length here, but let me sound a note of caution. From a comparative point of view it is useful to bear in mind that many Western philosophers are concerned with how early Greek thought led by stages to the development of scientific thought wedded to experimental verification—in other words, how Greek thought was transformed from "magic" to "science," and how the seeds sown by the Greek philosophers ultimately flowered in the scientific revolution of the seventeenth century, when "the analogy of mechanism" alone was exploited with respect to events in nature and when nature's laws were sought in mechanical conceptions. Indeed, when later Newton's theory of gravity was propounded, the Cartesians attacked him for propounding a theory of "attraction" in the occult idiom—that is, action at a distance without contact. The linear evolution and transformation of Western thought from the sixth century B.C. to the present day in the field of science should not be taken as an intellectual model when investigating the societies anthropologists study, unless at the same time one is deeply conscious of the underlying intellectual interests of the scholars who formulated it. Their interests were the foundations of scientific thought and of formal logic in Greece and the unique(?) development by which Greek analogical thought became subject to empirical verification, falsification, and deductive-inductive reasoning. Must analogical thought of the Azande necessarily be examined and its form and meaning unraveled in relation to these intellectual preoccupations?

In order to answer this question, let us examine carefully the kinds of analogies that exist and their uses. First of all, what do we mean by "analogy"? Basically, analogy depends on the recognition of similarities between the instances compared, and, as many philosophers have recognized, analogy stands as a prototype of reasoning from experience. J. S. Mill's paradigm serves well as a definition: "Two things resemble each other in one or more respects; a certain proposition is true of the one; therefore it is true of the other." Lloyd elucidating Keynes's thinking on the subject (in *A Treatise on Probability*) remarks that "both Bacon's own inductive method, based on the use of 'exclusions and rejections,' and Mill's Methods of Agreement and Difference, aim at the determination of the resemblances and differences between particular instances, at the determination of what Keynes called the Positive and Negative Analogies" (1966:173).

Hesse in an instructive essay (1963), on which I draw, lists four kinds of analogies. For my purposes, I shall modify her examples, and elaborate in new directions fundamentally two types of analogy—the *scientific predictive* and the *conventional persuasive*. First, let us bear in mind that "positive analogy" relates to properties shared or points of similarity between the things compared, "negative analogy" to their points of difference or properties they do not share, and "neutral analogy" to properties of the things compared of which we do not yet know whether they are of positive or negative character.

Of the two fundamentally different types of analogies that can be distinguished, one serves as a model in science generating hypotheses and comparisons which are then subject to verification inductively. In this use, the known or apprehended instance serves as the "model" and the unknown or incompletely known is the *explicandum*, the phenomenon to be explained by means of a theory.

Figures 2.1 and 2.2 show examples of analogies that might be used

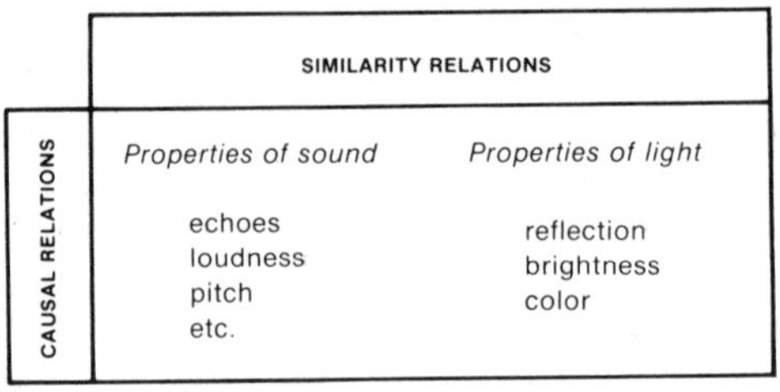

SIMILARITY RELATIONS	
Properties of sound	*Properties of light*
echoes	reflection
loudness	brightness
pitch	color
etc.	

(left vertical label: CAUSAL RELATIONS)

Figure 2.1. Examples of analogies that might be used in science, showing relations of similarity and causality.

in science. Following Hesse, I indicate in the figures two kinds of dyadic relations that should be recognized: the *horizontal* and *vertical* relations. If Figure 2.1 is to serve as a material analogy in science, the pairs of horizontal terms (echoes : reflection, and so forth) should be either identical or *similar,* and the vertical relations (between the properties of sound such as echoes, loudness) should be *causal,* which term given a wide interpretation should mean at least a tendency to *co-occurrence,* in that certain properties are necessary or sufficient conditions for the occurrence of other properties.

In the "looser" example given in Figure 2.2, the horizontal relation may show similarities of *structure* or of *function,* and the vertical relation that of whole to its parts depending on some theory of interrelation of parts, evolutionary or adaptive.

It is essential to note that analogies can usefully serve as theoretical models only if the horizontal dyadic relations are relations of similarity (that is, judged by identities and differences), if the vertical relations of the model are *causal* in some scientifically acceptable sense and if those of the *explicandum* also promise relations of the same kind, and if the essential properties and causal relations of the model have not been shown to be part of the negative analogy between model and *explicandum*. If these conditions are satisfied, then predictions can legitimately be made from any set of known—say, three—terms to an

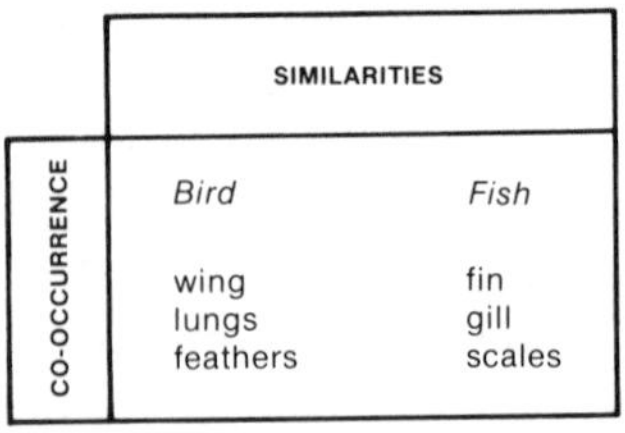

SIMILARITIES	
Bird	*Fish*
wing	fin
lungs	gill
feathers	scales

(left vertical label: CO-OCCURRENCE)

Figure 2.2. Examples of analogies that might be used in science, showing relations of similarity and co-occurrence.

unknown fourth. For example, in the case of the sound and light analogies in Figure 2.1, if we have established the similarity of "echoes" to "reflection," then from the known property of "loudness" in sound we may expect to find the "similar" property of "brightness" in light. Or in the bird and fish analogy, one can predict from the known parts of the bird skeleton to a "missing" part of the fish skeleton. To put it differently, the fun lies in extrapolating from the domain of positive analogy into the domain of neutral analogy, as these were defined above. Ultimately, of course, these predictions should be capable of verification or falsification in terms of observation statements.

There is another kind of traditional analogy used widely in human discourse that does not owe its genesis and use to the pursuit of "scientific" knowledge. It would therefore be ridiculous to weigh and measure its adequacy in terms of inductive verification. Consider the following analogy that may occur in political rhetoric: the employer is to his workers as a father is to his children.

$$\frac{\text{father}}{\text{children}} : \frac{\text{employer}}{\text{workers}}$$

Let us say that the purpose of this analogy is propagandist, that it is disseminated by employers in order to "evoke" attitudes in workers rather than to "predict" them.

It should be noted that in this example the vertical relations are not specifically causal; nor is it necessary that if three terms occur, the fourth also must. Even more important, there is not in this example any horizontal relation of similarity between the terms, except by virtue of the fact that the two pairs are up to a point *related by the same vertical relation*. (There may be other persuasive analogies in which, in spite of horizontal similarities between terms, the critical relation is still the vertical one.)

How must this analogy work if it is to succeed as political rhetoric? The relation of father to children bears some resemblance to the relation of employer to workers (positive analogy) in the sense, let us say, that just as the father provides for the material needs of his children so does the employer provide work and wages for his workers. Let us next say that the relation of children to father (and vice versa) is much more than this dependence; children should love their father, obey and respect him, and so on. These meanings are not necessarily implied in the employer-worker relation (negative analogy). It is precisely this expansion of meaning or the transfer of these additional values to the employer-worker relation that is sought by invoking the father-children analogy. Since in this case the ultimate aim is to make workers believe that they are like "children," there is a sense in which we can say that the operation consists in "transferring" (rather than "predicting") from the postulated three terms the value of "children" to the fourth term, the "workers." It is for this reason that this analogy and its variants are labeled "persuasive," "rationalizing," or "evocative."

It is my thesis that in ritual operations by word and object manipulation, the analogical action conforms to the "persuasive" rather than the "scientific" model. I shall later illustrate the argument that in Zande rites (as well as those of many other societies) the operation rests on the explicit recognition of *both similarity* (positive analogy) *and difference* (negative analogy) *between the vertical relations of the paired terms*. And the rite consists in persuasively transferring the properties of the desired and desirable vertical relation to the other which is in an undesirable condition, or in attempting to convert a potential, not-yet-achieved state into an actualized one. The manipulation is made operationally realistic by directing the transfer not only by word but, as in the Zande case, by bringing a material piece of the object in the desirable-desired analogy into contact with the object in need of the transfer. There are nuances in this basic manipulation which are best illustrated when dealing with the concrete cases.

Thus, a vital difference exists between the use of "analogy" in science and its use in ritual. Barring a few instances, in most Zande magical rites (especially those considered important by the people concerned), the analogical relation or comparison and the wished-for effect is stated *verbally* simultaneously with or before the carrying out of the "homeopathic" act (of influencing certain objects by manipulating other objects which resemble them). Why must the analogy of attraction be stated in word and deed for it to be effective? No classical philosopher or historian of science appears to have asked this when propounding that the principle of "like attracts like" activated primitive thought and action. In a laboratory of today, the only time a scientist may be found to foretell and verbally explain his actions while simultaneously doing his experiment would be, for example, when he is teaching a class the procedure involved in conducting that experiment. (And of course he does not expect that his words will automatically make the experiment come out right, as we know from the failed experiments in science classes we have attended at school.) Outside some such situation, his sanity would be suspect if he gave instructions aloud to his apparatus to do his bidding.

Note also how extraordinary the magical operation must look in terms of the traditional explanation (of like attracts like) when placed in relation to the use of analogy made by a scientist. Supposing a scientist constructs an electronic brain-model to "simulate" in some ways a human biochemically structured brain. The former is useful as a predictive model only in those areas where the material makeup of the analogue is not essential to the model (that is, constitutes the innocuous negative analogy) but where the pattern of mutual relation of the parts and the behavioral relations expressed by it are the essential features. If, say, a man is weak in arithmetic the scientist does not bring a brain-model that can add and place it in contact with the head of the former so that his additions may be thus "caused" to be correct. But this is precisely what we are told the primitive magician might attempt to do! (On the other hand, the scientist may demonstrate the working of an adding machine to our hypothetical subject, and it is possible that after sufficient demonstration of its workings the subject's abilities might increase. This is a technique of "persuasion" through contact. Could it be that this is the logic of the magical operations as well?)

Some Zande Analogies

I have already noted that for the first time, well toward the end of the Azande book, Evans-Pritchard (1937) broached the question of the analogical basis of magical rites as seen by the actors. It is, however, a pity that he did not compile a more thorough indigenous exegesis on why certain "medicines" were used, and what properties or features of the substance used were singled out as "similar" to those of the recipient of the rite. Hence, in the examples he cryptically cites, the logic of their use is open to an alternative interpretation that is as plausible as Evans-Pritchard's own implicitly theory-dictated view that the medicines and drugs, chosen on the basis of superficial resemblances and to which is given mystical significance, are empirically ineffective and scientifically false, although used as if they had automatic effects. Let us look at some Zande cases:

1. At a certain time of their growth the stems of the creeper *araka* lose their leaves. These are replaced by a double row of bands, joined to the stalks, which little by little dry, split, and fall in small pieces just as the extremities of the hands and feet disappear in "*la lèpre mutilante.*" This creeper is highly thought of as furnishing treatment for this kind of leprosy (p. 450).

I suggest that the analogical reasoning in this example is more complex than is implied by a simplistic "like attracts like," in that it brings to view both similarities and differences, positive and negative analogies, in the *vertical relations* of the terms (see Figure 2.3). In

	POSITIVE AND NEGATIVE ANALOGIES	
CO-OCCURRENCE	Araka creeper ————————— falling leaves etc. ————————— growth	Human being ————————— falling extremities ————————— disease (leprosy)

Figure 2.3. Zande analogies between *araka* creeper and human being.

the case of the creeper, the falling of its extremities is a *phase of its growth cycle*, whereas in the case of human beings the decay of limbs through leprosy is a *disease that leads to degeneration and death.* Thus, this comparison proceeds to use the *araka* creeper in the rite as a vehicle or agent of life, the message being: may the leprosy disappear and health appear, just as the shedding process in the creeper stimulates growth. The rite expresses the wish that one "vertical" relation that is undesired be replaced by another desired one; it itself represents symbolic, not causal, action.

2. Let us next take the celebrated example already cited of a man indulging "in the action of placing a stone in the tree and relating by a few words this action to a desired end." We should bear in mind that the man is on a journey and wishes to arrive home before sunset (pp. 468–469).

We can plausibly say that here the initial comparison is between the sun "traveling" toward sunset (in the sky) and a man traveling (on land) to his homestead (see Figure 2.4). The sun and the man are therefore similar in their situations, but their interests are not identical (the difference that constitutes the negative analogy). The man wishes to travel faster than the sun. It is in this context that we must view the operation of putting a stone in the fork of a tree and thus wedging it. It represents the desired positive effect of retarding the sun and the implicit counter effect (or negative analogy) of quickening

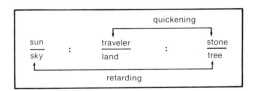

Figure 2.4. Zande analogies describing a man on a journey.

his footsteps home, which in fact the traveler actually does by performing this rite.

3. A third example is a case of "homeopathic" treatment of a disease. Ringworm in children is called *imanduruakondo* (*ima* = sickness; *nduruakondo* = fowl house). It is so called because the scabby patches of the disease resemble fowls' excrement. Hence, they appear to consider the disease a result of the afflicted child's having eaten food grown on a dung heap in the vicinity of a fowl house. Hence also they consider the remedy to consist in fowls' excrement dried and reduced to ashes and mixed into a paste with a little palm oil and applied to the ringworm (p. 485).

While the "like attracts like" argument would say that the fowls' excrement is (falsely) used to attract the scabs on the skin which it (falsely) resembles, I am tempted to say that the analogy is interesting and is capable of being acted upon creatively because, once again, of the positive and negative features it exhibits (see Figure 2.5). The relation of fowl to excrement is one of *elimination* of (unwanted) waste product, while that of scabby skin on child is one of (unwanted) *adherence* to body. Hence it is that the fowl's excrement can convey the desired idea of eliminating the scabs when applied to the body, because while in one sense similar to it, it is also essentially different.

4. Epileptic fits (*imawirianya: wiri* = small; *nya* = animal) are associated with the red bush monkey, which is thought to display certain movements resembling epileptic symptoms. Before sunrise this monkey seems to be in a torpor, but as he comes out of it under the warm rays of the sun, so does the epileptic slowly recover when placed in the warmth of a fire. One of the remedies for epilepsy is to eat ashes of the burnt skull of the red monkey (pp. 483–484). Superficially considered, it seems inconsistent and absurd that the ashes of the skull of the "epileptic" monkey can cure an epileptic man. But in fact the analogy moves in two steps, exploiting the fact that although the

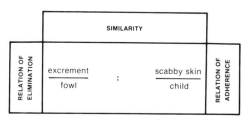

Figure 2.5. Zande analogies for the treatment of ringworm.

monkey's movements resemble epilepsy, yet it is a normal occurrence for the monkey to revive daily from its torpor under the warm rays of the sun, and the same recovery is desired in the patient. It is this capacity of the monkey to revive daily that is persuasively exploited by the rite of eating the ashes of the monkey's skull.

Enough Zande examples have been given to suggest how the analogical thought and action of the persuasive type are exploited. A well known example such as the cure of elephantiasis by the use of ashes from a piece of burnt elephant's leg looks much less bizarre when subjected to similar analysis. Nor is this underlying logic peculiar to the Azande. Numerous cases were documented by Malinowski: one example that neatly illustrates analogical action is that in which the Trobrianders, having postulated an analogy (or homology) between the yam house with yams stored in it and the human belly with food inside it, act upon the former in order to influence the latter. According to Trobriand logic (as we have already seen in Chapter 1), the rite is really a metaphorical analogy urging the human belly to restrain its hunger and greed for food. The application of "similarity and difference" analogically also serves to unravel the logic of some Trobriand food taboos.

Closer to the Azande, a number of examples can be taken from Turner's voluminous and excellent documentation of the symbolism exploited by the Ndembu in their rites. For instance, take the Ndembu *Ntambu* cult, which deals with the hunter's affliction of failure to kill animals. The mode of manifestation of the disease is that the afflicted hunter sees a lion in his dreams, and the ritual consists of the making of an effigy of a lion on a mound and the miming of the lion's actions by the hunter and the practitioner (Turner, 1968: 301). Or again, consider the simple persuasive analogy which exploits identity and difference between a Mujiwu tree which has many roots (empirically a true and desirable state of affairs) and a woman who wants to have many children (desired but not an empirically inevitable state of affairs). The Ndembu penchant for use of arboreal substances rests on such analogies and persuasive manipulations, which are cultural equations. There is no intrinsic reason why the tree should be similar to a mother and the roots to children, but the analogy which says that roots are to the tree as children are to the mother makes relational sense that can be used to "transfer" effects.

Finally, take this fragment from Dobuan magic (close in form to the Trobriand system) which displays a persuasive analogical act. Fortune (1932) writes: "The woman magician next breathes a spell into two or three water gourds containing (sea) water, and pours the water over the heaped seed yams . . . The spell breathed into the water gourds and continued while the water is being poured runs—

> murua octopus
> from its inner cave
> it thrusts a left arm out
> on the left side it lies, head inland,
> it thrusts a right arm out
> comes over and lies down . . ." (1932: 117)

The analogical pattern of this rite is crystal clear. Verbally a comparison is made between the octopus which has many tentacles and the yam which it is desired will sprout many roots and shoots (like an octopus). The seawater in which the octopus lives metonymically represents it, and it is realistically poured on the yam to transfer to it the desired properties of the octopus. This Dobuan example portrays equally well the underlying design of Trobriand analogical action.

How to Understand Ritual (Which Includes "Magic")?

I have perhaps so far only indicated negatively how "magic" should not be viewed, and not positively how it might be viewed in terms of a new perspective. I have argued that to view magic as an attempt at science that failed (or more crudely a "bastard science" in the manner of Frazer, or more sophisticatedly as a "closed" system of thought that allows for no verification and falsification of its principles *à la* Popper) is to assert that in their magic and ritual[2] the primitives tried to achieve results through "causal" reasoning and failed. I have also argued that while it is the case that much primitive magic is based on analogical thought and action as is Western science, the difference between them is that whereas in science the use of an analogy is closely linked to prediction and verification, and its adequacy judged in terms of inductive support, or of meeting standards of probability criteria, or of standing up to tests of falsifiability, and the like, the semantics of a magical rite are not necessarily to be judged in terms of such "true/false" criteria of science but on different standards and objectives. The corresponding objectives in (magical) ritual are "persuasion," "conceptualization," "expansion of meaning," and the like, and the criteria of adequacy are better conveyed by notions such as "validity," "correctness," "legitimacy," and "felicity" of the ceremony performed.

It is this latter assertion that I wish to elucidate now. In Chapter 1 I took some steps toward understanding the form and meaning of ritual in terms of its inner semantic frame and outer pragmatic frame. My starting point with regard to the former was that most "magical rites" (as indeed most rituals) combine word and deed and that the rite is devoted to an "imperative transfer" of effects, which some might phrase as the "telic" and others as the "illocutionary" or "performative" nature of the rite (Austin, 1962; Finnegan, 1969). The semantics of the transfer itself, the logic of construction of the transfer, in the Trobriand case depend 1) on metaphorical and analogical transfers by word, mediated by realistic contact transfer through objects used as "transformers," and 2) on imperative verbal transfer of energy to a "whole" through the metonymic naming of the parts. One of the points I made was that the same laws of association that apply to ordinary language apply to magical language—I reiterate this because one reader at least has managed to misunderstand my effort and thinks I tried to deal with the special character of "magical" utterances (Finnegan, 1969: 549), thereby also not appreciating my critique of the theory of "magical" language held by Ogden and Richards, Malinowski, and others. But fortunately, in compensation, Finnegan has led me to Austin (1962), whose ideas I shall exploit in an attempt to formulate a perspective, according to my own design, for viewing the form and meaning of ritual.

In Austin's *How To Do Things with Words* (1962), the chief topic of elaboration is what he calls the "performative" or "illocutionary" act, in which the uttering of the sentence cannot merely be described as saying something, but is, or is a part of, the *doing of an action.* When in a marriage ceremony the man says "I do take this woman to be my lawful wedded wife" (or some such formula), or the man says in a will "I give and bequeath . . . ," to utter these sentences in the appropriate circumstances "is not to *describe* my doing of what I should be said in so uttering to be doing or to state I am doing it: it is to do it" (p. 6).

What ultimately I think Austin arrives at toward the end of his exercise is a classification of speech acts, "the issuing of utterances in a speech situation," which makes any stating "performing an act." (This is close to Malinowski's approach of seeing speech as part of action; see Chapter 1.) How many senses may there be in which to say something is to do something, or in saying something we do something, or even by saying something we do something? The following classification of speech acts may help answer the question:

1. To perform a *locutionary* act: To utter a sentence with a certain sense and reference (an assertion, a descriptive statement of fact) which is *true or false in a referential sense.*

2. To perform an *illocutionary* act: This relates to an utterance which has a *certain conventional force*, a performative act *which does something* (as implied in promising, ordering, apologizing, warning). Usually the explicit illocutionary utterance is reducible or analyzable into a form with a verb in the first person singular present indicative active (that is, the "I," the "active," and the "present" seem appropriate). These statements cannot be subject *to the true-false test,* but are *normatively judged* as "happy"/"unhappy," valid/invalid, correct/defective, and so forth.

3. To perform a *perlocutionary* act: This refers to what we bring about or achieve by *saying something* (as connoted by convincing, persuading, misleading). It refers to both the intended and unintended *consequence* upon the hearer of words uttered by the speaker. (By saying it I convinced him . . .)

These three are analytically separate but in reality not exclusive categories: both locutionary and illocutionary acts can have consequences listed as perlocutionary; and an illocutionary act can have referring and predicating elements together with the performative.[3] We could perhaps say that an imperative illocutionary act attempts to get the world to conform to words, whereas "true" when ascribed to illocutions attributes success in getting words to conform to the world.

Adapting these ideas for our purposes, we can say that ritual acts and magical rites are of the "illocutionary" or "performative" sort, which simply by virtue of being enacted (under the appropriate conditions) achieve a change of state, or do something effective (for example, an installation ceremony undergone by the candidate makes him a "chief"). This performative aspect of the rite should be distinguished from its locutionary (referential, information-carrying) and perlocutionary (consequences for the participants) features.

It was quite evident to Austin that, while he focused on the role of speech in illocutionary acts, the utterance was not the sole thing necessary if the illocutionary act was to be deemed to have been performed, and also that *actions other than speech,* whether physical or mental, were entailed for the full realization of the performance. Indeed it is even possible at the other extreme to enact a performative act without uttering words at all—a hypothetical example would be the establishing of blood brotherhood by the physical exchange of blood (without an exchange of words).

The vast majority of ritual and magical acts combine word and deed. Hence, it is appropriate to say that they use words in a performative or illocutionary manner, just as the action (the manipulation of objects and persons) is correspondingly performative.

I shall attempt to formalize in a few words the essentials of what I see as the form and meaning of magical ritual acts. The rite usually consists of a close interweaving of *speech* (in the form of utterances and spells) and *action* (consisting of the manipulation of objects). The *utterance* can be analyzed with respect to its "predicative" and "illocutionary" frames. In terms of predication and reference the words exploit analogical associations, comparisons, and transfers (through simile, metaphor, metonym, and so forth). The illocutionary force and power by which the deed is directed and enacted are achieved through use of words commanding, ordering, persuading, and the like: "Whistle, whistle, I send you after a thief"—so commands a Zande spell. And a Trobriand spell combines both metaphor and illocutionary force by urging the *taytu* yam to throw out foliage like the spider spinning its web (Malinowski, 1965: 148):

> The spider covers up, the spider covers up . . .
> The open space, the open space between thy branches, O taytu
>   the spider covers up,
> . . . Shoot up, O head of my taytu
> . . . Make mop upon mop of leaves, O head of my taytu . . .

The action can be similarly analyzed. The objects manipulated are chosen analogically on the basis of similarity and difference to convey meaning. From the performative perspective, the action consists of an operation done on an object-symbol to make an imperative and realistic transfer of its properties to the recipient. Or to put it differently, two objects are seen as having resemblances and differences, and an attempt is made to transfer the desirable quality of one to the other, which is in a defective state.

It is clear that the words and action closely combine to form an amalgam which is the magical or ritual *act.* The interrelation between the two media—speech and object manipulation—can take different forms.[4] What I want to emphasize here is that this way of looking at "magical art" breaks through the Saussurean *langue/parole* distinction. On the one hand, the magical act bears predicative and referential *langue*-type meanings, and on the other it is a performative act. Both frames are coexistent, and it is as a *performative* or "illocutionary" act directed by analogical reasoning that magic acquires its distinctiveness.

It is *inappropriate* to subject these performative rites to verification, to test whether they are true or false in a referential or assertive sense or whether the act has effected a result in terms of the logic of "causation" as this is understood in science. Let me illustrate the point by considering the Thai rite in which a new house is blessed by Buddhist monks (so that evil spirits may be driven out and prosperity result) through the recitation of sacred verses and the performance of certain acts. Several conditions have to be satisfied if a performance of this rite is not, to use Austin's word, to become an "infelicity": there must exist a conventional procedure properly enacted only by authorized persons—for example, monks or householders; the monks who take part must be entitled to conduct the ceremony (as in this particular instance); and the actual ceremony must be executed both correctly and completely.

Quite another set of conditions relates to the *bona fides* of the actors. For example, the rite is intended for beneficiaries who expect to conduct themselves in certain ways and who have the right intentions. In fulfillment of this, it is necessary that the participants, in the actual rite performed, satisfy these expectations and actually so conduct themselves subsequently.

Now suppose that after the performance of the rite, it is found that one or more of these conditions were not fulfilled—the monks may have been bogus, the ceremony incorrectly performed, or the householder never intended to live in the house with his family but planned to use it for an illicit purpose. We cannot in these circumstances say that the rite itself was false or empirically ineffective in a causal sense. The ceremony *itself* cannot ever be said to have been proved to be false or untrue or ineffective; however, any particular enactment of it may be said to be void, unworthy, or defective. A bigamist who on false pretenses has gone through a second marriage ceremony does not on that account make the institution of marriage false, wrong, or ineffective; what can be said is that he has undergone the ceremony in bad faith and that he has not properly "married" a second time.

The conclusions therefore are that 1) while to particular instances of ritual enactments of the illocutionary or performative type *norma-*

tive judgments of efficacy (legitimacy, defectiveness, propriety, and so forth) may be applied, it is inappropriate to judge their efficacy in terms of *verification statements* and inductive rules, and 2) while ritual in general as an institution cannot be declared to be defective, particular instances of it may be so declared, if the proper conditions of performance were not met. It is at this point that I wish to take issue with Evans-Pritchard and Robin Horton.

Evans-Pritchard in his classic study of Zande witchcraft, oracles, and magic, having elucidated the coherence and close linkage of these systems of belief, felt it necessary to ask how they fitted into the observer-imposed ritual/empirical categories and how they related to Zande "practical" day-to-day activity. More pointedly, Evans-Pritchard, naturally interested in a "European" intellectual problem, asked how magic, which was oriented to achieving effects, compared with Western empiricism based on canons of proof and experimentation. Evans-Pritchard gave various reasons why the Azande did not cease believing in magic even when the expected or wished-for magical effect did not materialize. His answer was that although Azande may be skeptical about the skills and knowledge of particular witch doctors or their poor medicines or the correct performance of particular performances, and the like, their belief in the efficacy of the system itself was not thereby assailed. Whereas Evans-Pritchard gave this as evidence of why Zande magic cannot be empirically proven wrong, he did not perhaps fully appreciate that the answers he received were appropriate to all conventional performative and illocutionary acts—particular performances may for various reasons be "unhappy" or "incorrect" and therefore inefficacious while the convention itself is unassailable.

Robin Horton (1967) compounds the "error" in his challenging essays, suggestively entitled "African Traditional Thought and Western Science." On the one hand, Horton argues that African traditional thought (with its supernatural entities couched in a personal idiom) and Western science (with its concepts couched in an impersonal idiom) are similar in that reference to theoretical entities is used to link events in the visible, tangible world (natural effects) to their antecedents in the same world (natural causes). On the other hand, however—and here is the sting—this same African thought-system whose aim is explanatory and predictive (just like science) refuses to subject itself (like good science) to falsifiability and other verification tests. Indeed, African traditional thought (just as Evans-Pritchard elucidated it) is a "closed system." The believer cannot get outside the web of his thought, he cannot be agnostic, there is no vision of alternatives. Furthermore, it portrays unreflective thinking—that is, traditional thought lacks logic and philosophy and reflection upon the rules of explanation. Evans-Pritchard's demonstration is driven home in traditional thought by a process of *secondary elaboration;* other current beliefs are utilized in such a way as to "excuse" each failure as it occurs, and thus the major theoretical assumptions are protected even in the face of negative evidence. By comparison, the collective memory of the European scientific community is littered with the wreckage of discarded theories. This is true, but Horton's enthusiasm for Popper's idealizations may benefit from some of Kuhn's skepticism.

I think it is possible to differ from Horton on the basic assumptions of the comparisons between traditional and scientific thought. One cannot deny that traditional societies reflect the patterns he enumerates. But I think it is fundamentally mistaken to say that African religion and ritual are concerned with the same intellectual tasks that science in Western society is concerned with: this is a case of analogy abused. The net result of such comparative pursuit is to land oneself where Frazer found himself—magical rituals are like science with the difference that they are mistaken and false.

My counterargument is that to view most ritual and magical acts as if they were directed to the purposes of scientific activity—to discover natural causes, predict empirical consequences in terms of a theory of causation—is inappropriate and not productive of maximum understanding. The analogical thought of Western science and that of primitive ritual have different implications. Like "illocutionary" and "performative" acts, ritual acts have consequences and effect changes; they structure situations not in the idiom of "Western science" and "rationality" but in terms of convention and normative judgment, and as solutions of existential problems and intellectual puzzles. These orders of thought and action after all are to be found in Western societies as well—they coexist with science and thrive outside its field of action or relevance. (It would be interesting to know what Horton thinks is the relation between science and religion in Western society.)

But returning to the problem of magic itself: Have I merely evaded answering what magic is by embedding it in ritual and seeing it as an analogical cum performative act? By and large I think this embedding is a correct representation of it. But I must also go on to say that insofar as magical rites try to effect a transfer, they are often geared to achieving practical results—such as cure of disease or production of a fine harvest—as much as they are geared to effecting social results. Although we should not judge their *raison d'être* in terms of applied science, we should however recognize that many (but not all) magical rites are elaborated and utilized precisely in those circumstances where non-Western man has not achieved that special kind of "advanced" scientific knowledge which can control and act upon reality to an extent that reaches beyond the realm of his own practical knowledge. Let us not forget what Evans-Pritchard's conclusion was. Zande rites were most "mystical" where the diseases they dealt with were the most acute and chronic. These rites, then, are on a different wavelength from scientific technology; or at least in primitive societies it is better to assimilate witchcraft and magic to "ritual" rather than to "applied science."

Let us also not forget one of Evans-Pritchard's most pregnant observations: the Zande belief in witchcraft does not exclude "empirical knowledge of cause and effect," but it provides a social and cultural method of acting upon the world. "In every case witchcraft is the socially relevant cause, since it is the only one which *allows intervention* and determines social behaviour" (1937: 73; italics added). Thus, through ritual man imposes meaning on the world, anticipates the future, retrospectively "rationalizes" the past, and effects results.

It is perhaps because magic and applied science are, so to say, on different wavelengths, yet may (partially) overlap on the ground they cover, that the results of the spread of modern science and technology in "traditional" societies are complex, inconsistent, and nonlinear. An effective pesticide may over time render a "magical rite" for killing pests redundant and unnecessary. But a sacrifice which creates the cosmos persists because it "creates" the world in a sense that is different from that known in the laboratory. How does one understand the Hindu theory of sacrifice, which asserts claims vaster than the causal act itself? And in the new urban communities of developing societies, "drugs" may replace traditional "medicines," but scientific "skepticism" and "prediction" do not replace astrology, or consulting of oracles or of diviners, for the guidance of human actions and for providing meaning in perplexing situations.

But what may be true of non-Western societies may not be true of Western civilization in its recent past. And hereby possibly hangs a tale.

The Relevance of European Experience

In certain respects the history and experience of Western civilization are unique. There is the possibility that, perhaps because the Western anthropologist himself is so naturally grounded in his own civilization, he may at times project it as a potentially universal experience. Let me clarify. If Western anthropologists faced with certain ritual procedures of non-Western societies view them as "magic" that is empirically false and doomed to concede to the claims of science, they are right as far as their own history is concerned, irrespective of the truth of the assertion elsewhere. There is no denying that in Europe there is some kind of developmental sequence by which out of more "primitive" notions and "magical" practices, more "scientific" notions and experimentation were born. The process was by no means linear, but it is true that alchemy gave way to chemistry, astrology to astronomy, leechcraft to medicine. It is also to be borne in mind that old concepts from Greek natural philosophy (such as "atoms," "species," "force," "attraction") and from Greek medicine (especially the Hippocratic corpus) still persist (in form), although they have been transformed (in meaning) in the process. Somewhere in the middle of the transition it is very plausible that science differentiated out of magic, while magic itself was at the same time making "empirical" claims. It may very well be that the Western experience is a *privileged* case of transition from "magic" to "science."

It is further possible that the outlines of similar transitions and developments can also be discerned in other great literate civilizations, such as China and India. For example, the relation between early Vedic ritual and cosmological ideas and the concepts of classical Indian medicine of later times is comparable to the development in Europe, although the trend may not have gone as far. Filliozat (1964), who has examined the question with great scholarship (and who is interesting in that he thinks Indian medical ideas may have influenced the Greeks rather than vice versa), came to the conclusion that between the ideas of Vedic times and those of later periods of Indian developments in the field of medicine there were both discontinuities and continuities.

> Classical Indian medicine claims to explain by means of a coherent system the pathogeny and applies its therapeutics as a function of its theories; its design is entirely scientific, even though many of its doctrines are, in fact, erroneous. It cannot, therefore, have its bases in the pathology and the therapeutics of the Veda. It does not, however, follow that the classical medical texts are not rich in Vedic souvenirs. We have seen that a number of Vedic names of diseases are explained by naturally climbing back from their meaning in classical medicine to the sense possessed by them in the Veda. But in the Veda, we have not found the prefiguration of ulterior pathological doctrines. (p. 137)

Anthropologists should heed this warning in their comparative studies. By simply naming rituals of non-Western societies as "magic," and the substances they use as "medicines" and "drugs," one cannot thereby attribute to the phenomena so named, by virtue of that naming, characteristics that may be peculiar to one's own contemporary civilization. It is only a short step from here to go on to measure these same ritual practices and ideas as equivalent to, but of course misguided and falling short of, empirical science. It is not that such a perspective is wrong but that it may hide from view the positive, persuasive, and creative, though "nonscientific," features of analogical thought and action expressed in magical rites. The dangers of excessive historical universalization should be kept in view. The rise of industry, capitalism, and experimental science in Europe in recent centuries found its counterpart in sociological theorizing in Weber's doctrine of growing "rationality" and "rationalization" in Western civilization—an inevitable historical process toward efficiency of social forms like bureaucracy, toward pragmatic orientation whereby means were closely linked to ends, and toward the generation of context-free, neutral, and universal constructs and principles. I am merely indicating that this is a particular historical experience which need not and should not be universalized if it entails automatic projections of how things traditional inevitably become things rational.

3

A Thai Cult of Healing
through Meditation

In 1974, in Thailand's capital city of Bangkok, I encountered a cult predicated on the notion that illnesses of various kinds, both physical and mental, can be healed or relieved through the practice of meditation (*samadhi*). The interpretation of the cult takes place along two axes, which I call the *cosmological* and the *performative*. In my view ritual can be fully understood only when it has been scrutinized in terms of both these perspectives.

The cosmological perspective implies that ritual acts cannot be fully comprehended except as part of a larger frame of cultural presuppositions and beliefs which provide the phenomenological and subjective basis for engaging in the ritual in question. From this perspective ritual is seen as a translation of a cosmology, and the signs, symbols, and other components of the ritual act as vehicles for expressing cosmological meanings. I must admit that I find the claims of the cosmological perspective unassailable; for example, it must be admitted that Thai rites of various kinds, Buddhist as well as spirit cults, reveal much of their meaning when placed against the Buddhist cosmological scheme of the three *lokas* (worlds) and the corporeal, sensory, and mental faculties attributed to the various beings—the Buddha, gods, humans, demonic spirits, and so forth.

But I am also convinced that the cosmological perspective cannot exhaust the understanding of ritual, but must be supplemented by a performative model of ritual as communication. That is to say, there is a danger that because beliefs are taken to be prior to ritual action, the latter may simply be seen as derivative and secondary. Thereby ritual itself is in danger of being ignored, whereas in reality it has its own distinctive structure and patterning and serves as a vehicle in its own right in appropriate contexts and situations for transmitting messages and meanings, and for the construction and experiencing of cultural and social reality.

The elucidation of the rather evocative concepts "the social and cultural construction of clinical reality" and "medicine's symbolic reality" (Kleinman, Eisenberg, and Good, 1978) can in the Thai case be approached by first considering the religious *cosmological* scheme which has widespread ramifications for many areas of knowledge and life. This cosmological scheme embodies cultural presuppositions and beliefs which constitute a *theodicy* and give *meaning* to notions of illness and healing, fortune and misfortune.

The Thai cosmological scheme has several ramifications. It is, for example, a unified scheme which states correspondences, sympathies and antipathies, identities and differences, between nonhuman (deities/spirits) and human and animal creatures, between the microcosm of man and the macrocosm of the universe, and the dimensions in which they participate in each other's natures. In the Thai case (as in other South and Southeast Asian cultures) the Buddhist cosmology, and local systems of knowledge and technique such as meditation, astrology, alchemy, medicine (*ayurveda*), all share an underlying scheme of classification and hierarchy and hence a coherence that is absent in the knowledge systems of contemporary Western societies, with their separation of "religious" from "secular" realms of knowledge, and of "specialisms" from one another, thus making it difficult for specialist and layman alike to see an overall existential pattern.

Another distinctive feature of Buddhist cosmology and philosophy is that there is no separation between the workings of "moral laws" and "physical" or "natural laws"; the concept of *dhamma* encompasses both. This again gives valence to understanding existential conditions and the manner in which human actions and cosmological events are thought to be linked. Finally, the Thai cult employs a form or procedure of curing by which illness and its relief are projected against a generalized cosmic reality which is considered more "real" and "enduring" than the sensations, pains, and ordeals of "this-worldly" events. What do we make of this cultural mode of treating illness?

As to the performative features of the cult, it cannot be emphasized enough that the cosmological scheme is not simply an abstract mapping in the mind; the meaningfulness of the healing situation stems from the enactments of the ritual and healing process that translate and *create* the cosmology as an experiential reality for the participants. In other words, the healing situation, as the case study shows, includes an exchange of words, acts, and substances between healer and patient. Aside from technical questions of the efficacy of the substances used in a Western scientific-medical sense (upon which I am not competent to comment), surely one aspect of the cure consists in how words, acts, and manipulation of substances achieve a *performative validity* (to use Austin's concept) for the participants.

As part of the performative and communicative framework, we should consider—especially for the understanding of practitioner-patient relations—not merely the conditions that make one a patient (on this point the case study is sadly deficient) but also what propensities and capacities are believed to inhere in and are claimed by the successful healer in his actions. Thus, we have to study a culture's conception and realization of the supranormal or extraordinary person who strives to achieve its ideals as much as we do its conception and realization of those who fall below a norm. Such investigations also take us to the heart of a society's cultural concepts of power and potency, their sources and modes of manifestation, who the persons and subjects are who have potency, and how they affect persons and activities in all walks of life.

Case Study: A Thai Cult of Curing Illness through Meditation

Achan ("teacher") Bunpen was a major in the Thai police force; he had been a student in Australia, and had been introduced to meditation practice by a Thai friend. In 1974 he was the leader of a healing cult centered in Bangkok. The following is an incomplete account of the cult, but it is adequate for discussing certain issues.

In Bangkok the cult leader had a large following which was a cross-section of highly educated, professional, and wealthy persons as well as persons who were poorly educated, of working-class, artisan, and smaller-trader status. His disciples included Ph.D.'s from the United States, bankers, teachers, officers of the armed services—in other words, members of the urban elite who had been exposed to Western influence and were both good Buddhists and modernizers. I was told that he had some two to three thousand disciples throughout the country.

Achan Bunpen—I shall refer to him hereafter as the *achan*—was a teacher of one kind of meditation (*samadhi*) to lay people. Second, he preached and taught Buddhist precepts to his disciples; and on Buddhist *wanphra*—about four holy days in a month on which the devout gathered together at the Buddhist temple (*wat*) for worship—he held in one of his two homes a service attended by large numbers, the majority of whom were members of the above-mentioned educated and elite segments. Third, and perhaps most important, the *achan* cured patients (*khon khai pai raksa*) who complained of miscellaneous and varied illnesses, both physical and mental. The method of curing had many dimensions and features, which must be teased out from the case description. Here let me, by way of preface, state some of the *achan*'s claims:

1. The *achan* claimed that through the practice of meditation, he had access to two kinds of benefits—the benefit of *kuson* (which is "merit" in the Buddhist sense) and the benefit of *ithirit* (Pali: *iddhi*), or "mystical powers."

2. It was also claimed that the *achan* had enormous merit accruing to him from his actions in previous lives. This endowment was referred to as his *anuphab,* and it was this meritorious potency that enabled him to do many things at once: to command or secure the good offices of certain kinds of divine angels/deities in his curing; to acquire still more potency by his expert practice of meditation; finally, by virtue of his benevolence to transfer some of his merit to others and to use his mystical powers for curing patients. Insofar as *anuphab* was attributed to the *achan,* he was conceived of as a *mediator,* who could commune with the beings of the heavens and mobilize their potency to serve the ends of man.

3. The patients, for their part, had first to become the *achan*'s "disciples" (*luksit*), undergo a forgiveness and penance rite (which included making merit by giving food and gifts to the monks), and participate in meditation. There were persons who might come to the *achan* for the sole purpose of becoming adepts at meditation, and these became his inner core of disciples for whom he held special meditation classes and who acted as his assistants at these classes, at curing sessions, and at sabbath devotions. I was told that the *achan* had about ten such assistants, who were his advanced pupils in meditation. I met some of them; they were all educated, could speak English, and were professionals or high-level students.

4. The *achan*'s ethic of conduct approximated the benevolent Buddhist ideal of showing compassion and loving kindness (*karuna* and *metta*) and of being personally disinterested in the fruits of action. As was the case with Buddhist monks, the *achan,* though a layman, had renounced sex. He lived separately from his wife. In fact he was described as "living like a monk."[1] He charged no fees, solicited no gifts

for his curing. However, this did not prevent his disciples from giving him voluntary gifts. Indeed, the *achan* owned two homes which I suspected could not have been entirely financed from his private wealth and his police pay: he owned a house in Thonburi (a poorer section of the capital), where he held his public curing sessions and conducted sabbath devotions, and he had a new modern home in a more affluent residential neighborhood, where he held his exclusive meditation classes for elite pupils.

5. The *achan*'s cult, its idiom and technology, we can locate properly only by relating it to the Buddhist cosmological scheme.

The *achan* was through meditation not pursuing world renunciation and the path of *nibbana* (Pali; Sanskrit = *nirvana*), but more a Buddhist "technology" which was concerned with gaining merit, virtue, and potency and using them to transform this world. Thus, at the entrance to his Thonburi house there was a signboard which read "*Buddhasaat*"—that is, the "science" (Sanskrit = *sastra*) of Buddhism, in contrast to *Buddhasasana*, the Buddhist "religion." Under this appeared the words "*tham le lok*"—that is, *dhamma* (the Buddha's teaching) and its application to the world. These captions conveyed the this-worldly "instrumental" aspects of the cult.

The Achan's Meditation Technique

Meditation, the *achan* expounded, could be directed toward the benevolent objective of acquiring *kuson* (merit), which could in turn be used for benevolent purposes; meditation also led to the acquisition of mystical powers (*ithirit*), which could once again be used for benevolent purposes or for the practice of *saiyasat* of a malevolent sort, such as *kun* (which was a kind of sorcery or witchcraft that introjected an object into the human body and caused it to suffer illness).

The *achan* taught that he practiced meditation in order to use the consequent powers for altruistic purposes. In his admonitions, sermons, and lessons he advocated the practice of the Buddhist precepts (*puthanuphab*), making merit by giving gifts to monks, and so on. It was alleged that the acquisition and possession of *kuson* enabled the *achan* to enlist the services of the deities in curing disease.

Intensive meditation classes for closed groups of elite disciples were held in the *achan*'s new home three nights a week (Mondays, Wednesdays, Fridays). These meditation sessions would be attended by ten to twenty persons.

An informant's account of these meditation sessions is as follows. This information was reluctantly given because the *achan* had urged his disciples not to disclose or reveal the nature of the proceedings, on the ground that a prospective disciple should come to him with no prior expectations of what he or she might experience. It was clear that the meditation experience that was sought was of a mystical kind but in a "concrete sensory" manner, which again lent reality to the curing process.

The *achan* gave a drug to each disciple so that the early stages of meditation could be bypassed. The meditation employed the technique of controlled "breathing" while sitting with eyes closed in a still and relaxed posture. The meditators listened to the verbal instructions of the *achan* and thereafter to his account of what he saw. The deities were "seen" as concrete images, and their action was felt as real—as, for instance, the fall of a thin spray of water on the tongue and the smell of fruits which the deities brought with them for the disciples to eat.[2] As a disciple became more adept and advanced in learning and practice, he or she would begin to see more and more vivid, colored pictures—of the deities, of their previous lives, of their present activities. Advanced disciples of the *achan* had achieved this higher stage and helped interpret the meditation experiences of beginners who reported to them their experiences. My informant, who had a doctorate in educational psychology from an American university, insisted on the reality of these experiences, and said that although she was not yet advanced she did see changes in light: at the beginning of the session she felt a heaviness at the back of the head and saw things as a darkness, but at the end of the session she experienced relief and saw a white light. She had also tasted the flavor of the divine fruits.

The Illness of Patients

The patients who sought relief from the *achan* appeared not to be of any special sort: both men and women, young and old (but no children were seen),[3] educated and not so educated. Patients seemed to suffer from a range of disturbances, "mental" as well as "physical." It is possible that the majority of them had tried other systems of medicine—Western, ayurvedic, and Chinese—and that a fair number may have been suffering from chronic ailments. The few cases I cite below indicate that the illnesses were varied. I heard it said that even heart patients and persons suffering from cancer sought out the *achan*'s cure.

Whatever the kind of illness—and I who am medically ignorant do not want to name, describe, and classify these illnesses—all the patients viewed their illnesses in a larger cosmological Buddhist context of previous lives and the possible moral cum physical consequences of past actions on their present lives (*kam/karma*). They shared the belief that a person like the *achan* could transfer to them the benefits of his superior accumulated merit, and that their practice of meditation as well as engagement in meritorious actions could have direct physical and mental consequences for them. Moral laws and physical/mental laws were, so to say, not disaggregated. As one patient (No. 4 below) said of the logic of curing involved here: "Each of us has debts to pay incurred in previous lives. The *achan* can help us settle these debts and thereby attain good health, because the *achan* has great *bun* [merit] by virtue of his own *kam* [*karma*]. The patients in turn have to practice *samadhi* [meditation] with him." One of my main tasks in this chapter is to explain why this episteme is meaningful to many Thais for understanding their illnesses and for the expectations of being cured that it generates.

Let me now give some examples of the patients I encountered at the *achan*'s sessions:

1. My best example of illnesses for which relief was sought concerns a husband and wife, both university teachers with Ph.D.'s in educational psychology, which they obtained from a reputable American university. The husband—I shall call him X and his wife Y—suffered from severe aches in the spinal region. He had consulted and been treated by four or five doctors in the United States but without relief.

On their return to Bangkok the couple learned about the *achan*. It took them five months before they decided to attend his sessions. On their first visit, two of the *achan*'s assistants asked X questions while touching the place where he had pain. Within ten minutes the pain disappeared and never returned. The diagnosis given was that X was the victim of *kun* (sorcery): a T-shaped object had lodged in his spine and had been extracted. The *achan*'s assistants explained to X that it was not useful or necessary to inquire into who had been the agent; it was more important to concentrate on making *kuson* (merit) and using it beneficially. After that, X had become a dedicated disciple of the *achan*, and a practitioner of meditation.

Y, the wife, had had her share of illness of a more serious sort. While studying in the United States, Y underwent a surgical operation for cysts in the uterus. Some five months later, when she was back home in Bangkok, she had to undergo another operation of the same kind. When pains started yet again, Y was certain that she would die if she had to have surgery for a third time; she told me she calculated that if the second operation followed the first in five months, the third would be due in two and a half months, and so on leading to her death.

Y accompanied her husband to the curing session during which he had been so dramatically cured. She then became a conscientious disciple of the *achan,* as was her husband, but she conceded that her own cure had been slow and prolonged. She had been attending meditation sessions for some five years when I met her; she had been free of pain and had not needed any more operations. It was her husband's cure, she said, that had given her the capacity to endure the long process of cure. She is the informant who described changes of light during the meditation experience.

2. At one of the curing sessions I met a young student, who said he was representing his mother, who had an "enlarged heart." He had come many times on behalf of his mother.

3. On the same occasion I met an elderly Chinese man who said he lived in the town of Khon Kaen (located a few hundred miles away in the northeast) and that he suffered from a kidney disease; he attended the curing sessions frequently.

4. At the second curing session I attended, I sat next to a man, probably in his late thirties, who was a Buddhist. He said that he had attended regularly the *achan*'s curing sessions for the last four years because he suffered from "body aches" which the doctors had not been able to cure. He found relief through attending the *achan*'s sessions, and he also practiced meditation at home.

5. At the *wanphra* devotions that I attended I met two young men after the devotions were over: one man was described by his wife as suffering from a disease of the nerves (*rog prasat*)—that is, some kind of emotional disturbance or "neurosis." The second man, who was a student, suffered from epilepsy (*lom chak*).

Curing Session 1

The *achan* held his curing sessions twice a week on Tuesdays and Thursdays, from about 8:30 P.M. to 10:30 P.M. On Tuesdays the session was held in his Thonburi home and was open to all, and on Thursdays he held it at his new home for his chosen disciples and elite clientele.

The following is a description of an open curing session I attended on July 16, 1974. As Figure 3.1 shows, there were two structures in the compound, the main house (A) and a smaller house (B). Patients sat on the ground floor of the main house, and there was a large overflow into the compound itself. In the compound there was an altar to the Buddha (with statues), and a stand on which flower garlands were placed; lighted candles and joss sticks were planted on both stand and altar. The "new" patients coming for the first time sat in a

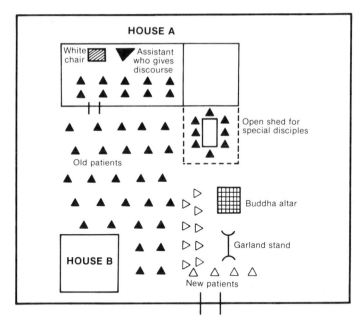

Figure 3.1. The setting for an open curing session by a Thai *achan*.

semicircle at this location. Being newcomers and not prospective patients, my assistant and I took our seats in the compound rather than inside the house.[4]

Each session had three sequences: 1) the induction of new patients, 2) the meditation and curing stage, and 3) the *gae kam* (dispelling the bad effects of *karma*) for the new patients. On this occasion there were at least 150 persons attending, of whom about fifteen were "new patients."

INDUCTION OF NEW PATIENTS

All patients, but in particular new patients, had to wear white clothes. All new patients had to bring with them nine white lotuses, two candles, and one packet of joss sticks. At the session I attended, the patients each held a tray on which these articles were placed, plus a glass of holy water (*namon*) which had already been prepared for them. An assistant of the *achan* instructed them to hold the trays up to their eye level and led them through a sequence of prayers, while they all faced *north*[5] and the altar.

The prayers began with those regularly used in Buddhist devotions—first paying respects to the Buddha, and then the *sangha* (order of monks).[6] Next was recited a long prayer called the *khau khama* (asking forgiveness), which was devised by the *achan* to be used in his curing sessions. This is a free translation of it: "We pay respect by offering these things to the five Buddhas, and we request that whatever merit we have made in our previous lives be offered to the Buddhas, the *pacceka* Buddhas,[7] *arhants* [saints on the path to *nirvana*), the *dhamma* [the moral teachings of the Buddha], the *sangha* [the monks], parents, teachers, *thewada* and *thepi* [male and female angels/deities], the *thewada* that brings victory, *achan* Bunpen [the cult leader and curer], the great god Brahma, the great *thewada*, the great Rishi, the Rishi Ai Nai, the great Prot, the great Devi, all the persons we are indebted to in our previous lives. We apologize for any acts that we may have done through carelessness or unintentionally. We request blessings to recover from sickness and be happy both in our gross material bodies and in our subtle [ethereal] bodies, and we request power [*anuphab*], the power of *thewada*, the power of Brahma, the power of the Buddha in order to acquire happiness and to avoid accidents." The new patients (or their representatives)[8] were asked to drink the holy water; their lotus, candle, and joss stick offerings were collected and placed on the altar; and they were then handed paper forms to fill in their names and addresses. They were urged to concentrate on the purpose of their visit and on recovery.

CURING THROUGH MEDITATION

The old patients (*khon kai gao*), who had come many times before, would bring with them either jasmine garlands, which were hung up in the stand near the altar, or nothing. They took little interest in the induction of new patients, and would wait for the collective meditation and curing sessions to begin.

A disciple and assistant of the *achan* took his seat next to a white-backed large chair (which was empty, and was the chair that would sometimes be used by the curer himself), and began recitations over a microphone.[9]

Before the devotions, everyone was asked to remove his or her shoes, slippers, socks, wristwatches, and eyeglasses. One informant explained that this was required because it is through all extremities of the body that negative influences affecting the patients (particularly *kun*)[10] are made to leave or are expelled.

The prayers offered earlier during the admission of patients were repeated: first *namo tassa* three times, then the request for the words of the *dhamma* (*aratana tham*), followed by the prayer of forgiveness invoking the help of the Buddhas, deities, parents, and so forth. During this sequence the patients adopt the worshipful *waj* posture.

Then followed the discourse, which lasted thirty to forty-five minutes, during which all the patients were directed to take the meditating position and concentrate on the words being said without losing attention or falling asleep. The discourse began as follows:

> You have come to this place to do merit, and to practice meditation; you don't have to pay any money; by meditating you will get merit [*dai bun dai kuson*].
>
> New patients should bring lotuses, but don't buy them from sellers outside this house. Next time you don't have to bring offerings, except perhaps garlands.
>
> Now we are going to do meditation; sit straight backed and in comfort, then close your eyes, and place the palms of your hands on your laps. Concentrate your mind on any "powerful" thing [*sing saksit*] that you normally respect—for example, the Emerald Buddha or the Luang Phau Sauthaun.[11] Concentrate.

The most important part of the discourse began now: the deities (*thewada*) were requested to come and cure the patients, and their coming and return was described in detail. Next more specifically the great Brahma and Great Thep were invited to descend—the invitation was repeated many times. Their coming was described—Brahma riding on his vehicle, and Thep riding on a *naga* (mythical serpent of the waters), one on the right the other on the left. The great rishi (*maha ruesi*) arrived too—and he came to rest in the "spirit house" in front of the compound.[12]

An interesting part of this description is that the gods and divine angels were described as giving injections and pills, curing cancer, extracting by surgery diseased bones. Many diseases were named. (Much of this description was based in large part on experience with Western medicine and surgery.) The deities were also described as giving the patients "water medicine" and fruits, and the patients were asked to open their mouths and extend their tongues.

While the assistant was giving this vivid and concrete description, the *achan* (curer) himself walked among the patients, smoking cigarettes profusely, touching the patients' heads or the backs of their necks, and blowing air on those spots. He came to me, and touched the base of my skull and blew air twice.

DISPELLING BAD KARMA (GAE KAM) OF THE NEW PATIENTS

The last sequence concerned the new patients again. While one disciple-assistant guided the patients through the meditation-discourse, another assistant sat near the new patients and busily filled in forms. By virtue of his own knowledge and powers, this assistant was able to diagnose for each new patient the weight of his or her offenses against various malevolent spirits and to assess the amount of merit he or she should do to dispel the negative effect. How much merit had to be done also depended on the patient's *chatha* (horoscope). The assistant would put down on paper the penance that was required. This penance consisted usually in the feeding of monks. Thus, a young boy representing his sick mother was instructed that servings of food to monks must be made three times—the first two times three monks had to be fed, and the third time five monks. Another patient, an old man, was instructed to feed on three occasions five, seven, and three monks respectively.

These recommended penances unambiguously allied this healing cult with the higher aspirations of Buddhism—by emphasizing that the healing was not practiced for monetary profit, and that the doing of merit by the material support of the monks was a way of making penance. It was also clear that the cult attributed the illnesses of patients not only to bad *karma* but also specifically to the action of malevolent spirits, who belonged to the lower levels of the cosmological scheme and stood in opposition to the benign angels. But this cult did not hold traffic directly with the malevolent demons as such, and therefore it was more elevated in its idiom compared to many of the *saiyasat* rites directly concerned with appeasing the demons.[13]

Curing Session 2

On July 23 I attended another healing session, during which I was able to observe additional features that I was unable to witness the first time. At the second session I gained a seat inside the house and also was able to witness the audience which the *achan* gave his disciples at the conclusion of the session.

As Figure 3.2 shows, some patients sat inside the house on the ground floor; a staircase led to a shrine room, where the *achan* himself sat in meditation (*samadhi*), while the assistant gave the discourse and verbal description of the meditation experience. The shrine itself was elaborately stocked with Buddha statues under a canopy. The quite obvious implication was that the *achan*'s own meditation and the employment of his powers were effective in unveiling the heavens, and in mobilizing the cooperation of the deities. This assistant, then, was describing events which were the product of the *achan*'s concentration. On this occasion, the *achan* meditated right through the discourse, without walking among the patients and touching them. The

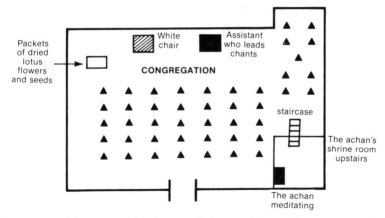

Figure 3.2. The setting for the concluding audience of an open curing session.

achan sat in meditation upstairs, higher in elevation than anyone else in the congregation. In Thailand a person of superior status has his head in a higher position than that of an inferior. A person upstairs symbolically and literally has his feet above the congregation's heads. The *achan* in this instance was spatially in an elevated position.

After the collective session was over, the *achan* held an audience upstairs in a large room in which stood a number of Buddha figures, which the *achan* garlanded with jasmine garlands offered him by his disciples. His disciples worshipped (*krab*) him just as they would a monk, but I had the strong impression that the *achan* was being treated like a royal personage or even like a deity. Dressed in red Chinese pyjamas and a red shirt, he sat like a benign deity in an imposing wide chair while about twenty-five disciples, many of them members of the urban middle class, sat decorously on the floor with expressions of utter devotion. Two male disciples (one who suffered from an "emotional disturbance" and another from epilepsy) sat at his feet massaging his legs right through the audience.[14] Several disciples came up to him in person wanting him to give advice or bless various objects.

As I entered the room I saw the *achan* whispering into a dish of jasmine flowers and handing it back to a couple, man and wife. I was told that he had made the flowers "powerful" (*sek*).

Another client handed the *achan* an envelope containing a small Buddha amulet (*phra khryang*); he extracted the amulet and whispered words over it with his eyes closed. He commented that the image was a good one (meaning it was now efficacious).

Next a woman asked his advice concerning her old mother, who had a stomach ailment and indigestion. He told her to try this remedy: "Put a piece of ripe papaya in a glass of warm water and stir it; drink it once a day early in the morning. At other times drink warm water in which dried lotus has been soaked." She then requested him to bless her (on behalf of her mother). While she kneeled and prostrated before him, the *achan* cupped his hands in front of his mouth, chanted some words softly, then brought down his joined hands and moved them from the woman's head outward toward her spine four times, blowing air at the same time. Then he touched her shoulder and asked her to get up.

I was in turn introduced to the *achan*, who was cordial toward me. He said that the previous week he had touched me because he felt some kind of affinity toward me. He said I could practice *samadhi* (meditation) on my own, and there was no need for a teacher. A teacher was necessary for persons who felt "dependent." If one was self-reliant and believed in oneself, things become possible. He invited me to attend the Sabbath devotions which he would be conducting in a few days time, and said that I would be able to meet an American disciple of his on that occasion.

Regarding the *achan*'s "technology," it was through the medium of words and substances that the *achan* transferred potency and efficacy. The power of the words was in fact transferred as if it were a "physical" entity, by hand gestures and blowing air.

Wanphra Devotions

I shall close the description of the cult proceedings by describing the devotions that were staged by the cult leader on a Buddhist sabbath. Normally such devotions, which include a sermon, are conducted in a Buddhist *wat* by monks. The *achan,* significantly, conducts the same devotions at his home. This is by no means improper, in that Buddhist practice allows laymen, if they are versed in the chants, to conduct the service.

But the extraordinary aspect of these sabbath devotions is that they are very much an affair for an urban, sophisticated congregation largely drawn from the educated elite circles,[15] and while some of them are patients as well, a number of them attend because of their interest in "meditation." The congregation thus consists primarily of meditation disciples.

On the day I attended (27 July) the Thonburi compound and house were crowded with 125–150 disciples all dressed in white; some of the women were wearing in addition traditional shawls and sashes. About 85 percent of the congregation was female[16]—there were women of all ages, including girls in their teens.

The devotions were interesting because it was the cult leader himself who gave the sermon, and also because four new meditation pupils were inducted.

The sequences of the sabbath devotions followed in general those I have documented for the curing session, except that the discourse or sermon was of a different type.

In the beginning, recitations were the same: 1) *namo tassa;* followed by 2) the prayer of giving merit to various supernatural and human beings (*khau tawai kuson*); 3) the request for the forgiveness and blessings of those same beings (*khau paun*); 4) the request by a layman for the sermon (*aratana tham*); and 5) the sermon itself.

This is an abbreviated paraphrase of the sermon given by the *achan* and cult leader:

> We the disciples have assembled here to practice meditation. From my meditation insight I am aware that some of you are adept and some of you are less adept, while still others fall asleep. It is neither easy nor difficult to practice meditation. You have to believe in yourself. Don't be taken in or misled by what others tell you. Don't be easily satisfied with those things that accrue to you now by virtue of meditation. Don't be satisfied with the images of various kinds you see; don't be frightened by certain visions that look frightening; try to advance further through practice. If you reach a certain stage you can have peace of mind [*khwam sangnob suk*].
>
> Even I have to practice and learn more to reach a higher stage. That I have already reached a certain high level is known to my disciples. The disciples have an example of this in a certain incident that took place. Once a divine spirit [*thep*] possessed a young boy and came here bearing no malice but at the same time wanting to inspect and test how powerful I was. I was able to talk with the spirit and to come to a conciliatory agreement with it. Thereafter the spirit left the boy.[17]
>
> All the divine spirits [*thep*] are kind and would like to help humans. The disciples should not be discouraged but continue practicing. Meditation is also a way of making merit [*kuson*].

6. The sermon was immediately followed by the initiation of new meditation disciples. The *achan* lit candles and joss sticks at the altar;

then each new candidate's name was read by an assistant, and he or she went up to the *achan*. The candidate presented him with a bunch of white lotuses and repeated (after the assistant) the *khau kama* prayer asking for forgiveness for past sinful acts. Then the *achan* said some words (which could not be heard), and with his finger made the *cherm* mark on the forehead of each candidate, which it was explained to me would make meditation easier and would in fact serve as an "object" of meditation.

7. Next was recited publicly by the entire congregation the prayer requesting forgiveness. After seeking the pardon of the Buddhas and the deities, the congregation requested the forgiveness of the *achan*, and then turning in all four directions each worshipper requested the forgiveness of his or her immediate neighbors. The request was followed by the worshipful *waj* gesture. The *achan* then absolved all by saying words of forgiveness while adopting the *waj* gesture toward the congregation.

8. The next sequence was the chanting of *suad mon* by a disciple in the manner of a monk—that is, he recited certain *paritta* verses from the usual chants monks recite in their morning devotions.

9. Finally, the entire congregation closed their eyes and sat silently in meditation for a period of about ten minutes.

After the formal devotions were concluded, the *achan* held his usual audience in the manner already described; his disciples presented jasmine garlands with which he decked the Buddha statues; devoted young men massaged his legs, while he gave advice to the needy.

There are a couple of points regarding this sabbath worship that I want to draw attention to.

On the one hand, the *achan* was fully aware that the worship at his home "substituted" for devotions monks conducted in temples, and in his sermon he first made the doctrinally more elevated assertion that meditation is part of the salvation quest (there are stages superior to the mystical states of *iddhi* to which the meditator should ascend). But the *achan* in the same sermon affirmed to the congregation the fact that he was able to exercise *iddhi* by citing the incident of his encounter with the boy possessed by a *thep*. Indeed most of his disciples and patients came to him because he had demonstrated his charisma and continued to demonstrate it by curing. But the *achan* was also catering to those nonpatient disciples who were more interested in practicing meditation as a way of liberating themselves from the bonds of this world.

Finally, in addition to affirming the reality of his own power gained through meditation, the *achan* also affirmed the existence of the divine angels and the reality of the images seen during meditation.

Interpretation

Interpretation of this cult must begin by placing it in the context and against the backdrop of the Thai Buddhist cosmological scheme, for it is both integrally implied and also creatively enacted in the curing and meditation sessions. This cosmological scheme constitutes a *theodicy* in the Weberian sense, and therefore provides a system of *meaning* for Thai Buddhists, for locating and understanding and even modifying their existential problems.

Cosmology

The cosmological scheme has been described in detail in many works; here I need only refer to those aspects that are directly relevant.[18] It has many facets: it first of all gives a picture of the universe in terms of space, time, matter, and causality; second, it translates this physical universe into a pantheon of deities, humans, animals, and demons to which can be attributed ethical and moral qualities; finally, the cosmology gives a dynamic picture of the nature, workings, and purpose of the universe in terms of the motion of the personifications in the pantheon, this motion up and down (and bursting out of the universe altogether) being propelled by ethical acts and spiritual force and energy. Thus, it might be said that the cosmological scheme says figuratively and in terms of metaphorical images the same kind of thing which is stated in abstract terms in the doctrine. The basic doctrinal concepts of Buddhism such as *karma* (ethical causation), *samsara* (cycle of rebirths), *nirvana* (final extinction), and *dukkha* (suffering), which are alleged to explain man's predicament and to direct his religious action, are also embedded in the cosmology (and its associated pantheon).

There is a close connection between cosmology and ritual. Cosmological and supernatural categories are embedded in the rituals I have described; they chart the geography and define the architecture of sacred space and are expressed in the material symbols that are manipulated in the rituals. In the rituals we see cosmology in action. Ritual is symbolic action that has a telic or instrumental purpose—to effect a change of state. The cosmology and ritual are closely connected because the cosmological concepts and categories are translatable and translated into an action medium that employs symbols of various kinds—verbal, visual, auditory, graphic, tactile, alimentary, and so on.

According to Buddhist cosmology, there are innumerable world systems or galaxies. Each system has its own sun and moon, and its earth containing continents and oceans, with a mountain in the center called Mount Meru. Upward from the mountain extend the heavens, downward the hells. These world systems are periodically destroyed and reformed in cycles of vast stretches of time (*kalpa*). In modern astrophysics this characterization would be called the theory of the pulsating universe.

The world system consists of thirty-one planes of existence divided into three major categories: *kama loka* (in which there is form and sensual desire, pleasure and pain); *rupa loka* (in which there is form but no sensual enjoyment, only a kind of intellectual enjoyment); and the *arupa loka* (in which there is no perceptible bodily form and no sensation). The order in which they are presented here is hierarchical from the lowest to the highest. The scheme is based on a progression from corporeality to incorporeality, from body to intellect.

These three major planes of existence subdivide into the thirty-one more specific planes in a complex manner. And in order to describe the ordering, I must start from the center of the world system.

Mount Meru stands in the center of the earth, and it is the pillar of the world. Between Meru and the great rocky circumference which is the wall of the earth are alternating concentric circles of seven mountain ranges and seven oceans. A last (eighth) great ocean adjoining the rim contains four continents at the cardinal points; the southern continent is Jambudvipa (which represents our globe, with the Indian subcontinent as the center). It is the most sacred in the time cycle in which Gotama Buddha was born.

KAMA LOKA

The *kama loka* plane of existence expresses the cosmology that is directly relevant here. This plane of bodily form and sensual feelings is divided into eleven *loka*: six are heavens inhabited by gods (*deva loka*); five are worlds, four of which are inhabited by human beings, animals, ghosts, and demons. The fifth world consists of eight major (and other subsidiary) hells, situated in the interior of the earth, in which intense torment and pain are experienced.

The six heavens (deva loka). The first heaven is below the summit of Mount Meru and is the residence of the four guardians of the world (*lokapala*). The second heaven (*Tavatinsa/Tawutisa*) is on the summit of Meru, over which presides god Sakka, or Indra. These two heavens must, in fact, be taken together because Indra presides over the four guardians, and together they impinge on the world of men and animals. In myth and ritual Indra always appears as the presiding deity. Around and just below Indra's abode at the summit of Meru are the four mansions of the world guardians.

Beyond and higher than the second heaven of Indra are four other heavens that fall within the definition of *kama loka*. Of these, only one need be mentioned here: the fourth, called *Tusita*, in which resides the all-compassionate *bodhisattva* (Buddha-to-be) Maitreya, awaiting the time when he will come down into the world of men as the next Buddha and savior. The *Tusita* heaven is regarded as the most delightful of the heavens, in which all desires are satisfied. In it grows the *kalpavriksha* tree (in Thai, *karaphruk* or *kamaphruk*), which produces fruits of gold, silver, and jewels that gratify all desires. The tree appears frequently in Thai rituals.

The five worlds. The four lower worlds of men, animals, *asuras* (demons), and ghosts (*preta*) stand in contrast to the heavens. While life in the heavens is unadulterated pleasure, the lower worlds are increasingly painful. Human beings and animals as forms of life require no commentary at this stage.

The *asuras* are in Buddhist (and Hindu) mythology the archenemies of the gods. They are demigods themselves and are of the underworld, living under Mount Meru. The *asuras* were finally subdued by Indra, and it is the task of the four guardians to continue to ward off their attacks. Rahu and Ketu are the much-feared *asuras* which swallow the moon and cause eclipses. The *asuras* as the classical opponents of the deities have found other expressions in contemporary Southeast Asian countries: *yakkha* in Sri Lanka, *nats* in Burma, *phii* in Thailand (in all these countries the gods are called *devas*).

Whereas the *asuras* are a permanent category of supernatural being, the *pretas* are of a different status. They are ghosts of dead humans who have recently inhabited the earth. They are condemned to live in a kind of hell or may wander about on earth, haunting the places where they formerly lived. Although in themselves not harmful to man, their appearance and attributes are disgusting. They are of gigantic size; they have dried up limbs, loose skin, enormous bellies. They continually wander about, consumed with hunger and thirst, yet are never able to eat or drink because of their small mouths, constricted throats, and the scorching, boiling heat that emanates from their bodies.

Some writers have seen in *pretas* the inversion of the Buddhist monk (Yalman, 1964). The *preta* condition of perpetual hunger and thirst may possibly signify the extreme punishment for withholding food from monks and for being stingy in merit making.

Finally, the eight major hells of the fifth world are fiery places of intense misery and pain. One has only to see the murals on the walls of Buddhist temples in Thailand and Sri Lanka to understand that hell is no mere abstract concept but is imagined in all its horror and sadism. In heaven handsome men and women embrace and walk around in a garden of wishing trees (*kalpavriksha*) studded with diamonds and other gems; in hell people burn in raging fire and their sides are pierced with weapons by demons.

THE RUPA LOKA, ARUPA LOKA, AND NIRVANA

Whereas the six lower *deva* heavens belong to the domain of form and sensation (*kama loka*), there are twenty other, higher heavens.

The next level upward is that of the *rupa loka*, consisting of sixteen heavens where there is form but no sensual enjoyment. Beyond them are the four *arupa* heavens, with no form at all. These last are of minimal significance in myth and ritual. Finally, beyond the *arupa* heavens one bursts through the boundaries of the cosmos of existence to reach *nirvana*—salvation, void, annihilation, and liberation from rebirth.

It is important to note about Buddhist (and Hindu) conceptions of deity, man, demons, and spirits (these conceptions may be less explicitly or differently stated in other religions) that all the beings of the *kama* world of corporeal form and sensory experience are fundamentally of one kind, though divided into hierarchical levels on the basis of moral worth and therefore physico-sensory and mental makeup. We cannot fully appreciate the logic of the cultic acts described here without understanding that they are premised on the fact that all these beings in the *kama* world directly interact, affect one another, and from above or below invade the world of men as well as coexist with men on the same plane.[19] The field of everyday action and experience for a Thai includes and takes into account as an existential fact that it is not merely confined to humans or merely an interaction between man and nature, or that the supernatural is a separate and distant domain altogether. The field of existence includes six forms of existence—god, demon, man, animal, ghost, soul in hell—whose distinctions are only of temporary duration and through which all human beings (except those who have entered the path leading to salvation) may at one time or other pass. The god may be reborn as demon, an animal as man, and so forth; a change of condition is a realistic possibility, depending on one's *karma* and ethical status. At any one point in time, the stratification can be expressed as a gradient extending from pure bliss and tranquillity enjoyed by the gods to black torment suffered by those in hell. The gods, especially those in the six lower heavens, exist in subtle corporeal forms. Although they are not omnipotent, they are capable of beneficial acts toward human beings. They, too, are subject to the universal law of dissolution and rebirth. They appear in the cosmology mainly as protectors of the faith, ready to help believers or to testify to the true doctrine. In turn, the other orders of existence can descend or go upward. The ghosts and demons are not perpetually condemned; they may harm men but they are also subject to the law of rebirth and can change their status for the better.

Implications of the Cosmology

This cosmological scheme contains certain fundamental ideas which are reflected in religious pursuits, ritual actions, and various systems of instrumental knowledge such as meditation, alchemy, astrology, and healing.

The scheme implies a single vertical gradient that links the various levels of existence in "this world" (*laukika*), and then pierces through at the summit into the hypercosmic "otherworldly" plane (*lokottara*) of liberation from sentient existence (*nirvana*).

Thus, the liberation from rebirth and existence is achieved through a pilgrim's progress of ascent and progressive liberation from the limitations of embodiment and confinement in space and time and from enslavement to sensory desires and organic processes that by definition are victims of time and decay.

The salvation quest which is a progressive liberation from such boundedness, and from subjection to sensory desires, is best implemented by the practice of meditation, which seeks an ascending liberation through the control of and distancing from sensory experience. Cosmologically, this journey can be viewed as a passage from *kama* world to *rupa* world to *arupa* world to *nirvana*. We shall have to examine later, therefore, the theory of meditation as currently held by Thai Buddhists, but here let me mention some ideas that lie at the heart of rituals and other "technologies" practiced in Thailand, Sri Lanka, Burma, and other Buddhist countries.

THE DIALECTIC BETWEEN SELF-CONTROL AND POWER

A critical set of postulates revolves around the nature of the *interrelation* between restraint and power, or perhaps, in the Buddhist case, between increasing control over actions and sensations, liberation from limitations of time and space, and decreasing subjection to bodily organic processes on the one hand, and on the other the fact that liberation paradoxically enables the exercise of more *power* over those placed lower in the gradient. "Paradoxically" because exercise of power would imply increased involvement with the world.

The answer to this paradox possibly lies in the Buddhist concept of *iddhi*,[20] which explains that the ascetic meditator by the very process of gaining control over his volition, senses, and consciousness liberates himself from the limitations and transitoriness of corporeal and sensory existence. Hence, this gain of control is literally a metaphysical victory. He, therefore, has mystical powers which transcend, so to say, the ordinary laws of "physics" which pertain to the material world. It follows as a corollary that the higher the meditator is in the ascent, the greater his liberation and the greater his *iddhi*-power.

But if he wants to go up and up, he should become disinterested in using *iddhi* which involves him with the world. But the benevolent gods and the meditators who have achieved *iddhi*, although superior beings, are still in the *kama* world, and they can and do exercise *iddhi* for the benefit of the world. This is precisely what the cult leader is claiming to do; and as there is precedent for this among Hindu ascetics and rishis, the adept at meditation may reach a stage equal to and even superior to that of the gods, and thus be able to mobilize, if not command, them. This again is what the *achan* is claiming to do, as the meditation discourse during healing vividly relates.

But doesn't this logic lead at first sight to a contradiction? If the higher one is on the liberation ladder the more *iddhi* one has—in the form of power associated with the "subtle" bodies and "intermediate" unembodied states—then how is it that the antagonists of men (and gods), the malevolent ghosts and spirits, have such power to cause harm, disease, and suffering, if they are the lowest on the same ladder? The clue to the combination of demerit and malevolent "power" consists in this: the demons and ghosts are the most "substantialized" and therefore also the most *uncontrolled* in their expression of their sensory desires; they are embodied with that corporeal density of entities imprisoned and confined in the webs and cubicles of time, space and form, and sense. Hence, they manifest themselves in all the forms of decay and transitoriness and illusion from which men must escape. It is precisely these antithetical expressions of control over body and sense and the subtle mystical "powers" of *iddhi* on the one hand, and, on the other, the uncontrolled gross malevolent "power" of the demons of distorted and excessive proportions, that come to focus when we compare this Thai cult centering on meditation and mobilizing the benevolent powers of deities with a Sinhalese exorcism cult, which addresses itself to demons and their expulsion from the patients whom they inflict or possess.

Sinhalese exorcism rites have been frequently documented (see Wirz, 1954; Gooneratne, 1865; Pertold, 1930; Sarathchandra, 1953). Let me therefore briefly refer to a ceremony called the *Mahasohona Sumayama*. Mahasohona is the Great Cemetery Demon who afflicts humans with disease just as many others in the demon hordes do, the most potent of whom are the Black Demon (Kalu Yakkha), the Blood Demon (Riri Yakkha), the Demon of Sacrifice (Billa Yakkha), the Demon of Sorcery (Huniyam Yakkha), and the Illness Demon (Sanni Yakkha).

The ceremonies addressed to these demons, whose names are indicative of their grossness, violence, and vileness, are much alike. Indeed a ceremony addressed to one demon includes propitiations to the others as well. The demonic attack is phrased in terms of *dishtiya* (a "manifestation" or "look") cast on humans, as well as in terms of direct possession. The cure, true to the cosmological hierarchy and arrangement of the pantheon, invokes the notion of conditional warrant granted by the superior deities to demons to inflict illness in order to gain from their human victims what they crave; they are therefore bribed to leave the patient by offerings of fried and burnt meats, liquor, opium, and live sacrifices; by flattery and false praise in songs; by frenzied dancing with firebrands and flame throwing; by equally heightened drumming—in fact, by the most intensified and even "uncontrolled" use of the media in concordance with the demons' crass cravings. Their expulsion is facilitated by the invocation of the gods to come to the officiants' and patients' aid, and by the commanding and compelling *mantras* recited that recall the results of ancient cosmic encounters when the Buddha and the deities subjugated the demons. A part of the logic of the cure is that the patient's illness is externalized and objectified as the affliction caused by revolting and antisocial and even comical agents. The patient wards them off and rejects them and makes them depart by granting gifts consecrated by him.[21]

Both the Thai healing cult and the Sinhalese exorcism rite, the latter more directly, raise the question why gods—especially those placed high in the cosmic hierarchy—if they are less corporeal and more mental, more still and less moved by sensory propulsion, have the power to control the malevolent spirits and even engage with them in combat and defeat them. How do they combine virtue and merit with power, or, in the Hindu idiom, purity with power?

As is well known and widely discussed, the Sinhalese Buddhist pantheon is built on the notion of *varam* (warrant, or delegated entitlement): the Buddha, though he has reached *nirvana,* is "powerfully" present in the world in the form of *dharma kaya* (the body of his teachings)[22] and *rupa kaya* (the material presence of his relics); he has given *varam* to the gods to enable them to live their ordained lives, and the deities in turn have given warrant to the demons, this time to inflict humans with illness and misery, subject to this condition: that when humans satisfy the gross desires of demons with strong foods and drink and frenzied and bawdy entertainment, the demons must remove themselves and their evil influence.[23]

But that is not all. There is the additional point that one's control over one's senses and desires and therefore one's ability to transcend substantiality not only give access to mystical powers associated with the "subtle" body and mind, but also enable when necessary that entity to assume and surpass the very forms and potencies of the adversary demon and thereby quell him. This is of course a temporary assumption of the gross body and senses which by definition can be left behind and transcended once the task is over. Thus, the deities of the *kama* and the *rupa loka* who are capable of manifesting themselves in human affairs have the paradoxical strengths of differential virtue and control over corporeality—a transcendence that enables them to assume the gross powers of the lower beings in order to meet and subdue them on their own terms.[24]

THE PLACE OF HUMANS IN THE COSMOLOGY

Human beings have a unique position in the cosmic hierarchy. On the one hand a human is placed in *kama loka,* a prisoner of corporeality and sensory desires; on the other he is placed interstitially between the deities of various kinds above him and the malevolent *asuras,* demons, *pretas* of the hells below him. The latter are able to attack him, his susceptibility being graduated according to his merit; and the former can be called upon to assist him to resist the demons and to enjoy good health, wealth, and fine complexion. To the gods he must voluntarily make gifts and transfer the merit of his good actions in this life; with the devils he can strike bargains and pay a fee or a bribe for their letting go.

But there is more that makes man the centerpiece in the cosmological scheme. As Buddhist doctrine makes clear, the human state alone makes possible the attainment of liberation. *Nirvana* is beyond the reach of animals and demons; gods, especially those bound by limitations of substantiality, though superior to man, nevertheless enjoy the heavenly pleasure only until their merit runs out, and they must be reborn as men in order to make further ascent; their heavenly state does not necessarily make them want to break through their bonds. Even a god must in his terminal life in the cycle of rebirths be born of a woman of human status in order to make the final leap to *nirvana*. But man alone can through the exercise of volition enter the path of liberation—usually through the practice of meditation—and can launch himself upward through all the worlds and burst into the unconfined state. (Incidentally, it is more common in Hindu than in Buddhist mythology to encounter the phenomenon of the ascetic in the forest achieving through meditation subtle powers which make the seats of the gods hot and make them aware of their human rival).

A typical Hindu formulation is that the practice of self-mortification and austerities (*tapas*) releases "heat" as energy, and this potency can find expression as sexual potency, the powers of fertilization as well as destruction. Thus, the conservation of energy enables a potent expenditure of it (see O'Flaherty, 1973, for the myths about Shiva). The Buddhist formulation, which is for instance common in Thailand, is that the practice of meditation (rather than austerities) results in two fruits. The first is *kuson* (merit), the benefits of which the meditator can, if he so wishes, transfer to humans and even gods. The second is *ithirit* (mystical powers), which, however, precisely because of the explanation given earlier (the transcendence of substantiality enables its manifest realization when necessary), allows the possessor to employ it as a "technology" (*saiyasat*) of the benevolent kind (curing) or of the destructive kind (sorcery). Hence it is that in Tantric Buddhism, adepts in occultism are distinguished between those who follow the "right-hand path" of "white magic" and the "left-hand path" of "black magic" (Evans-Wentz, 1960). And in Burma there exists a hierarchical distinction among healers and exorcists between the "master of the upper path" (*athelan hsaya*), who is committed to the Buddhist discipline and aspires to become a *weikza* (reminiscent of the *arahat*), belongs to a *gaing* sect, and practices alchemy, and the master of the inferior path (*aulan hsaya*), who tries to control harmful supernaturals (Spiro, 1967: 325). As I have remarked elsewhere (1970: 325), the remarkable aspect of Spiro's description is that the *athelan hsaya* uses Buddhist *gatha* prayers, the monks' *paritta* verses, and invokes the trinity in his encounter with the possessing spirit; in one sense he is using the power of the Buddha's *dhamma*, but he can use it so efficaciously only because he is himself an adept follower of the Buddhist path. I invoke these comparisons to suggest that the *achan*, who cures through meditation and uses the potency of the Buddha's works, can be seen as comparable to the "master of the higher path."

Doctrinal Buddhism, while thus placing man as the actor imbued with *intentionality* and capacity for the complete transcendence of substantiality, also asserts as a fundamental principle that men are born unequal, so to say, because their present lives reflect the sum of virtues and demerits of past lives. The principle of *karma* implies that therefore men have different capacities not only for resisting misfortune but also for practicing the higher pursuits of Buddhism. There is thus a dialectical play between that aspect of early Buddhism in India which freely recruited monks from all castes, freed the monk from preoccupation of worldly hierarchy, and even went so far as to declare the doctrine of the nonexistence of the self, and the countervailing assertion of the inequalities in capacities and susceptibilities created by *karma* and previous lives. One of Thailand's most famous propagators of meditation, a former abbot of the largest and very famous *wat* in Bangkok, once expounded on this to me:

> One needs merit [*bun*] in order to be able to practice *vipassana* [meditation]; if a man's store of *bun* is great he can become an adept in seven days; if he has less, then it takes seven months. But some men don't make it at all for lack of merit.
>
> There are different kinds of humans, or as the Buddha said four kinds of horses harnessed to a carriage: the horse which knows where to go by the horseman's simply pulling at the reins; the horse at which the horseman points the switch and threatens to prod it in order to make it go; the horse that actually has to be prodded and punished to make it go; and finally the horse that cannot be made to move at all. It is the human of this last kind who cannot be taught *vipassana*, and such humans constitute the majority of mankind. However, in society an equilibrium is reached because the minority with wisdom can guide and control the majority. There is a saying that the wise are in number like the horns of a buffalo, and the ignorant like its hairs.
>
> Or, to put it differently, it is said that there are three groups of human beings: the *upalimakai* group are the upper part, the neck and head of the body; *majjimakai* are the middle, from neck to waist; and the *hettimakai* are the lower, from waist to legs. The three groups have to be educated accordingly. All three are necessary. But if we educate them all to be heads, the body will not be able to walk.

There is in Buddhist thought a fundamental tension in the evaluation of the place and role of man in the cosmic process. One should not be beguiled into a too easy acceptance of the Buddhist cosmological scheme as being a simple graduated pyramid with human beings placed somewhere lower down in the *kama loka*. Be this as it may, human beings also become the centerpiece of the cosmic process—by virtue of their interstitial position between the heavens and hells, by virtue of their preeminent ability to act voluntarily and with intention in such a way as to transcend their status and break through, as no one else can, the chain of being. But this is counterweighted by the assertion that humans themselves are not equally endowed with the virtue and capacity to understand the nature of the existential problem and to act so as to resolve it.

THE EPISTEMOLOGY OF CURING

We are now better informed to ask what kind of cure is implied in the Thai cult of healing, especially after taking note of the Thai Buddhist view that all men are not equally endowed with merit and therefore with capacities. This view leads to an elitist postulate that a minority of superior men can by virtue of past merit and present practice transcend the impingements and limitations of the world. They can thereby also help their less fortunate fellow beings who constitute the majority of mankind and who are highly susceptible to miseries by virtue of their enmeshment in the world.

The cult does not pay great attention to the biographical details of the patient who comes to be cured. It does not deal in detail with individual symptoms and the course of the illness. To all patients and disciples it presents a timeless, generalized, cosmological goal as the only enduring reality.

Let us begin uncovering the *raison d'être* of this perspective at the most abstract philosophical level. Buddhist phenomenology accords no essence or substantiality to the notion of self. There is no actor, but there are actions that are themselves decomposable into chains of interactions until we come ultimately to the *dharmas,* elements which are themselves process (Stcherbatsky, 1923; Conze, 1970). Thus, entities such as "persons" and "things" are not set against and contrasted with "events" and "processes," and no well-defined "self" is accorded the status of a fact. All this results in a resolute depersonalization of "self," and change itself is considered a continuous and uninterrupted process, a succession of new *dharmas* rather than the transformation of a preexisting entity. It is also very unlike Western phenomenology in the sense that the individual, the acting person, and his subjective orientation to the world in which he finds his way and makes his choices, are not the focal point of imaginative analysis. Nevertheless, as I have previously remarked, *intentionality* is accorded a primary place in Buddhism, and the intention behind an act is given crucial value in the moral evaluation of the act and the "fruit" it produces. Thus, Buddhism, while not reifying the conscious self by virtue of considering it as a temporary synchronic configuration of the five *skandhas* (form, feeling, perception, impulses, and consciousness, the last being the central entity and the rest depending on it in "conditioned coproduction"), does attribute to this synchronic configuration a volition and intentionality, which is the starting point for the quest for wisdom and liberation.

The next point to note about Buddhist phenomenology and subjectivism is that one dissolves the world by acting upon oneself—upon one's subjective processes of creating and attaching oneself to the world—rather than by acting independently upon the world. Thus, Buddhist phenomenology is not some kind of Western physical science but a religious meditative technology that becomes the field of experimentation and manipulation. Such a technology leads to the involvement with paranormal experiences, the doctrines of "intermediate" worlds and "subtle" beings, and of "powers" generated by mental practice.

Western conceptions of the effective cure of psychobiological stress share certain presuppositions with the Western (classical) conceptions of tragedy. There has to be a plot, a development of the character of the hero/patient, who (though he may suffer from an initial fatal flaw) goes through a series of crises, out of which comes a denouement and a reintegration. Mental therapy in particular, therefore, must probe the details of the case, biographical and circumstantial, and therefore engages in a dialogue between patient and curer and in a prolonged process of curing. This is so because these data and processes are considered "real" and "causal" and "relevant," and because the individual as an entity is also considered "real," autonomous, and of unquestioned value per se.

But in the Buddhist healing cult discussed here, we note a dual perspective that sees illness and cure in a different way. On the one hand, the doctrine of *karma* and the consequences of actions in past lives are invoked as a powerful blanket explanation of a patient's present condition; on the other, the tenets of the cosmological scheme are such that the experience of illness, pain, and misery is viewed as a real manifestation of one's "substantial" and corporeal enmeshment. Relief and liberation from this condition come not from dwelling upon its momentary and illusionary, though experientially painful, manifestations, but from transcending them, ideally through meditation, which enables one to leave one's mortal coil behind. The modes of normal awareness are obstacles to the progress of the mind toward its empty-ing and reaching tranquillity.

Hence it is, I suppose, that the cult leader and his assistants do not amass case histories of patients; they make them do penance for past *karma*, and then immediately engage them in the experience of medi-tation. It is the meditative ideal of leaving form and sense behind that is considered the true enduring reality, and the forms of worship, dis-course, sermons, and meditative exercises are alleged to lead the dis-ciple to a truer and more permanent mode of being than is the framework of contingent individual existences. And since all patients and disciples are subject to the same ritual routine of signs, gestures, words, postures, and recommended attitudes, this stereotyping im-plies—I hypothesize—that the curing routine does not so much ad-dress itself to the conscious passions and emotions of the individual patient but, through a general notion of appropriateness, to important aspects of his latent emotional life.[25]

In the Buddhist context the individual and personal aspects of ill-ness are assimilated to an enduring cosmic paradigm of theodicy and tranquillity. Thus, a transition is expected from the individual details of motion and turmoil (imbalance) to a generalized state of stillness and bliss.

But this is only half the story; for while the cult leader advises the patients and disciples not to dwell on the "causes" of their present ill-nesses and exhorts them to transcend their present conditions and merge with a cosmic paradigm, he and they know that they can do this at best only approximately and temporarily. And the cult leader and his assistants, who, as meditation adepts, are further along the way of transcending substantiality and earning merit, must provide relief for their dependents by employing their mystical powers of *iddhi*. Thus, it is at this level of transfer from the upper reaches of the cosmological scheme to the lower reaches that the ritual is more open to circum-stantial developments and inventive realism. The meditation cum cur-ing discourses realistically describe diseases and the techniques for curing them, which include those borrowed from Western medicine (techniques such as injections and operations, and diseases identified as cancer and thrombosis).[26] Furthermore, realism enters in the way the *achan* literally substantializes the power of his words and his mys-tical power and transfers their potency to his patients. Although the transcendental truth of otherworldliness is the path of searching and not easily arriving, this world of *laukika* is the plane of actual life in which good fortune and good health are sought and experienced, and they are the springboards for the higher quest.

Thus, what Eliade (1958) wrote of yoga is appropriate to the Thai meditation cult as well: "But let us recall a few of the techniques designed to arrest the flow of time. The commonest, the one that is indeed pan-Indian, is *pranayana,* the rhythmicisation of breathing. It should be noted that, although its ultimate aim is the transcendence of the human condition the practice of Yoga begins by restoring and improving that condition. For all forms of Yoga include a preliminary transformation of the profane man . . . into a glorious man with perfect physical health, absolute mastery of his body and his psycho-mental health . . . It is man thus made perfect that Yoga seeks finally to suppress . . . In cosmological terms . . . it is by starting from a perfect cosmos that Yoga sets out to transcend the cosmic condition as such."

THE PERFORMATIVE EFFICACY OF THE CURING RITUAL

Certain details of the curing session reveal much about the efficacy of the curing technique as a "performative act." In Chapter 2 we saw that ritual acts as *conventionalized enactments* (employing words and acts as an interlaced amalgam) attain much of their "illocutionary force" by their very performance. The enactment of the ritual is a "doing" in itself and an instrumental attainment of a new state; this performative effect is separable from other functional consequences the ritual may have upon the world, though of course efficacy cannot be judged apart from them.

The healer derives his warrant of legitimacy not as a prototype renouncer but as a proven meditation-adept who is using the mystic powers he gains from meditation to effect results in this world of sensory existence. But the healer, by virtue of his renunciation of sex and his religious concerns, no doubt partakes of the capacities and qualities of an ascetic; he is very nearly a monk (*bhikkhu*). In the sessions I observed, there was a second feature stemming from the healer's lay life that in fact supported and reinforced his instrumental role: he was also a police major, and a policeman, especially in a country like Thailand, quite conspicuously wields power and employs force in his dealings with the public. There is still a third feature of significance which may lend a moral validity and potency to the healer's role.

In the Buddhist cosmological treatise *Traiphum,* the description of the levels of heavens and hells is followed in the middle of the text by the appearance of the universal monarch, who, wielding the potent bejewelled discus (*cakkavatti*), renders a sermon as befits someone considered as introducing order in a chaotic world. The *achan* as healer, I suggest, participates in this image of a merit-laden figure acting on behalf of the world with kindness (*metta*) and without selfish interest in the fruits of his action. Moreover, like the ideal sage king, who is born by virtue of worthy past lives with potency (*rajanuphab*) and acquires merit by religious observances and acts, the *achan* too is credited, as we have seen, with similar great merit of past lives which enables him to use power (*anuphab*). (Note that the same elevated concept of *anuphab* customarily employed to characterize divine and royal personages is used to describe the healer's potency.) We can thus fruitfully ask whether the healer's curative acts are, at the widest limits of meaning, similar to the benevolent acts of the universal king toward his subjects—that is, whether a rich and potent Buddhist religio-political analogy is in play in the curing session. Details I have already described, such as the healer's giving audience in the manner of a "king" or a "deity," and the respectful and worshipful treatment of him by his clients, may serve to reinforce this interpretation.

Be that as it may, what is emphasized in the ritual itself is the classical relationship between teacher and pupil. The healer is literally called "teacher" (*achan*) and he calls his followers disciples (*luksit*). The traditional norm is that the teacher-disciple relation is a personal bond, in which the disciple submits to the discipline of obedience, loyalty, service, dependence, and trust, and that in return the teacher reveals progressively over time the secrets of his knowledge. This pattern of oral transmission and "closed" dyadic relationship is emphasized in all contexts of transmission of knowledge. The healer, especially with regard to the teaching of meditation, actively invokes these norms and patterns. Moreover, the curer-patient relation is assimilated to the culturally more encompassing and historically more universal relation of teacher and disciple, just as insofar as illness is sought to be cured through meditation, it too is assimilated to the encompassing notion of suffering (*dukkha*) and its relief to an enduring cosmic paradigm of tranquillity through the dissolution of individual selfhood.

Furthermore, the teacher-pupil relation is the crucial pathway which is traversed by the enactments of the curing session itself. On the one hand, it is the disciple-patient who is called upon to make the *cosmic ascent* by practice and action—he must engage in *intentional action* concretized as motivated but selfless gift giving to monks as penance, and he must learn through meditation to transcend the unreality and transitoriness of sensory corporeal existence. He thus places himself in the stream of cosmic process. On the other hand, there is in the opposite direction a descent of the superior levels of the cosmos into the human world; when the teacher transfers the merit of his mystical powers in altruistic fashion, the deities themselves descend and bring to bear their subtle bodies and qualities upon the gross material world. And in complementarity to the patient's progressive "receptivity" to the cosmos by losing his self-preoccupation, there is the concretely realistic experience of the higher subtle powers and forces impinging on the patient and transforming him. To put it a little differently, while meditation is a way of meaningful understanding of the illness by repudiating the transitoriness of the present, transcending bodily and mental pain, and affirming the timeless cosmic impersonal truth, the healing itself does the opposite by accentuating the auditory and visual and tactile sensations of the subtle bodies and forces which are experienced, so to say, as the inrush of the spiritual/mental into the corporeal and gross. Thus, intention, selflessness, and detachment are matched by the reward of experiencing subtle essences.

I will now turn to certain details of the curing session and see how the "ascent" and "descent" in the exchange between disciple and teacher are enacted and experienced in the curing session in a "realistic" way. One of the main features of this ritual realism is the way in which words and acts are interrelated in the ritual.

Certain features of the induction of new patients are crucial. Following are those I noticed in Curing Session 1: The patients wear white, which is the appropriate color for Buddhist laymen worshipping at the temple (*wat*). They offer objects which are standard articles of offering at worship: candles, joss sticks, and lotuses. (The lotus is a multivalent Buddhist symbol, one remarkable signification being that it stands for liberation from gross materiality, just as its roots stand in mud and its flower rises above the water and reveals its beauty.) During the induction the patients first hold and later imbibe sacralized water, which physically transfers its virtue to them. The handling of these objects is accompanied by a recitation of the forgiveness prayer. The flowers are placed on the altar, the candles and joss sticks lit and the water imbibed at the conclusion of the prayer.

The prayer itself is easy to follow. It begins, interestingly, by asking the sick patient (who is deficient in merit) to transfer his merit to all those he is already indebted to—the Buddhas, monks, deities, *achan*, parents, and so forth—not because the latter need it but because it represents for the patient an expression of the *benevolent intention to give*, which is doctrinally highly emphasized. Next the upper half of the cosmological scheme and pantheon, from the highest Buddhas and saints to deities and superior humans, is invoked (the lower half of the pantheon and cosmology, consisting of sinful humans, malevolent spirits, and so on, is irrelevant to this situation).[27] Thus, the universe of beings and relationships that the patient and curer accept as meaningful is not simply constituted of the social world of humans, but also of deities and the Buddhas themselves. The patient is made to apologize for his careless and unintentional sinful acts, and then to request the power (*anuphab*) of the beings propitiated so that he can enjoy good fortune and avoid misfortune. The patient's illness is unambiguously linked to his sinful acts in his past and present lives, and hence moral aspects of conduct and psychophysical illness are dynamically linked.

The prayer, though simple, has a contrapuntal pattern: it plays the patient's present, conscious intentionality of gift giving against his or her past, unconscious unintentionality of sinful acts (a formulation which is comforting in that past sins are not seen as deliberate). It insists on the patient's transfer of merit to his or her ethical superiors (Buddhas, deities, and humans), and this superfluity earns the bounty (*anuphab*) of the latter.

Following the prayer comes the curing through meditation. In order for the meditation sequence to work—a sequence that relies heavily on words stimulating the auditory and visual imagination of the patients—the patient must remove from the extremities of his body material objects (like shoes and wristwatches) that would obstruct the expulsion of negative influences. The negative influences are objectified as material things embedded in the body, which are later realistically extracted. And this extraction is complemented by the healer's conveying his potency by touching the most sacred parts of the patient's body and introjecting into it by blowing breath. These are the realistic physical manipulations.

The words of meditation produce their effects in various ways. Note that potency/power is concentrated upon or invoked instrumentally. The patients are asked to focus on a powerful object (*sing saksit*), such as a Buddha image, as a meditation support. And then the words stimulate the auditory and visual imagination—as, for instance, in the description of the gods and divine angels. Furthermore, even the physical sensations of taste and touch are activated by describing the administration of medicines and injections, and the ingestion of fruits and water in their subtle form.

Thus, in one sense the words stimulate the same sensory modalities as the actual physical manipulations of touching and breath blowing, and, in this sense, these media complement each other. This reinforcement is an aspect of intensifying effect through "redundancy." Another manifestation of this redundancy is that the meditation sequence begins by repeating the forgiveness prayer already recited at the induction of new patients. This *recursive* occurrence of ritual sequences is a characteristic of most complex rituals which attempt to cumulatively increase the performative effect by repetition.

The last sequence, the dispelling of bad *karma* (*gae kam*), has a number of central features. Here there is a return to the recurring basic theme of the cult: the bad effects of past *karma* acts must be expelled, and are efficaciously expelled by intentional acts of penance in the form now of feeding Buddhist monks. The dispelling sequence uses the patient's horoscope as a diagnostic of his *karmic* state (the scale of credits and debits resulting from past acts). Insofar as the horoscope postulates a relation between the configuration and motion of planetary deities and the configuration and trajectory of individual human lives, the cosmological scheme again reveals its encompassing presence, and macrocosm and microcosm are again brought into correspondence.

It is interesting that in this sequence the patient's illness as a result of his bad *karma* is simultaneously represented as and conflated with the action of malevolent spirits who have become angered. For the first time the lower half of the pantheon and cosmological scheme is directly confronted, and appeased—not directly but in a more elevated or sublimated manner.

There thus occurs once again another somewhat recursive pattern, but with an important shift. Whereas in the first induction sequence the new patients make offerings to and seek the forgiveness of their ethical superiors located in the upper half of the cosmological scheme, in the last sequence they again make gifts, but as appeasement, to the malevolent spirits who are attacking them in the form of illness, in order to remove and neutralize these spirits. It is appropriate that the sequential structure of the curing session should follow the hierarchical pattern of the pantheon and deal first with the deities and superior humans and last with those malevolent ghosts inferior to man.

THE UNITY OF KNOWLEDGE AND EXPERIENCE

Buddhism, both in its canonical literature (*sutta*) and in its discursive commentarial literature, implies a nondualism or monism that can be spelled out in various ways. There is first of all the notion of *dharma*, which in its most encompassing aspect does not separate moral laws from the laws of nature: *dhamma* is the "nature of things"; it is also moral law (including the teachings of the Buddha) and the fruits of its observance. One outcome of this globalism is that human actions, events in nature, and cosmological notions are considered to be interrelated and to affect one another. Second, unlike Western thought, which not only separates natural (physico-chemical) laws from moral laws but also the user of knowledge—the "scientist"—from the impersonal truth value of "objective" scientific knowledge, Buddhism considers them inseparable. Knowledge implies and is wedded to practice, and it is intimately related to the capacities of the knower.

A second implication of the unity of knowledge is that just as the *sutta* (Pali; Sanskrit = *sutra*) literature is the nonarguable ground of truth as taught by the Buddha, and the *abidhamma* the arguable commentarial literature that ensues from it, so do the *sastras* (discursive systems of knowledge) also stem from and branch out of religion (*sasana*). Thus, there is a single tree—no doubt a hierarchized tree—of knowledge, and this tree encompasses religion, and other systems of knowledge and practice such as meditation (*samadhi* and *vipassana*), alchemy, medicine (*ayurveda*), and astrology. The concept of knowledge, *paññā*, includes all these related systems, and it is precisely because they are considered bodies of genuine systematic knowledge that even many Western-trained Thai intelligentsia, whatever their positivistic and empiricist training in the United States, have resorted to them when necessary. Participation both in Western systems and their own traditional systems of knowledge is not fraught with conflict for them, a state of affairs that is aided by the fact that these systems have different contexts of relevance and are therefore insulated from direct confrontation. Buddhasat (the "science" of "applied" Buddhism, the systematic practice of Buddhist knowledge) is also for them not a contradiction in terms between "religion" and "science"; therefore they see no reason why all systems of knowledge could not coexist, without one system finding it necessary to supplant another according to some exclusive criteria of falsifiability and experimental proof.

A third implication is that all these systems of traditional knowledge set up correspondences, sympathies and antipathies, identities and differences, between the entities that are posited as composing the cosmos. There are relations formulated between "nonhuman," human, and animal creatures, and between man as microcosm and the universe as macrocosm. The universe itself is capable of being coded simultaneously in purely physicalistic terms (as in ayurvedic medicine) or in terms of planetary deities (as in astrology). Apart from these correspondences, meditation, medicine, and alchemy all share a language of successive ascending purifications and transformations along a vertical gradient, and a corresponding discarding of gross material waste products. A remarkable feature is that the theory of indigenous medicine (*ayurveda*) postulates the progressive "cooking" and transformation of food from chyle (*rasa*) to blood to flesh and so on, until ultimately the highest and most potent form of body substance—semen (*sukra*), which both men and women secrete in their bodies—is produced. Meditation, especially in the form known as Kundalini Yoga, concerns itself with the transformation and progressive purification through ascent of this same semen into another kind of vital fluid and its conservation as energy. Other forms of meditation, such as the Buddhist theory of *vipassana* or *samadhi*, posit the attainment of insight and wisdom and final liberation as an ascent by which form and sense are progressively left behind, and with them impermanence, suffering, and experience of self. Again alchemy, operating on base metals, "cooks" and purifies them through successive firings, and analogically relates the chemical operation on metals to the practitioner's own progressive purification of mind and attainment of mystical powers. Astrology in turn shares the same "episteme" in Foucault's sense: it is one's *karma* that determines the time and circumstances of one's birth, and the configuration of planets in their interrelations of potencies "mirrors" and reflects one's destiny to accumulate merit and avoid demerit (Nash, 1965), and makes "visible" the invisible action of one's past lives. Astrology, thus fitting into the Hindu-Buddhist cosmological scheme, serves as a diagnostic system and an indexical symbol, and permits remedial action, which is phrased in the best ethical language of giving, merit making, and cleansing oneself of impurities and sinful states. Furthermore, the coding of planets as deities, and of misfortune as the action of malevolent spirits (which mirrors one's own sinful state), allows for astrology too to fit into a single cosmology and belong to the same tree of knowledge and practice.

4

A Performative Approach to Ritual

In commemoration of A. R. Radcliffe-Brown, one of the great founders of social anthropology, I shall take as my point of departure certain passages not from the pages of his mature, lean, and lucid essays but from some casual and inconclusive yet thought-provoking musings in his octopodous work *The Andaman Islanders* (1964), first sketched out in 1908 in a thesis, then revised and extended in 1913, and finally published in 1922. They relate to the improbable subject of dancing, a topic on which he briefly scintillated but to which, as far as I know, he virtually never returned in his subsequent writing.

Limiting himself to treating dance as "a form of social ceremonial," Radcliffe-Brown notes the unexceptionable fact that "the essential character of all dancing is that it is rhythmical," and that this rhythmical nature of dance enables "a number of persons to join in the same actions and perform them as a body" (p. 247). From there he proceeds to suggest something more complex, something that can be extrapolated from dance to most cases of collective ritual: "Any marked rhythm exercises on those submitted to its influence a constraint, impelling them to yield to it and to permit it to direct and regulate the movements of body and even those of the mind" (p. 249). Fixed rhythm and fixed pitch are conducive to the performance of joint social activity. Indeed, those who resist yielding to this constraining influence are likely to suffer from a marked unpleasant restlessness. In comparison, the experience of constraint of a peculiar kind acting upon the collaborator induces in him, when he yields to it, the pleasure of self-surrender. The peculiarity of the force in question is that it acts upon the individual both from without (as a collective performance) and from within (since the impulse to yield comes from his own organism).

The next theme of interest is that in the Andaman Islands, dancing is always accompanied by song; indeed, every song is composed with the express intention of being sung at a dance (p. 334). Here Radcliffe-Brown not only draws our attention to the use of multiple media in ritual, but even goes so far as to suggest a motor or visceral theory of the effects of song and dance. Some very dubious speculation on the co-origins of music, dance, and song is followed by a pioneering foray into how dance and song engage the faculties: dancing not only brings into play the muscular system of the dancer, creating in him a condition of physical tension, but also engages two chief senses, that of sight to guide the dancer in his movements and that of hearing to enable him to keep time to the music. Radcliffe-Brown offers this hypothesis of visceral effect: "Recent psychology [note that "recent" here is no later than 1914] shows that what are called the aesthetic emotions are largely dependent on our feeling the music as movement, the sounds appealing not to the ear only but to stored-up unconscious motor images." Similarly, dance—even the simple dance of the Andaman Islanders—creates in the dancer "partly by the effect of the rhythm, partly by the effect of the harmonious and balanced tension of the muscles, a direct appeal to that motor sense to which the contemplation of beautiful forms and movements makes only an indirect appeal" (p. 250). It would be nice to imagine that Radcliffe-Brown's abortive visceral theory prefigures Lévi-Strauss's more elaborate and scintillating excursus on how music makes its effects (*The Raw and the Cooked*, 1970), except that Radcliffe-Brown sees both dance and music as creating effects in the same way.[1] Be that as it may, Radcliffe-Brown broached many decades ago the tantalizing question of how and with what effects different media are frequently combined in ritual, a question that has received little systematic attention in anthropology, in spite of all the obsession with ritual in our time.[2]

The Problem

The macro-problem I shall grapple with here is the dual aspect of rituals as performances. On the one hand, it can be said in general that a public ritual reproduces in its repeated enactments certain seemingly invariant and stereotyped sequences, such as formulas chanted, rules of etiquette followed, and so on. On the other hand, every field anthropologist knows that no one performance of a rite, however rigidly prescribed, is exactly the same as another performance because it is affected by processes peculiar to the oral specialist's mode of recitation, and by certain variable features such as the social characteristics and circumstances of the actors which (aside from purely contingent and unpredicted events) affect such matters as scale of attendance, audience interest, economic outlay, and so on. It is therefore necessary to bear in mind that festivals, cosmic rituals, and rites of passage, however prescribed they may be, are always linked to status claims and interests of the participants, and therefore are always open to contextual meanings. Variable components make flexible the basic core of most rituals.

But because this duality of ritual cannot be examined all at once, I want to probe in the first part of this discussion the basis for the formalized dimension of ritual, and to take the question of contextual meaning subsequently. Rituals tend to take a certain form wherever and whenever they occur in human societies. In making this statement I am quite aware of the variable ideological and symbolic designs of societies and of the pitfalls of approaching the variability of cultural conceptions with a pretentious set of analytic concepts drawn from a parochial Western experience. I am, for instance, aware that Balinese life, so suggestively painted for us by Bateson and Geertz, is more ritually patterned, more suffused with aesthetic values than contemporary American life, and that English society during the time of Jane Austen was more "conventionalized" than it is today. I am aware that within a single society, as well as between societies, rituals can vary in their degree of formalization, in their openness to context and contingent demands and meanings, and in their use of multiple media—words, music, dance. Nevertheless, I am persuaded that human beings everywhere commonly structure certain events which they consider important in a similar way, events which we can recognize as *ritual*, and that there are good reasons why they should do so.

How then do we recognize ritual in general terms by its form?

Identifying Ritual

Anthropologists cannot in any *absolute* way separate ritual from nonritual in the societies they study. But *relative* contrastive distinctions (rather than *absolute* distinctions) help to distinguish between certain kinds of social activity. For example, although symbolic elements surround the activity of a scientist conducting an experiment in a laboratory—he may wear a white coat and observe a certain etiquette with his colleagues—yet there is a difference between the scientific experiment and a Roman Catholic mass with regard to the way words and acts are implicated, "verification" procedures invoked, and results interpreted.

Although neither linguistically nor ostensively can one demarcate a bounded domain of ritual (separated from other domains) in any society, yet every society has named and marked out enactments, performances, and festivities which one can identify as typical or focal examples of "ritual" events. They constitute paradigmatic instances of the phenomenon I want to focus on here.

In the Thai language the prefix *pithi,* usually translated as "ceremony," demarcates certain events. *Pithi taengan* means marriage ceremony, *pithi phaosob* means cremation rites, and *pithi wajkhru* means the ceremony of honoring one's teacher. Again the prefix *ngān* signifies some kind of festivity, and can label a temple fair (*ngān wat*) or a feast at home (*ngān liang*). Although differentiating ceremonies or festivities from other events to which these labels are not attached, these examples do not differentiate "religious" events from "nonreligious," for in no Thai *pithi* or *ngān* is some feature of Buddhism or the supernatural not invoked.

Consider the following expressions in the English language: graduation ceremony, church service, prayer meeting, Republican Convention, communion rite, football match. The words "ceremony," "service," "convention," "meeting," "match," and so on mark the events as being of a particular kind. Indeed, these events appear to share some features—an ordering or procedure that structures them, a sense of collective or communal enactment that is purposive (devoted to the achievement of a particular objective), and an awareness that they are different from "ordinary," everyday events.

Some examples from India and Sri Lanka illustrate another feature associated with rituals, especially those of a festive kind—namely, the charged use of certain vehicles and devices of communication as a mode of experiencing and activating the extraordinary and extramundane. The word *līlā* in North India means "play," and as such labels games and dramas. But *līlā* is also used to describe one of the great cycles of religious festivals, the Rām Līlā, at which the epic Rāmāyaṇa is enacted. In this context, *līlā* means no "ordinary" play, no "ordinary" theater, but communicates the fact that the gods and the divine are becoming *activated and manifest in this world,* and thus stands for an intensified *experience* of the divine, characterized by a heightened use of many media of communication and a charged and expectant mass participation. The Tamil equivalent for such a religious festival is *thiruvilaiyādal,* and in neighboring Sri Lanka festive rites performed for gods are called *deiange sellama,* "the play of the gods." And it is perhaps not too far-fetched to say that the Tikopians express in a different idiom, immortalized by Raymond Firth, "the work of the gods," a similar sense of prescribed communal activity and an intensified experience during the ritual cycle when their gods initiate and regulate the cosmic round of activities.

We can of course find similar examples in the ancient Greek world, where ritual, festival, and play belonged to a paradigmatic set (in the Saussurean sense). A brief reference to Johan Huizinga's *Homo Ludens* is apposite here. Asserting the refreshing proposition that "play activity is the basis of civilisation" (as a view of contest it is at least a nice antidote to Konrad Lorenz's attributing the same role to aggression), Huizinga enumerates many features characterizing "play" in the classical Greek period, of which the following are examples: play constitutes a stepping out of real life into a temporary sphere of activity with a disposition all its own ("limitation of time"); it also takes place in a marked-off space, the playground and ritual stage sharing this "limitation of space"; it assumes a fixed, culturally ordained form, constituted of "elements of repetition and alternation (as in a refrain) [which] are like the warp and woof of a fabric"; it is a "contest for something" as well as a "representation" of something . . . it "creates order, and is order," and in an imperfect world it brings temporary perfection. All these characteristics fit like a glove the examples of ritual I earlier cited.

But Huizinga himself saw that there were elements of tension, uncertainty, and chanciness of outcome in play, a feature which Lévi-Strauss, continuing the challenging comparison between ritual and play,[3] singles out as the distinctive difference between them. In a famous passage in *Savage Mind* (1966) Lévi-Strauss remarked, "All games are defined by a set of rules which in practice allow the playing of any number of matches," while ritual is played "like a favoured instance of a game, remembered from among the possible ones because it is the only one which results in a particular type of equilibrium between the two sides" (p. 30). "Games thus appear to have a disjunctive effect: they end in the establishment of a difference between individual players or teams where originally there was no indication of inequality. And at the end of the game they are distinguished into winners and losers. Ritual, on the other hand, is the exact inverse; it conjoins for it brings about a union . . . or in any case an organic relation between two initially separate groups, one ideally merging with the person of the officiant and the other with the collectivity of the faithful" (p. 32).

Although no anthropologist will take Lévi-Strauss's formulation to be true of all rituals known, yet his comparison helps one understand how the Trobrianders (in Jerry Leach's marvelous film *Cricket in the Trobriands*) have transformed the English competitive (and ritualized) game of cricket—a "rubbish" game from the Trobriand point of view—into an elaborate formalized *kayasa* display, where not an outright win but a near equivalence of exchange (with the host team enjoying a slight edge) is the outcome.[4] The Trobriand transformation of a competitive game that evolved in an individualist Western society to a near-balanced reciprocity of formalized display and exchange does hint at a general, if not universal, feature of ritual: ritual usually specifies in advance not only the procedural rules but also the sequences of events, and in this sense stands in stark contrast to the unpredictable and unequal outcomes of sports (as they are understood in our time), with the jubilation of victory and the humiliation of defeat, all too well known in soccer and other sports today.

Obviously such ritual enactments as various forms of divination, astrological consultations, and mediumistic sessions do not predict their outcomes in advance, yet their ordering is very different from the uncertainties of a game. For they have as their aim the enabling of the client to effect a cure or a reconciliation, to make a decision, to avoid a danger, and in this sense the object of the exercise is to make a fruitful exchange between the occult and the human via the mediation of the officiant, a fruitful conjunction that will help produce an orderly, ongoing social existence.

Following is a working definition of ritual which highlights the features I have touched upon:

Ritual is a culturally constructed system of symbolic communication. It is constituted of patterned and ordered sequences of words and acts, often expressed in multiple media, whose content and arrangement are characterized in varying degree by formality (conventionality), stereotypy (rigidity), condensation (fusion), and redundancy (repetition). Ritual action in its constitutive features is performative in these three senses: in the Austinian sense of performative, wherein saying something is also doing something as a conventional act; in the quite different sense of a staged performance that uses multiple media by which the participants experience the event intensively; and in the sense of indexical values—I derive this concept from Peirce—being attached to and inferred by actors during the performance.

The Integration of Cultural Account and Formal Analysis

The above definition insists on ritual's being a culturally constructed system of symbolic communication—that is to say, its cultural content is grounded in particular cosmological or ideological constructs. The definition also insists on ritual's portraying certain features of form and patterning, and using certain communicational and semiotic vehicles. Can a "cultural account" and a "formal analysis" be fused in one and the same analysis? Can the formal features of ritual in general be reconciled with the particular cultural contexts in which rituals are created and enacted? Are they not conflicting analytical frames? I hope to demonstrate that cultural considerations are integrally implicated in the form that ritual takes, and that a marriage of form and content is essential to ritual action's *performative* character and efficacy.[5]

At first sight this theoretical aim seems daunting, because it appears as if the battle lines have already been drawn between two schools of thought, the neo-Tylorians and the proponents of a semiotic theory of ritual. The neo-Tylorians (for example, Horton) conceive the critical feature of religion, and therefore of (religious) ritual, as being belief in, and communication with, the "supernatural" world or a "transtemporal" other world. In contrast, the semiotic school views the category "ritual" as spanning sacred-secular, natural-supernatural domains, and as having as its distinctive feature a tendency toward certain forms and structures of "communication."

My view is that we can liberate ourselves from the limitations of the neo-Tylorian natural-supernatural dichotomy by first recognizing that all societies have cosmologies which in their *several different classificatory ways* relate man to man, man with nature and animals, and man with the gods and demons and other nonhuman agencies. The inevitability of the cosmological perspective was graphically stated by Wittgenstein in this aphorism: if the flea were to construct a rite, it would be about the dog. We must also clearly realize that cosmological conceptions are not merely—or even importantly—to be understood in terms of the subjects' stated "beliefs," as the neo-Tylorians tend to do, but are most richly embedded in myths, rituals, legal codes, constitutional charters, and other collective representations. Moreover, when beliefs are taken to be prior to ritual action, the latter is considered as derivative and secondary, and is ignored or undervalued in its own right as a medium for transmitting meanings, constructing social reality, or, for that matter, creating and bringing to life the cosmological scheme itself. In other words, ritual's performative and creative aspect as an enacted event tends to be lost sight of in neo-Tylorian discussions.

Thus, while we must grant the importance of cultural presuppositions, of cosmological constructs, as anterior and antecedent context to ritual, we must also hold that our understanding of the communicative aspects of ritual may not be furthered by imagining that such a belief context adequately explains the form of the ritual event per se. But the clue for synthesizing this seeming antinomy has already been revealed, in the fact that cosmological constructs are embedded (of course not exclusively) in rites, and that rites in turn enact and incarnate cosmological conceptions. The integration of cultural account and formal analysis is revealed in this mutuality: if a society's major rituals are closely associated with its cosmology, then we can legitimately ask *what* a society seeks to convey to its adherents in its main performances, which leads us to ask why certain communicational forms are chosen and used in preference to others as being more appropriate and adequate for this transmission.

By "cosmology" I mean the body of conceptions that enumerate and classify the phenomena that compose the universe as an ordered whole and the norms and processes that govern it. From my point of view, a society's principal cosmological notions are all those orienting principles and conceptions that are held to be sacrosanct, are constantly used as yardsticks, and are considered worthy of perpetuation relatively unchanged. As such, depending on the conceptions of the society in question, its legal codes, its political conventions, and its social class relations may be as integral to its cosmology as its "religious" beliefs concerning gods and supernaturals. In other words, in a discussion of enactments which are quintessentially rituals in a "focal" sense, the traditional distinction between religious and secular is of little relevance, and the idea of sacredness need not attach to religious things defined only in the Tylorian sense. Anything toward which an "unquestioned" and "traditionalizing" attitude is adopted can be viewed as sacred. Rituals that are built around the sacrosanct character of constitutions and legal charters or wars of independence and liberation, and that are devoted to their preservation as enshrined truths or to their invocation as great events, have (to borrow a phrase from Moore and Myerhoff) a "traditionalizing role," and in this sense may share similar constitutive features with rituals devoted to gods or ancestors.[6] No wonder an American sociologist—Bellah—has coined the label "civil religion" to characterize some American national ceremonials.

Thus, suppose we say that the main and critical points of articulation in many (if not all) cosmologies[7] are (to give a few examples): the insistence on unquestioned acceptance of conceptions that cannot be subject to the criterion of independent validating experience, the promise held out that the committed members will experience a greater cosmic reality and truth if they will suspend doubt and simply follow the prescribed practices; the postulation of a relation between life and death, between a "this world" and an "other world," between the realms of gods, ancestors, humans, and creatures of nature; the predication of a morally evaluated hierarchy of all creatures that make up the cosmos, and the transactions between them, both desirable and undesirable, deserved and undeserved; the enshrinement of events of sacred beginnings and climactic events. Supposing we say this, then certain corollaries necessarily follow which inflect and mold ritual action, which has for its objective the communication with and mediation between these culturally distinguished agents, levels, domains, and events which compose the cosmology.[8]

Formality, Conventionality, Stereotypy, and Rigidity

This dynamic nexus between such cultural constructs and ritual as a mode of social action generates the set of features which in my definition I referred to as formality, conventionality, stereotypy, and rigidity. If cosmological constructs are to be taken on faith and considered as immutable, then it is a necessary corollary that the rites associated with them be couched in more or less fixed form, be transmitted relatively unchanged through time, and be repeatedly enacted on ordained or crisis occasions. Moreover, especially in cosmic rites, but also in many rites of passage and in curing cults of mediumistic possession, the cosmogony is repeatedly enacted and the archetypes constantly reiterated in order to achieve the double feat of projecting concrete present time into mythical time (Eliade, 1959: 20) and bringing the superior divine realm or moments of beginning into the present human world to achieve a cleansing and a charging with moral potency.

These objectives and constraints directly shape certain features of form in ritual as a medium, features which by a happy convergence of ideas more than one anthropologist have in recent times identified.[9] In some respects, of course, these recent discussions return to Malinowski's treatment of magical language as a distinct mode, separate from ordinary speech. For example, Rappaport (1971, 1974) enumerates a conjunction of features as distinctive of ritual, such as formality (including stylization and repetition), invariance of liturgical form which generates sanctity (the quality of unquestionable truthfulness), and certainty of meaning. Bloch (1974) makes a similar identification. Moore and Myerhoff in a more recent work (*Secular Ritual,* 1977) refer to ritual as a "traditionalizing instrument" and single out repetition, stylization, ordering, evocative presentational style and staging, and so forth as formal features which enable ritual to imitate the rhythmic imperatives and processes of the cosmos and thereby to attach permanence and legitimacy to what are actually social constructs. Moore and Myerhoff make the telling observation that even in the case of a newly invented ritual (or a ritual performed only once), the ritual is constructed in such a way that "its internal repetitions of form and content make it tradition-like" because "it is supposed to carry the same unreflective conviction as any traditional repetitive ritual" (pp. 8–9).

I want to begin my commentary by elaborating the point that the formalization of ritual is linked to ritual's being *conventionalized* action, and that this conventionality in turn psychically *distances* the participants from the ritual enactment. This very fact puts in jeopardy the usefulness of the intentionality theory of meaning for understanding ritual.[10] Let me explain.

Rituals as conventionalized behavior are not designed or meant to express the intentions, emotions, and states of mind of individuals in a direct, spontaneous, and "natural" way. Cultural elaboration of codes consists in the *distancing* from such spontaneous and intentional expressions because spontaneity and intentionality are, or can be, contingent, labile, circumstantial, even incoherent or disordered.

If for the purposes of exposition we draw a crude distinction between "ordinary" communicational behavior and "ritual" behavior (accepting of course that both kinds are equally subject to cultural conventions), then we could say (forgetting the problem of insincerity and lying) that ordinary acts "express" attitudes and feelings directly (for example, crying denotes distress in Western society) and "communicate" that information to interacting persons (the person crying wishes to convey to another his feeling of distress). But ritualized, conventionalized, stereotyped behavior is constructed in order to express and communicate, and is publicly construed as expressing and communicating certain attitudes congenial to an ongoing institutionalized intercourse. Stereotyped conventions in this sense act at a second or further remove; they code not intentions but "simulations" of intentions. People can act meaningfully in stereotyped ways because they have "learned to learn" (in Bateson's sense of deutero-learning) and because the enactment of ritual is the guarantee of social communication. Thus, *distancing* is the other side of the coin of conventionality; distancing separates the private emotions of the actors from their commitment to a public morality. In a positive sense, it enables the cultural elaboration of the symbolic; but in a negative sense it also contributes to hypocrisy, and the subversion of transparent honesty.[11] The whole point about a vigorous culture as a social product is that it is capable of elaborating several orders of conventionality, superimposing and interweaving them, and juxtaposing several dimensions of meaning.

This of course means that any theory of ritual as directly modifying sentiments, as enabling persons to "act out" their aggression or frustration and thereby reach a cow-like, placid state is too simplistic and naïve. Radcliffe-Brown himself, at certain points in *The Andaman Islanders*—for example, in his discussion of the peace-making ceremony (p. 238)—viewed ritual as replacing aggressive feelings with those of "friendship and solidarity."[12] But he clearly saw that the objective was not achieved directly; for example, he commented that Andamanese ceremonies "are not spontaneous expressions of feeling; they are all customary obligations to which the sentiment of obligation attaches" (p. 246).[13]

Suzanne Langer (1951) saw very well how formalization in ritual involved the adoption of conventionalized gesture as opposed to improvised action, and how critical the phenomenon of psychic distancing of the participants was. She noted that ritual, usually bound to set occasions, is a "presented idea"; ritual as symbolic activity involves "conceptions" rather than an immediate relief of feelings, which may or may not take place. Ritual, Langer continued, was a culturally constructed expressive act, "expressive in the logical sense"—that is, "not as a sign of the emotion it conveys but a symbol of it; instead of completing the natural history of a meaning, it denotes the feeling, and may merely bring it to mind . . . when an actor acquires such a meaning it becomes a *gesture*" (pp. 123–124).

In other words, Langer's point was that ritual's distinctive characteristic is not the evoking of feelings in an immediate psychological sense, not the inducing of a catharsis in the Aristotelian sense, which it may or may not do, but the "articulation of feelings," and "the ultimate product of such an articulation is not a simple emotion, but a complex permanent attitude. This attitude, which is the worshippers' response to the insight given by the sacred symbols, is an emotional pattern, which governs all individual lives. It cannot be recognized through any clearer medium than that of formalized gesture." Ritual is not a "free expression of emotions" but a disciplined rehearsal of "right attitudes."[14]

All of a piece with the elaboration of the formalized gesture is the development together with ritual of what Hymes has called the "polite style," as opposed to the normal unmarked colloquial and slang. The polite style, the style of rhetoric, the use of superior forms of address and pronouns and of inflated vocabulary, comes to be preferred in important, serious ceremonies. "The style becomes a formal marker of occasions of societal importance where the personal relationship is minimized" (Ervin-Tripp, 1972: 235). I might add that where, as in many complex serious ceremonies, slang and low comedy—the indicators of "vulgar" persons—are introduced at certain points, these "crude" sequences make their import by unfavorable comparison with, and subordination to, the high style associated with the refined, the honored, and the high-ranked *persona*.[15]

If we push this line of thought far enough, a certain conclusion follows: when quintessential rituals are enacted, their meanings retreat further and further away from an "intentional" theory of communication and meaning, as developed by philosophers of language.[16] We can keep aside as more or less irrelevant the Gricean theory of intentional meaning, because in conventional ritual like marriage the immediate intentions of the officiating priest or of the bride and groom do not explain the meaning and efficacy of the rite itself (or the unintended meanings). Whether a man is marrying because he has made the girl pregnant, or whether the ceremony is being performed by a fallen, drunken priest (of the sort so powerfully depicted in Graham Greene's *The Power and the Glory*), is immaterial to the validity of the sacrament performed, provided certain conditions are satisfied (the priest has been ordained into his office, the couple are not marrying bigamously, and so on).[17] Thus, if we postulate a continuum of behavior, with intentional behavior at one pole and conventional behavior at the other, we shall have to locate formalized ritual nearer the latter pole. Although this leaves intentionality as such behind, there is a strong temptation to adopt and adapt the Austinian notion of performative acts and the Gricean notion of conventional (and nonconventional) implicature in this scheme for understanding the social meaning and efficacy of ritual.

At this point I can conveniently introduce the first of the three senses in which I consider ritual to be performative. This first sense obviously derives from Austin's well-known notion of the performative utterance, in which the saying of the illocutionary speech act is "the doing of an action"; this act, "conforming to a convention" in "appropriate circumstances," is subject to normative judgments of felicity or legitimacy and not to rational tests of truth and falsity.

Adapting Searle (1969)[18] for my purposes, I can say that rituals as performative acts may be subject to two different sorts of rules, *regulative* and *constitutive*. This distinction is not watertight, but it does afford some analytic mileage. Regulative rules regulate (perhaps "orient" is a better word) a preexisting activity, an activity whose existence is logically independent of the rules—as, for instance, when dinner-table manners regulate the eating of food. Constitutive rules constitute (and also regulate) an "activity the existence of which is logically dependent on the rules" (pp. 34–35), as in the case of the rules of football or chess.

To Austin's classical examples of constitutive acts, such as greeting, baptizing, naming a ship, and marriage vows—all of which are created and understood within the bounds of the conventions themselves— one can add several anthropological examples: the installation of a Tallensi chief, Ndembu circumcision rites, Lodagaa mortuary rites, a Japanese tea ceremony, a Catholic Mass, and a multitude of cosmic rites and festivals which are self-constituting events and of which there are several classic descriptions.

To these classic constitutive ritual acts, whose very performance achieves the realization of the *performative* effect, can be attached two kinds of *perlocutionary* (functional) consequences. There are certain constitutive rites in which certain *perlocutionary* effects are presupposed by the illocutionary force of the acts and actually take place: when a Tallensi chief is properly installed certain results must imperatively follow upon his exercise of the powers of office. The valid performance of Lodagaa mortuary rites must imperatively lead to the distribution of the rights and duties and property of the dead man to his declared heirs (Goody, 1962). But there are also constitutive acts which, although they realize their performative dimension, may yet be uncertain of realizing their expected perlocutionary effects. A classic example is curing rituals in cases of spirit possession, which, though performatively valid, may or may not induce a cure in the patient, traffic with the supernatural being notoriously uncertain.

The way to account for people's continuation with "magical" rites that empirically may produce false results is a classic anthropological chestnut that has exercised, to give a few examples, the minds of Tylor, Frazer, Evans-Pritchard, and, more recently, Horton. Against this main-line tradition, I earlier submitted that it might be misplaced to judge such rites solely against the perspective and truth canons of Western scientific rationality, for as constitutive and persuasive acts they cannot be "falsified," though individual instances of them may be declared normatively infelicitous or illegitimate (see Chapter 2). If anthropologists insist on seeing magical rites as acts launched by the actors to achieve practical results by suspending the laws of motion and force as we understand these laws in modern physics, then obviously such acts must be declared false. But insofar as anthropologists are open to the proposition that magical rites are conventional acts which should also be examined within a performative frame of social action, then a new horizon opens for viewing the logic of such purposive acts and the canons for their validity from the actors' point of view.

But this performative view also faces fuzzy instances which it must situate within its framework. Where curing rites are intertwined with the use of herbal and other medicines and practical health care (as in many traditional societies), it may make sense to view the ritual component as having a strong "regulative" character. In such cases, an improvement in medical techniques may render the older rites *obsolete* rather than proving them false or wrong. An example is the virtual disappearance of the rites addressed to the smallpox goddess in Sri Lanka in the face of the dramatic success of Western medicine in eradicating smallpox. Another frequently observed fact can also be cited in this context. Curing rites, divinations, rain-making rites—all promising an empirical result but not falsifiable on that account—are prone to proliferate, compete with rivals, and come into and go out of fashion quickly, depending on their alleged results. But rival cults do not seek so much to "disprove" as to outbid one another, and usually a great number of redundant cults coexist and are simultaneously resorted to by clients.

Certain special considerations apply to that second class of performative ritual acts which I have called *regulative,* in the sense that they orient and regulate a practical or technical activity, and address themselves to the aesthetic style of that activity, or act as its diacritical features, without actually constituting it. The procedures for rice cultivation among the Kachin, which may entail ploughing in certain directions or allocating different roles to men and women, regulate or orient cultivation without constituting it. Again the Trobriand canoe-making ritual or agricultural rites, interwoven closely with practical technical acts of boat building or gardening, do many things such as organizing labor, encoding aesthetic values and mythical associations, timing the work phases, and providing an anticipatory statement about the success to be achieved in Kula or yam harvests to be distributed as *urigubu*—yet these rites supplement and regulate the technical activity which is a separate strand in the coil.[19]

Thus, regulative rituals have two characteristics. By themselves they can be seen to have a "constitutive" element; but they are in fact interwoven with practical activity, and therefore the constitutive element does not exhaust the whole amalgam, which is canoe building or gardening in Trobriand terms. Second, the expected perlocutionary effect of the rites may happen uncertainly, but this does not undermine their performative validity.[20]

The Application of Information Theory to Ritual

I have so far explored some of the conditions that contribute to the formalization, conventionalization, and distancing of ritual as a medium of communication. One set of features that frequently accompanies the foregoing in most complex rituals consists of various kinds of abbreviations and elisions which are referred to in the literature as *condensation* and *fusion*. A second set consists of repetitive and recursive sequences which tend to be labeled *redundancy*, a labeling that derives its reason by association with information theory. In actual fact condensation and redundancy are linked, dialectically related processes that produce intensification of meaning as well as the decline of meaning.

Information theory has been promiscuously invoked by analysts of ritual, an invocation that is further compounded by different "readings" of the theory that are then applied to the interpretation of ritual. It is necessary therefore to make a few preliminary clarifications even at the risk of sounding pedantic.

Information theory (Cherry, 1961; Miller, 1951) relates strictly to communication engineering, which is concerned with the technical problem of making the most economical use of the capacity of a transmission channel (or, to put it another way, of transmitting the maximum number of messages through the channel in the shortest possible time). In this technical science, the notion of "information" has a precise statistical meaning. The amount of information carried by a unit in a code is a function of the probability of its occurrence; in fact, information content is inversely proportionate (and logarithmically related) to probability.[21]

Other concepts that are central in information theory are "noise" and "redundancy." "Noise" refers to any interference in a channel that affects the correct reception of signals. The use of "superfluous" symbols to make sure that the message will be received correctly is known as redundancy. Redundancy is considered a necessary vice in information theory; some degree of it is thought to be desirable because of the interference upon the medium or channel of unpredictable physical or other disturbances, which would lead to a distortion or obliteration and loss of information.[22] "Redundancy, like the unemployed worker, is unproductive, but only when the message is to be sent through a perfect noise-free channel to a perfect receiver" (Corcoran, 1971: 33).

Messages can be repeated in many ways. They may be transmitted over several channels simultaneously, permitting the recipient to compare the several received messages and arrive at the correct message. More often it is necessary to use a single channel several times in a row, in which case either the entire message may be relayed and then repeated, or one section of the message may be repeated before proceeding to the next section.[23]

At first sight the fact that ritual has various features of redundancy and high probability of occurrence invites an application to it of information theory. But there are good reasons against a literal and limited application of that theory to ritual as communication.

The passage of new information as such from one person to another is only one aspect of social communication, and in ritual, which is formalized and predictable, this aspect may be subordinate and of little relevance. But one should not think that because most rituals are not concerned with transmitting new information, they therefore lack any referential, propositional, and analogical meanings at all.[24] A further limitation is equating information as such (in the technical sense) with the concept of "meaning."[25] Indeed, the various ways "meaning" is conceived in anthropology are a deadly source of confusion.

Social communication, of which ritual is a special kind, portrays many features that have little to do with the transmission of new information and everything to do with interpersonal orchestration and with social integration and continuity. The orchestrational and integrational aspects of the communicative process (Birdwhistell, 1970: 86–87) includes many operations: the "phatic" feature which keeps the communication system in operation, the certainty of message which eases an interpersonal anxiety or affective lesion, the battery of linguistic and other cues which act as triggering mechanisms and context markers, the regulative etiquette which orders what is considered as proper communication between persons in equal or asymmetrical statuses—these are a related set. Another set relates to features that cross-reference and link particular messages to enable their comprehensibility and reception as larger totalities, and features that relate the particular context of communication to the larger cultural context(s) of which it is a part. Here one can also appropriately invoke and apply to ritual Jakobson's enumeration of functions of verbal communication—referential, poetic, phatic, emotive, conative, and metalingual, all of which in varying proportions are served by verbal communication. The coding of emotive elements in ritual speech through prosodic features of intonation and stress, emphatic vocal prolongations, and so forth, and the supplementary use of paralinguistic features such as kinetic movements and gestures, whether conventionally required or unconsciously manifested, are familiar indices that reveal the emotional attitudes of the officiants and participants. In Thailand one has only to compare the still, emotionless, detached postures of the Buddhist monk and the convulsive, overwhelmed movements of a spirit-possessed medium to realize instantly the different involvements being communicated. But rituals may also convey the metalanguage function of definitional, glossing learning, as for instance manifest in certain initiation and mystery cults whose initiates are "taught" mysteries and identities and given new knowledge from which they were previously excluded.[26] Examples of such teaching of the cultural code in graduated terms are the Baktaman (Barth, 1975), who progressively introduce initiates into the secret mysteries, and the Bemba, who in their Chisungu rite use mnemonic devices and songs for teaching young girls (Richards, 1956).

These things notwithstanding, I wish to elucidate and underscore one understanding of "meaning," defined not in terms of "information" but in terms of *pattern recognition* and *configurational awareness*. A hallmark of the arts and crafts—poetry, painting, dancing, music, pottery design, and so on—is the reduction of the random by restraint (as Bateson put it)[27]—indeed, the creation of recognizable patterns and unanticipated tensions and outcomes, by means of redundancy and recursive loops. And of course a prime aesthetic censor which prevents the deterioration of art forms into degenerate banality is *controlled modulation*. One recognizes, in this characterization of meaning in terms of pattern recognition, a positive characterization of the role of redundancy in art forms. The antithetical image of this positive projection of meaning as pattern is the communication engineer's postulation of unpredictability and low probability of occurrence of an item as constituting its high information content.

I must now introduce a certain amount of rigor into the discussion of what I mean by "redundancy" in ritual. Those who have done detailed studies of complex rites and ritual cycles are keenly aware of various kinds and patterns of repetitions that occur, sometimes causing boredom with their seemingly insistently unvarying recurrence, and sometimes subtly stimulating a sense of creative variation and attentive expectation. In this chapter I can only barely suggest the dimensions of the problem, locate some of the meaningful patterns, and urge the need for a closer analysis of them before one indulges in gross generalities. There are, just to enumerate at random, repetitions of the same sequence, both within a long rite and between a series of related rites. But there are many rites in which redundancy, rather than being mere tedious repetitions of the same thing, can be demonstrated to be interesting and complex in the work it does.

A standard example is "parallelism," the pairing of couplets, which Robert Lowth identified and made famous in the second half of the eighteenth century as being characteristic of Hebrew poetry, and which more recently Jakobson (1966) analyzed in his work on Finnic and Russian oral traditions.

Parallelism in its more general sense refers to the poetic artifice of "recurrent returns" at the semantic, syntactic, and phonemic levels of expression, and in its specific canonical sense refers to a compositional device wherein "certain similarities between successive verbal sequences are compulsory or enjoy a high preference" (Jakobson, 1966: 399). Parallelism expresses mainly a relation of symmetry, the two halves of the pair being slightly distinguished from each other by syntactic or semantic variations or slight differences in function or by other substitute devices.

In a recent survey Fox (1977) enumerates the occurrence of canonical parallelism in its various forms and patterns, and reports its widespread occurrence in both literate and oral cultures distributed in time and space, in as diverse instances as Hebrew, Vedic, Chinese, Dravidian, and Mayan poetry, in the ritual language occurring in Vietnam, Mongolia, and Hawaii, and among the Todas, the Walbiri of Australia, the Navaho, the Kachin, the Thai, the Buang of Papua New Guinea, the Merina of Madagascar, the Rotinese of the outer Indonesian Islands, and the Chamulas of the Chiapas Highlands of Mexico.

What is of particular interest here is that parallelism is a pervasive device and idiom of formal speaking, chanting, and singing, and of greetings, farewells, petitions, and courtship overtures. Especially throughout the world's oral traditions, it is a "speech form or language stratum reserved for special situations: for the preservation of past wisdom, for the utterance of sacred words, for determining ritual relations, for healing, and for communication with spirits" (Fox, 1975: 127–128).

The question of why such a language form should be considered appropriate for formal occasions, especially as a component of ritual language, could be approached from many angles.

Let me briefly allude here to the creative role of the "formula," a term applied by Lord (1958), and Parry before him, to "repeated word groups" that express an essential idea, in generating and producing an actual recitation as performance. The Slavonic singer of epic poetry has in his possession "basic patterns of meter, word boundary, melody," and he is adept at using these compositional devices: "the linking of phrases by parallelism, [the] balancing and opposition of word order," and the substitution of key words (Lord calls this paradigmatic operation a "substitution system"). Lord has eloquently stated that "for the oral poet the moment of composition is the performance." He has demonstrated how the oral poet, whose basic capital is a stock of memorized formulas, varies and ornaments his songs, lengthens or shortens them, according to the demands and character of the audience and other situational circumstances, and how in fact he preserves the tradition by the constant recreation of it. Indeed, such a dynamic performative approach should refute the overly simplistic view that, because oral specialists say and believe their sacred words are fixed and invariant, their actual renditions are reproductions of an invariant text. It surely cannot be the case that, although guided as well as constrained by sequencing rules and other prescriptions regarding language expression, the political orator—including those in the Merina and Balinese instances (Bloch, 1975)—produces set congealed speeches.

In ritual, too, not only would the outputs of different specialists allegedly performing the same rite be different in certain respects, but the outputs of the same specialist—especially if he is not confined to the recitation of a written sacred text—would be variable at separate performances of the same rite. Indeed, complex rites, and long recitations, usually have some sequences more open than others, more open in terms of structure and more open to new contents. Even in the Trobriand case, Malinowski remarked that in the main body (*tapwana*) of the spell—which in content was constructed by combining and varying action words with metaphors and metonyms—there was a certain amount of freedom regarding the order in which words were uttered, whereas words were not liable to "even the smallest alteration" in the first part (*u'ula*) of the spell, which was usually a recitation of ancestral names that established the magician's charter. Thus, in summary, let us suppose that whatever the permissible features of creativity and variability in the "production" of rites as performances, such features 1) function on a base or core of stereotyped or conventionalized formulas and "substitution systems" and/or 2) can to some degree be accounted for in terms of contextual demands and indexical factors.

Whatever the importance of these compositional considerations, I have yet to tackle here why *ritual language* resorts to, and how it exploits, redundant and patterned devices, of which parallelism is an example. An ethnographic illustration opens a window onto the problem by revealing why a certain people views a particular linguistic construction as an effective communication device with the divine. The Chamulas of highland Mexico consider formal ritual speech as "heated" discourse (in comparison with the "cool" discourse of ordinary times). Heated discourse is an intensified medium which serves to establish contact with the higher holy entities, which are themselves symbols of cyclical heat, a principle of great importance in Chamula thought. This ritual speech, rendered with voice modulations from higher to lower pitch with great regularity, is constructed in pairs, and multiples of pairs, which enter into numerous combinations in "song," "prayer," "language for rendering holy," and sometimes "true ancient narrative," as these genres are distinguished by native speakers.

From the point of view of text or discourse construction, the "stacking" (as Gossen calls it) of the parallel couplets one after the other enables the performers to extend texts, give them embellishments (within stylistic bounds), explore nuances of multivocal meanings; and from the point of view of performative efficacy the structure of the entire recursive recitation may be seen as an iconic analogue of the cycles of creations of the cosmic order in their temporal and spatial regularity and cumulative effect.

I would like briefly to recall the structural pattern of the Trobriand spells in order at least to confront, if not solve, the basis for the Trobriand view that their magical spells are "verbal missiles" launched by man as "magical power towards the entities or forces which they were meant to affect" (Malinowski, 1935, vol. 2: 248–249). At least part of the explanation for the "creative metaphor of magic" and its persuasive potency lies in the verbal construction of the spell, the mode of its recitation, and the physical manipulations which accompany it. As Malinowski put it: in the main part of the spell (*tapwana*) "several key words are repeated with inventory expressions" in such a way as to produce the effect of "rubbing" the verbs of action into a succession of dazzling metaphors drawn from diverse sensory domains, or into the enumerated parts of the object—whether it be a tuber or a yam house—assembled as a whole through step-by-step metonymic recitation. The contours of this magical operation have already been described (see Chapter 1; also Nancy Munn, n.d.), but here I want to suggest the mechanisms by which this kind of redundant rhetoric "generates" the magical missile. The formulaic pattern of the Trobriand spells insistently introduces a variety of metaphorical expressions or metonymic parts into a stereotyped stream of repeated words intoned with modulations of speed, loudness, and rhythm, thereby foregrounding them as well as telescoping or fusing them into an amalgam that is given motion and direction by compelling illocutionary words of command and persuasion or declaration. Malinowski's characterization of this process as a "rubbing" effect is felicitous, for indeed in Trobriand magic the verbal creation of force is made more realistic and operational by using substances (which themselves have metaphorical associations named in the spell) metonymically, so that a transfer of effect is made through blowing, rubbing, smoking, and various tactile manipulations. The cross-linkages in this art are manifold, and combine to produce an arrow-like thrust.

The Trobriand formulaic structure and ritual operations are by no means idiosyncratic. The spell symbolism and structure of the Melpaspeaking people of Mount Hagen in New Guinea are remarkably similar as described by the Str, therns (1968). Michelle Rosaldo (1975), with the Trobriand precedent in mind, has suggested that the effectiveness of the magical spells of the Ilongot of Northern Luzon, Philippines (who are hunters, headhunters, and swidden agriculturists), "depends on the fact that they invoke images from a number of diverse areas of experience and that these images, in turn, are regrouped and organized in terms of a small set of culturally significant and contextually desirable themes," and that this "new organization," the creative product of the spell, itself depends on "the repetitive and formulaic quality of magic" (p. 178).

One upshot of these analyses is that the ordering and the pattern of presentation of the ritual language, physical gestures, and manipulation of substances is the *form* of the ritual: form is the arrangement of contents. Therefore I think Rappaport (1974) is mistaken—in the same way that McLuhan is mistaken—in thinking that the "surfaces of ritual" whose features are stereotypy, liturgical invariance, and so on can be dealt with apart from the symbolism of ritual or, as he puts it, "the relations among the symbols that may appear in rituals." If then the neo-Tylorians err in accenting beliefs to the detriment of the ritual action, there is one extreme semiotic school that supposes that form can be tackled apart from the presentation of contents and the interpretation of symbolism.

Let us now review another order of redundancy which consists of recurrences that are not simply mechanical in their appearance but occur in *recursive* fashion to start new sequences or combine unit acts into different "syntactic" sequences within the same rite.

There are in all complex rites discernible "sequencing rules" and "co-occurrence restrictions." Sociolinguists in the United States have shown that almost all kinds of speech events constitute forms of discourse with their own sequencing rules: telephone conversations have their predictable sequencing (Schegloff, 1972; see also Sacks, Schegloff, and Jefferson, 1974: 696–735); therapeutic discourses have their coherent sequencing (Labov and Fanshel, 1977).[28] Since ritual discourse is in fact a more conventionalized event, one should not be surprised to find that it has even more conspicuous sequencing rules. Moreover, because the rituals I am focusing on are considered public, serious, and festive by the actors, various "co-occurrence restrictions" and "bound relations" in the proceedings are to be expected, precisely because on the one hand the communication reflects and realizes cosmological and liturgical concepts and principles, and on the other hand that same communication is between persons in "status marked situations" of authority and subordination, of competence and eligibility, of "power and solidarity" (to repeat the famous phrase from Brown and Gilman, 1960)—persons variously called priest, officiant, patient, communicant, addressor, and congregation. In other words, if ritual events are performative acts (in a much stronger sense than ordinary speech acts, which also do something with words), then the connections between the unit acts and utterances of the ritual, the logic of the rules of obligatory sequences of the ritual acts per se, cannot be fully understood without realizing that they are the clothing for social actions; and these social actions cannot in turn be understood except in relation to the cosmological presuppositions and the social interactional norms of the actors. Once again, the form and content of ritual are necessarily fused, and the problem here is to devise a conceptual system that sees the message "as both itself internally patterned and itself a part of a larger patterned universe—the culture or some part of it" (G. Bateson, 1972: 132).

There are two more general points to be made regarding the study of redundancy and patterning. The notions of sequencing rules and co-occurrence restrictions have to do with horizontal relations, the linear syntagmatic connections between actions and utterances as they unfold from beginning to end. The classical framework in the anthropological study of rites in this mode is of course the tripartite scheme of Van Gennep—segregation, liminal period, and reaggregation—and Mauss's earlier scheme for sacrifice—entry, act, and exit. This scheme, if employed mechanically, can mask certain perceptions. For example, there are certain rituals of curing which are patterned into two halves, the second half being a repeated but stronger and more potent version of the first half. Or again there are both cosmic festivals and rites of affliction which have internal recursive loops, and shifts in the media emphasized, and a combined pattern of progressions and reiterations, whose subtleties are not revealed by a prior commitment to the tripartite straitjacket as the point of departure. A generative syntactic approach, or a pointillist dissection, or a configurational approach devoted to seeing how the whole is built up from, but is also greater than, the parts—all these perspectives will concentrate on how lower-level units build up into or fuse into higher-level units and processes, how different media are made to converge, and how total experiences are produced.

In other words, the horizontal relations and connections dynamically act upon one another to constitute the *vertical* dimension by which higher-level integration is achieved by "the interplay of variation" (T. Turner, n.d.), by the dialectic of paradigmatic "oppositions" and syntagmatic "contrasts" (Jakobson), and by the condensation of messages sent through "the switching of metaphoric and metonymic modes" to produce a "single experience" and a single "message" (Leach, 1966, 1976). Thus, the second sense in which I see ritual as performative is as a dramatic actualization whose distinctive structure including its stereotypy and redundancy has something to do with the production of a sense of heightened and intensified and fused communication. The objectives of such intensification have been variously phrased: as the submission of persons to a compelling "constraint" (as Radcliffe-Brown put it), or as their transportation into a supranormal, transcendental, "antistructural," "numinous," or "altered" state of consciousness, or as a euphoric communion with one's fellow beings, or as subordination to a collective representation. If such is the case, then anthropologists have to delve deeper than they have done so far into the manner of interplay of the horizontal and vertical dimensions of the ritual, and the manner in which media such as chants, songs, dance, music, verbal formulas, and material gifts are employed in the service of heightening communication. These media may, according to cultural definitions, be considered "heated," "compelling," "forceful," and "pleasing" to demons and deities; and at the same time they may be seen as making certain kinds of impacts on the officiants and participants as both senders and receivers of the message.

The media may, especially in their repetitive and/or punctuational use, serve to initiate and leave sacred time or to enter and leave supranormal states. The employment of certain musical instruments for this purpose has been aptly noted by Needham (1967). Another classical example is the verbal formulas of Buddhist meditational exercise by which their mindful repetition is held to enable the achieving of the detached mental state of "one pointedness of mind" (Maha Boowa, 1976), or the *mantra* of Hinduism which "are now mainly regarded as aids or means to meditation and concentration" or as "instruments of therapy intended to bring about a change in mental state" (Staal, 1975: 27–28). Whether or not they are literally meaningful[29] (some are and some are not), the prime value of these repeated sayings is their therapeutic value as "focusing" mechanisms. But their efficacy is of an intriguing sort. I previously referred to ritual's formalism as enabling the "distancing" of actors, and participation in it as engaging not raw emotions but "articulated" feelings and gestures. In a similar vein it makes sense to suggest that the repeated verbal formulas as "supports of contemplation" or transporters into a trance state perform these functions not by a direct assault on the actor's senses and inflicting an immense psychic toll on him or her, but by a more indirect conventional illocutionary employment of them as instruments of passage and as triggering mechanisms.[30]

It is time now to give some ethnographic body to these pontifications, and at least to illustrate some of the complexities suggested. Sinhalese exorcism rites have been amply documented (for example, Wirz, 1954; Pertold, 1930; Gooneratne, 1865; Kapferer, 1977; Obeyesekere, 1969) and provide a good example of the employment of multiple media and the devices of redundancy. Their study will perhaps give some clues as to how ritual attempts to persuade its clientele, and reveal what some of the patterns and positive effects of redundancy in its various forms might be.

A Sinhalese Exorcism Rite

In the southwest low country of Sri Lanka, there is an elaborate set of beliefs and cults concerning illnesses that are believed to be caused by demons.[31] The demonic attack is referred to as a "manifestation" (the Sinhalese term is *dishtya*, a look cast upon the victim). The attack itself takes place because the victim is in a vulnerable situation on account of bad *karma*, planetary influence, or sorcery. The entry of the demon is forced and therefore involuntary on the patient's part, and this alien resident dislocates the host's capacity for normal communication with his fellow beings.

The theory of cure presupposes a Buddhist pantheon in which gods are superior to demons, and in which the Buddha as the supreme entity has delegated powers to demons to indulge their crass cravings on the condition that they leave their human victims when appropriate gifts are made to them in an appropriate state of mind. In the exorcism rite gods, as benevolent agents, are invoked by the officiants to act together with them in the expulsion of the demons. Part of the dynamic of these transactions lies in the Buddhist notion that demons and humans as well as some of the gods (especially those who belong to the *kāma* realm of form and desire) are capable of bettering their futures in the cycle of rebirths by meritorious conduct.

The exorcism rite which I am describing is addressed to Mahāsohona Yakkha, the Great Cemetery Demon. In theory, there are a number of major demons who (with their retinues) can individually cause diseases in which they specialize. These demons have horrifying names such as the Blood Demon (Rīri Yakkha), the Sorcery Demon (Sūniyam Yakkha), and so on. But usually, although a ceremony is performed for one demon as the major disease agent, many other demons are also addressed and propitiated because they all act in concert.

The curing ceremony, which lasts from sunset of one day to the dawn of the next, is a "public" occasion in many senses of the word. The definition and contour of the illness are public knowledge; the patient has to make a public rejection of the introjected agent, witnessed by the local community of kin and neighbors, whose failure to attend may lead to suspicion of sorcery against them. This rejection is made normatively desirable because the ritual represents the demons as gross and loathsome, confined in the cubicles of space and time and desire as the lowest form of life in the Buddhist cosmos. The demons and their acts of indulgence of their gross desires are represented with maximal sensory intensity, and this representation dovetails with the less obvious cathartic enjoyment of the spectacle by the human participants and spectators. The ritual itself is best understood as a system of meaning to which the patient is made to relate existentially and attain his own cure according to his lights.

Given these cosmological and therapeutic concepts and conditions, the task of the ritual is to create the demonic "other reality" and to achieve its manifestation in the human world—in that very village compound prepared as an arena for the invasion and retreat of the enemy without that has become the enemy within. The demons' presence is commanded by *mantra;* they are attracted by offerings of food, fire display, whirling convulsive dance, praise songs, flattery, and smutty jokes. When surfeited, they are sent away. As William James once remarked, the notion of the devil enriches our lives, provided we

have a foot firmly placed on his neck. In this seduction, the main officiant offers successive surrogates of the patient, including himself, and
tricks the demons (who are not very bright) into believing that they
have made off with their human victim. Paralleling this adventure is
the other journey by which the patient, by suggestion and ultimately
by self-awareness, is made to recognize the disease inside him and to
reject it as loathsome.[32]

With this introduction, I shall get down to the nitty-gritty of how
this ritual employs multiple media and redundant structures and sequences.

According to native account, meticulously documented by Michael
Egan, the Mahāsohona Samayama is divided into eleven major named
sequences, and these sequences in turn are divided into named subsequences. In these circumstances the analyst cannot ignore the society's fine-grained attention to segments and their subdivisions that
are combined in various ways to produce dramatic twelve-hour outcomes.[33]

The major sequences are:

Divination—performed at the *beginning*

(1a. Preliminary silent prayers to Buddha and the gods)
1. *Kalu Yakkha* (Black Demon) *Pidēniya* (offering)
2. *Dāpavilla* (to lie down and offer body, then rooster, to
    many demons)
3. *Mahāsohona Natanavā* (dance to Mahāsohona)
4. *Mangra Pela-Pāliya* (a procession in honor of God
    Mangra—comic sequence)
5. *Mahāsohona Pidēniya* (offering to Mahāsohona)

Divination—performed in the *middle*

6. *Dera Hāva* (reclining on a stretcher, a mock funeral)
7. *Sanni Yakkha Pidēniya* (offering to Disease Demon)
8. *Avatara* (manifestation or apparition of the Demons—
    the most dramatic sequence in the rite)
9. *Daha-ata Pāliya* (eighteen-part sequence in which
    gifts are brought by a messenger of the gods and are
    given to demons: low comedy)
10. *Sūniyam Yakkha Pidēniya* (offering to the Sorcery
    Demon)
11. *Mahāsohona Baliya* (the effigy of Mahāsohona to
    which illness is transferred)
(11a. Final prayer)

Here is a nonexhaustive listing of some of the sequencing patterns and bound relations (co-occurrence rules):

1. The rite as a whole is divided into two halves. There is an augury taken at the very beginning (by reading the pattern produced in a pot of boiled rice), and another taken at the middle (between sequences 5 and 6) to check on the effect achieved to that point. The second half of the rite is in a sense an amplified version of the first.

The first half consists of the invocation of gods and demons, their propitiation, the "consecration" of the patient's offerings (in the sense that they are identified with him or her by being passed over his or her head). There is much recourse to multiple media, and there is a buildup to a climax which consists in the fearsome creation and manifestation of the demons on stage by means of furious whirling dance and sensational play with fire and resin; then follows the offering of the officiant himself as a corpse to the demons, followed by a substitute live rooster whose head is bitten off on stage.

The second half of the rite is the *avatara,* or manifestation of the demons—the officiant, seeing the devils come physically, becomes them himself, and rushes headlong into the cemetery at the village's edge, where, changing his role again, he shakes them off and commands them to remain in their natural habitat. After this fearsome collective dispelling of the demons, there follows a second expulsion of them in a comic mode. Since they have already been vanquished, there can now be a second sendoff in a masked play in which they are fearlessly and derisively represented as loathsome clownish savages. This last phase of ordinary low speech and banter, a marked descent from the language of invocations and praise songs, is an apt prelude and transition to the everyday world.

Thus, the second half of the rite is an amplification of the first half in the sense of featuring speeded up dance and spectacle, and evoking stronger emotions of fear and revulsion. But it is also its mirror image, in that while the first half coaxes the demons to come from the other realm to be realized in human company, the second half moves from their energetic manifestation to their unceremonious ejection.

There is thus also a triadic structure of three watches[34] embedded in the dual division. Propitiation of demons in the early part of the night leads to their manifestation at midnight, and manifestation is followed by their satiated departure in the small hours of the morning.

Why should sensational dancing and fireplay become, at the climactic moment of demon manifestation, the dominant medium of communication, surpassing language? Because, to extend Radcliffe-Brown's thesis further, dance is a superb vehicle for realizing the sense of force and power through "ritual gesture," through physical motion that gives the illusion of the conquest of gravity, and through movements that create spatial tensions ¡between the dancers. Thus, humanly created and unleashed movements become the manifestation of forces outside and beyond the performers, and beget the illusion of emotions and wills in conflict.

2. Tension alternates with relief. There are actually two comic interludes nicely and significantly spaced in the rite. Sequence 4 near the beginning is a *perahera* procession mounted on behalf of God Mangra, who rules over the demon Mahāsohona; sequence 9 near the end is the smutty and repulsive masked play at the demons' expense. Curiously, the praise of the gods is staged as a farce, all kinds of mistakes being committed in the protocol. In fact, the two balanced comic phases stand in a relation of inversion. The gods' procession is farcical not because the gods are funny but because humans are clumsy when they presume to create and represent the divine realm; but the demonic farce is at the cost of the demons, who are represented as uncivilized when compared with the more refined humans.

3. Right through the ritual an *invariant sequencing* rule is followed—namely, the gods have to be propitiated before the demons. Although the rite's main concentration is on the demons, this sequencing rule is dictated by the hierarchical rules of the pantheon.

4. As stated earlier, there are demons other than Mahāsohona who are considered to play a collusive role in the illness. The most frequent sequence in the entire rite (amounting to four of the eleven sequences) is called *Pidēniya* (offering). And apart from this sequence which is devoted to Mahāsohona (sequence 5), virtually identical sequences[35] are devoted, at spaced intervals, to the Black Demon (sequence 1), to the Disease Demon (sequence 7), and to the Sorcery Demon (sequence 10).

5. This commonest *Pidēniya* sequence, extremely repetitive and additive from one point of view, is in fact internally composed of all the verbal genres of speech and song that appear, and all the media that are exploited, in the entire rite. It begins with *mantra* (spells) that "command" the demonic presence, then shifts to invocations of gods and demons (accompanied by dancing), which have for their purpose the consecration of the patient's offerings. Then follow songs of praise and flattery (*kavi*) couched in lyrical prose and addressed to the gods and demons; next follows a fire dance to please the demons, concluding with food offerings. The following *pidēniya* is addressed to the Black Demon, and the recognized subsequences are:

1. *Mantrima:* spells which contain a reference to the origin myth of the demon, relating how the demon was subjugated, and which state that by the power of that act the officiant is giving an offering and commanding the demon's submission.
2. *Kannalavva:* invocation of the God Mangra, who controls the Mahāsohona demon, by means of song to the accompaniment of drums; the officiant circles the offerings over the patient's head while the audience acclaims the consecration by shouting *aiboo* ("long life").
3. *Yaddina:* invocation of the demon in question (similar to 2 above); the origin myth of the demon is sung, and to the accompaniment of drums the officiant dances and waves offerings over the patient's head.
4. *Ata Kona Kavi* ("eight-sides" poem): a song that summons the demon from the eight directions of the universe.
5,6,7. *Kavi:* songs of praise of many kinds, sung to the demon. The officiant dances and sings, and the lyrical poem recounts the life of the demon and asks him to bestow blessings on the invalid. A second song directly refers to the idea of *varam* (delegated and conditional power to harm), the reason for making offerings, and the necessary efficacy of that act by analogical transference from the original myth. A third song requests the demon to depart from the patient's body.
8. *Natanavā:* the *edura* dances a frenzied dance of whirls and leaps to the accompaniment of drums, to please the demon.
9. *Mal Bulat Dīma Moona Pisa Dämīma:* the officiant takes offerings of flowers and betel to the invalid, touches the invalid's fingertips and face, and offers his gifts with prayer to the demon, to the accompaniment of public acclaim.

All the verbal forms enumerated have as their substantive ground a pool of mythical stories of origin, but they clearly display a *progression* embodying different principles of literary composition and *logic of persuasion*, from command to invocation, to praise, followed by a shift to a kinetic and visual medium (dance), and then finally to food, which appeals simultaneously to taste, smell, sight, and alimentary needs.

All the verbal forms, moreover, reiterate in one way or another the proposition "Because then . . . therefore now"; this proposition is doctrinal and cites a primeval precedent by which the demon became bound to the Lord Buddha's authoritative act and must submit now when that precedent is recalled and enacted; it is a presumptive proposition that derives its legitimacy from an ethical principle, which is axiomatic for the Buddhists and which Mauss declared to be universal: if a gift is given with good intentions, that act must be reciprocated. But true to the ritual format, this ethical proposition is incorporated in the wider elocutionary and illocutionary constructs of command, invocation, or flattery.

While the *Pidēniya* as a microcosm encodes the full variety of forms and media exploited in the entire rite, there are other effects achieved *between sequences* by means of *accenting* different modalities, by making one of them dominant in turn while the others are subordinate.

There is, for instance, an attempt to create a *staggered effect in adjacent sequences:* in sequence 5, words (in the form of invocations, *mantra,* praise songs) dominate; in sequence 6, which is a mock funeral, offerings of betel, flowers, food, human corpses, and roosters dominate; and in sequence 8 (demon manifestation) frenzied dance and physical manipulations dominate. Here we see, then, the modalities of speech, dance, and food being juxtaposed and brought into relief serially.

Or again, not surprisingly, the primary demon, Mahāsohona, is the focus of attention in three of the eleven major sequences, but each of these concentrates on a particular mode and thus a *cumulative* effect on the demon is sought. He is danced to (*natanavā*) in sequence 3, he receives offerings (*pidēniya*) in sequence 5, and the illness is transferred to a clay image of him (*baliya*) in sequence 11.

Finally, let me briefly highlight the variety of sensory acts that in a complementary manner achieve the same performative outcome. For example, a set of paradigmatic acts is engaged in to *attract and please* the demons: the blowing of a whistle to summon them; the burning of flaming torches that illuminate the offerings; the sacrifice of a live bird, and the offering of smoked foods that are considered polluted; the singing of *kavi* and dancing.

A contrastive paradigmatic set of acts is thought to overcome and dispel the demons: the throwing of fire and flames at them, the stroking of the patient's body with limes and their cutting, the pointing of the *īgaha* wand (Isvara's metal-tipped arrow), the recitation of spells.

This by no means complete analysis shows how some structural features of a ritual—the sequencing rules, the recursive as well as cumulative repetitions, the interplay of variations, accentuations, and progression of sensory modalities by opposition and contrast—how all these redundant patterns fuse into one configurational totality, one cumulative experience, one superimposition of successive sequences.

Ritual Involution

But there is more to the extensive use of redundant structures in this Sinhalese ordeal of the night than a creation of a totalized sensory experience. There is in the whole construction unmistakable evidence of what I call *ritual involution,* a seeming overelaboration and overprolongation of ritual action woven out of a limited number of "technical" devices and stylistic complexes. One must confront not only peasant inventiveness but also peasant tedium.

From New Guinea to the northwest coast of the United States, societies have manifested and still manifest this feature: the *longer* a rite is staged and the grander the scale of the ritual's outlay and adornment, the more important, the more efficacious the ceremony is deemed to be. The psychology and logic of this extension in time and elaboration in space to the point of inventive exhaustion, aesthetic overstylization, and pecuniary bankruptcy has exercised the interpretative ingenuity of many an anthropologist. Let me review some of the explanations of ritual redundancy, looked at from this perspective of ritual involution.

Stanner (1958–59) has remarked thus on the New Guinea cargocults' manifestation of exaggerated elaborations: "not only is the valuation of the cargo exaggerated; every element has a consonant augmentation," and the components of the cult take on a "larger than life" appearance. Stanner interpreted this factitious elaboration in terms of an "inordinate valuation" that the participants put upon the cargo; therefore they acted beyond themselves in a futurist sense, in a situation where the desires were extreme and the wealth promised by novel means was great. To this motivational feature of inordinate valuation, Stanner added a *social transactional* factor: the ritual acts are really "incomplete transactions" with the supernatural, and "we are dealing with a one-sided subjective valuation, with expressive-persuasive rather than manipulative conduct."

Mike Egan (n.d.) sought an answer for the Sinhalese exorcism ritual's repetitive length in somewhat similar terms, from an external observer's point of view. Using the language of cybernetics, Egan speculated that the Sinhalese healer, the *edura,* while controlling the technical processes of input as into a computer, received no informational feedback concerning the progress of the operations. "Thus, what is lacking in ritual techniques is any sort of direct and immediate empirical feedback from the occult about the effects the ritual techniques are having on them, and in consequence the *edura* (as control mechanism) lacks the necessary information for knowing when to stop one set of operations and start another." Furthermore, the *edura,* motivated to succeed, tries to achieve his objective in as many ways as possible. Egan concluded: "The *edura,* then, can be compared to an individual stranded on a desert island with only a radio transmitter, but no receiver."

Imaginative and ingenious as these comments are, they seem to me to illuminate only part of the truth. From the point of view of the actors, it cannot be said that there is no feedback from the supernatural—for mediums of gods do become their emissaries and speak in divine tongues, patients do become possessed by spirits and experience their expulsion as a reality, a congregation feels it has received grace from a priest's sacramental act. All this feedback happens because the senders of the messages are also their receivers acting within a context of accepted axioms and meanings. Nor is it adequate, it seems to me, to treat a culturally structured collective representation from the motivational perspective of a single individual officiant as if the phenomenon can be explained in terms of an individual consciousness and motivation. A single officiant, even a single culture or society may be mistaken, but to say that so many societies should persist in futile converse with the supernatural is to contribute to the slogan "All religions are illusory." Finally the frustrations of a sender of messages who receives none from the supernatural cannot explain the complex creative patterns of redundancy that I revealed earlier.

This brings me to another challenging attempt to explain redundancy and stereotypy as structural features of ritual—that of Maurice Bloch (1974). Because Bloch's essay is important, I feel it necessary to state my objections strongly in the spirit of critical appreciation rather than of fierce denunciation. Bloch's assertion that "religion is the last place to find anything 'explained' " contradicts the role of complex cosmic schemes that many religions have constructed to explain fundamental existential problems, including those of theodicy, as Max Weber so eloquently taught us. Starting with the proposition that ritual language is a medium wherein syntactic and other linguistic features of articulation are reduced, Bloch ends up by arguing that ritual speech, being predictable speech, has no propositional force at all. Starting with the argument that formalized speech is nonlogical in the (limited logical positivist) sense that it admits of no alternative formulations for establishing truth value, Bloch concludes that ritual speech has "no semantics." Again asserting that "with increasing formalization (of speech) propositional force decreases and illocutionary force increases," that the two types of meaning vary inversely, he, I think, misinterprets the tenets of linguistic philosophers like Searle (1969)—namely, that in speech acts the propositional locutionary aspect is usually present but is embedded within the illocutionary act, not that there is an inverse variation between them.[36] Finally, lumping ritual speech (such as formal oratory, intoned spells) together with song and dance, Bloch sees in song "the total lack of individual creativity" and in dance a complete control of body movements; he then concludes that "art is an inferior form of communication."[37] Bloch's answer to ritual involution would be that since ritual lacks propositional or logical meaning, all ritual can do to persuade is to repeat itself for emphasis over and over again like a broken record.[38]

The ultimate inspiration for Bloch's view lies in seeing formalized modes of communication as the handmaid (perhaps even a basis?) of political authority, and in the further extrapolation that religion is an extreme form of political authority. Formalization in a *political action context* becomes an engine of power and coercion, because it admits of no argument, and of no challenge to authority, except by total refusal to accept the conventions of authority. Formalized communication, concludes Bloch, which is common to both traditional authority and religion, serves to "hide reality."

My quarrel is not with a Marxist formulation as such but with that kind of formulation which sees a prior "real world" of "brute facts" that religion, as a mystification, seeks to hide, as if there are some privileged orders of institutional facts which have a presymbolic or precultural existence; see Sahlins (1976) for a critique of such assumptions. Moreover, for me, the exciting kind of analysis is that which sees ritual involution not so much as a diabolic smoke-screen but as an ideological and aesthetic social construction that is directly and recursively implicated in the expression, realization, and exercise of power.[39] Therefore, I suggest that in addition to all the answers so far given for the phenomenon of ritual involution, a powerful impulse for it lies in the fact of ritual's duplex existence, as an entity that symbolically and/or iconically represents the cosmos and at the same time indexically legitimates and realizes social hierarchies. I think functionalism in all its guises—I include here the old-fashioned and some of the neo-Marxist and ecological versions—fails to comprehend fully the message of ritual in a double sense: that there is on the one hand an ontological and experiential constraint that leads to formalization and archaism through the performance of cosmological archetypes, and, on the other hand, a social constraint that allocates to persons in ranked positions and relations of "power and solidarity" a differential access to and participation in a society's major rites, and a differential enjoyment of their benefits. Let us see now how in actual analysis the two constraints operate, so that we can combine the semantic and pragmatic frames of analysis.

Indexical Symbols and Icons as Duplex Structures

How is ritual directly and recursively implicated in differential relations of power and status? I would like to examine this question in terms of the Thai classical ceremony of topknot cutting (now virtually obsolete). I shall employ the concepts of *indexical symbol* and *indexical icon* in the following ways.

A most useful notion that has emerged from Peirce's three-fold classification of signs (symbol, icon, and index) in relation to the objects they signify is the concept of *indexical symbol* as proposed by Burks (1949), or alternatively *shifter* as labeled by Jakobson (1971), following Jespersen.[40] The main point about *indexical symbols* or *shifters* is that they have a duplex structure, because they combine two roles: they are symbols which are associated with the represented object by a conventional semantic rule, and they are simultaneously also indexes in existential pragmatic relation with the objects they represent.[41]

By extension, then, an *indexical icon* also possesses two dimensions of meaning—by iconically representing an object according to a conventional semantic rule of likeness, and by being existentially linked to it as well. Thus, the concepts of indexical symbol and indexical icon are useful for showing how important parts of a ritual enactment have a symbolic or iconic meaning associated with the cosmological plane of content, and at the same time how those same parts are existentially or indexically related to participants in the ritual, creating, affirming, or legitimating their social positions and powers. The duality thus points in two directions at once—in the semantic direction of cultural presuppositions and conventional understandings and in the pragmatic direction of the social and interpersonal context of ritual action, the lineup of the participants and the process by which they establish or infer meanings. The sense in which I imagine actors to infer indexical meaning is similar to Grice's formulation of "conversational implicature," in that by saying or enacting something a certain meaning is *implicated,* which can be readily understood (conventional implicature) or is capable of being "worked out" (nonconventional implicature), given certain contextual features and certain communicational understandings.[42]

Variants of the Topknot-Cutting Ceremony in Thailand

The topknot-cutting or tonsure ceremony in Thailand is old, and was performed widely until the early decades of this century. (The principal source for this discussion is Gerini, 1976.) The ceremony was performed for boys in their early teens before they were initiated as Buddhist novices (*samanera*), and for girls before the onset of puberty, it being considered a disgrace if they had not undergone it. Both Buddhist monks and Brahman priests officiated at the ceremony, the monks reciting the Pali *paritta* chants of blessing and protection from danger and being ceremonially feasted, and the Brahmans being the actual officiants supervising the haircutting of the youths, their aspersion, and other rites, concluding with the disposal of the hair by setting it adrift on water.

The tonsure rite considered in its semantic symbolic aspect had a constant characteristic: the rite *whenever* performed and for *whomever* performed followed certain obligatory sequences and used certain ritual articles called "the implements of the *mandala.*" The origin of the tonsure rite is associated with certain myths, principally the stories of the tonsure of his elder son, Khanda Kumara, by his divine father, Shiva. And the symbolism of various sequences of the rite is quite clear.[43] I want to refer here only to the actual site of aspersion; it is said to represent Mount Kailasa, where god Shiva resides and where the initial archetypal tonsure took place.

The level of meaning that I want to focus on concerns not the stable underlying semantic structure of the ritual, but the *variation* in lexical usages, in the structure of the site of aspersion, and in the *scale* of the ceremonies (pertaining to their magnificence, their duration, the number of officiants participating, the place of staging, and so on)—for it is these *indexical* features which directly show how interpersonal aspects of rank and privilege are validated and enacted by the symbolism and requirements of the ritual itself. This *indexicality* is the third sense in which ritual can be seen as performative.

As regards rank, it is sufficient to note that the first division in traditional Thailand was between commoners and nobility[44] on the one side and royalty on the other, and that the royal princes and princesses undergoing the tonsure were divided into three grades: the highest, *chao fa* princes and princesses (children of the reigning king by princesses of *chao fa* or *phra ong chao* rank); the intermediate, *phra ong chao* (children of the king by mothers who were not princesses); and the lowest, *mom chao* (children of the princes of the above two ranks by mothers holding the rank of *phra ong chao* and *mom chao*, or by concubines). For the sake of simplicity I shall hereafter refer to them as Grades A, B, and C.

There was first of all a linguistic variation in the names by which the ceremony was called by different status groups.[45] The tonsure ceremony for the commoners and nobility was called *kan kon chuk* (forelock shaving) or *kan tat chuk* (topknot cutting); for the Grade C royals it was called *kesa kanta* (*keca kan* = cutting hair); and for both grade A and B royals it was called *sokan*, a word probably of part Khmer derivation, Khmer being since Ayuthaya times the fashionable court language. Additionally we may note that while the commoners referred to the hair that was cut as *chuk*, the court referred to it as *chula* or *moli* (both derived from Pali).

The ceremony for commoners and nobility was staged at their homes while that for all the royals was held usually in the royal palace, including the palace of the "second king" (*uparat*).

The actual duration of the rites varied by rank. In the case of the commoners and nobility the proceedings occupied two days[46]—with the hair being sent afloat normally on the third morning. In striking contrast were the festivities for a prince of the highest grade (*chao fa*), which stretched the same sequences over seven days: "Of the seven days the first eve is devoted to the preliminary rites of consecration of the site; the first, second and third to the rehearsal of the same Buddhist texts, attended on each occasion by the candidate in state. The forenoon of the fourth day is appointed for the tonsure; the afternoon of the same day and of the two immediately following (5th and 6th) being assigned to the *Somphot* or propitiation of the *Khuan* (spirit essence) and consecration of the neophyte by the waving of the lighted tapers round his person. Finally, the morning of the seventh day is reserved for the rite of floating away the severed hair. This terminated the festival" (Gerini, 1976: 65).

In between fell the festivities for a prince of Grade B: "The pageant has only four days, the eve and the first three being occupied as before, the ceremonies concluding on the fourth or tonsure day, in the afternoon. The solemnities of the 5th, 6th and 7th days are omitted" (p. 64), though of course the hair was disposed of in the usual way.

One item in the ritual itself was a focus of much attention and was a carrier of much meaning of an iconic-indexical sort. This was the place of aspersion, which consisted of a construction that was said to be an iconic representation of Mount Kailasa. But the representational constructions used in the ceremonies differed in the physical likeness they bore to the cosmological mountain, ranging from simple cano-pied platforms to an elaborate man-made hill.

The commoners and nobility made at one end of the hall in the house a square five-storeyed platform surmounted by a flat or pyrami-dal canopy. All Grade B and C royals were bathed on top of a perma-nent stone hillock, some ten feet in height, situated by a pond, within the precincts of the royal palace. But the aspersion of the Grade A princes of the highest order took place with much pomp, entertain-ment, and procession on a specially built Kailasa hill. A spectacular example of such an artificial mountain was the one constructed by King Chulalongkorn in 1892 for the tonsure of his son and crown prince, Vajiravudh. The forty-foot hill constructed of bamboo covered with gold, red-gold, and silver tinsel had on its summit a gilt pavilion decorated with colored glass and tapestries. And the artificial moun-tain was embellished with rare specimens of ferns and calladium to represent the rare flora of the mythical mountain.

It is clear that these variant representations carried two kinds of meaning simultaneously. The more the constructions resembled Mount Kailasa itself, the more efficacious, auspicious, and potent were deemed the effects of the ceremony for the candidate and his family. This instrumental or performative effect was at one end pegged to iconic (and metaphoric) likeness, but the fruits of the ritual were at the other end firmly pegged to social rank, for the details pertaining to the scale, magnificence, and splendor of the rite were diacritical privi-leges of rank and barred from use by socially inappropriate persons. The linguistic variants, the differences in duration from two to seven days, and the variant representations of the sacred mountain tell the same story of the belief in greater instrumental potency of scale and duration of ritual and of the mutual implication between ritual forms and social privilege. The greater the scale and the longer the cere-mony, the more frequent the redundant recitations, the more numer-ous the cohorts of priests, the greater the outlay and distribution of wealth and food, and the larger the publics entertained, edified, and educated in the human relevance of a cosmic vision. These facts clearly bespeak a ritually involuted society where the domains of reli-gion, polity, and economy fuse into a single total phenomenon, and where truth claims and normative canons are conflated, appearance transformed into reality, "is" made into "ought," solidarity and power brought into accord however uneasily, and the institutional assimilated to the natural.

Having documented the symbolic and indexical (conventional) meanings of the tonsure rite, I shall now allude to a historical instance of a "nonconventional implicature" (whose emergent meaning, however, once recognized and routinized, changed the status of the enactment to a conventional symbolic index for later times). That the rule of succession in the traditional Siamese kingdom was notoriously ambiguous and unstable is well known, as was the frequent occurrence of rebellions and usurpations. Although in traditional times, well into the mid-nineteenth century, reigning kings did hold grand tonsure rites for their highest *chao fa* princes (especially the prince who by birth was most eligible to be a future king), the concept of an undisputed crown prince and future heir did not emerge in Thailand until after the mid-nineteenth century, when King Mongkut so marked out the future King Chulalongkorn.[47] The factors that made possible this undisputed succession were historical developments whereby in the course of the nineteenth century, while other southeast Asian kingdoms were swallowed by Western imperial powers, the Bangkok dynasty secured more and more centralized patrimonial power *pari passu* with colonial contact, and with the ensuing expansion of the rice trade after the Bowring Treaty (1855). What I am interested in here is the additional, probably unprecedented, meaning that King Mongkut managed to impart to the tonsure ceremony of his son, Prince Chulalongkorn, in 1866. He made one major change in the ceremony: customarily a representative of the king acted the part of God Shiva and received the prince on the summit of Mount Kailasa and aspersed him. This custom of the king's representative substituting for him as a temporary king was analogous to Hindu practice, in which the permanent deity was believed to remain inside the temple and a secondary, movable deity was taken out on procession. In the case of real kings, whose heads were notoriously uneasy, their confinement within the palace was a protection against assassination and the gaze of impure commoners.

King Mongkut broke precedent by himself personally taking the part of God Shiva and aspersing his son. This innovative step (which he repeated in other cosmic rites)[48] had three implications. There was the "modernizing" motive by which the king, to impress the foreigners, allowed himself to be seen by his people in public without their having to cast their eyes down on bended knee; there was the political statement of the king's increased exercise of power and personal sense of security which enabled him to emerge in public, for a king confined to his palace relies on the dubious eyes and ears of his favorites; and there was the ritual motive, in that the king's personal presence in this tonsure and his acting as chief officiant marked the occasion as special and made the rite especially efficacious for the initiate.

In addition, in the course of the festivities Mongkut invested the prince with new titles, crowned him with a magnificent coronet (a coronet, but not of such splendor, was traditionally put on a prince's head), and all but pointedly announced to his court that his son was the crown prince and heir to the throne. This was the emergent implicature riding upon a traditional ceremonial form, some details of which were not so much changed as amplified and given a special stress. Thereafter the practice became customary, and in the next reign King Chulalongkorn himself staged an even more lavish tonsure ceremony for crown prince Vajiravudh[49] in 1892, by which time the ceremony was publicly understood as the occasion for presenting to the court the crown prince and heir to the throne. Thus, emergent meaning once recognized usually becomes conventional meaning, and is incorporated into the existing framework of conventions.

The foregoing example makes possible a statement about "emergent" meanings in conditions of historical continuity. Emergent meanings ride on the already existing grids of symbolic and indexical meanings, while also displaying new resonances. Although he stretches or transforms or even violates particular customs or norms, the innovator is not attempting and is not viewed as acting to upset the overall framework of customs. King Mongkut was enlarging the institution of kingship, not wrecking it, and the significance of his substitutions and elaborations in the tonsure ceremony was readily inferred and acquiesced in by his courtiers. At the next round they became conventional customs.

The Limits of Inventiveness and the Freezing of Styles

With this analysis of the Thai haircutting ceremony as an example of how symbolic or iconic and indexical meanings may intertwine in a helical process, let me return to the issue of ritual involution and confront the conditions in which there can be a decline of meaning.

I can think of three related symptoms of ritual involution in its negative decadent aspect:

1. One occurs when a complex rite seems to repeat certain sequences and actions to the point of compulsive tedium, so that even

when all the dimensions of performative force and meaning have been taken into account, a creative exhaustion seems to have been reached.

2. A second symptom might occur when the same (or a similar) rite is repeated in many contexts and situations as a primary mode of achieving results.

3. A third clue might be the reliance placed by a society upon a limited set of ritual modes, such that its entire corpus of rites appears to be composed of certain standard actions, idioms, and symbols. Thus, an unmistakable ritual style crystallizes and affects the layout of the rites with regard to entries into and exits from sacred time, and the "rhetoric" of persuasion employed in the propitiation of superiors and the powerful. In certain extreme conditions of ritual involution a limited number of stable complexes may be used again and again, for all kinds of purposes, seemingly with little relation to the logic of their composition.

An actual instance of ritual that appears to portray the three symptoms of involution listed above will allow me to carry the discussion further.

Thai mortuary rites that are performed in Bangkok today for the *affluent* are a good example. Soon after death the corpse is brought to the *wat*, ceremonially washed, and placed in an elaborate coffin in a *sala* (hall) lavishly decked with flowers and wreaths. There, on seven consecutive nights, four monks intone for one and a half hours each time precisely the same collection of Pali chants called *suad phra apitham;* moreover, at each recital the monks have to chant the same collection of chants four times in succession. After seven days the corpse is stored for fifty days or one hundred days, at which point elaborate cremation rites are held, accompanied by chanting; and in between the storage of the corpse and the final cremation anyone might (if he wanted to make more merit for the dead) sponsor additional chanting by monks every seventh night as well. Even this doesn't exhaust the amount of repetitive chanting monks are called upon to do at the death of the rich and elevated. This deliberately stereotyped and unvarying performance clearly signifies that the more times the monks chant the same sacred verses, which alone are appropriate for the occasion, the more potent is the effect of making merit for the deceased as well as for the living sponsors. This performative logic is evident to the Thai, for they are acutely aware that if the dead person was poor, his or her kin can afford only three nights of chanting in all, followed by cremation on the third day. Thus, the scale of the repetitious chanting is not only a pointer to the degree of performative potency but also an indexical pointer to the social status, affluence, and rank of the deceased and the bereaved. But this duplex structure of meaning alone does not exhaust the implications, for Thais also have recourse to almost identical and unvarying chanting by monks (who are feasted and given gifts) at those numerous, almost uncountable occasions when merit is made and blessings sought—at housewarmings, at the foundation of a business enterprise, at the opening of Parliament, on a return from a trip, before a couple are married, in order to dispel bad luck, to celebrate a birthday, to commemorate a dead person, and so on.

The development of circumscribed ritual styles—to the point of banal predictability—has to be understood in part at least in relation to the dominant ethical and normative preoccupations of the actors in question. A key to the reiteration may be found in the wider cultural definition of what kinds of existential problems are felt by a society to be recurrent and important, and why a certain ritual style is considered efficacious. The Thai, for instance, are so preoccupied with the fruits of merit making and well-intentioned giving that their frequent recourse to monks seems monotonously inevitable. Thai Buddhists seek contact with their monks because by reason of their ascetic life these monks are seen to acquire virtues and energies they can transfer to the laity imprisoned in desire and sensory gratification. Thus, ritual formalization in this case is closely related to the native theory of charisma.

Such a native understanding of performative potency clearly militates against a simplistic application of linguistic theory. It is tempting to say that ritual incantations repeated again and again on the proper occasions carry no semantic and referential information as such, and can have only functional, "indexical" uses. Such an inference is all the more persuasive when the ritual speech is in a sacred language largely not understood by the congregation, or in a high style laced with archaic expressions and weird vocabulary. But it is also relevant to point out that such recitations by appropriate officiants are believed by the actors to be powerful in themselves, irrespective of their unintelligibility and predictability (see Tambiah, 1970: ch. 12), and that this conception of power is related to understandings and valuations of the superiority of the monk's salvation quest and the powers it enables him to acquire, and the belief in the quality and efficacy of the semantic truths coded in the sacred Pali words, even if they are not literally understood.

There is, however, an entirely different factor that contributes to the phenomenon under discussion.

Ritual circumscription and involution may also be rooted in a tendency pertaining to the *ritual medium per se*—namely, the processes

of *condensation* and *fusion,* which are the other side of the coin of redundancy. Configurational patterning and meaning intensification,
the positive features of redundancy in its creative aspects, are so dialectically bound with the processes of meaning condensation and fusion, that the more a rite becomes formalized, conventionalized, and
repeated the more it also seems vulnerable to the *rigor mortis* of
meaning atrophy.

Condensation and fusion can be approached from seemingly different theoretical perspectives, but they all seem to point to the same
conclusions. A structuralist might be prone to hold up the image of a
palimpsest: meaning as achieved not merely through the combined
use of metaphor and metonym, but more so through the double
switching and transformation from one mode into the other and back
again (see, for example, Leach, 1976: 25). Thus, all varieties of ritual
may be seen as involving multiple condensations; and since different
sensory channels are used simultaneously, the participants "pick up
all these messages at the same time and condense them into a single
experience which we describe as 'attending' a wedding, or 'attending'
a funeral" (p. 41).

Suzanne Langer (1953, ch. 10), who represented another tradition
of symbolic interpretation, coined the phrase "the principle of assimilation" in order to explain the fusion that takes place when words and
music are brought together in vocal music. She argued that in song,
whether it be choric or operatic, "when words and music come together . . . music swallows words; not only mere words and literal sentences, but even literary word-structures, poetry." In this instance
music is the "commanding form," and words "are no longer prose or
poetry, they are elements of the music" because "song is music." In a
general sense, then, assimilation, fusion, and condensation relate to
the mutual effects and outcomes—such as the relations of domination
and subordination between modes conjoined, erasure or loss of meaning of originally different modes, the blurring of boundaries between
separate modalities through their mixing.

The "texture" of ritual is also the subject matter of allegedly "pragmatic" approaches which argue that ritual is best understood not in
terms of a multilevel analysis (that is, how lower-level units make up
higher-level units as adopted in descriptive linguistics) but in terms of
its being experienced by participants as made up of fused higher-level
entities or whole chunks as single events. One writer has called them
"praxemes" (C. Bateson, 1974).[50] Many processes contribute to this
fused numinous experience. One is the addition of meaning through
the cumulation of similar or related connotations. This needs little

elaboration in the face of Victor Turner's rich treatment of "conden-sation" of meaning. A second is the atrophy of the meaning of compo-nents and their "coefficient of weirdness" (to use Malinowski's expression) because of their archaic character: the freezing of ritual language makes it drift out of meaning and makes it insensitive, as Maurice Bloch has remarked (1974), to the processes of historical linguistics. A third process, already referred to, is the blurring of boundaries between separate units or modalities through the mixing of modalities.[51] A final feature contributing to the sense of total fused experience is the hyper-regular surface structure of ritual language: the poetic devices such as rhyme, meter, assonance, and alliteration generate an overall quality of union and a blurring of grammatical boundaries (as is already implied in Jakobson's discussion of the po-etic function).[52]

If one picks and ties together into a single bouquet the flowers and weeds found in the garden patch of ritual—invariant form attached to archetypal cosmic truths, constitutive convention-bound acts, predict-ability and stereotypy, intensification of meaning and its condensa-tion, the duplex structure of indexical symbolism or indexical iconicity and the tendency toward atrophy of meaning, creative use of multiple media and the stagnancy of an exhausted style—and if one views both the fragrant and the fetid as being characteristic of ritual action, one must conclude that ritual oscillates in historical time between the poles of *ossification* and *revivalism*. All the substantive features which nourish the formalism of ritual also conspire to empty it of meaning over time. Cosmological ideas, because they reflect the epistemologi-cal and ontological understandings of the particular age in which they originated, and because they are subject to the constraint of remain-ing accurate and invariant, are condemned to become dated over time and increasingly unable to speak to the minds and hearts of succeed-ing generations facing change and upheaval. During these periods of ossification, rituals may increasingly lose whatever semantic meaning they previously had and may carry primarily indexical meanings which derive from rules of use and from pragmatic or functional con-siderations.

But one should guard against attributing to all ritual the priority of functional pragmatics over semantics. For in periods of religious reviv-alism or when new cults are forged by charismatic leaders, there is a deliberate attempt to coin new doctrinal concepts and mold new ritu-als bursting with meaning attached to the contents of the acts per se. In such times of promise and hope the semantic meanings of words uttered and object-symbols and icons manipulated matter terribly, and the esoteric lore of doctrine and rite is taught with punctilious care to disciples. And the ambitious aim—so solemnly cultivated by the Quakers—is pursued to breathe meaning and fervor into each article of faith and each act of communal worship. But these enthusiasms of revivalism can be relatively short-lived. For the most part between messianic hope and indolent routine, the rituals of ordinary times carry both symbolic or iconic and indexical meanings in different mixes, and the participants too understand these meanings in varying measure, according to their lights, interests, and commitment.

One task, then, is to specify the conditions under which rituals—which ordinarily convey both symbolic or iconic and indexical, referential and pragmatic meanings—take opposite turnings: to the right when they begin to lose their semantic component and come to serve mainly the pragmatic interests of authority, privilege, and sheer conservatism; and to the left when committed believers, faced with a decline of referential meaning but with a surfeit of manipulated "implicatures," strive to infuse purified meaning into traditional forms, as often happens during the effervescence of religious revival and reform. Such a dynamic view might make it possible to transcend the seeming dissonance between two perspectives: the approach which sees redundancy as contributing to pattern emergence, and the use of multiple media as resulting in message intensification; and the other approach, which, wearing the garb of realism, sees in formalism and redundancy a decline of semantic meaning, and the sovereign presence of power buttressing itself with ritual speech, and the exploitative strategies of priestly castes building castles out of esoteric knowledge. The concepts of indexical symbolism and indexical iconicity might serve as a bridge for studying the dynamic interrelation between these two kinds of meaning.

II

Cosmologies and Classifications as Thought and Action

5

Animals Are Good to Think and Good to Prohibit

The ethnography of certain segmentary societies contains the paradoxical situation that marriage and fighting go together. Thus, Megitt (1965) says of the Mae Enga, "We marry the people we fight," and Middleton (Middleton and Tait, 1958: 217) writes of the Lugbara, " 'We marry our *juru*' and 'We fight our *juru*' are consistent axioms even though the *juru* may not be coterminous." This thesis can be even more dramatically confirmed with respect to headhunting societies. It would appear that in these instances oppositions such as exogamy and alliance, war and peace, bridewealth and bloodwealth are closely linked at the level of thought.

The voluminous literature on Indian caste has reiterated that there is a strong correspondence between commensality and connubium, between cooking and marriage; rules regulating whom a person is permitted to marry ordinarily correspond to rules regulating with whom he or she is permitted to eat, though the two ranges may not be actually congruent (compare Mayer, 1960). The Indian situation is an elaboration of the analogy found in many societies between sexual relations and eating, often expressed in the language itself. In villages in Sri Lanka, for example, the fact that a woman "cooks food for a man" is a public statement of a conjugal relationship.

Contemporary anthropology's most contentious debate revolves around a related but different problem: under the aspect of totemism has been debated the meaning of the association of animals with social groups, especially when this association is phrased in terms of food prohibitions or taboos. Rules concerning what may or may not be eaten are, of course, not unique to totemic societies. Lévi-Strauss (1966) has formulated a view (also formulated by others) which can be taken to apply in general to food taboos—namely, that "there is an empirical connection between marriage rules and eating prohibitions" and that this "connection between them is not causal but metaphorical."

In this chapter Lévi-Strauss will remain offstage until the very end, when the implications of this inquiry can be related to his theoretical assertions. My problem is to try and make sense of the dietary rules relating to animals in a village in northeastern Thailand. My investigation takes its cues from the ideas of Mary Douglas and Edmund Leach. Douglas (1957) first developed her notion of "anomalous" animals with respect to the Lele and systematized it in a subsequent volume (Douglas, 1966). Stated briefly, the theory argues that dietary prohibitions make sense in relation to a systematic ordering of ideas (a classification system), as exemplified for example by the abominations of Leviticus. Leach, partly building on Douglas, postulates a theory of taboo—"Taboo inhibits the recognition of those parts of the continuum which separate . . . things"—and, using this postulate, demonstrates for the English and the Kachin the correspondence among three scales of social distance from Ego, pertaining respectively to marriage and sex relationships, spatial categories, and edibility of animals.

Prima facie, both Douglas and Leach are relevant to my investigation. On the one hand, Thai villagers place living creatures which are individually identified into certain named hierarchically ordered groups which appear to comprise a system of classification (with some curious anomalies). On the other hand, they have a varied set of rules that relate to the edibility of animals. Some animals are tabooed. A case in point is the taboos, said to be imposed by Buddhism, that prohibit the eating of ten kinds of meat—*Tham (dhamma) haam sib yaang:* human, horse, dog, tiger, snake, crocodile, elephant, monkey, leopard, and otter. There are other taboos which are not justified in terms of Buddhism but are nevertheless of strong intensity, such as those relating to the eating of vulture and crow. A third kind of rule applies to the eating of animals provided that certain forms of etiquette are observed; some domestic animals appear to be a focus for such rules. Last, some animals are not considered as food at all; following Leach, we may say that these are unconsciously tabooed.

Two major issues are raised by the Thai data, and I shall use two frames of analysis to investigate them. The first is: What is the relation between dietary prohibitions concerning animals and the animal classification scheme? More specifically, what kind of fit is there between dietary taboos relating to certain animals and their position or location in the scheme of classificatory categories? The second issue is the relation between rules concerning the eating of animals and the rules pertaining to sex and marriage.

Although the first problem is in one sense more general, in that it entails the description of the animal world as seen by the actors and therefore deserves prior attention, I shall begin with the second because, having worked through the data, I find that it holds essential clues for making sense of the first.

Sex Relationships, House Categories, and Dietary Rules

In Leach's essay the three series correlated are human beings categorized in terms of sex relationships, spatial or ecological categories (for example, house, field, forest), and a scale of dietary rules relating to animals of certain kinds (for example, domestic, farm, forest). The English and Kachin, of course, structure these series differently. Leach selected from the entire animal world known to the actors only certain categories of animals because they were associated with spatial and ecological concepts which also served to distinguish human beings.

The three series I shall correlate are marriage and sex rules, house categories, and a set of animals called *sad baan* (domesticated animals or animals of the house or village) and *sad paa* (animals of the forest), which are two of the three categories into which *sad* (animals) are subdivided. *Sad paa* and *sad baan* constitute for the villagers two opposed categories within a single related series. The middle series relating to house categories is spatial in that it relates to the ordering of the different parts of the villager's house and compound. This series in fact links the concepts relating to marriage and sex with those relating to animal edibility. In content this spatial series is different from that which appeared in Leach's essay, because in the Thai case the spatial ordering of the house is a domain of conceptualization which is closely related to their conceptualization of sex and dietary rules.

The Village of Baan Phraan Muan

Baan Phraan Muan is located in northeastern Thailand between Udorn town and the Mekong River, which forms the boundary between Thailand and Laos. The name of the village, which means "village of Muan the hunter," is deceptive as a representation of present-day life, for the people are peasant rice growers. Their economy is a monoculture centered on rice, and hunting as such is of marginal interest. Villagers rear domestic animals such as buffaloes, pigs, ducks, and chickens, and they derive a good part of their day-to-day animal food from the flooded fields, canals, and perennial swamps, which are significant landmarks in a dry country that depends on insecure monsoon rains.

Villages are clustered. The settlement (*baan*) is surrounded by fields and water sources; farther out are patches of rapidly dwindling forest. The region is dotted with villages spaced a few kilometers from one another. Settled agriculture of the kind described tends to make a village inward-looking, but villages have had traditional social contacts with each other through a network of marriages and by participating in both Buddhist festivals and regional cults. Most marriages, however, are made within individual villages.

The clustered village itself is residentially broken up into fenced compounds in which dwell closely related families. Since marriage is normally uxorilocal, the typical compound tends to be composed of the household of the parents (and their unmarried children) and the family of the daughter who has most recently married, plus other households of older daughters previously married. A later stage of the domestic cycle would result in two or more households related by ties of siblingship (commonly sisters, or even brothers and sisters). In 1961 Baan Phraan Muan had a population of 932 persons constituting 182 families, 149 households, and some 80 compounds.

The Concept of the Marriage Ceremony

The words for "marriage ceremony" in Phraan Muan village explicitly allude to the connection between eating and sexual intercourse, in the frequently encountered sense of the man being "the eater" and the woman "the eaten." Villagers refer to the marriage ceremony as *kin daung*, which has the following range of meanings:

1. *Kin* means to eat; *daung* is an abbreviation of *kradaung* meaning tortoise (or turtle) shell.

2. *Daung*, tortoise shell, means female sexual organ. This is a slightly vulgar usage, but by no means so vulgar that villagers are inhibited from using it in company. Thus, *kin daung* means "to eat the female sex organ"—that is, to have sexual intercourse.

3. *Kin daung* also means the marriage feast (at which many guests are present). Thus, the most usual meaning of the concept is the marriage ceremony including the feast which ratifies the marriage.

Orthodox marriage transactions in the village follow this sequence.

Old respected elders (*phuu thaw*) representing the groom visit the bride's parents, and, if the marriage is acceptable to the latter, the marriage payment (*khaa daung,* "the price of the female sex organ") they would receive from the groom's parents is agreed upon. The *khaa daung* is the payment to the bride's parents for the transfer of the girl and can be claimed in whole or part by the husband under specified conditions if there is a separation in which the blame rests with the wife or her parents.

The evening preceding the marriage ceremony, relatives on both sides assemble separately in the respective parental houses, and they give money gifts to the parents. The gifts are called *phau daung* ("to help hold the marriage ceremony"). The next morning elders from the bridegroom's house go to the bride's, where they meet the elders representing her parents, and, after some ritual haggling, the *khaa daung* is counted and accepted. This is followed by the bridegroom's procession to the bride's house, the holding of the *sukhwan* ceremony to call the soul essences of the couple (see Tambiah, 1970), and the paying of respects by them to each other's parents and relatives (*somma phuu thaw*), who tie their wrists with cord and give them money gifts (*ngoen sommaa*). The ritual concludes with the marriage feast.

The implications of the concept of *kin daung* are not exhausted at this verbal metaphorical level, but appear in a ritual sequence connected with one kind of disapproved marriage which I shall discuss later. One of the objects used in the rite is the tortoise shell, and some additional linguistic facts need to be set out in order to interpret its role fully.

Mary Haas (1951) presented a number of names used among northeastern Thai which sound vulgar or impolite in the Bangkok dialect (Central Thai). One such is "*tâw*" or "*tàw,*" which means "tortoise" or "turtle" both in Bangkok and the northeast, and in Bangkok has as one of its additional meanings "vagina." In this sense it is a very obscene word. It is noteworthy that the northeasterners also see in the tortoise or turtle a metaphor for vagina, but use part of the animal, the shell (*daung*), for it in this context; therefore, for them *tàw* as such is not obscene.

The Categorization of Humans in Relation to Sex and Marriage

People (*khon*) are differentiated in diverse ways. I am concerned here with the ordering of persons with respect to sexual accessibility and approved marriage.

The kinship system of the villagers is bilateral. The ordering of persons in this system is along two axes—the vertical generational and the lateral sibling. Kinship terminology is widely applied, and the village population is arranged into generational strata: grandparents, parents, siblings, children, and grandchildren. Within these generational hierarchized layers, ranges of kind are distinguished by distance, especially within one's own generation.

Incest and marriage prohibitions are combined in different permutations in village thought. While marriage across generations and also marriage which breaks the rule of "relative age" (the rule that the husband must be older than his wife) are prohibited, especially if the partners are close kinsmen, marriage and sex regulations are usually formulated on the lateral axis differentiating categories of persons in Ego's own generation. Kinsmen in one's own generation (including affines) divide into two categories, *phii* and *naung,* older and younger sibling, and the concept *yaad phii-naung* in its widest reference means "kinsmen." It is thus the *phii-naung* series, subject to further differentiation into named subcategories to which attach rules of sexual conduct and marriage, that is under consideration here. It is the series that closely reflects village formulation:

1. *Phii kab naung* (blood brothers and sisters, siblings). Sex relations (*see*) between siblings are forbidden. If siblings engage in such relations, they must be forcibly separated. Marriage (*aw kan,* "to take") between them is impossible. These attitudes are axiomatic and are therefore not the focus of verbal elaboration. In short, both sex and marriage are prohibited with *phii kab naung.*

2. *Luug phuu phii naung* (first cousins). Sex relations between first cousins are forbidden. If first cousins engage in such relations, they must be forcibly separated. Marriage is forbidden. The expressions used in discussing these prohibitions are worth mentioning: *awkan baw dai* ("cannot marry") because *bau yuen pid booran* ("impermanent and against custom," "impermanent" here meaning that one or the other partner will die); *haam gaad sum diawkan* ("strictly forbidden, descended from common ancestor"); *bau kam bau khun bor mang bau mee* ("they will not be prosperous, not be rich"); *haa kin mai saduag, chibhaai, mai ram mai ruay* ("insufficient livelihood, ruin [loss of possessions], not wealthy"). These attitudes simply deny that stable and prosperous marriage is possible between first cousins. It is axiomatic that a marriage ceremony cannot take place (*tham pithii baw dai*), and that if two first cousins live together and refuse to be separated, they will be disinherited and disowned. Villagers appear to observe these rules strictly. No marriage between first cousins was encountered.

3. *Phii-naung* (classificatory siblings, second cousins). Second cousins, though not separated from third cousins by a special term, nevertheless make up a special category in regard to sex and marriage, a transitional ambivalent category. Sex between second cousins is not a serious matter if of temporary duration. In this village, however, since sex usually follows courtship and courtship is a prelude to marriage (in fact ideally there should be no intercourse before marriage), sex relations between second cousins carry the possibility of marriage.

There are cases of the marriage of second cousins in the village, but they are infrequent. The attitude toward such marriages is ambivalent. *Tham prapheenii haam tae aw dai khaw chaub ragkan,* "custom forbids but they can marry if they love each other." They can be married ceremonially in the orthodox fashion, but if second cousins break the relative-age rule (that the woman be an "older sibling" of the man), they must go through a certain ritual to overcome the effects of incest. In normal usage a husband can be referred to by his wife as *phii* ("older sibling") and can refer to his wife as *naung* ("younger sibling"). Thus, a marriage that contravenes relative-age distinctions creates an unacceptable linguistic asymmetry between husband and wife.

In the corrective ritual the couple are made to eat rice from a tortoise shell. The symbolism is that dogs commit incest and ignore relative-age distinctions, and that eating in the fashion of dogs misleads the punishing moral agents into thinking that the couple are not humans but animals. *Riagwaa khaw pen maa cha dai yuu diawkan yuen,* "they are called dogs so that then they can live long together." The ritual not only invokes the dog but physically employs the tortoise shell *(daung)*. I have already indicated that *kin daung* means a marriage ceremony, and that *daung* linguistically and metaphorically means vagina. The words and metaphor which are normally associated with acceptable marriage are now used instrumentally in an unacceptable marriage. The ritual implies that the couple are eating from (born of) the same tortoise shell (the same vagina), and that in eating together (having sexual intercourse) they are behaving like incestuous dogs.

We may note two relevant features. At the range of second cousins, rules concerning marriage become ambiguous in terms both of closeness of kinship and of relative age and can be broken with the aid of proper ritual action. Second, the ritual cited reveals explicit connections between "eating" and "sex," tortoise and vagina, and doglike behavior and forbidden sex or marriage relations.

4. *Phii-naung, yaad haang.* The second term, *yaad haang,* means distant relatives. Third and more remote cousins fall into this cate-

gory. Marriage is recommended or approved within this range, and sex relations are possible.

5. *Khon ouen,* "other people"—that is, nonkinsmen. Typically they are persons of other villages in the region. It is possible to marry them and thereby convert nonkin to kinsmen.

6. Finally, there is the unknown "outsider" who marks the limit of sex relations and marriage. He stands at the edge of the social universe, rather than constituting a special forbidden category. Outsiders may be superior, powerful, wealthy persons or inferior, unfamiliar strangers. Witchcraft is attributed to remote villagers. This category also includes the urban world, to which power and wealth and also poverty and degradation belong. There is no single term for outsiders. There are, however, such named groups as Cheg (Chinese), Kaew (Vietnamese), Khaeg (Indians), and Farang (a word which denotes white-skinned foreigners and is derived from *farangseed,* meaning the French).

The Social Significance of House Categories

The house categories which refer to the physical arrangement of the rooms and floor space have for the villagers a direct association with the human series already described and also a relevance for the manner in which the domesticated and forest animals are conceived. The architecture of the house becomes a central grid to which are linked categories of the human and animal world.

All village houses, with very few exceptions, are raised from the ground on wooden stilts or pillars. Access to the house (*baan*) is by a ladder. The space on the ground under the floor is used for keeping animals and storing household goods.

The village settlement (also called *baan*) breaks up ecologically into compounds. Physically a compound means a house or a collection of two or three houses enclosed by a fence with one or two entrances. The people who live within the same fence (*juu nai wua diawkan*) comprise a compound group. The village concept for compound is *baun baan* ("the place where the house is") or *baun diawkan* ("shared place"). A compound typically takes its name from the oldest member, who may be a female if the male head is dead (for example, *baun baan Phau Champee*).

The description of the physical layout of the house requires a preliminary statement of certain aspects of kinship, marriage, and residence. Bilateral kinship in the village is combined with certain residence customs. Whereas inheritance of rice land is bilateral, resi-

dence and inheritance of house and compound follow different rules.
First residence after marriage is usually uxorilocal. The son-in-law and
married daughter spend a few years in the latter's parental house,
until they are displaced by the second daughter's marriage. Commonly, the displaced daughter and husband then build their own
house in the wife's parental compound. The youngest daughter and
her husband usually remain as part of the stem family, looking after
the parents in their old age and inheriting their house and an extra
portion of rice land. Any house where parents have adult children is
thus likely to include a son-in-law and married daughter.

Figure 5.1 (top) sets out the floor plan of an orthodox village house.

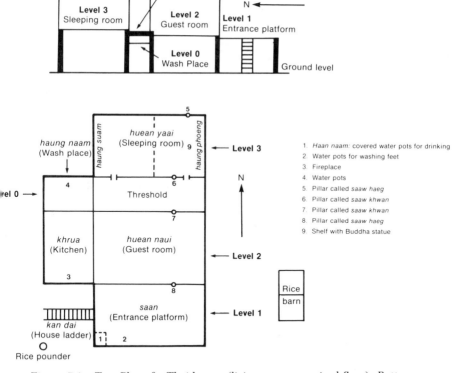

Figure 5.1. Top: Plan of a Thai house (living space on raised floor). Bottom: Profile of house showing levels.

The major features of the layout are the following. A ladder (*kan dai*) leads up to the *saan,* an unenclosed and roofless entrance platform which I call "threshold." From the entrance platform one enters the *huean naui* ("little house") or *bawn rab khaeg* ("place for receiving guests"). This guest room is roofed and has walls, except on the side which gives onto the open entrance platform. The limits of the guest room are fixed by two pillars, *saaw haeg* and *saaw khwan* (*haeg* means "first" and *khwan* refers to the "spiritual essence" of a human being). From the guest room one enters the *huean yaai* ("large house") or *baun naun* ("place for sleeping"). This sleeping room likewise has two important named pillars, *saaw khwan* and *saaw haeg* (their arrangement being the reverse of those in the guest room, so that both *saaw haeg* are at the extremities). The area between the two *saaw khwan* is the second "threshold" in the house, separating the sleeping quarters from the guest room. The sleeping room is internally divided into *haung phoeng* (room of parents) and *haung suam* (room for son-in-law and married daughter), but this room has no actual partition, only an invisible one constituting the third "threshold." To the left of the guest room are the kitchen (*khrua*) and adjoining it the washing place (*haung naam*), an open platform on which are pots of water used for bathing and for cooking. It is a place for cleansing and is used by members of the household only.

Another major fact relating to the architecture of the house is that all the floors of the named divisions are on different levels (see Figure 5.1, bottom). The washing place (*haung naam*) is the lowest in level (level 0). The entrance platform (*saan*) is at the next level (level 1); the kitchen is also on this level. The guest room (*huean naui*) is higher (level 2), and the sleeping room (*huean yaai*) is at the highest level (level 3). These levels are not accidental but are symbolic of the various values assigned to the divisions of the house.

The compass points as indicated in Figure 5.1 have symbolic values. Ideally, a person entering the house would face north, and the entrance platform is at the southern end and the sleeping room at the northern end. The directions can be reversed, but never must the sleeping room be placed toward the west. The kitchen and the washing place are always on the western side of the house. The four directions have the following values. East is auspicious, represents life, is sacred (the Buddha shelf of the house is always placed in the easterly direction), and is the direction of the rising sun. East is also, when one faces north, the direction of the right hand and represents the male sex. West is inauspicious and represents death, impurity, and the setting sun. It also represents the left hand and the female sex.

North is auspicious and is associated with the elephant, an auspicious animal because of its size, its natural strength, and its associations with royalty and Buddhist mythology. South is of neutral value.

The sleeping room or "large house" (*huean yaai*), the most sacred place in the house, is divided in two by an invisible partition. The *haung phoeng* (the parents' room) is always the eastern half, the *haung suam* (the room for son-in-law and married daughter) is always the western half. Thus, the relation of the parents to the son-in-law and married daughter in the house is expressed by values associated with east and west. The linguistic meaning of *phoeng* and *suam* is obscure. Villagers cannot describe what *phoeng* means (the dictionary meaning is "lean-to"); they explain that *haung phoeng* is the parents' room. Similarly *suam* evokes no linguistic meaning except that *haung suam* is associated with son-in-law and married daughter. In the language of central Thailand *suam* means "lavatory." The villagers of Baan Phraan Muan are aware of this and are somewhat embarrassed by this connotation but explicitly deny that the association holds for them.

When the house is located in the ideal direction (with the *huean yaai* at the northern end), the *haung phoeng* is, for a person facing it, on the right and the *haung suam* on the left. We have seen that right in village formulation is auspicious and also associated with male; left is inauspicious and associated with female (in any assembly of both sexes, men ideally sit on the right and women on the left). There are always two doors leading into the *huean yaai*—one into the *haung phoeng* and the other into the *haung suam*.

The most conspicuous social feature of the division in the sleeping quarters is that a son-in-law must not enter the sleeping quarters through the doorway of the parents-in-law; furthermore, once inside the room he must never cross over into their "room." This taboo does not bear on children of either sex, or on the married daughter. There is only one occasion on which the son-in-law ever enters through the doorway of his wife's parents: at his wedding ceremony, he is ceremonially led through that door by the ritual elders (*thaaw*) for the ritual of *sukhwan* (binding the soul essence to the body). This symbolizes that he is accepted into the house by the bride's parents and that he is legitimately allowed into the sleeping quarters as a son-in-law. There is no reciprocal taboo on parents-in-law crossing over into the *haung suam*. The taboo on the son-in-law represents an asymmetrical "avoidance," with all its sex and incest connotations.

The sleeping arrangements inside the *haung yaai* emphasize further the precautions taken against incest and prohibited sex. Father and mother are so placed that the father sleeps at the right in the east, with his wife beside him on the left. The male children sleep on the side of the father, the female children on the side of the mother. When sons reach the age of adolescence they are sent out to sleep in the room outside (the *huean naui*); when daughters grow up they move to the western half of the room, the parents to the eastern half. This anticipates the arrangement when the daughters marry.

After the marriage of a daughter, the son-in-law would, in an ideally placed house, sleep in the western corner with his wife to his right, while the wife's father would sleep in the eastern corner with his wife to his left. These spatial arrangements readily convey the precautions taken against separating the junior and senior generations. Furthermore, while the father and mother keep the orthodox right-left position, the son-in-law is placed left with respect to his wife. This reversal symbolically places the son-in-law in an inferior position in the house. It should be noted that a man is strictly forbidden to have sex relations with his wife's sisters; by being put in the western end of the room he is spatially removed from them. While there is no social avoidance, he must not joke with them in any manner suggestive of sexual connotations.

Apart from the members of the household (normally parents, children, and son-in-law) who sleep in the *haung yaai*, only siblings of parents (*phii kab naung*) and first cousins (*luug phuu phii phuu naung*) are allowed to enter the *haung yaai*, though they are not permitted to sleep there. These two kin categories, as we have seen, are considered so close that sex and marriage with them are forbidden. These spatial restrictions, which apply in everyday life, are not operative on ceremonial occasions like death, marriage, ordination, and merit-making ceremonies in the house, when monks are invited. On such occasions the ritual proceedings take place inside the sleeping room (*haung yaai*), and all guests can enter. Ritual occasions temporarily obliterate the restrictions of everyday life; marriage, for example, recreates and adds to the social structure of the house, whereas death disturbs and diminishes it.

The *huean naui* is the place for receiving and entertaining guests (*baun rabkhaeg*). Typically these guests are second and more distant cousins, neighbors, and friends from the same village, and those from nearby villages. These categories (*phii-naung* and *yaad haang*) are eminently marriageable and may be sex partners. They are forbidden to enter the sleeping quarters (*huean yaai*), unless they enter into a marriage relationship with a member of the household. They are divided from the sleeping quarters by a threshold space represented by the two *khwan* pillars which stand between the two rooms.

The *haung naam,* or wash place adjoining the kitchen, is a platform with water jars. It is used for washing and bathing by family members only; it is considered unclean, but the dirt is "private" and pertains to the family.

The kitchen (*khrua*) is not a particularly private or sacred space. Cooking, however, is normally a female task. Hence, the kitchen is predictably placed in the west and to the left.

The *saan* (entrance platform) is another threshold, giving entry into the house proper. It is a place for washing one's feet before entering the house. Pots of water are placed on the floor (the boards of which are loosely spaced to permit water to flow through), and persons coming from the outside are normally expected to cleanse their feet. Only persons who are invited or are socially admissible can mount the ladder and step on the *saan. Khon ouen,* or "other people," are normally excluded from entering the house, unless invited.

The compound fence marks the boundary of private property. Outsiders are not expected to enter the compound (*baun baan*).

There is clearly a close correspondence between the marriage and sex rules pertaining to the human series and the house categories, which say the same thing in terms of living space and spatial distance. The house and kin categories are linked in turn to an animal series.

Animal Series: Sad Baan and Sad Paa

Animals are classified into *sad baan* (animals of the house or village) and *sad paa* (animals of the forest). They are listed in Table 5.1.

By *sad baan* the villagers mean animals that are reared or looked after (*liang*) by them. It is therefore appropriate to refer to them as domesticated animals. It should also be noted that, while domesticated and forest animals are opposed categories (which in turn are internally differentiated), there is an overlap between them in the forest animals which villagers say are the "counterparts of domesticated animals."

The domesticated animals *par excellence* in the village are the dog (*maa*), cat (*maew*), ox (*ngua*), buffalo (*khuay*), pig (*muu*), chicken (*kai*), and duck (*ped*). The goose (*haan*), though found in the village, is rare. The horse is not found in the village or surrounding villages as a domesticated animal, and will therefore be excluded from further discussion (like the elephant, it is associated with royalty and

Table 5.1. *Sad baan* and *sad paa.*

Sad baan (domesticated animals)	Sad paa (forest animals)
	Wild counterparts of *sad baan:*
Khuay (buffalo)—edible with rules	*Khuay paa* (wild buffalo)—edible
Ngau (ox)—edible with rules	*Ngua paa* (wild ox)—edible
Muu (pig)—edible with rules	*Muu paa* (wild boar)—edible
Maa (dog)—not edible (taboo)	*Maa paa* (wolf)—not edible
Maew (cat)—not edible	*Chamod* (civet cat)—edible (ambiguous)
Kai (chicken)—edible	*Kai paa* (wild fowl)—edible
Ped (duck)—edible	*Ped paa* (wild duck)—edible
Haan (goose)—edible but rarely eaten	Other animals:
	Kuang (deer)—edible
	Faan (barking deer)—edible
	Nuu paeng, nuu puk (forest rat)—edible
	Kahaug (squirrel)—edible
	Kadaai (hare)—edible
	Ling (monkey)—not edible
	Animals of the deep forest, rarely seen:
	Saang (elephant)—not edible
	Sya (tiger)—not edible
	Sya liang (leopard)—not edible
	Mii (bear)—not edible

also appears in some episodes in the Buddha's life). Of the domesticated animals found in the house and compound, only the dog and the cat actually live together with human beings inside the house. This is consciously pointed out by villagers and sets these two animals apart as a subcategory.

The village house, as already described, stands on pillars or stilts. The house categories—sleeping quarters, guest room, wash place, kitchen, and entrance platform—pertain to the house floor above the ground. The house thus has space and ground underneath which is called *tai thun,* the subdivisions of which have no particular names but are referred to as ground under the entrance platform, sleeping room, and so on (see Figure 5.2). These spaces are demarcated on the ground by the pillars. The domesticated animals other than the dog and cat are housed, especially at night, underneath the house; this space is also used for storing certain kinds of property. There is a pat-

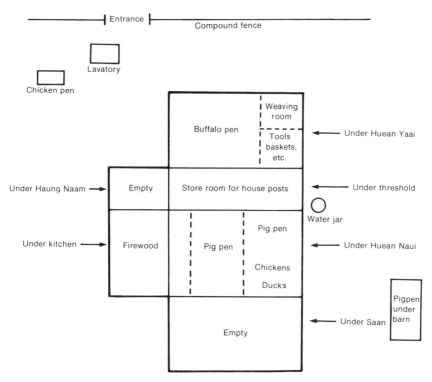

Figure 5.2. Space under a Thai house (ground level).

tern in the arrangement of animals and property under the house, and the villagers have explicit ideas about it.

A part of the ground under the sleeping quarters (*huean yaai*) is blocked off by posts and divided into three sections. In one is stored the weaving loom; weaving, a female activity, is done in this spot. In another section are usually stored baskets, agricultural equipment, and other miscellaneous property. The remaining and major portion of the space is used for tying up buffaloes, especially at night, and is considered the right place for them.

The pigpen is located in the space under the *huean naui*, the place for entertainment of guests. Chickens and ducks may also be housed there or elsewhere in the compound; they are never kept at night under the sleeping room.

During the day, buffaloes (and oxen) and pigs can be tied anywhere in the compound, but at night special precautions are taken. The spaces under the entrance platform (*saan*) and especially the wash place (*haung naam*) are regarded as dirty and wet, and one of the most inauspicious things that can happen to the house is for a buffalo or an ox to sleep there at night. Should the animal do so by accident, a ceremony for removing bad luck (*sia kraw*) must be conducted.

The spatial facts concerning the domesticated animals make it possible to infer a gradation among them in the context of their association with the values attached to the house categories.

The dog (*maa*) and the cat (*maew*) enjoy almost human privileges in the freedom allowed them to move in and out of the house. They sleep in the house or outside as they wish. Of all animals, they are in a sense closest to human beings. But there is a telling difference between the attitudes displayed by the villagers toward the two animals.

The dog is in one sense a friend of man, but it is not a "pet" as understood by Westerners. It is treated casually, given great license and little care. It is, in fact, an animal that arouses paradoxical attitudes which are symptomatic of its close bearing on human relationships. The dog is not edible; this is not simply a neutral attitude but a definite taboo. Verbal attitudes represent the act of eating dog as revolting. Furthermore, this animal, though close to man, is viewed as a "low creature" (*pen khaung tam*); it eats feces (*khii*) and is therefore unclean and inedible. The dog is regarded as the incestuous animal *par excellence;* canine parents and children copulate. It is, as already noted, a metaphorical vehicle in the ritual by which the mystical dangers of a wrong marriage are nullified—the bride and groom eat like dogs from a turtle shell and become dogs to hoodwink supernatural agents. It seems clear that in Phraan Muan village the dog is treated as a "degraded human"; its inedibility corresponds to notions of uncleanliness and incest. One of the strongest insults that one villager can hurl at another is to say that a dog has had intercourse with his parental and maternal ancestors (*maa sii khood phau khood mae myng*). Other animals do not figure so effectively in insulting language.

The cat, objectively no different from the dog in its food habits or sex behavior, evokes none of the negative attitudes directed at the dog. The cat is not as frequent a village animal as the dog, and it, too, is not a "pet" in the Western sense. In fact, it is "neutral" in its implications for man. The cat is also not eaten. Villagers say that there is no taboo on eating cat but that they do not eat it (*mai haam tae mai kin*). It is not eaten because it is useful to man; the Buddha created the cat in order that it may eat the rat, which is harmful to man because it gnaws his clothes. There is also an attitude—by no means elaborated into a theory—that the cat brings coolness to the house. Though I have not witnessed it, I have heard that a cat is used in rainmaking ritual; the exposure of a cat to the sun or the washing of a cat attracts rain. It thus seems that the cat and dog, both of which live with man in the house, represent opposed values centering around a single problem. The dog is debased, unclean, tabooed as food, and incestuous; eating it is as repulsive as incest. The cat is clean, useful, and cools the house; its appearance in rainmaking ritual also connotes valued fertility.[1] Not eating it appears to be associated with its positive metaphorical representation of proper and prosperous family relationships. This point is reinforced by statements made by villagers that they do not like the dog to enter the sleeping quarters (*huean yaai*). If it is seen in this room it is quickly expelled. The cat, on the other hand, is given full freedom to enter and sleep there.

The ox (*ngua*) and the buffalo (*khuay*) are not opposed animals; the same attitudes are expressed toward them. The ox, however, is rare in the village, whereas the buffalo is commonly found as a work animal. Since I am more familiar with the role of the buffalo, I shall largely confine my comments to it. Of all domestic animals—in fact, of all animals—the ox and the buffalo are differentiated most in terms of age and sex distinctions. For most domesticated animals, as well as their wild counterparts, distinctions are made between adult males, adult females, and young animals of either sex by adding to the name of the animal a second word meaning "male," "mother," or "small"—for example, *maa puu*, *maa mae*, and *maa naui*, respectively, for dogs. Similar distinctions are made for the ox and the buffalo: *ngua thoeg*, bull; *ngua mae*, cow; *ngua naui*, calf; *khuay thoeg*, bull buffalo; *khuay mae*, cow buffalo; *khuay naui*, buffalo calf. However, two additional age and sex discriminations are made for the ox and buffalo alone—namely, *bag* (young adult male) for a bullock and *mae nang naui* (virgin or unmarried female) for a heifer, the very same words that are used to represent the comparable human statuses.

The ox—in the form of a cow and its calf—appears as the central character in a story of village origin that has wide circulation in the region in which Phraan Muan village is located:

> This is the story of an ox called Hoo-Saparat. A rich merchant [*seethii*], who lived at the spot which is now the swamp [*bueng*] called Chuean, owned a pregnant cow. The rich man asked his servant Siang to take the cow out to graze. The cow disappeared. Siang and others tried to track it, and the place where they did this was called the village of Noon Duu [which

means "upland" and also "to look"]. The cow was not found there, and its tracks were followed until it was found at the village of Phakhoo [*pha* = "meet"; *khoo* = "ox"]. The ox was then taken to graze at the village of Naam Suay ["beautiful water"]. The herders stopped to eat and the cow disappeared again, because it wanted to find a place to calve. Siang then went to see a hunter called Muan to ask whether he had seen the cow. Muan was not able to help. Muan lived in the village that was called Baan Phraan Muan ["village of Muan the hunter"]. The tracks of the cow were discovered again and followed; the cow was eventually found and its legs were securely bound at the village of Ngua Khong [*ngua* = "ox"; *khong* = "rope to bind legs"]. The cow calved at this place, and Siang took the placenta to wash at the village of Nam Kun [*naam* = "water/pond"; *kun* = "not clear/muddy." The word used for placenta is *naung*, which is explicitly recognized as the same word as *naung*, meaning "younger sibling." In the village the placenta is eaten and relished]. The cow and calf were taken back to the owner in Bueng Chuean.

All the villages mentioned in the story actually exist today, and the story links them in a regional complex by means of linguistic play, and by using the cow and calf as its vehicles. The cow and calf, mother and child, as associated with the founding of human settlements, and we may well ask why in the Thai context the ox or the buffalo appropriately serve as effective vehicles for such an origin story.

The buffalo is of vital importance as a work animal in agriculture, especially for plowing rice fields. It is looked after with great care. A frequent sight is that of a buffalo pasturing, accompanied by a man (or less frequently a woman) or a young boy or girl as its protector—and, I am tempted to say, its companion. By and large, it is the task of young boys to graze the buffalo. They ride the animal and sleep on its back in the hot afternoons. The buffalo needs a human protector not only because it must be fed properly but particularly so that it may not stray and be stolen by strangers. It must be prevented from invading the fields during the time when rice is growing there.

The buffalo's hardest work period is during the plowing season. Thereafter it is free of work, except to pull carts. So important is its economic role that it is the only animal that is included in religious ritual devoted to ensuring good crop yields. Before plowing starts, the village holds a ritual for its guardian spirit; the villagers ask for good health for themselves and their buffaloes and for generous yields. After the harvest, there is a thanksgiving rite that is addressed to the spirit for boons granted.

The close association of buffalo with human beings is also manifest in the fact that to the buffalo alone of all animals is attributed *khwan* ("spiritual essence"), a preeminently human possession (although *khwan* is also attributed to rice, the staple food). The buffalo enters the realm of Buddhist religion; one of the taboos associated with the Buddhist sabbath (*wanphraa*) is that no plowing should be done on that day. It is said that this should be a day of rest for the buffalo as well as for humans and that it would be sinful (*baab*) to make it work. Here the buffalo is again singled out as a being toward which man must act ethically; it is in a sense assimilated to the human ethical code. However, there is no counterassertion that the buffalo acts ethically toward man.

What is the attitude of villagers toward the buffalo and the ox as a source of food? It is said that the buffalo is a ceremonial food—the most appropriate food to be served at feasts. This statement is partly related to the fact that it is a big animal that can provide meat for a large number of guests, but its ceremonial appropriateness is more than this practical consideration. A buffalo or an ox is killed to provide meat for village Buddhist calendrical festivities such as Bun Kathin and Bun Phraawes (large-scale collective merit-making rites), and also for household and family rituals—for example, house blessing, marriage, mortuary rites, and the ordination of a son of the household. The killing of the animal in these rites is not a sacrifice in the classical sense; it is simply the most appropriate food.

However, there are important ritual attitudes connected with the killing of buffalo and ox. Villagers claim that, in the case of a collective village ritual, no animal that belongs to the village may be killed; it must be acquired from another village. In the case of a family or household ritual, no animal reared in the house may be slaughtered; it must be acquired from another household in the village or in another village. If this norm is broken, certain evil consequences will allegedly follow for the village or household: *chibhaai*, loss of animals through death and disease; *liang yaag*, difficulty in rearing animals, especially young ones; *phae luug*, infertility of animals, in the sense that few calves will be born. These are the same words and concepts used by the villagers to describe the consequences of breaking marriage and sex taboos.

The attitudes toward the buffalo and ox with respect to their killing and eating thus show a correspondence to the attitudes relating to proper marriage and sex relationships among human beings. Sex rela-

tionships within the *baan* (house) are legitimate if the marriage partner comes from another *baan* and is outside the range of prohibited
kin; marriage is the event that initiates this desirable state of affairs.
The buffalo and the ox that belong to the house must not be killed and
eaten (paralleling prohibited marriage and sex); killing and eating the
buffalo and ox in an approved manner corresponds to the rules of correct exchange in marriage and sex relations. It might be said that the
food taboo concerning the dog parallels negative attitudes toward sex
and incest, whereas the ritual attitude relating to the killing and eating of the buffalo and ox parallels positive attitudes concerning marriage and sex. The buffalo, like the dog, appears in verbal insults with
sexual connotations—for example, *ii naa hua khooi,* "your face is like
the head of my penis." *Khooi* here sounds like *khuay* (buffalo) and is
a pun. However, compared with the incest insult in which the dog appears, this insult is mild and innocuously Freudian. Might the insulter
here be saying that he has procreated the insulted? Beef or buffalo
meat can be eaten on ordinary as well as ritual occasions. Villagers,
however, rarely eat beef; their normal protein needs are provided by
animals of the water (*sad naam*). Nevertheless, they can buy meat in
the town or from other villagers if an animal has been killed, though
this rarely occurs in the village except for ceremonial purposes. Under
conditions of protein scarcity, as when there are no fish in the ponds
and swamps, the villagers may kill a buffalo and share the meat or sell
it in the village, but these facts do not negate the everyday ritual attitudes.

Attitudes toward the pig are similar to, but weaker than, those that
the villagers show toward the buffalo and ox. Whereas the latter are
housed under the sleeping room, the pig is usually kept under the
room in which guests are entertained. Though sharing none of the
quasi-human attributes of the buffalo and ox, the pig is nevertheless
the focus of the same attitudes in connection with killing and eating.
Pork is a ceremonial meat, though only as a second preference. If a pig
is killed for feasting, the same rules apply as those concerning the
buffalo and ox. Hence, the same interpretation holds of the relation
between marriage and sex on the one hand and killing and eating on
the other. Unlike the buffalo and ox, however, the pig is reared chiefly
for commercial purposes, to be sold to middlemen for slaughter. The
pig does not figure in verbal abuse.

The duck and the chicken are the commonest feathered creatures.
Technically they are not "birds" (*nog*); the villagers do not invest
them with the same values. The duck is, in fact, associated with negative ritual attitudes which contrast with those toward the chicken on

the one hand and the buffalo on the other. Like pigs, ducks are reared to be sold in the marketplace. Like other domestic animals, they are rarely eaten as ordinary food. But unlike other edible domesticated animals, duck should not be eaten at feasts—occasions at which the eating of buffalo or ox or pig is appropriate. Villagers say that duck must not be served to assembled guests because if they eat it they will not come together again; they will lose interest in one another (*bya kan*). Duck should not be served at marriage feasts, or the marrying couple is likely to separate. This prohibition is explained thus. The duck lays eggs but it ignores them and does not bother to hatch them; it is lazy. A hen must then be made to sit on the eggs and hatch them. The duck is compared to a lazy wife and mother, the hen to a responsible wife and mother, and their behavior is seen as appropriate for making metaphorical statements about human relationships. The avoidance of eating duck at marriage transmits the message that husband and wife should not separate but must be a responsible pair as spouses and parents. In situations of emergency, if duck must be served, its beak and legs are cut off and buried (in village ritual, burial has the implication of neutralizing ritual danger and pollution). There is no prohibition about killing a duck that belongs to the house. No ritual prohibitions are associated with the chicken. It can be eaten as ordinary food and can be served at feasts to supplement other, more desirable meat.

The dog and the cat are not sacrificial animals. The village of Phraan Muan, apart from Buddhist rites, observes a cult addressed to the village guardian spirits and also rites to appease malevolent spirits (*phii*). In the appeasement of malevolent spirits, who act capriciously, part of the offering usually consists of cooked chicken or duck. The village guardian spirits are propitiated in two contexts: first, in collective rituals held twice a year, to request a good harvest and as thanksgiving after the harvest, at which occasions, ideally, a whole cooked chicken must be offered; and, second, in individual rites of affliction, where gifts of food are offered to the guardian spirits that they may withdraw their usually righteous anger. In cases of the latter type, the offerings are graduated according to the severity of the offense committed and may range from a chicken for a minor fault to a pig's head for a serious one. The buffalo is sacrificed on only one occasion—in connection with the practice of the one major regional cult—when the guardian spirit of the largest swamp in the region (Bueng Chuean) is propitiated with a buffalo sacrifice before the plowing season in order to ensure good rains. Many villages participate in this sacrifice, and they all contribute money for the purchase of the buffalo. If, in the communication of man with the supernatural, animals can be considered as acting as sacrificial intermediaries and as substitutes for the sacrificer, we can observe their gradation on a scale of increasing values: chicken and duck, pig, buffalo. This gradation corresponds to their ideal spatial location in the house compound.

Animals of the forest (*sad paa*) are opposed in village thought to domesticated animals in terms of their habitat and of man's relations to them. The latter live in the village and are cared for by man; the former live in the forest and are wild. As a class, forest animals have a greater variety of members than the domesticated category. In village classification, however, there is an important overlap between them which can serve as a starting point for the discussion of the edibility of forest animals. Villagers say that every domesticated animal has its forest counterpart; the wild buffalo, the wild ox, the wild boar, the wolf (called *maa paa*, "forest dog"), the civet cat (called *chamod* or *maew paa*, "forest cat"), wild fowl, and wild ducks.

The rules regarding the edibility of these forest counterparts are guided by the rules relating to the corresponding domestic animals. All are edible except the wolf, which resembles the house dog and is therefore obnoxious, and the civet cat, about which there is some ambivalence. I have noted that the house cat, though not eaten, is not rejected on the same grounds as those advanced for the degraded and incestuous dog; the civet cat is eaten by the villagers but is forbidden to pregnant women. Furthermore, the civet cat attacks domestic fowl, and such attacks are considered inauspicious. When it leaves the forest and enters the village, it is an animal out of place. One major difference between the wild and domestic species, however, must be noted: all the edible forest counterparts can be hunted, killed, and eaten at any time without ritual restriction. A wild buffalo or pig is consequently not the same as its domestic counterpart.

There is a range of other forest animals that are perfectly edible and can be hunted at will. Examples are the deer, barking deer, forest rat, forest squirrel, and hare. One point of interest is that the forest rat becomes edible by virtue of being a forest denizen, even though it is recognized as a kind of rat (*nuu*) which, when found in the house or in the field, is not recognized as desirable food.

There is another class of animals of the deep forest which are considered inedible. They are the elephant, tiger, leopard, lion, and bear. These animals represent to the villagers the power, danger, and might of the forest as opposed to human settlement, and they are viewed with admiration and awe and fear. Villagers hardly ever encounter them in their wild state, and hence they seem almost mythical to them. Inedibility here simply refers to their existence in a world remote from the human. All except the bear are included in the list of Buddhist food taboos. However, or perhaps because of their special status, they are used as vehicles for expressing certain ideas and values. The elephant, tiger, and lion, together with mythological creatures such as the mythical sky bird (*krut* or *garuda*) and the mythical water serpent (*naag* or *nāga*), appear in astrological charts; the elephant stands for inherited size and strength (*waasaana maag*), the tiger has natural power (*amnad*), and the lion is said to hide away in a deep cavern. The elephant and the tiger are singled out for further elaboration. The elephant, when caught and domesticated, becomes a royal animal and is then an animal useful to man. As one informant put it, "It also helped Lord Buddha to subdue Phaya Maan" (Mara). In the astrological chart the tiger (*sya*) is opposed to the domesticated ox, representing the antithesis of forest versus village, of wild beast versus man. It is thus appropriate that *sya* (tiger) is the title given to gangsters and bandits (Wijewardene, 1968). Philanderers are also called *sya phuuying*.

The attitude of the villagers toward the monkey is intriguing and suggests that the villagers see in some of the forest dwellers an imitation of themselves. Eating monkey is forbidden in the village, and the taboo is said to derive from Buddhism. Interestingly, the monkey is avoided as food not because it is a "friend of man" (*ling pen sieow manud*), but because it is "descended from man" (*ling maa chag khon*). This inversion of the Darwinian evolutionary theory is formulated in a story: "There is a story called *Nang Sibsaung* [A Woman with Twelve Children]. This woman with so many children was too poor to support and feed them. The children therefore had to go into the forest in search of food, and they ate the wild fruits there. In the course of time, hair grew on their bodies and they became monkeys." Monkeys are thus in a sense lost and degenerate human beings; their affinity to humans make them improper food. Yet it is whispered in the village that some people do eat them. Their animal and semihuman status is a bar to open "cannibalism."

Relationship among the Three Series (Human, Animal, and House Categories)

I have spelled out marriage and sex regulations as a scale of social distance, house categories as a scale of spatial distance with social implications, and rules that apply to the eating of domestic and forest animals as a scale of "edibility distance." The three series are in general, if not in a very precise manner, homologous or isomorphic. Table 5.2 summarizes the main features of the three series. Each row read horizontally states the distance gradient; each column read vertically states the pattern of metaphorical equivalence between the three series. Some of the nuances in the text cannot, of course, be included in the table, but the kind of equivalent statements that can be read from it are:

1. Incest between siblings : a son-in-law crossing over into the wife's parents' sleeping quarters : a buffalo leaving its place and wallowing in the mud of the washroom : eating dog.
2. Marriage of first cousins : persons allowed to enter the sleeping room abusing the privilege and sleeping there : slaughtering a buffalo reared in the house for a wedding feast.
3. Recommended marriage : entertaining kin in the guest room : feasting on buffalo reared by another household.
4. Marriage with nonkin (other people) : visitors entering the house and cleansing their feet on the house platform : eating edible animals of the forest.
5. Outsider : compound fence : powerful or degraded forest animals.

As long as we say that the three series imply correspondence, or that each series makes statements that have their equivalents in the other series, we are on safe ground. But the price of security is formalism. If, adopting Lévi-Strauss's terminology, we say that the three series "constitute codes making it possible to ensure, in the form of conceptual systems, the convertibility of messages appertaining to each level," so that the realm of men's relations to one another becomes in some manner related to the seemingly different realm of man's relations with nature (animals), we are faced with the following questions: What is the relationship between the two realms? And what is the logic and basis of the conversion of the message from one realm to the other? We must reserve consideration of these questions until the classification of animals has been examined.

Animal Classification, Unaffiliated Classes, and Anomalous Animals

The villagers of Baan Phraan Muan have a scheme of six major categories into which they spontaneously place living creatures (see Figure 5.3). The six are *khon* (people), *maeng* (insects), *nog* (birds), *sad*

Table 5.2. Relationship among three series: marriage and sex rules, eating rules, and rules of etiquette concerning house categories.

Human series	Blood siblings	First cousins (second cousins are ambiguous)	Classificatory siblings beyond second cousins	Other people	Outsiders
Marriage and sex rules	Incest taboo	Marriage taboo; sex not condoned	Recommended marriage (and sex)	Marriage and sex possible	No marriage
House categories	Haung phoeng and haung suam	Huean yaai (sleeping room)	Huean naui (guest room)	Saan (platform)	Compound fence
Rules relating to house space	Sleeping rules separating parents from son-in-law and married daughter	Rights of entry but not sleeping	Taboo to cross threshold into huean yaai	Visitors wash feet if invited in	Excluding outsiders
Animal series	Domestic animals that live inside the house	Domestic animals that live under the house (and have been reared there)	Domestic animals belonging to other households	Animals of the forest: counterparts, deer, etc.	1. Powerful animals of the forest 2. Monkeys
Eating rules	Inedible and taboo	Cannot be eaten at ceremonials	Eminently edible at ceremonials	Edible	Inedible and taboo

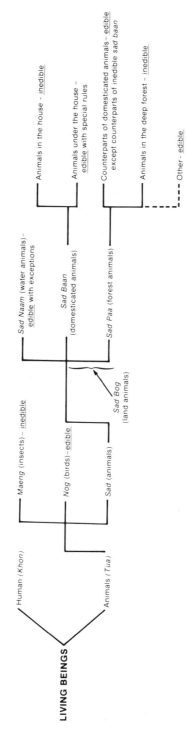

Figure 5.3. A Thai classification of living creatures.

naam (water animals), *sad baan* (animals of the house and village—that is, domesticated), and *sad paa* (forest animals). There are other named classes of animals which are not placed in any of these major categories; these I shall refer to as "unaffiliated" (or unique) classes.

Although I use the phrase "living creatures," this does not represent an explicit label in the local language, though the sense can be conveyed discursively. But there are linguistic usages which clearly distinguish human from nonhuman living beings and posit a common characteristic for all forms of the latter. An important linguistic marker is the use of classifiers with nouns, chiefly as complements and for stating numerical quantities, in the Thai-Lao language (see Noss, 1964, for the rules).

Khon means "people" or "human beings" and is also the classifier for them. This classifier is never used for any other being, whereas a single common classifier, *tua*, is used for all other living creatures (*sad, nog, maeng,* and the unaffiliated types). A primary meaning of *tua* is "body." This shows that in one respect all nonhuman living creatures are equated in a single universe; however, *tua* as a classifier is not used solely with respect to them.[2] The English labels which I have given in parentheses for the categories of nonhuman living creatures which share the classifier *tua* should not be construed as equivalents. They are given to aid the non-Thai speaker, but the reader is advised to think in terms of the Thai categories, for these show some startling discrepancies when matched with English folk usage.

Maeng (Insects)

A large number of individual species (ant, bee, mosquito, butterfly, cockroach, and so forth)[3] are placed in the class *maeng.* For the villager, *maeng* by and large connotes animals that are not eaten, but I have encountered two exceptions: *tak taen* (grasshopper) is eaten, and one kind of red ant (*mod daeng*) is crushed to make a vinegary sauce.

Nog (Birds)

Individual birds are described in terms of characteristics such as feathers, wings, or two legs, but from the point of view of the villagers an important semantic load carried by the word *nog* is that "all *nog* are edible." The habitat of *nog* varies and is not a principle that enters into the definition of the class. Linguistic usage unambiguously identifies *nog* by using it as a prefix before individual names. In the list I compiled of *nog* familiar to the villagers,[4] all *nog* were said to be edible with one exception, the owl, whose distinctive properties (for example, that it is active and moves around at night) are conveyed in its names, *nog khaw maew* ("bird like a cat") and *nog huug* ("bird that makes the sound *huug*").

For someone operating with English classificatory usages, it will come as a surprise that domesticated ducks and chickens and their wild counterparts are not classed as *nog* but as *sad*. More spectacularly, the vulture (*ii haeng*) and crow (*ii kaa*) are not defined as *nog* and are not affiliated with any major first-order category. Their unique prefix (*ii*) sets them apart linguistically.

What place do *nog* have in the diet of the villagers? Although "all *nog* are edible," they are not part of the common diet, since the villagers rarely engage in hunting or trapping. *Nog* are a delicacy but they are not served, even if available, on ceremonial occasions. Though not taboo, they are simply not an appropriate ceremonial food. Finally, there are no special rules regulating the eating of *nog*. By and large, in village dietary rules, *maeng* are inedible, and *nog* are edible, and thus in a sense they constitute two opposed though peripheral domains in the universe of living creatures.

Sad Baan, Sad Naam, and Sad Paa

The word *sad* is rendered in dictionaries as "sentient being, "beast," "animal creation" (McFarland, 1944), and as "animal," "beast" (Haas, 1964). The villagers are firm and clear in their use of the word. *Maeng* (insects) and *nog* (birds) are definitely not *sad*. Scrutinizing the variety of creatures which are called *sad*, one might say that they include all mammalian quadrupeds, the majority of aquatic animals, and domesticated fowl and their wild counterparts.

The three classes which bear the prefix *sad*—namely, *sad baan* (animals of the house or village), *sad naam* (animals of the water), and *sad paa* (animals of the forest)—are based on three distinct ecological realities: the village settlement, water, and the forest.[5] Water is in an important sense associated with the rice fields, and the village settlement is separated from the forest by the intermediate ecological features of field, canal, and swamp. Just as the rice fields provide villagers with their staple cereal, it is water (and the fields) that provide them with their everyday protein food. As a well known Thai saying has it, "There is fish in the water and rice in the fields." What follows is an amplification of this statement.

In the village during the monsoon rains and for some time afterward, when the rice is growing, the paddies are full of water; bordering the fields are a large canal and several subsidiary ditches which drain off the excess water. When the fields are transformed into a sheet of water they teem with multiple varieties of fishes (*plaa*), shrimps (*kung*), crabs (*puu*), and frogs (*kob*), which constitute highly appreciated food. There is another ecological feature in the region which is a perennial source of food—the permanent swamps (*bueng*), which (especially in the harsh, hot, dry season, a time of water scarcity) are symbols of rain and are associated with rainmaking ceremonies. In the dry season, fishing in the swamp is a major activity for both men and women.

Although the vast majority of water animals[6] are eaten, there are interesting exceptions. The water leech is considered inedible because it sucks human blood; the villagers use the word *khiidied* ("hate") to describe their reaction to this animal. The crocodile (*khee*) is inedible because of a Buddhist taboo—largely theoretical because crocodiles are not found in the area. The most important prohibition is associated with the otter (*naag*), which is tabooed on two grounds, one linguistic and the other based on its resemblance to the house dog. The word *naag*, or *nāga*, ordinarily denotes the mythical water serpent which dwells in the swamps and rivers and is associated with rain; it appears in Buddhist mythology as a servant and protector of Buddhism, and in rainmaking ritual and mythology as an opponent of human beings. I have discussed *naag* symbolism elsewhere (Tambiah, 1970); it is a multivalent symbol representing rain and fertility, as well as enmity and benevolence toward man. The second objection to the otter is its resemblance to the dog (*maa*), which is strongly tabooed. One can thus appreciate the vehement assertions of hatred (*khiidied*) which villagers direct toward this truly strange-looking creature of the water.

The tortoise (*taw*) poses problems. I have already noted that the tortoise shell (*daung*) is associated with the female sex organ, whereas the word *taw* does not carry the vulgar connotation of vagina as it does in Central Thai. The tortoise is normally edible in Phraan Muan village, but one variety is tabooed. It is called *taw phii* ("tortoise belonging to the spirit"—that is, the turtle associated with the guardian spirit of the swamp and also by extension with the guardian spirit of the village), or alternatively *taw san lang diaw* ("tortoise with a single stripe on its shell"). Tortoises with more than one stripe are edible, whereas villagers say that the *taw phii* is specially forbidden by the intermediary (*cham*) of the guardian spirit whose animal it is. As a water creature and by virtue of its association with the swamp spirit, the tortoise symbolizes water. I am unable to suggest why it is particularly associated with the swamp spirit, or whether sexual symbolism has anything to do with one of its varieties being tabooed as food.

Among water animals, the otter and the tortoise can be viewed as a related and opposed pair: the otter, which is doglike and shares the same name as the mythical and sacred water serpent and perhaps represents its negative features, and the sacred tortoise, which represents perennial water (and perhaps also female sexuality) and is associated with the guardian spirit of the swamp.

The other two categories with the *sad* prefix—*sad baan* (domesticated animals) and *sad paa* (animals of the forest)—have already been discussed in detail. The status of these three classes *vis-à-vis* the major classes *maeng* and *nog* presents an analytical problem from the point of view of formal classification theory which apparently is not unique to the Thai situation.[7]

From a formal standpoint, one might suppose that the villagers first divide nonhuman beings (distinguished by the classifier *tua*) into three major classes—*sad, maeng, nog*—and then subdivide *sad* into two categories, *sad bog* (land animals) and *sad naam* (water animals), and the former of these again into two subclasses, *sad baan* and *sad paa*. But the perceptual field of the villagers is somewhat different. Although at a certain level *sad* as a generic term may be contrasted with *khon* (roughly "beasts" versus "men"), from their own spontaneous statements it is clear that for them *sad baan, sad naam,* and *sad paa* are basic major classes of the same order as *maeng* and *nog.* It would appear that the various classes of *sad* are of major interest to them (far more than other kinds) and that, whatever the formal logical operations and the place of classes in the scheme for the classification theorist, the actors assign different weights to divisions of the natural world on the basis of relative interests, so that their own perceptual field collapses certain parts of this scheme and magnifies or upgrades the place of certain logically lower-order categories to the status of others of a logically higher order. For these reasons I shall refer to *maeng, nog, sad baan, sad naam,* and *sad paa* as "major classes," although a formal elucidation of the scheme may state things slightly differently.

The formal scheme based on the explicit and implicit ideas of the actors (but subject to the limitations discussed) is represented in Figure 5.3 and can be elucidated as follows. All living creatures divide into two basic categories: human beings (*khon*) and nonhuman beings (characterized by the classifier *tua*). The world of nonhuman living creatures is first divided into three major categories: *sad, nog,* and *maeng. Maeng* are largely inedible, *nog* are largely edible; they are differentiated at this level of classification.

At the next level of differentiation, although a contrast between land animals (*sad bog*) and water animals (*sad naam*) may be invoked in certain situations, it is more often perceptually and verbally overridden by another formulation. All *sad* are divided, on the basis of three ecological locations (house and village, water and fields, forest), into *sad baan, sad naam,* and *sad paa,* the water animals being separated off and declared edible, with some important exceptions. Although water animals are further subdivided (into kinds of fish, frogs, and so on) they are not grouped into higher-level kinds attributed to domestic and forest animals.

Domesticated animals divide implicitly into those that live in the house together with humans (inedible), and those that are reared apart from humans under the house (edible with special rules). Forest animals divide into those that are counterparts of domestic animals (edible without rules except for counterparts of inedible domestic animals), and animals of the deep forest credited with extraordinary properties (inedible). There is a residue of animals, such as the deer and forest rat, which are all edible.

One problematic fact emerging from this classification is that the *sad* categories are not constructed around a single dimension of edibility, as is largely true of *maeng* (insects) and *nog* (birds). This is especially so of domesticated and forest animals; edibility rules concerning domestic and forest animals cannot be meaningfully considered apart from their relation to other social facts, such as concepts of social distance, marriage rules, and house categories—that is, their relation to other systems of human classification.

But does the concordance among the three series established earlier help us understand the logic of the dietary rules which apply to creatures which are neither domesticated animals nor forest animals? I think that it does, but must first set out the problem.

Unaffiliated Classes and Anomalous Animals

I have used the term "unaffiliated classes" for the types of animals that the Thai villagers do not include in what they conceive to be the major categories of *maeng, nog,* and the threefold division of *sad.* Table 5.3 presents some examples, together with their position as regards edibility. These unaffiliated classes are problematic in two ways. From a formal point of view the snake (*nguu*), vulture (*ii haeng*), rat (*nuu*), and so forth are classificatory categories of the same order as *nog* and *maeng,* but clearly the villagers do not see them as being of the same magnitude as the major classes. These animals are also problematic with respect to their edibility, as indicated in Table 5.2. A second type of dietary problem is posed by the animals, such as the owl

Table 5.3. The edibility of unaffiliated classes of animals.

Giant lizard (*khapkae*)	Medicinal food for children
Lizard (*khiikiam*)	Not eaten, but no aversion to it; too small to constitute food
House rat (*nuu sing*)	"Only small children eat"; possibly eaten by adults but not admitted
Chameleon (*chiikapom*)	Medicinal food
Field rat (*nuu thaung khaau*)	"Only small children eat"; adults eat privately
Monitor lizard (*laeng*)	Edible, but dangerous to mothers after childbirth
Water monitor (*hia*)	Inedible (aversion)
Snake (*nguu*)	Inedible (aversion)
Toad (*khan khaag*)	Inedible (aversion)
Vulture (*ii haeng*)	Inedible (aversion)
Crow (*ii kaa*)	Inedible (aversion)

and the otter, that are inedible members of a largely edible class. For my purposes I shall call both types anomalous, the first being a kind of classificatory anomaly in that it is neither placed in a major class nor given an equivalent major status, the second being anomalous within its class. The problems they pose can be discussed in terms of a single theoretical framework. To account for the observed facts, I shall put forward a theory in the form of a series of related propositions. The theory relates classification or conceptual order, dietary attitudes, and omens or inauspicious signs in one scheme of ideas which represents an adaptation and extension of ideas propounded by Leach and Douglas.

> *Proposition 1.*
> An animal that is not placed in an ordered system of major classes receives further signification as ambiguous food. To find out the exact dietary signification given to it, we must investigate to what named major class it is penumbral and what dietary value is given to that class.

Creatures like the giant house lizard (*khapkae, tukae* in Central Thai), the house lizard (*khiikiam, chingchaug* in Central Thai), and the house rat (*nuu sing*) are not placed in any major class. Villagers say that these animals are found in the house, and therefore resemble *sad baan* (domestic animals), but that they are not reared by people, so they are not *sad baan*. Thus, they are prenumbral to *sad baan*, with which they share one property (location) but not the other (human care). Moreover, they live inside the house like the dog and cat, and these animals are tabooed as food. What is the status of these creatures as food? The house rat, though it is sometimes eaten, is not relished, nor do villagers like to admit to eating it. They state that young children, being what they are, are allowed a laxity that is not respectable in adults. It is interesting that throughout Thailand children are addressed as *nuu*. The giant lizard is likewise not ordinary food but is considered a medicinal food for children. The small lizard is definitely not eaten. There appears to be an analogy between creatures that are small and marginal to the house and unsocialized children. On the whole, Proposition 1 holds in regard to these creatures which live in the house but are not of the house.

Much the same attitudes concerning edibility are exhibited toward the chameleon (*chiikapom*) and the field rat (*nuu thaung khaau*). These animals live on land (*sad bog*) and are found in the compound, in the village, and in the fields, but they are also not domesticated animals. The chameleon is said to be eaten only for medicinal purposes. While villagers are known to eat the field rat, they publicly say that it is the young children (*deg num num*) who eat it. The idiosyncratic status of these animals again corresponds to their ambiguity as food objects.

We now come to a set of animals which the villagers say are unplaced in the major classes because they share characteristics of two ecological categories, water (*naam*) and land (*bok*). The monitor lizard (*laeng, takuad* in Central Thai) and the water monitor (*hia*) are remarkable examples of such anomalous animals. The *laeng,* a land animal, is normally regarded as edible but is sometimes forbidden to nursing mothers because it is considered poisonous and may cause illness or dry up the mother's milk. It is found in the peripheries of the village, in the forest. The *hia* is regarded as physically uglier than the *laeng* and is considered altogether inedible; it is, moreover, the focus of intense hatred. Both the *laeng* and the *hia* pose classificatory problems to the villagers. When asked why they do not assign them to a major category, they reply that although the land and water monitors are physically similar, one lives in the water and the other on land. Moreover, the tabooed and hated *hia* moves on land as well as in the water and thus straddles both ecological habitats. In Central Thai, *sad khrueng naam khrueng bog*—"animals partly water partly land"—expresses their anomalous properties. This phrase, though known in northeast Thailand, is not used there.

Proposition 1 to some extent accounts for these animals' ambiguous status as food, but the *hia* (water monitor) is the focus of attitudes which require an additional proposition to account for them. The *hia* is both inedible and hated. To call a person a *hia* is one of the worst insults possible, though perhaps not as extreme as calling him or her a dog (*maa*). Finally, the *hia* is a bad omen: its appearance in the village and entry into the compound is a highly inauspicious event, which in some instances may require a ceremony to dispel bad luck. It is an animal "out of place" (see Proposition 2, below).

Snakes, distinguished by the class name *nguu*, parallel the case of the monitor lizard. When asked why snakes do not belong to a major category, villagers answer that there are both land snakes and water snakes. Snakes are considered entirely inedible, however, and this cannot be fully explained by Proposition 1. The villagers regard snakes as enemies, as poisonous and injurious to man, which is objectively true for a number of them.

Proposition 1 does not account for the special attitudes of the villagers toward such unaffiliated animals as the toad, water monitor, vulture, and crow. It must be supplemented with a second idea, which I derive from Douglas's statement that "dirt is matter out of place" but apply in a new manner.

Proposition 2.
An unaffiliated animal, if it is seen as capable of leaving its location or habitat and invading a location or habitat of primary value to man, will be the focus of strong attitudes expressed in the forms of a food taboo and a bad omen or inauspicious sign.

In the case of the inhabitants of Phraan Muan village, the habitat of primary value is their village settlement and home (*baan*).

Like the water monitor, the toad (*khan khaag*) has no place in the major classes and arouses attitudes of hatred among the villagers, who consider it ugly. (Linguistically, hatred and ugliness are coupled, the words being *sang* and *naa sang*; an alternate word for hatred is *kii-diad*.) The villagers resist linking the toad with the edible frog, and point out that it is a land animal. Their "aversion" to the toad is linked to the fact that one of the most inauspicious things that can happen to a house and its members is the entry of a toad into the house. If this happens, a special ceremony must be held to get rid of the bad luck (*sia kraw*). A toad that steps over the threshold is an animal out of place and a bad omen. It is the supreme symbol of the unwanted and unclean outsider entering the house. The appearance of a snake in the house is similarly interpreted.

The vulture (*ii haeng*) and the crow (*ii kaa*) are not considered *nog* (birds)—one of the surprises of the classification scheme to an outside observer—and they are both inedible. Their names carry the prefix *ii*, which has implications of abuse, insult, and low social status.[8] On the vulture are focused attitudes very similar to those relating to the toad. It arouses aversion, and if a vulture alights on the roof it is an inauspicious invader of the house, and a *sia kraw* ceremony must be held forthwith. Vultures, which are common in northeastern Thailand, behave quite differently from *nog*. They fly very high, soar in the sky, and swoop down to eat carrion, dead cattle, and dogs. In alighting on the roof of a house, they are very conspicuously out of place.

The crow is not edible, but it does not evoke aversion. It is a scavenger and an unwanted but everyday intruder and therefore too common to attract ritual attitudes centering around bad luck. The vulture and the crow are not only unaffiliated with *nog* but also inedible. The former brings bad luck by virtue of its rare but unwelcome invasion of the village and house. The latter, though not rare, is simply not food and not *nog*.

The same kind of logic works with animals which are affiliated with a major class but which can at times be out of place and thus viewed as signals or omens of misfortune. The ominous significance of the buffalo that leaves its appointed place in the house at night to wallow in the mud of the wash place has already been noted. This event requires a rite to dispel bad luck. Another inauspicious sign—though not one which requires a ritual—is the crossing of a civet cat from its forest habitat into the village. A modification of the two propositions already stated will make it possible to express the attitude toward animals which, although firmly placed in the major classificatory classes, are yet anomalous within their class.

Proposition 3.
An animal that is placed in a class because it shares certain dominant properties of that class may yet be seen as exceptional or anomalous and therefore ambiguous as food or inedible (even if other members of its class are edible) if it shares one or more characteristics with animals of another class which carries strong values and is considered inedible.

In the Thai case, the strong values in question relate to domestic animals of the inedible class—the dog and cat. The proposition applies to the animals of the forest (*sad paa*) which are viewed as counterparts of the domestic dog and cat—namely, the wolf and the civet cat. It also applies to the hated otter, which, though clearly an animal of the water, obviously resembles the dog. The owl, too, though in one sense clearly *nog,* is one of the exceptional inedible *nog* because it is a night bird and is recognized as resembling the domestic cat, which also sees at night. It is, in fact, called "cat bird." The owl is inauspicious because it is thought to steal the *khwan* (spirit essence) of the inmates of the house which it approaches; more intriguingly, it is viewed as the representation of the *khwan* of an inmate of the house who is wandering outside at night.

> *Proposition 4.*
> An animal that belongs to a class that is edible and positively valued, if it also shares one or more characteristics with a member of another positively valued and edible class qualifies as an auspicious and eminently edible animal.

This permutation of Proposition 3, though it has no manifestation in Phraan Muan village, deserves to be stated to make the scheme complete. Such an animal may even be considered unique and a multifaceted symbol, as in the celebrated case of the pangolin among the Lele (Douglas, 1957). Perhaps positive mediators are compounded of such stuff. Unique classes or creatures of a different sort, on the other hand, may perhaps be generated from a cluster of characteristics which combine the positive features of an edible class and the negative features of an ambiguous or inedible class, thereby becoming the foci of restrictive rules of eating surrounded by ritual precautions. The Karam cassowary (Bulmer, 1967) is an apt illustration.

My discussion indicates that Douglas's theory of classificatory anomalies and their relationship to dietary rules is inadequate as it stands. Propositions 2 and 3 are needed as additional principles to explain the Thai facts. A further lesson is that simple intellectual deductions from a society's formalized scheme of animal categories will not take us far unless we can first unravel the core principles according to which people order their world and the valuations they give to the categories (see also Bulmer, 1967). In my analysis the core principles lie in the domain of primary social interests and values connected with the ordering of kin, incest and marriage, and conceptions of social distance. This is why an exposition of the nexus linking the three series (human sex and marriage discriminations, spatial categories of the house and compound, and the internal differentiation of domesticated and forest animals) is critical for unraveling problems posed by the formal system of ordered categories (classification). It also has implications for the more general problems posed at the beginning of the chapter: man's relationship to the animal world and the role of dietary regulations in the ordering of social relations.

Conclusion

The Thai village I have described is not a totemic society, and the totemic controversy in the strict sense does not apply to it. But insofar as this controversy has also focused on dietary rules relating to animals and ritual or religious attitudes toward animals, I must relate my ethnography and its implications to the larger theme. Hence, in these concluding comments, Lévi-Strauss comes back on stage.

By and large this discussion has affirmed the Lévi-Straussian approach: the attitudes toward animals as expressed in dietary rules do not make total sense in terms of Radcliffe-Brown's narrow notion of social or utilitarian value, but they represent a systematic mode of thought that corresponds to other systematized conceptual systems in the society. But is it enough to show correspondence or homologies between relational sets, or resemblances between systems of differences, and go no further?

If, as Lévi-Strauss accepts, there is a general connection of a metaphorical nature between sex and marriage rules and eating prohibitions, and if both are sets of ethical rules, we need to investigate why human beings find it apt to make this particular connection. Why are the killing and eating of an animal a focus for representing sex relations? Lévi-Strauss has appreciated that totemism is more than a system of signs, in that dietary rules relating to totemic animals have ethical and normative behavioral implications. He has, in fact, raised and tried to answer the question: If totemic representations amount to a code, why are they accompanied by rules of conduct?

His answer is disappointing because he either bypasses the question or resorts to the argument of the lowest common denominator. He counters the problem that totemic media of representation are frequently associated with eating prohibitions on the one hand, and with rules of exogamy on the other, by arguing that these are not necessary relations, because any one of them can be found without the others and any two of them without the third. He argues that dietary prohibitions are not intrinsic to totemism since food prohibitions either do not always coexist with totemic classifications or are found in the absence of totemism. Therefore, they are either extra- or para-totemic (Lévi-Strauss, 1966: 99) or logically subordinate (1966: 108). Moreover, "eating prohibitions and obligations . . . seem to be theoretically equivalent means of 'denoting significance' in a logical system some or all of whose elements are edible species" (Lévi-Strauss, 1966: 103). Finally, his most radical conclusion is that the rationale why some species are permitted and others forbidden lies in the concern to introduce a distinction between "stressed" and "unstressed" species. Prohibiting some species is merely one of several ways of singling them out as significant, but the logic can work in terms of practical rules of behavior or in terms of images. The two modes are analogous and of equal weight. In fact, taboos regarding death names, sex rules, and dietary prohibitions are all analogous modes for stressing significance. They can be redundant, supplementary, or complementary. An impoverishment of semantic content in the interest of form is thus accomplished.

Lévi-Strauss is evasive and even begs the question, for it is precisely the nature of the "significance" denoted that is never established. It could be said that his treatment of totemism is concerned with a single polemic—the demolition of those anthropologists who have seen dietary prohibitions as an intrinsic element and as symbolizing man's sense of identity, affinity, or participation with animals. The classic question of Radcliffe-Brown (1922, 1952) as to why man should have a ritual attitude toward animals still remains a haunting problem.

The inability of Lévi-Strauss to deliver the complete answer is, one suspects, linked to the position he has taken in regard to the question of the relation of man to animal. In *Totemism* (1962: 101), when discussing man's "triple passage (which is really one) from animality to humanity, from nature to culture, and from affectivity to intellectuality," he says: "It is because man originally felt himself identical to all those like him (among which, as Rousseau explicitly says, we must include animals) that he came to acquire the capacity to distinguish *himself* as he distinguishes *them,* i.e., to use the diversity of species as conceptual support for social differentiation." While no doubt justifiably criticizing those anthropologists who have conceived the relation between man and animal to be of only a single kind—identity, affinity, or participation—Lévi-Strauss places this sense of identity of man with animal sometime in the historical past when man for all time made his passage from nature to culture. Thus, he phrases the process in sequential terms: "The total apprehension of men and animals as sentient beings, in which identification consists, both governs and *precedes* the consciousness of oppositions between, firstly, logical properties conceived as integral parts of the field, and then, within the field itself, between 'human' and 'non-human' " (Lévi-Strauss, 1962: 101–102). It is because man is seen as once and for all having made the passage from affinity with the animal to separation from it, which state is equated with the primacy of the intellect, that Lévi-Strauss can see in nutritional prohibitions a refusal by men "to attribute a real animal nature to their humanity." Thus, he interprets these prohibitions as symbolic characteristics by which humans distinguish different animals, which then provide a natural model of differentiation for human beings to create differences among themselves.

Whereas *Totemism* and the earlier chapters of *The Savage Mind* are addressed to the devaluation of man's sense of identity with animals as expressed in dietary rules, it is intriguing and gratifying that Lévi-Strauss (1966: ch. 7) adopts a quite different conception of man's relation to animals when he discusses French conventions regarding the naming of animals. Happily for him, dietary prohibitions do not enter into this issue.

His scintillating analysis of the logic of French naming of birds, dogs, cattle, and racehorses is conducted with the aid of two concepts, metaphorical and metonymic relations based on principles of contiguity and resemblance. In Chapter 1, taking a hint from Jakobson, I used the concepts metaphor and metonym in a slightly different manner to decode the logic of Trobriand magic. This magical system postulates metaphorical or symbolic similarities (usually verbally in the spells) and simultaneously uses material parts of the symbol metonymically and realistically in the rite to achieve a transfer both in thought and deed. I shall use these concepts once again to sum up the Thai situation.

The Frenchman's relation to animals is discussed by Lévi-Strauss in the following terms. Birds are separated from human society, yet they form a community that is homologous to or resembles human society. The world of birds is thus a metaphorical human society, and the procedure for naming them is metonymic in that human Christian names are given them. The relation of bird names to human names is that of part to whole. Birds are metaphorical human beings.

The case of the dog is the exact reverse. Dogs do not constitute an independent society but are, as domestic animals, a part of human society, although they are accorded a low position in it. The relation of dogs to human society is metonymic, and they are given metaphorical stage names drawn from the paradigmatic chain of language, since it would cause uneasiness or mild offense to give them human names. Dogs are metonymic human beings.

The social position of cattle is metonymic since they form part of the technical and economic system of man, but different from that of dogs in that they are treated as objects. Cattle are thus metonymic inhuman beings and are given descriptive names from the syntagmatic chain of speech (metonymic).

Racehorses are metaphorical inhuman beings. They are products of human industry but lead the desocialized existence of a private society. They are disjoined from human society and lack intrinsic sociability. Their names are vigorously individualized and are metaphorical, drawn from the syntagmatic chain of speech and transformed into discrete units.

In this analysis, Lévi-Strauss is dealing with the complex relation between the Frenchman and the animal world, which involves principles of contiguity and similarity (negative and positive), of symbolic relations and participation (why else is dog meat tabooed?), and of exchange of similarities and differences between culture and nature.

I submit that the Thai villagers' relation to the animal world shows a similar complexity which expresses neither a sense of affinity with animals alone nor a clear-cut distinction and separation from them, but rather a coexistence of both attitudes in varying intensities which create a perpetual tension. And I submit that dietary regulations are intrinsic to this relationship. They provide a clue to the ritual attitude toward animals, to linking eating rules with sex rules, to man on the one hand drawing nature into a single moral universe and also at the same time vigorously separating nature from culture.

A backward glance at the ethnography reported will illustrate. Looking at the first-order classificatory categories reveals first that *maeng* (insects) and *nog* (birds) are separated off into inedible and edible categories; they are at the same time declared distant to man. The next process of elimination is applied to creatures of the water (*sad naam*), which by and large constitute the everyday animal diet, with some conspicuous exceptions whose logic of exclusion lies in the next level of differentiation.

It is with respect to the universe of land animals—domestic and wild—that the Thai villager thinks and feels in a complex fashion; it is with respect to them that attitudes of affinity and separation, opposition and integration, fuse to produce the complex correspondence of sex rules, house categories, and animal distinctions.

The dog, by virtue of the fact that it lives in the house and has a close association with man, has a metonymic relation to human society. The taboo on eating dog has a metonymizing role; it cannot be physically eaten and incorporated because it is in a sense incorporated into human society. But at the same time the dog is considered degraded and incestuous and thus stands for the antithesis of correct human conduct. This degradation to a subhuman status is used by the villager to perform a metaphorical transfer on the basis of an analogy. Man imposes on the behavior of the dog the concept of incestuous behavior, thereby attributing a human significance to the sexual behavior of dogs. This then allows man to copy the behavior of dogs metaphorically—for example, eating food from a tortoise shell—in order to correct the moral consequences of his own improper incestuous marriage.

The ox and the buffalo have a metonymic relation to man that is, unlike the relation to the dog, highly valued in a positive sense. The metonymizing behavioral acts that express this relation are that humans must act ethically toward them (for example, not working them on the Buddhist sabbath), and that concepts of human statuses are applied to them. These metonymizing acts are man-made and are possible because there can be no real confusion of man and animal. The ox and buffalo are not "human"; they do not reciprocate in a human idiom. They are edible with rules.

The ox and the buffalo have a metaphorical significance for man, different from that of the dog, by virtue of their positive valuation. There is almost a precise reversal in the ritual idiom. An impure act of an ox or buffalo (for example, straying into the dirt of the wash place at night) has by a direct metaphorical transference a bad consequence for humans (for example, a bad omen that has to be dispelled by ritual). It corresponds to improper sexual relations on the part of the inmates of the house. Again the taboo on eating the meat of the ox or buffalo of the house at a marriage feast is a metaphorical statement of proper marriage, which conjoins eating with sex and marriage regulations.

The domestic pig partakes, in a somewhat weaker fashion, of the attitudes toward the ox and buffalo. The duck has only a marginally metonymic relation to man. The avoidance of eating duck at a marriage feast is a metonymizing act which expresses a metaphorical significance of a negative kind (for example, the human wife should not behave like the unmotherly duck).

The wild animals of the forest have a different significance for the Thai villager. The elephant and the tiger have no physical relationship with man (nonmetonymic), but their attributes have strong metaphorical significance for him. They provide the imagery for the uncommon man, royalty and bandits, the social and antisocial heroes. That they are considered inedible is a statement of their extreme distance and difference from man.

The anomalous animals derive their significance either as recognizable imitations of domestic animals (or even man himself) or as inauspicious intruders into the ordered life of home and village. The otter resembles the dog physically, but has no metonymic relation to man. Hence, it is doubly hated and rejected as food. It is anomalous within the class of water animals which is eaten by man.

The vulture, the toad, and the snake do not belong to any major class. They are unplaced at this level of classification. But they are prone to leave their normal habitat and intrude into the habitat of man. In doing so, they are seen as performing metonymizing acts that establish unwanted contact with man, thereby bringing bad luck and misfortune. They are negatively valued sacred things that threaten to be out of place and to attack the established order of the universe. In a less dramatic way the civet cat presents the same threat, and the crow represents an unwanted association with man that has to be lived with.

The monkey, a creature of the forest, has little contact with man (nonmetonymic). But it is seen as bearing a metaphorical resemblance to man and portraying his descent into savagery. The taboo on eating it represents this physical and social rejection.

In sum, animals are effective vehicles for embodying highly emotionally charged ideas with respect to which intellectuality and affectivity cannot be rigidly separated as representing human and animal modes of conduct. If we are to answer adequately the question of why man has a ritual attitude toward animals, why values and concepts relating to social relations are underpinned to rules about eating animals, we have to inquire for the society in question why the animals chosen are appropriate means in that context for objectifying human sentiments and ideas. Lévi-Strauss has nobly defended the primitive as capable of contemplating nature independently of the rumblings of the stomach and of using natural models of differentiation to express social relations; he has at the same time substituted for crude utilitarian needs the nebulous concept of "interest" as dictating that contemplation. In the event, this interest turns out to be man's need to express and order social relations, to forge a system of moral conduct, and to resolve the problem of man in nature.

Between Lévi-Strauss's message- and sign-oriented intellectualism, represented in the statement that natural species are chosen not because they are good to eat but because they are good to think, and the actor-oriented moralism of Fortes (1967), represented in the statement that animals are good to prohibit because they are good to eat, lies scope for an imaginative reconstitution and reconciliation of the structural properties of symbolic systems qua systems and the effectiveness of symbols to bind individuals and groups to moral rules of conduct. Cultures and social systems are, after all, not only thought but also lived.

6

From Varna to Caste
through Mixed Unions

George Gaylord Simpson in *Principles of Animal Taxonomy* (1961) describes two forms of classification: *hierarchy* and *key*.

Hierarchy is a systematic framework with a sequence of classes at different levels in which each class except the lowest includes one or more subordinate classes. At each level from higher to lower there is a splitting or separating into subordinate discrete classes. The Linnaean hierarchy of dividing into seven levels—kingdom, phylum, class, order, family, genus, and species—is a classical example. Or more simply, the bear (*ursus*) subdivided into brown bear, polar bear, and so on is an example of hierarchical taxonomy.

In contrast, a *key* is an arrangement produced by the *overlap* of classes: it is a systematic framework with a sequence of classes, at each level of which more restricted classes are formed by the overlap of two or more classes at the next higher level. Thus, two separate classes of animals such as horned mammals and two-toed mammals can by a process of *overlap* or mixture generate the class of horned two-toed mammals.[1]

Conklin (1964), who distinguishes five methods of classification, confirms the basic distinction between a taxonomic hierarchy (whose constituent taxa or entities are arranged vertically by nondimensional class inclusion and whose hierarchical positions are *not permutable*) and a key which is a multidimensional and hence often *permutable* arrangement of attribute oppositions, which by their hierarchical application help locate the entities being identified.[2]

What relevance do these two taxonomic schemes have for anthropological writings? Mary Douglas in *Purity and Danger* (1966) has in mind a classification based on a hierarchy of classes. According to her, "anomaly" or "dirt" or "abomination" is that which does not fit into an ordered system of categories or is an imperfect member of its class. In fact, she generates a theory of impurity and taboo in terms of anomalies which interfere with keeping categories separate and bounded.[3] Her exegesis of the underlying logic of the Abominations of Leviticus is in terms of a hierarchical scheme of discrete classes.[4]

Edmund Leach in his seminal essay "Animal Categories and Verbal Abuse" (1964) admits his debt to Mary Douglas, and explains the nature of taboo from a perspective similar to hers. He gives a diagrammatic representation of taboo in terms of a Venn diagram of two intersecting circles, with the overlap area being the ambiguous tabooed entity.[5] Leach's exposition of English and Kachin attitudes toward animals as food is based on hierarchical taxonomies, the tabooed entities being those that are interstitial to the discrete classes.

Although Mary Douglas and Edmund Leach have made an important contribution to the theory of taboo, this theory stemming from classification in terms of the logic of hierarchy is not exhaustive or comprehensive. For the *key* form of classification proceeds on the reverse principle and generates new classes by the mixing or overlapping of prior classes. The area of intersection which is tabooed in Leach's Venn diagram is precisely the new class (approved under certain circumstances, disapproved under others) generated by the *key* form. And if one pursues these implications further, one can illuminate a basis for taboo that is unexplored by the Douglas-Leach scheme and which may add to their major contribution.

From a substantive point of view, an example of the generation of a classification by a systematic mixture of classes is to be found in certain portions of the Indian Dharmashastric literature dealing with *varna* and their mixing in approved and disapproved forms of marriage to generate *jati,* occupational groups, and so forth.[6] The close study of this classificatory technique in Indian materials may make possible a substantive contribution to caste theory concerning the relation between *varna* and *jati.*

Let me explain. The relation between *varna* and *jati,* though declared to be crucial by two of the most important figures in Indian sociology (Srinivas and Dumont), is never systematically demonstrated by them.

Srinivas (1952) has stated that the *varna* "provides an all-India framework into which the thousands of *jati* may be fitted"; it was efficacious for the assessment of the status of *jati*-members from one region by those of another; and it provided a scale of upward social mobility for ambitious groups following the route of "sanskritization." Such a weighty statement of the relation between *varna* and *jati* nevertheless fails to clarify their precise linkage.

Following Dumézil, Dumont has given us a formulation of the Indian social hierarchy in terms of the dialectical opposition and combination of the *varna* categories: the Brahman is first defined in opposition to the Kshatriya; these two then collaborate in opposition to the Vaisya; and all three combine to form the twice-born in opposition to the Sudra. Phrased differently, Morality and Religion are superior to and legitimate Politics; and Politics in turn encompasses the Economy. It is this scheme of values that Dumont sees as unique in the Indian system.

But how do the *jati* (castes) fit into the *varna* (status orders) system? Dumont sees the *varna* system and the caste order as having *homologous* structures, both culminating in the Brahmans at the apex. In fact, Dumont compares the relationship between *varna* and *jati* to that between Marx's basic dichotomization of political classes into the bourgeoisie and the proletariat and the more complex social class systems of his historical writings.[7]

Some additional insights into the contributions of these giants can be gained by a close study of the system of ideas expressed in some of the Dharmashastric texts which have been only too familiar to students of Indian society—namely, the *purusha* myth of the creation of *varnas,* and the origins of *jati* through the mixing of *varnas* (*varnasamkara*).

In some ways I am simplifying the texts and crediting them with an unwarranted clarity when I say that they contain a theory of the *generation* of castes (*jati*) and occupational and other groups from the original scheme of *varna* orders. However, I shall lean on Kane (1941), who holds that despite the textual complexities, the underlying import of the texts is as I have described it. Here is Kane's description of the theoretical objectives of the Dharmashastric writers such as Apastamba, Gautama, Baudhayana, Vasistha, Manu, and Vishnu who dilated upon mixed castes and their avocations: "The ancient writers on dharmashastra strive very hard to account for the bewildering ramifications of the caste system from the four varnas that were spoken of in the *sruti* (revelation). There is unanimity on the theory that the numerous castes actually found in the country arose from the unions of males of different varnas with women belonging to varnas differing from their own. The divergences (and they are many) among the several smrtikaras relate only to details" (pp.

50–51). But there is no doubt that the texts present us with certain difficulties. While the categories *varna* and *jati* (caste) are sometimes clearly distinguished (as in Yajnavalkya 11.69), very often they are confounded. In Manu, for instance, we find examples of *varna* being used in the sense of mixed castes (*jati*), and conversely *jati* is used for *varna* (Manu X, 27, 31, 41; III, 15, 177; IX, 86).

Despite these lax usages, it is clear that *varna* and *jati* meant different things and were being brought into a scheme of correlation. As Kane informs us, *varna* is known from the time of Rgveda. In its first appearance, the basic dichotomy expressed by *varna* was that between Arya and Dasyu (both in terms of difference in skin color and culture); subsequently, especially at the time of Brahmana literature, the four *varnas* as we know now were differentiated, with the Shudras probably consisting of Dasyus subjugated and brought into the fold. *Jati*, on the other hand, as a concept hardly appears in Vedic literature and becomes fully developed only among the *smrti* legal writers (for example, *jatidharma* = laws of caste). But the Vedic period, though lacking *jati*, did not lack named crafts and occupational groups, and many of these names later become identified as castes in the *smrti* literature (Kane, 1941: 43ff) and remained so for hundreds of years.

Kane surmises that the *smrti* view of the derivation of numerous castes from the mixture or confusion (*samkara*) of the four *varnas* was not entirely hypothetical or imaginary, for the writers were trying to propound a social theory to account for certain facts on the ground. But the *smrti* writers could not possibly account for all the castes and subcastes in terms of mixed unions. They catalogued and gave the derivation of a limited number, merely suggesting that further numberless mixed castes arose from the repeated unions of the progeny of mixed unions.

It must be recognized that there is great diversity among the *smrti* writers about the actual names and status placement of progeny of mixed unions, about the interpretation of the rules of upward and downward caste mobility (*jatyutkarsa* and *jatyapakarsa*), and about the constituents of the label "mixed castes" (*varnasamkara*) itself.[8] Nevertheless, they all agree on the basic ideas of the hierarchical ordering of the *varnas,* the permissibility of *anuloma* hypergamous unions, and the disapproval of *pratiloma* hypogamous unions, and manifest a remarkably consistent theory of caste generation through mixed marriage.

In the fashionable language of today, we can say that a few *base categories*—namely, the *varna* categories—themselves arranged in a hierarchical order, are subject to combination by means of the application of certain operations or rules, such as *anuloma* (approved) and *pratiloma* (disapproved) unions, and primary marriage and secondary marriage; they thereby generate a number of new ranked categories which we can identify as *jati* (castes) or their analogues.[9]

In terms of classification theory, we can say that the Indian scheme begins with a hierarchical ordering of *varna* categories, and then uses the overlap (key) technique to generate further classes which derive their hierarchical value from the value attached to the prior classes that are mixed. The procedure is represented in Figure 6.1. This figure is based essentially on Manu who, of all the classical writers, has the most elaborate discussion and enumeration of mixed castes. "Manu refers to six *anuloma,* six *pratiloma* and twenty doubly mixed castes and states the avocations of about twenty-three" (Kane, 1941: 57).

Mixed Marriage and the Generative Rules

The generative rules that I shall set out systematically are those contained in *The Laws of Manu* (particularly in Chapters III and X), supplemented by other writers wherever appropriate.

But this consideration must be prefaced with a reference to the all too familiar *purusha* myth, according to which the four *varnas* (status orders) sprang from the primeval man's body—the *Brahmans* (priests) from his mouth, the *Kshatriyas* (warriors) from his arms, the *Vaisyas* (husbandmen) from his thighs, and the *Shudras* (who are condemned to serve them all) from his feet. The *varnas* and their hierarchical ordering are explicit in this origin myth. The *shastric* texts such as Manu enumerated the graduated societal functions of the *varnas* as follows (Manu 1, 87–91; hereafter, all citations from Manu are from Bühler, 1886).

> But in order to protect this universe, He, the most resplendent one, assigned separate (duties and) occupations to those who sprang from his mouth, arms, thighs, and feet.
>
> To Brahmans he assigned teaching and studying (the Veda), sacrificing for their own benefit and for others, giving and accepting (of alms).
>
> The Kshatriya he commanded to protect the people, to bestow gifts, to offer sacrifices, to study (the Veda), and to abstain from attaching himself to sensual pleasures.

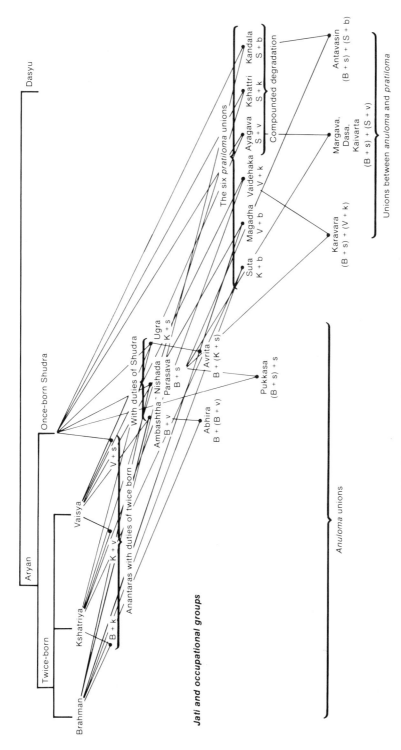

Figure 6.1. From *varna* to *jati* through mixed unions.

The Vaisya to tend cattle, to bestow gifts, to offer sacrifices, to study (the Veda), to trade, to lend money, and to cultivate land.

One occupation only the lord prescribed to the Sudra, to serve meekly even these (other) three castes.

The following restriction, built into the above verses, is reiterated and made more explicit later: "Let the three twice-born castes (varna), discharging their prescribed duties, study the Veda; but among them the Brahmana alone shall teach it, not the other two; that is an established rule" (X, 1).

These ideas I have represented in the upper region of Figure 6.1 as partial evidence for an initial hierarchical scheme of classification by which Manu (and others) postulate a successive scheme of division, first between Aryans and Dasyus, then the Aryans into the twice-born *varna* and the once-born Shudra *varna*, and then again the twice-born into Brahman, Kshatriya, and Vaisya *varnas*. The four *varnas* are explicitly ranked, and it is from this base that the mixture of *varnas* according to the key or overlapping technique is exploited to generate *jati* categories, which are represented in the lower portion of Figure 6.1. This initial ranking of the four *varnas* is a crucial feature in the subsequent generation and ranking of hybrids.

Now let us consider the generative rules for the production, ranking, and placement of hybrids.

There are two basic distinctions which the texts reiterate—that between the Aryans and the non-Aryans (for example, the Dasyus), and among Aryans the distinction between the twice-born Brahmans, Kshatriyas, and Vaisyas and the once-born Shudras. The Dasyus are those "tribes" excluded from the community of those born from Brahma (that is, the four *varnas*), and they are of that status irrespective of whether they speak the language of Mlekkas (barbarians) or that of Aryans.

Consider, for instance, the following rulings:

1a. "He who was begotten by an Aryan on a non-Aryan female may become like to an Aryan by his virtues; he whom an Aryan mother bore to a non-Aryan father is and remains unlike to an Aryan" (Manu X, 67). Thus, only one kind of union—that between an Aryan male and a non-Aryan female, is countenanced; for on the basis of the doctrine of male superiority, an Aryan female (who is higher in status) is polluted by mating with a non-Aryan male who stamps his qualities on the progeny (the ruling that a man can mate beneath him but not a woman beneath her is best understood in terms of the rules stated below).

1b. Marriage between the twice-born and the once-born Shudra is also discountenanced: "Twice-born men, who, in their folly, wed wives of the lower Shudra caste, soon degrade their families and their children to the state of Shudras" (Manu III, 15). It is particularly the unions between Brahman male and Shudra female[10] that are virulently castigated as producing the consequences of hell, loss of rank upon the birth of a child, and so on (see Manu III, 16–19).

2. But this blanket condemnation is softened by the notions of "primary" and "secondary" marriages. The judgment in 1b applies particularly if the union of a twice-born with a Shudra constitutes the only marriage. "For the first marriages of twice-born men, wives of equal caste are recommended, but for those who through desire proceed to marry again, the following females, chosen according to the direct order of the castes, are most approved."

"It is declared that a Shudra woman alone can be the wife of a Shudra, she and one of his own caste the wives of a Vaisya, those two and one of his own caste the wives of a Kshatriya, those three and one of his own caste the wives of a Brahmana" (Manu III, 12–13). Vishnu (XXIV, 1–4) states: "Now a Brahmana may take four wives in the direct order of the (four) castes; a Kshatriya three, a Vaisya two, a Shudra one only."

I shall adopt the following notation in which the capital letter stands for male and the lowercase for the female; a plus sign (+) signifies an additional spouse, and an equals sign (=) signifies the progeny of the union between man and woman.

	Male	Female
Shudra	S	s
Vaisya	V	v
Kshatriya	K	k
Brahman	B	b

Then the differential advantages of marriage or union that fall to the different statuses can be written thus:

$$S : s$$
$$V : v + (s)$$
$$K : k + (v + s)$$
$$B : b + (k + v + s)$$

The higher *varnas* have a greater range of access to women than the lower *varnas*. This differential advantage of access to lower-*varna* women weighted in favor of the higher *varnas* also implies that the Brahman followed by the Kshatriya could generate more kinds of progeny (of mixed-union status).

3. There are listed some eight kinds of marriage but the two basic

categories are, first, the approved or prestigious rite which involves the gift of a daughter to the bridegroom after decking her with costly garments and honoring her with jewels (as in the Brahma and Daiva rites); and, second, the disapproved or nonprestigious rite which involves the bridegroom in giving as much wealth as he can afford to the bride and her kinsmen. The basic distinction is between the "gift" of a virgin together with "dowry," and the "sale" of a girl for "bride-wealth": the first is approved for Brahmans, the second (Asura) is approved for Vaisyas and Shudras, while to the Kshatriya is allotted marriage by capture, or Rakshasa (Manu X, 12–35).

Manu says: "No father who knows the law must take even the smallest gratuity for his daughter; for a man who, through avarice, takes a gratuity is a seller of his offspring" (III, 51). I shall note later how in hypergamy the wife taker also profits by receiving a dowry, a fact which benefits the man of superior status.

4. An underlying distinction which acts as an axiom in the evaluation of mixed marriage is that between male "seed" and female "field" or "soil" in the theory of conception. It is declared that between the two, the male seed is *more important,* but not exclusively so, for "seed sown on barren ground perishes in it," while "good seed, springing up in good soil, turns out perfectly well" (X, 69, 71, 72).

The implications of the relative statuses of male seed and female field in which it is sown are critical for caste theory—critical but also problematic, for a male's superiority cannot automatically lift his progeny from the taint of an inferior mother. Thus, "Sons begotten by twice-born men on wives of the next-lower castes they declare to be similar to their fathers, but blamed on account of the fault inherent in their mothers. Such is the eternal law concerning children born of wives one degree lower than their husbands" (Manu X, 6). "Blamed" in the above rule, which relates to men marrying women of status immediately below them, is interpreted by one commentator as "excluded from the father's caste."

From this evaluation of "seed" and "field" for the status of progeny, three rules can be deduced which are of enormous importance:

4a. Ideally, father and mother should be of the same status, and a child derives the same status bilaterally. "In all castes (*varnas*) those children only which are begotten in the direct order on wedded wives, equal in caste and married as virgins, are considered as belonging to the same caste as their fathers" (Manu X, 5).

4b. But since male seed is superior to female field, it is not repugnant (especially as secondary union) for a man to mate with a woman of lower status, though the child thus born is tarnished. It constitutes an act in the acceptable direction, or "with the hair" (*anuloma*).

4c. The reverse is repugnant and causes a contradiction in and a confusion of hierarchical categories: seed of an inferior-status male cannot fall on the field of a superior status female. It constitutes an act in a nonacceptable direction, or "against the hair" (*pratiloma*).

Anuloma and Pratiloma

The consequences of *anuloma* (a superior-caste man uniting with an inferior-caste woman) and *pratiloma* (an inferior-caste man uniting with a superior-caste woman), usually known in anthropology as hypergamy and hypogamy, are dramatically different and are the subject of much fine categorization and commentary. The "mathematical" permutations and derivations of new castes through mixed unions and the assignation of status positions to them on the basis of *anuloma* and *pratiloma* principles are worth following in detail because they exemplify a mode of formal derivation of a complex system of classification.

ANULOMA

1. *Sons begotten on wives of the next-lower ranks.* I cited earlier (in 4, above) the rule that sons born of wives of the next-lower ranks, though "similar to their fathers," are excluded from their father's caste. Manu defines this more clearly (X, 14) thus: "Those sons of the twice-born, begotten on wives of the next-lower castes, who have been enumerated in due order, they call by the name Anantaras (belonging to the next-lower caste) on account of the blemish inherent in mothers." Many commentators agree that sons of this type of union belong to the mother's caste.

The status of sons born of such unions can be represented according to my system of notation as follows:[11]

The kind of union	Valuation of sons by Manu	Valuation of sons by Baudhanya
B + k	K	B
K + v	V	K
V + s	S	V

But it is to be expected that sons born of wives of the next-lower castes will be in an *intermediate position,* which can be evaluated a little differently on the basis of the superiority of male seed and the rules of hypergamy. Thus, according to the school of Baudhanya, sons begotten on wives of equal or the next-lower caste are called Savarnas ("of equal caste"). However, this evaluation is not confirmed by Vasishtha, who supports Manu's judgment.

In sum, although *B, K, V, S* are regarded as separate *varna* categories, there is room for evaluating more or less positively the product of the union of immediately adjacent categories which are closest in status. They are ambiguous but *acceptable* intermediate categories. Further support for this will appear below.

2. *Sons born of wives of two or three degrees lower.* Sons born of wives of two or three degrees lower are on the one hand begotten on the *anuloma* principle but on the other represent the union of *varna* categories somewhat removed in status. Hence, such unions lead to the generation of *new* castes (or groups). A Brahman male begets on a Vaisya female a son called Ambashtha; on a Shudra female, a Nishada or Parasava. A Kshatriya begets an Ugra son on a Shudra female.

$$B + v = \text{Ambashtha}$$
$$B + s = \text{Nishada}/\text{Parasava}$$
$$K + s = \text{Ugra}$$

These sons are distinctly downgraded (because the unions are more explicitly in violation of the law) and are said to have the "duties of Shudras." The principle which compares sons born of wives of one lower degree and those born of wives of two or three degrees lower is clearly enunciated by Manu (X, 41): "Six sons begotten by Aryans on women of equal and the next-lower castes (Anantaras) have the duties of twice-born men; but all those born in consequence of a violation of the law are, as regards their duties, equal to Shudras." Thus, these six sons born of the following unions have "duties of twice-born":

$$
\begin{array}{ll}
B + b & B + k \\
K + k & K + v \\
V + v & V + s
\end{array}
$$

But three sons born of the following unions have duties of Shudras:

$$
\begin{array}{ll}
B + v & B + s \\
K + s
\end{array}
$$

(The son of a Brahman and a Vaisya female, the Ambashtha, is assigned the occupation of healing by Manu.)

It is clear from the above that the twice-born/once-born, pure/polluted distinction applies with force to Brahman and Kshatriya unions with Shudras (Manu assigns the degrading occupations of catching fish and killing animals to their issue).[12] But the Vaisyas, who are at the bottom of the twice-born hierarchy but adjacent to the once-born Shudras, appear to be allowed an acceptable crossing of the barrier.

But on theoretical grounds we could expect the judgment equally well to go the other way, and the Shudra women to be declared beyond the reach of all twice-born men. Thus, Vasishtha declares that the twice-born must keep within their bounds: a Brahman is permitted three wives according to the order of castes $(b + k + v)$,[13] a Kshatriya two $(k + v)$, a Vaisya *one only* (v), and the Shudra the same (s). Vasishtha pointedly asserts that although some schools declare that twice-born men may marry even a Shudra female, "Let him not act thus" for "the degradation of the family ensues, and after death the loss of heaven" (I, 24–27).

3. *Further anuloma mixed unions.* Theoretically, it should be possible to have further *anuloma* unions between (pure) twice-born men and the female issue of preceding acceptable mixed unions. But the texts do not appear to be interested in multiplying these "permutations." Thus, for instance, there is no listing of the result of the union of a male Brahman with a female born of a Brahman-Kshatriya union $(B + [B + k] = ?)$, or with a female of a Brahman-Vaisya union $(B + [B + v] = ?)$ and the like $(K + [K + v] = ?; V + [V + s] = ?)$.

Curiously, the texts concern themselves with the consequences of Brahman union with females who themselves were born of the union of superior males with women two or three degrees lower (women of Ambashtha and Ugra status). According to Manu, the union of a Brahman with an Ambashtha female produces an Abhira; that with an Ugra female, an Avrita:

$$B + (B + V) = \text{Abhira}$$
$$B + (K + s) = \text{Avrita}$$

Another mixture which, though in the acceptable *anuloma* direction, contravenes the distinction between twice-born and Shudra is the union of a Nishada male with a Shudra woman to produce a Pukkasa: $(B + s) + s = \text{Pukkasa}$. Why the texts are more concerned with these less acceptable unions will be discussed below.

4. *The upward mobility of anuloma issue through repeated marriage.* There is a truly remarkable statement in Manu (and other *shastric* writers)[14] concerning the possibilities of upward and downward social mobility (*jatyutkarsa* and *jatyapakarsa*, respectively) through certain kinds of *repeated* marriage conforming to the rules of *anuloma*. I am particularly interested here in the rules for achieving improvement of status upward.

"If a female of the caste, sprung from a Brahmana and a Shudra female, bear children to one of the highest caste, the inferior tribe attains the highest caste within the seventh generation. Thus, a Shudra attains the rank of a Brahmana, and in a similar manner a Brahmana sinks to the level of a Shudra; but know that it is the same with the offspring of a Kshatriya or of a Vaisya" (Manu X, 64, 65).

According to Bühler, the various schools of law essentially put two interpretations upon the question of the mechanics of upward mobility. In the one case, if a female child of a Brahman male and a Shudra female—that is, a Parasava (or Nishada) female—and her descendants all marry Brahmans, the offspring of the sixth female descendant of the original couple will be a Brahman. The second interpretation goes thus: if a Parasava son (offspring of a Brahman male and a Shudra female) marries a most excellent Parasava female and his descendants do the same, the child born in the sixth generation will be a Brahman (see Figure 6.2, left and right).

The remarkable aspect of this mechanism of upward mobility is that, as in interpretation 1, the inferior female is encouraged to unite consistently with a superior male. This, of course, is the blueprint for hypergamy which exists even today in India, not so much across distant castes but either between ranks within a caste or between adjacent castes. Hypergamy is consistent with male superiority; it is in the

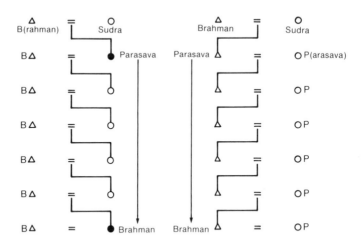

Figure 6.2. Two interpretations of upward mobility in Indian society. (After Bühler, 1886.)

right *anuloma* direction. The second interpretation promises a rise in status as a result of consistently impeccable endogamy—that is, marriage with persons of an equal status after the initial asymmetrical one. This is the preponderant rule of marriage among most Hindus. Thus, the two interpretations can be placed within the orthodox hypergamy-endogamy parameter.

True to the differential evaluation of the *varna* orders and the differential advantages accruing to them, the offspring of a Brahman and Vaisya union are promised Brahman status in the *fifth* generation, and of a Brahman and Kshatriya union in the third generation, if they follow the path of recommended repeated marriage on the lines discussed above.[15]

PRATILOMA

Unlike *anuloma,* it is *pratiloma* unions which, going "against the hair," are "in the inverse order of castes" and therefore cause a true "confusion of castes." Though heavily censured, paradoxically they are enumerated in some detail. I shall later attempt to account for this paradox and its implications for the theory of caste classification.

The aversion to and moral condemnation of *pratiloma* is evidenced in this pronouncement by Manu: "By adultery committed by persons of different castes, by marriages with women who ought not to be married, and by the neglect of the duties and occupations prescribed to each, are produced sons who owe their origin to a confusion of the castes" (X, 24). Manu lists six *pratilomas*[16] which can be placed in the following hierarchical order (from high to low) as gleaned from rules subsequently stated.

Son of a Kshatriya male and a Brahman woman: $K + b =$ Suta
Son of a Vaisya male and a Brahman woman: $V + b =$ Magadha
Son of a Vaisya male and a Kshatriya woman: $V + k =$ Vaidehaka

Son of a Shudra male and a Vaisya woman: $S + v =$ Ayogava
Son of a Shudra male and a Kshatriya woman: $S + k =$ Kshattri
Son of a Shudra male and a Brahman woman: $S + b =$ Kandala, the lowest of mortals

Vasishtha also heartily disapproves of these unions "from the inverse order of the castes" and therefore "destitute of virtue and good conduct" (Bühler, 1882, pt. II, ch. 21). It is declared that a Shudra who "approaches a female" of the Brahman caste is thrown into a fire, and the (polluted) woman concerned is shaved, her body is anointed with butter, and she is then placed naked on a black donkey and conducted along the highroad in order to be purified. Vaisya and Kshatriya males cohabiting with a Brahman woman merit the same punishment; the only difference as far as the woman is concerned is that a yellowish and then a white donkey are correspondingly substituted (black, yellow, white are colors of decreasing impurity).

In Manu, all *pratiloma* issue are declared to be *excluded* from the Aryan community. However, among them there is a rank order of *pratiloma* which can be listed as follows: among twice-born, the *varna* statuses of the superior female and inferior male count with respect to the ordering of their *pratiloma* children; thus, a Suta is superior to a Magadha, who is superior to a Vaidehaka. But when there is a crossing of the twice-born/once-born barrier, and inferior Shudra males unite with superior twice-born females, then there is a *reversal* in the principle of degradation, which operates by "geometrical progression": the sons of a Shudra man's union with higher females are rated *lower* than his sons by more inferior women, so that an Ayogava rates higher than a Kshattri, who in turn is superior to the Kandala, who is the son of a Shudra and a Brahman female and is the lowest of mortals.

The principle of *compounded degradation,* which is truly an inversion of the ordinary *anuloma* status rules, is unambiguously stated.

First and foremost, all possibility of *mobility* (accessible to *anuloma* issue) through successive correct and superior marriages is denied *pratiloma* issue: "These six Pratilomas beget similar races (varna) on women of their own caste, they also produce the like with females of their mother's caste (gati), and with females of higher ones" (Manu X, 27).

Second, not only is mobility denied but a repetition of *pratiloma* unions *compounds the degradation.* "These six . . . also beget, the one on the females of the other, a great many kinds of despicable sons, even more sinful than their fathers, and excluded from the Aryan community (vahya)" (Manu X, 29). "Just as a Shudra begets on a Brahmana female a being excluded from the Aryan community, even so a person himself excluded procreates with females of the four castes (varna) sons more worthy of being excluded than he himself" (Manu X, 30).

Although a second repetition of the deprecated *pratiloma* union is denounced, the law texts go on to state precisely the mathematical properties of such mixtures: "Men excluded by the Aryans (vahya) who approach families of higher rank beget races (varna) still more worthy to be excluded, low men (hina), still lower races, *even fifteen in number*" (Manu X, 31, italics added).

One of the interpretations given of the above rule (favored by Bühler following Raghavananda, Narada, and Kulluka; see *Laws of Manu*, p. 409)[17] illustrates the simple calculation adopted. The ruling is taken to apply to the six *pratiloma* issue of wrong *varna* unions already enumerated. The lowest among them, the Kandala $(S + b)$, may produce with females of the five higher *pratilomas* five *more degraded* races, the Kshattri $(S + k)$ similarly with the four above him, the Ayogava $(S + v)$ with the three above him, the Vaideha $(V + k)$ two, and the Magadha $(V + b)$ one. The total of more degraded races is thus $5 + 4 + 3 + 2 + 1 = 15$.

"More degraded races" born of repeated confusion of castes. The law texts list numerous castes of still other *pratiloma* mixtures which compound the error: thus, men who are progeny of *pratiloma* unions unite a) with superior women of the four *varna*, b) with superior women who are the issue of *anuloma*, c) with women who are themselves products of previous *pratiloma* unions, and so forth.

The distinctive character of these *pratiloma* progeny is that they are assigned to an infinite number of base occupations practiced in general today by various polluted castes, the majority of them falling into the category called Harijans.

I give below an incomplete list of such castes (stating in parentheses the details of their mixed origin in terms of the notation I have adopted). They are all declared to be "base-born of Aryans," or produced in consequence of a "violation of the law" (*ap-adhvamsaya*), who shall subsist by occupations reprehended by the twice-born. They shall not only be known by their occupations of the most demeaning kind but also by their place of residence, food, clothing, and the like: "Let these tribes dwell near well known trees and burial grounds and in groves, known by certain marks and subsisting by their peculiar occupations" (Manu X, 50). They are to dress in garments of the dead, eat food from broken dishes, wander from place to place; they are not allowed at night in villages and towns; they are compelled to transport corpses of dead who have no relatives, and act as executioners of criminals; the most outcaste of them (such as the Kandalas and Svapakas) are condemned to dwell outside the village, and their wealth shall be dogs and donkeys.

We can summarize the generation of degraded castes in three steps.

1. Following are the occupations of the six archetypal *pratilomas* who derive from the confusion of the four basic *varna* categories:

Suta $(K + b)$	Management of horses and chariots
Magadha $(V + b)$	Trade
Vaidehaka $(V + k)$	The service of women (guardians in the harem)
Ayogava $(S + v)$	Carpentry
Kshattri $(S + k)$	Catching and killing animals living in holes
Kandala, the lowest of mortals $(S + b)$	Dwelling outside the village, their wealth being dogs and donkeys

2. Following are the occupations of the heavily censured issue of *anuloma* unions, which though in the right direction yet cross the barrier between the twice-born and once-born, a crossing which is particularly heinous for the Brahman and Kshatriya (but not for the Vaisya) according to some schools.

Nishada $(B + s)$	Catching fish
Ugra $(K + s)$	Catching and killing animals that live in holes
Pukkasa $(([B + s] + S)$	Catching and killing animals that live in holes

3. Let us enumerate the implications of still more confused unions between the progeny of *anuloma* and *pratiloma* unions.

The unions between issue of "unacceptable" *anuloma* and despised *pratiloma,* and of double *pratiloma* unions, reproduce and frequently increase the initial degradation. Technically there can be three kinds of these unions:

a. Male issue of (unacceptable) *anuloma* mating with female issue of *pratiloma* to produce children—for example:
Nishada male and Vaideha female $(B + s) + (V + k)$
= Karavara, leather worker.
Nishada male and Kandala female $(B + s) + (S + b)$
= Antyavasayin,[18] employed in burial grounds, despised even by those already excluded.
Nishada male and Vaideha female $(B + s) + (V + k)$
= Ahindika, occupation not given.

Nishada male and Ayogava female $(B + s) + (S + v)$
= Margava, Dasa, or Kaivarta, who subsist as boatmen.

b. Male issue of *pratiloma* unions mating with females produced by (unacceptable) *anuloma* unions to produce children—for example:
Kandala male and Pukkasa female $(S + b) + ([B + s] + s)$
= Sopaka, who follows "sinful occupation" of Kandala.

c. Double *pratiloma* union—for example:
Kandala male and Vaideha female $(S + b) + (V + k)$
= Pandusopaka, who deals in cane.

Non-Aryan ethnic groups located in terms of confusion of castes.
The Aryans in India are alleged to have encountered diverse alien ethnic groups variously called Dravida, Dasyu, and so on. Here is an example of how two such alien ethnic groups—the Andhra of the Deccan and the Meda of southeast Rajput—are placed on the margins of the classification grid by characterizing them as products of sexual unions in "the inverse order of castes." Thus, an Andhra is said to be the product of a union between a Vaidehaka male and a Karavara female: $(V + k) + ([B + s] + [V + k]) =$ Andhra. And a Meda is described as the product of a union between a Vaidehaka male and a Nishada female: $(V + k) + (B + s) =$ Meda. Finally, a Dasyu (non-Aryan) male unites with an Ayogava female $(S + v)$ to produce a Sairandhra, who is described as living like a slave and subsisting by snaring animals.

The Social Implications of the Classification Scheme

We have seen in detail how a scheme of ranked castes (and analogous groups) has been generated through the systematic mixing of categories (the *key* forms of classification). But the beauty of the total scheme is that because we start with four ranked *varna* categories (derived on the basis of hierarchical taxonomy) and because the procedures for mixing are themselves evaluated as approved or disapproved and so on, the categories progressively generated are themselves in turn automatically ranked. This makes it possible to comprehend a whole universe of numerous castes, all in principle capable of being *ranked* and *interrelated* into a single scheme.

Although several kinds of permutations and mixtures are possible in a mathematical sense, and although the classical legal theorists considered both approved hypergamous mixing and disapproved hypogamous mixing, paradoxically the theorists were more concerned with the generation of castes and occupational groups through the unsanctioned and repudiated forms of intermixing. How can we explain this paradox?

It seems to me that *pratiloma* is a convenient intellectual device for generating various disapproved categories, assigning them degraded positions, and ideologically explaining and rationalizing why so many groups in the caste hierarchy are placed in low or downtrodden positions. In other words, the rationale of a formula which mixes the basic *varna* categories in approved and disapproved ways to produce a classificatory scheme becomes understandable in a hierarchical society which has a steep gradation of statuses. Although caste society may or may not in its actual demographic composition constitute a pyramid, its evaluation of statuses and ritual and occupational roles must necessarily be pyramidal. The pure statuses are few, the impure are legion. The economy of the distribution of purity and impurity makes this inevitable. This is the reason why the law books show little interest in permuting the unions of the approved *anuloma* type between the twice-born beyond a point (for high-level positions in a society are necessarily few) and show an unexpected preoccupation with permuting *pratiloma*-type unions, for these, though morally condemned, are in fact the vehicle for producing the many lowly positions in society.

There is another closely related point. In the catalogue of *anuloma* and *pratiloma* unions and further derivations from their mixtures, the participation of the Brahman *varna* exceeds that of the Kshatriya and Vaisya *varnas*.[19] From the point of view of caste theory this is remarkable, for what we have here is the purest and highest *varna* being in a sense the most lax of the twice-born strata! But there is a method to this madness. The consequence of this mythical derivation of castes propounded by Brahmans is that a number of castes, many of them indeed beyond the pale, can and do relate their mythical origins to a Brahmanical ancestor, male or female, who was degraded. Ethnographers have reported many of these origin myths of low castes.[20] This mythical charter which the impure use to bolster their claims also implicitly and tacitly reinforces the fact that the Brahmans are—because they are the point of reference—the fountainhead of purity and the apex of the pyramid.

From the perspective of classification theory, we can predict over what issues the classical lawyers would disagree or show discrepant judgments. We know that the important boundaries in the categorical system are those between Aryan and non-Aryan, between twice-born and once-born, and among the three *varnas* within the twice-born. The phenomena which are the subject of discrepant interpretations by the *shastric* writers are precisely those mixtures which create ambiguities, as a) when adjacent rather than more distant categories mix (Is the child of a Brahman male and a Kshatriya female—who is like his father but bears his mother's blemish—a Brahman or a Kshatriya?); and b) when *adjacency* permits union, but when at the same time the distinction between twice-born and once-born is a barrier (Does the product of a Vaisya male and a Shudra have or not have the "duties of the twice-born"?).

Toward an Interactional View of Pollution Rules

I shall try to demonstrate that the two rules of *direct order and inverse order of castes* applied to the four basic *varna* categories are the underlying design of the various *shastric* formulations on pollution.

My task has been to a great extent made easy by Orenstein's three articles on ritual defilement in Hindu Sacred Law (Orenstein, 1965, 1968, 1970). Although Orenstein's discussion of the pollution rules is illuminating, it is my view that his labels for the three types of pollution he isolates are unsatisfactory and that he fails to see some of the logic of the underlying design.[21]

I do not pretend that I can unravel the underlying design of all the pollution rules stated by the *shastric* writers, since certain statements show inconsistencies. I merely want to show the path to an interactional view of pollution based on the "interrelation of castes," both approved and disapproved, and to do so I shall exploit Orenstein's analyses.

Relational Pollution (Especially between Varna/Caste Equals)

By "relational pollution" Orenstein referred particularly to pollution incurred by virtue of relations of kinship on the occasions of birth and death. Ego is polluted for a stipulated period of time irrespective of physical nearness—for example, whether or not he has had contact with the deceased is of no account in death pollution. The graduated periods for observance of pollution depending on closeness of kinship (*sapinda*) and affinity are well known. The texts talk of pollution spreading through the group whose members are considered as being "connected by particles of the same body."

From a *varna* point of view, Orenstein formulates the following paradigm as regards "relational pollution": "Holding constant such factors as degree of relationship, the amount of pollution incurred is inversely proportional to the rank of the *varna* in which the event takes place." The principle that the lower the *varna* the greater the birth and death pollution is well attested by the law codifiers. Thus, according to both Vishnu and Manu, the impurity of a Brahman caused by the birth or death of a *sapinda* lasts ten days, of a Kshatriya twelve days, of a Vaisya fifteen days, and of a Shudra one month (Manu V, 83; Vishnu XXII, 1–4).

In his 1968 essay Orenstein adds a few more details which make problematic the exposition of relational pollution he gave in 1965. There are internal differences among Brahmans which make them unequally subject to relational pollution: a Brahman who knows the Vedas and tends the sacred fire achieves purity in the event of birth and death pollution in one day, a Brahman who knows the Vedas but does not tend the fire achieves purity in three days, and a Brahman who does neither in ten days. A similar decreasing scale applies to the four *ashramas:* the householder is most subject to relational pollution, then the student, then the forest hermit, and least of all the *sannyasi.*

The rules of pollution associated with birth and death apparently provide some sort of puzzle for caste theorists. They force even Dumont into a quite uncharacteristic explanation which he deplored in Dubois and James Mill and which he has dubbed "voluntaristic" (1970: 23–34). This is the species of explanation which attributes certain customs and "superstitions" to a deliberate invention by priests for their benefit. Let us allow Dumont himself to comment on certain rules which are for him "incomprehensible from the point of view of purity":

> But above all, starting from the Dharmasutras of Gautama and Vasistha, one finds illogical injunctions, which later became very widespread. These are those which prescribe, all other things being equal, an increasing period of impurity for decreasing status: in the case of death, close relations are impure for ten days for Brahmans, twelve for Kshatriyas, fifteen for Vaishyas and thirty for Shudras.
>
> . . . But, going by the nature of the system, we would expect the contrary, for impurity is more powerful than purity, and the higher the degree of purity to be regained, the more severe should be the effect of impurity. Either we have not yet managed to enter into the spirit of the system, or else *the Brahmans*

have here transformed into a privilege what ought to be a greater incapacity. (Pp. 70–71, italics added.)

I believe that there is a simple and more acceptable explanation for the rules of relational pollution which reasonably follows from the requirements of "the direct order of castes."

First, we know that the higher the *varna* position, the higher the natural condition of purity (under normal circumstances). Death and birth pollution essentially refer to the bodily and therefore *kinship connection between status equals*. Death and birth pollute kinsmen by virtue of this connection alone. Hence, it would be completely antithetical to the basis of *varna* status differentiation if death or birth conferred on a Brahman greater impurity than on a Kshatriya and so on down the line, for this would attack the very doctrine of the sharing of "particles of body" and kinship which makes a Brahman superior to Kshatriya, a Kshatriya to a Vaisya, and so on. It is clear that the normal doctrine that pollution attacks the pure more than the impure *cannot* be allowed to work here, for it would *undermine the hierarchy itself.* The premises of hierarchy stem from the logic of the "direct order of castes" and the differential dominance it implies.

How do we explain the fact that the Brahman who knows the sacred Vedas and tends the sacred fire is less prone to relational pollution in the event of birth and death than one who is less virtuous; and that a *sannyasi* is less prone than a forest hermit, who in turn is less prone than a student, who in turn is less prone than a householder? This is strictly in line with Hindu religious aspirations: the more virtuous and religious, the more removed from the chains of the physical and organic world and the physical and organic body. Therefore, this detachment from the world which increases with the progressive renunciation of a gross householder's or a nonreligious man's state also means *greater immunity from the bodily connections of kinship.* Thus, at the highest peak of achievement the true *sannyasi* renounces the world, transcends family bonds and caste status, and becomes a detached individual in a hierarchical group-minded society.

Birth and death within the kinship group thus have different polluting potencies not only for different *varnas* but also among men of different religious achievements. The more sacred the personal status the less subject to social bonds; the higher the caste status the less polluting the bonds of kinship (particles of body) shared by that status group.

A marvelous confirmation of the thesis that pollution rules relating to death and pollution are based on the privileges of "direct order of castes" is to be found in the following rules formulated by Vishnu (XXII, 19, 21–24).

> 19. Wives and slaves in the direct order of the castes (those who do not belong to a higher caste than their lord) remain impure as long as their lord.
> 21. If *sapindas* of a higher caste (are born or have died) the period of impurity has for their lower-caste relations the same duration as for members of the higher caste.
> 22. A Brahmana (to whom) *sapindas* of the Kshatriya, Vaisya, or Shudra castes (have been born or have died) becomes pure within six nights, or three nights, or one night, respectively.
> 23. A Kshatriya (to whom *sapindas* of the) Vaisya or Shudra castes (have been born or have died) is purified within six and three nights, respectively.
> 24. A Vaisya (to whom *sapindas* of the) Shudra caste (have been born or have died) becomes pure within six nights.

What verse 19 establishes is that we are dealing with *anuloma* unions. Particularly relevant here are verses 21–24, which refer to kinship between *varnas* as a result of *anuloma*. How do we interpret the fact that while the superior *varna* or caste regains purity in less time according to the degree of inferiority of the affine, the lower-status affine observes pollution for his superior affine for the same duration as this superior's own caste members? For example, although a Brahman achieves purity in ten nights where a fellow Brahman kinsman is concerned, he achieves purity in six nights, three nights, and one night where the kinsman is a Kshatriya, Vaisya, and Shudra respectively. But these last three achieve purity in ten nights where a Brahman kinsman is concerned, thereby being subject to impurity for the same period as members of Brahman status.

What this asymmetry seems to be saying is this. From the Brahman's point of view, the strength of his kinship or *sapinda* relationship to persons of inferior *varnas* is *weaker* than is the case from the point of view of the lower-status affine for whom it is *stronger,* as strong as it is for equals in the superior varna! This asymmetrical valuation of "affinal" link becomes comprehensible when we see it as finding concrete expression in the Nambudiri-Nayar *tali*-tying relationship. For the Nambudiri, the relationship if consummated is concubinage; for the Nayar, it is marriage. The Nayar woman and child must observe death pollution when the Nambudiri man in question dies, but he does no such thing when the linked Naya woman dies. Here are differential evaluations of the strength of the same relation according to the dominance and differentiated privilege implied by the "direct order of castes."

There is one special sort of death pollution that I must allude to briefly. The texts minimize or curtail pollution, or declare the total absence of pollution falling on kinsmen in cases of suicide (including those who die by fasting, taking poison, or hanging), and in cases of death penalty or killing administered by the king or by Brahmans, presumably for offenses or polluting actions (Orenstein, 1968: 32, for textual references). Here the texts seem to be asserting that the relationship of kinship or *sapinda* does not bear the burden of sharing the blame and impurity of violent deaths, or deaths meted out for crimes which are matters of "personal" rather than "collective" and "relational" responsibility, in the same way as, for instance, "self-pollution" induced by personal circumstances does not spread to others if the person polluted keeps himself separate from others and avoids social contact.

The second major class of pollution rules Orenstein isolates are given the label *act pollution* (called in the 1965 essay *transitive pollution*). This involves some kind of interaction or contact with biological phenomena, life substance, and process. Orenstein subdivides act pollution into internal pollution and external pollution.

Internal Pollution

Here "ego as subject acts upon an object" and incurs impurity particularly by inflicting injury on living things, especially by destroying life. The pollution incurred by the sinner is proportional to the purity of the victim's *varna* or sacredness. The penance imposed for killing a Brahman is heavier than that imposed for killing a Kshatriya and so on. Thus, one may say that defilement is proportionate to the magnitude of the crime, which in turn is measured according to the purity or sacredness of the victim. The classical acts condemned as mortal sins (*mahapataka*) under this rubric are killing a cow or a bullock, or a Brahman, committing adultery with a guru's wife, stealing gold from Brahmans, drinking Sura (Manu XI, 55). Other acts condemned include reviling the Vedas, eating forbidden food, drinking spirits, committing incest with sisters by the same mother, having intercourse with unmarried maidens, slaying kine, and committing usury (see Manu XI); these range over a wide spectrum of injuries, crimes, sexual deviations, use of violence, and the like. We may construe these acts as primarily signifying attacks launched or injuries inflicted by a person on other persons or objects, the most serious of which are those "mortal sins" committed by inferiors on persons or things of a superior status.

In the light of this perspective, what Orenstein labels "act pollution: internal pollution" is also relational in my terms, in that it deals with disapproved "social" contact between persons and things. Orenstein further fails to see that the logic of this class of offenses is based on the principle of the "direct order of castes" in two reinforcing senses: first, the higher the status of the person, animal, or object injured the greater the penance/punishment/impurity that befalls the offender; second, the higher the status of the offender usually the less severe the punishment meted out than for offenders of lower status for the same crime or offense. In this sense the scheme for calculating the degree of punishment guards the privileges of those of higher status.

External Pollution

External pollution is simply the reverse of the above, in that a person becomes polluted by coming into contact with an inferior or a defiling object. "The extent of Ego's external pollution is proportionate to the defilement of the *varna* he contacts; for example, a Vaishya's corpse defiles more than does a Brahman's" (Orenstein, 1968: 116).

The implication of these rules is that the high castes are required to undergo more thorough purification and rituals than the low castes: the paradigm of external pollution is that "holding constant the things with which Ego interacts, he is polluted in proportion to the rank of his *varna*" (Orenstein, 1965: 7).

Translating this into our idiom, we may say that these rules which punish the higher castes more than the inferior for engaging in polluting contacts appear to follow the logic of "the inverse order of castes" in order to prevent the "confusion of castes" and other similar consequences. The law books devote much space and verbal skill to defining the pollutions through contact against which men of caste must guard with eternal vigilance: drinking from an untouchable's cup, eating foods that have been eaten by low castes, having sexual intercourse with women of low caste, living in the house of a degraded caste man, or coming into contact with a corpse, with a menstruating woman, or with polluting substances.

The familiar arithmetic is brought into operation in the stipulation of penance. If a Brahman eats the leavings of a Shudra's meal, a Vaisya's meal, a Kshatriya's meal, and a fellow Brahman's meal, he must do penance by living on milk for seven days, five days, three days, and one day respectively. If a Kshatriya eats the leavings of a Shudra's meal and a Vaisya's meal, he does similar penance for five days and three days respectively. A Vaisya who eats the leavings of a Shudra's meal must live on milk for three days.

The logic of these rules stems from the simple precept that the higher the purity status of a man the greater his defilement by impurity, especially that stemming from a lower-level person or object. Conversely, the logic says that a lower-caste person insofar as he is permanently more polluted than a higher-caste person does not proportionately heap more pollution upon himself through defiling contact, and can return to his status quo ante more easily than a superior-status person, whose fall is proportionately steeper and the purification entailed correspondingly more elaborate. This logic is, of course, the precise reverse of that entailed in relational pollution resulting from birth and death.

Finally, what Orenstein calls self-pollution, where Ego pollutes himself through substances secreted from his own body, and where a man defiles himself by eating, defecating, or urinating, naturally comes within the scope of "inverse order of castes": the higher the status of the person in question the more elaborate the ablutions, the baths, the sipping of water. In these instances a person "contacts" and contaminates himself. As may be expected, the severity of purification required is not only proportionate to the superiority of *varna* status but also of spiritual status. A student, an ascetic, a hermit respectively undergo more stringent purification than a (Brahman) householder.

With respect to self-pollution, Orenstein faces a puzzle for which he produces a convoluted and cumbersome answer but for which perhaps a simpler one can be found. He is puzzled by the problem of "compounded pollution," as formulated by the *shastric* writers. Why do they pay special attention to the combining of "self-pollution" with "external pollution" (that is, coming into contact with defiling persons or objects while suffering from self-pollution) in that order, and why do they compound the resulting pollution to an extent that is more severe than the individual acts taken singly? "In general, it appears that if one has polluting contacts with others while in self-pollution, the result is not as if one 'stain' were simply added to another; rather one is much more defiled" (Orenstein, 1970: 28). A final question posed by Orenstein is why the theorists deal only with "compounded pollution" caused by the mixing of self-pollution with external pollution, and not by the mixing of other kinds of pollution.

The answers to all these problems are possibly already given in my previous account of the generation of mixed castes.

There I pointed out that while many forms of *anuloma* and *pratiloma* mixing between the *varnas* were theoretically possible, the theorists were more interested in generating the more degraded forms, and of these degraded forms the most severe "compounded degradation" possible was the doubling of the principle of "inverse order of castes."[22] A good example of compounded degradation in mixed unions resulting in exclusion from the Aryan community was the union of a man, who was the product of a Shudra father and a Brahman mother, with a Brahman woman, $(S + b) + b$: a case of double or repeated "confusion" of *varnas,* or of "inversions" of *varna* or caste order. Similarly, of all the permutations of pollution possible in Orenstein's classification, there is only one mixing in which the theorists would predictably be interested, because it represents a repeated compounding of the "inverse order of castes" (the higher the *varna*/caste status the greater the resulting defilement). This is the mixing of self-pollution with external pollution. The other two forms, relational and internal pollution in Orenstein's classification, are based on the "direct order of castes."

The *shastras* conceived of self-pollution as rendering a person vulnerable; women particularly were very vulnerable in this state; and external pollution defiled a person much more in this state than in ordinary circumstances because excretions and adhesions associated with bodily processes were dangerous marginal stuff that acted as powerful conductors of impurity, multiplying or compounding the intensity of pollution.

Toward a View of Purity and Pollution

The above discussion of the rules underlying the *shastric* theory of the generation of castes shows how far the underlying design is from a *taxonomy* which implies progressive *segmentation* into less inclusive classes that are kept separate and discrete and considered nonpermutable. I have also indicated that there is a correspondence between the structure of hierarchical taxonomy and that of Douglas's approach to pollution and purity: the corollary of the keeping of categories mutually separate is the generation of marginal stuff, intermediate substances, anomalies of taboo objects, and so on.

While we must recognize the importance of this perspective and take into account the manifestation of inclusion and exclusion in caste behavior, we must also take into account the implications of another perspective if we are to understand caste behavior more fully. The caste system also emphasizes the *rules for and consequences of the interrelation of castes*. In other words, the Indian caste mentality is very much concerned with the implications of approved and disapproved contact or relation between differently valued and hierarchically ordered categories. Like all law codes, the classical Dharmashastra texts generate a grammar of "ungrammatical" (immoral/unlawful/disapproved) conduct. They are concerned more with what ought not to be done rather than with what should be done.

It is only in this perspective that one can appreciate not only the basic rules relating to contacts that are in accordance with the direct order and the inverse order of castes, but also the fact that many of the situations against which the law codes legislate are *unrealistic*. It is as improbable for a Brahman to eat a Shudra's leavings as for a Western factory owner to eat with his trash collector. Much of Manu's code shows the mind of a lawyer writing up rules for exigencies and emergencies rather than for everyday life. On reading these rules, one might imagine that an Indian village would consist of highly exclusive groups having much less social contact than peasant communities which are not weighed down by rules of purity and pollution. This is objectively false. Despite Srinivas's characterization of Indian village social relations as "back to back" rather than "face to face," the quantitative aspects of social interaction in an Indian village are probably no different from that in other stratified societies. The interrelation between castes is best seen in the *jajmani* relationships, in ritual exchange, in graded participation of castes in temple festivals, and in the rites of passage staged by superior-caste patrons. The rules of commensality and connubium can thus be seen as focusing on contact rather than segregation.

How does the picture look when we view *pollution* as disapproved contact between superior and inferior entities, or as the disapproved movement or overflow of a defiling entity onto a purer or uncontaminated entity, and when we define *purity* as signifying approved contact between entities, or as the approved withdrawal from preexisting contact with the impure?

The difference in focus is best illustrated in relation to the notorious body substances—saliva, body hair, nail parings, urine, excreta—that inevitably make their appearance in any discussion of impurity. Rather than think of them always as marginal stuff or ambiguous substances and therefore anomalous and impure, I suggest that they be considered somewhat differently, as *boundary overflows* which threaten to flow from their sources to adjacent entities, or which conduct back to the host the condition of others—that is, as substances that relate or join adjacent entities to produce either good or bad effects.

Boundary overflows which may connect two adjacent entities or categories can be both negatively and positively evaluated. Where negatively evaluated they constitute pollution, as exemplified by contact with body impurities, impure foods, and so on. These are all overflows from beings or objects whose natural condition is one of more or less pollution, but pollution nevertheless.

The overflows from a pure object can, however, be eminently purifying, as in the case of the five sacred products of the cow; or, less dramatically, the leavings of food offered to and eaten by the pure gods; or, more dramatically, the water with which a saintly guru's feet have been washed. Within the sphere of everyday caste life, the same principle is at work when the food leavings of the Brahmans are acceptable food to polluted castes, or when various categories of cooked food may pass from superior patrons to inferior clients.

The inevitable consequence of undesirable direct contact is that pure beings are polluted by the impure. There are, however, compensating remedial actions. Water is a primary vehicle of cleansing. Objects can be given relative values in terms of their resistance to the action of impurity. In this sense, gold is purer than silver, and silver purer than iron; silk is more pollution resistant than cotton; brass cooking vessels are less attacked by dirt than clay vessels. Such permanently graded objects and substances are the *wedges*, the *vehicles*, and the *conductors* by which polluting contact is neutralized and purity restored. But religious acts and the acquiring of sacred knowledge are also eminently cleansing, and the texts fuse "spiritual" action and "instrumental" action with the aid of objects. Thus, Vishnu says (XXII, 88): "Sacred knowledge, religious austerities, fire, holy food (*Pankagavya*), earth, the mind, water, smearing (with cow dung), air, the morning and evening prayers and other religious acts, the sun, and time (by the lapse of ten days of impurity and the like) are purifiers of animate objects."

These are but the preliminary steps toward a *transactional* theory of purity and pollution, which is more in accord with McKim Marriott's (1968) analysis of the logic of food transactions between castes than with Mary Douglas's speculations on the same subject.[23] Mary Douglas's argument runs as follows: "In India the cooking process is seen as the beginning of ingestion, and therefore cooking is susceptible to pollution, in the same way as eating. But why is this complex found in India and in parts of Polynesia and in Judaism and other places, but not wherever humans sit down to eat? I suggest that food is not likely to be polluting at all unless the external boundaries of the social system are under pressure" (1966: 127). She proceeds to argue: "We can go further to explain why the actual cooking of the food in India must be ritually pure. The purity of the castes is correlated with an elaborate hereditary division of labour between castes. The work performed by each caste carries a symbolic load: it says something about the relatively pure status of the caste in question . . . But the point at which food is prepared for the table is the point at which the interrelation between the purity and the occupational structure needs to be set straight. For food is produced by the combined efforts of several castes . . . Before being admitted to the body some clear symbolic break is needed to express food's separation from necessary but impure contacts. The cooking process, entrusted to pure hands, provides this ritual break. Some such break we would expect to find whenever the production of food is in the hands of the relatively impure" (pp. 126–127).

At best this is only half the story about "Indian pollution symbolism regarding cooked food." An important index of caste status arises from the *passage of food between castes,* and it is through food transactions that relative positions are demonstrated and validated. It is this *dynamic* aspect of relationship between castes through food exchange that is missing in Douglas and present in Marriott.

Marriott (1968) argues that the attributional index (the possession of qualities and the practice of customs) is not a consistent guide to the logic of ranking of castes practiced by the villagers of Kishan Garhi. He finds this key in the matrix of food transactions (a transactional index). Ultimately, Marriott's argument rests on social dominance and dependence deriving from the direction of giving and taking. "Gaining dominance over others through feeding them or securing dependence on others through being fed by them appear to be comprehensive goals of actors in the system of transactions" (p. 169). Marriott's model "is based on an implicit local postulate of the symbolic equivalence of transactions in any medium between any two castes, *high rank always deriving from the giving, low rank from the receiving of foods*" (p. 170).

Although Marriott's displaying of the mechanics of mutual ranking through food transactions is revelatory, we should note that in caste relations it is not in all spheres that the giver is superior to the receiver. This is largely so with food and other material transactions, but the logic is *reversed* in marriage and sexual unions. *Anuloma* unions, hypergamy, and the like rest on the principle that a woman is freely given as a gift to a superior man, and the latter honors the giver by receiving. Nevertheless, although the directions of the passage of women and of food are reversed, they both express the same principle of dominance based on the interrelation between castes. It is now time to explore other aspects of this dominance and differential privilege according to the principle of the "direct order of castes" as it is expressed in marriage, mating patterns, and sexual transactions.

The Direct Order of Castes, Hypergamy, and Dominance in Modern India

By dominance deriving from the principle of direct order of castes I mean the privileges and immunities—material, political, occupational, sexual, and legal—that accrue to the superior *varnas* or castes in relation to the inferior.[24] I am here mainly concerned with the sexual/marital privileges and their consequences, which derive from the notion of primary and secondary unions and the principle that the higher the *varna* status of a male the greater his access to the women of inferior *varna*. Today this differentiated privilege is reflected in India in the institution of *hypergamy*, which although usually defined as women of lower status marrying men of superior status can just as well be viewed as a privilege allowing men of superior status a *greater access* to a wider range of women of their own and inferior statuses than it allows men of inferior status.[25]

While it is obvious that the classical theory of mixed unions is a rationalizing theory of caste generation and fission rather than a true historical account, in the matter of marriage and other forms of sexual union some of the major classical premises, suitably modified, can be seen to be still operative in India.

The preponderant rule in India is endogamous marriage between persons of the same caste or subcaste status, but *hypergamous* unions of the classical *anuloma* type are also widely institutionalized in different parts of India. These unions are an expression of dominance, in that upper-status males have legitimate access not only to women of their own status but also to women of immediately inferior statuses; and this accessibility, sometimes coinciding with lord-vassal, landlord-tenant, and other hierarchical politico-economic relationships, is a superb instrument within limits of political incorporation.

Hypergamy in India manifests two forms which for the sake of convenience (but not very accurately) I shall call the northern and southern forms. While I am aware that the suffix "-gamy" implies marriage, I shall use the words "hypergamous unions" and "hypergamous concubinage" to describe certain mating patterns traditionally practiced in Malabar.

The hypergamy practiced by the Rajput clans of northwest India (Blunt, 1931; Tod, 1832; Parry, n.d.), the Patidari of Gujarat (Morris, 1968; Pocock, 1972), and the Rarhi Brahmins of Bengal (Hutton, 1951; Dumont, 1970) is largely between ranked groups (clans/lineages/circles) within caste (with some crossing of caste boundaries at the lower edges in the case of the first two). In these instances, insofar as the father can lift up his child to his own group's status despite the slight inferiority of the mother, the unions follow the logic of "sons of the twice-born, begotten on wives of the next-lower castes," as propounded by Baudhayana.

In contrast, in the South Indian Malabar instances where the hypergamous union is between castes (and between subcastes within castes) and the children are relegated to the status of the mother as the inferior partner (while merely enjoying the "honor" of being sired by superior fathers), the logic of placement follows the interpretation as propounded by Manu.

I do not wish to embark on the intricacies and implications of Indian hypergamy. The authors I have cited are better guides; see, for instance, Morris's brief but perceptive discussion on the dilemmas of hypergamy (1968: 97). However, a few words are in order.

Obviously the two strategies of hypergamy are connected with different institutional features. In North India, where the accent is on status competition and improvement, marriage as alliance must be kept open, and these aspirations approximate *in spirit* the mechanics of social mobility stated in Manu: "If a female of the caste, sprung from a Brahmana and a Kshatriya, Vaisya, or Shudra female, repeatedly bears children to one of the highest caste, the inferior person or group attains the highest caste within certain specified generation."

In South India, the contours of the social structure are kept intact by senior sons engaging in alliance marriage with equals, while non-succeeding sons may unite more flexibly with women in a downward direction. This is consistent with ranked lineages, the core lineage at the top continuing intact through a closure best represented by prescriptive cross-cousin marriage (Dumont, 1957; Schneider and Gough, 1961).

In the case of the intercaste *anuloma* unions in Malabar, it is clear that the relegation of children to the mother's status fits in beautifully with a situation where the patrilineal Nambudiri indulge in socially accepted concubinage while the matrilineal castes find the same unions appropriate for the placement of the progeny in the mother's matrilineage and caste or subcaste (Schneider and Gough, 1961: 320; Dumont, 1961).

Rather than discuss familiar and well documented cases, I have represented in Figures 6.3 and 6.4 the hypergamous marriages of the Rarhi Brahmans of Bengal and the hypergamous marriage and concubinage patterns among the Malabar castes in such a way as to show how men of superior status have access to a wider range of women than men of lower status, this being a statement of dominance and privilege. In Appendix 2, I quote excerpts from Morris (1968) on the ideal Patidari hypergamy scheme.

The spirit of *anuloma* has also been preserved in parts of India in historical times in the institutions of primary and secondary marriages, whereby the primary marriage of the male bearer of status is with an orthodox and excellent equal, and his secondary marriages are with females of lower status within the same caste, these unions in turn generating offspring of unequal status allocated according to the statuses of their mothers. This is consistent with the existence of ranked lineages, and with the fact that the core lineage at the top ensures its interests through a closure best represented by "prescriptive" cross-cousin marriage (Dumont, 1957). In another variant of this, the children of *anuloma* unions are assigned to a third caste different from that of the parents (Karve, 1961; Harper, 1968).

There is no need to belabor the point that Indian society guards zealously against the degradation of *pratiloma* unions whereby a woman mates with a man of inferior status (hypogamy). Practice by

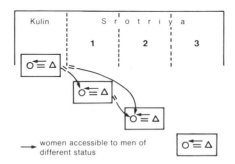

Figure 6.3. Hypergamy among the Rarhi Brahmans in Bengal. (Adapted from Dumont, 1970: 120.)

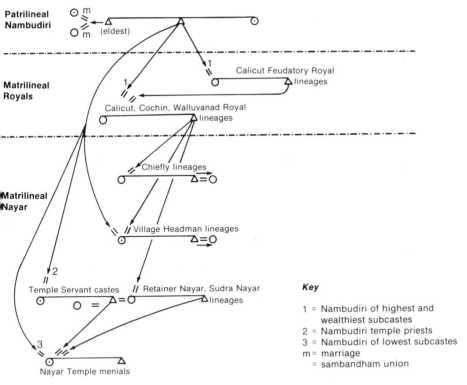

Figure 6.4. Hypergamy and concubinage among the upper castes of Calicut, Cochin, and Walluvanad. Note: The Nayar Retainer castes, the largest in number among all groups, gave less than 10 percent of their women to all superior castes. (Based on Schneider and Gough, 1961: 319–322.)

and large matches the rule; and wherever unsanctioned hypogamous unions take place, the progeny present problems of placement because they are truly "anomalous." They may be assigned to the father's inferior caste, or they may be considered to have no caste at all depending on the fate of the mother.

In Hindu society, therefore, hypergamous unions of the sanctioned and institutionalized kinds present no problems regarding the placement of children of "mixed unions"; the soft spots in the system relate to the placement of children born of unsanctioned hypogamous mixed unions (or of unions which, though *anuloma* in direction, are still unacceptable—for example, unions of partners of highly disparate status such as the union of a twice-born male and a woman of polluting caste).

The satisfactions derived by the parties to hypergamous unions of the Nambudiri-Nayar type are crystal clear. I shall therefore conclude this section by stating why, given the Indian rules and preferences, hypergamy of the North Indian type rather than hypogamy gives a "payoff."

Sanctioned hypergamy. 1) From the woman's point of view: if she takes a husband of higher status, then her children take the status of their father, and her natal lineage enjoys the prestige of having affines of superior status. 2) From the man's point of view: if he takes a wife slightly lower in status, his children still retain his status (no "decrease" in value); he is compensated by a sizable dowry which his wife brings (economic advantage); and his own marriage ensures the hypergamous marriage of his sister. Thus, hypergamy is mutually advantageous to a man and his status group as well as to his spouse and her natal status group.

Unsanctioned hypogamy. 1) If a woman marries a man of lower status, her children do not enjoy her status ("decrease" in value) but are at best assigned the status of her inferior husband. 2) If a man marries a woman of superior status, his children cannot enjoy their mother's superior status, only his own. Furthermore, he cannot expect to receive a dowry because he has no advantage of status to give in exchange. Thus, hypogamous unions are disadvantageous to both men and women.

An essential feature of the caste system is that men cannot *increase* the status of their children through their own marriage, but they can increase their material assets through marriage. At the same time, men cannot allow the *decrease* of the status of their children by marrying women lower than the prescribed, preferred, or permitted status range. But there are indirect ways by which a man can raise the status of his group and its descendants. By strict control and manipulation of the marriages of his sisters and daughters, by successfully denying them to males of equal (and, of course, inferior) status and marrying them to superior males, a man can in turn aspire to marry his sons to women previously inaccessible to his own group.

Typically, hypergamy as found in certain parts of North India lends prestige to the wife givers not through the conversion of affinal bonds over time into bonds of consanguinity, but through keeping up the bonds of affinity (without repeated marriage) for three generations through prestations. After three generations the affinal obligations are dissolved, and the strategic possibilities exist for renewing marriage with the same group or for achieving marriage with a group whose females were previously inaccessible. Structurally, repetitive marriage alliance *coupled with dowry* is inimical to the spirit and aspirations of North Indian hypergamy, for it would fix and make enduring the relative statuses of wife takers and givers, thus denying the possibility of social mobility. However, enduring and repeated hypergamous transactions coupled with bridewealth are possible among social groups or statuses whose positions are relatively *fixed* and unchangeable—for example, a king taking women from chiefs, they in turn from petty chiefs, and so down the line, where political patronage is coupled with political allegiance.

In the long run, hypergamy of the North Indian kind is unstable for various reasons. A primary problem is the escalation of dowry, so that the groups participating may attempt to reverse the trend and introduce egalitarian trends by forming endogamous marriage circles or legislating about dowry (Pocock, 1972; Morris, 1968; Parry, n.d.). Furthermore, there is always the problem of an excess of women at the top, for there are no males of higher status available to marry them; this results in female infanticide, multiple marriage such as "Kulinism," and the like, which are not enduring solutions. But despite the strong counterpressure of leveling tendencies, hypergamy fits into the general Indian aspiration for maintaining and increasing status and honor through the institution of marriage.

Marriage is thus at the heart of Hindu society. It is usually considered the most important event in a man's life; it is in the forefront of Hindu "consciousness"; and it is a focal point of the social system. Marriage is directly integrated with caste, which is the basis of a Hindu's primary status position in his society. A man's caste is first of all decided by the status of his parents, and subsequently maintained or modified by his own marriage and sexual encounters.

The Marriage of Purity and Power

This chapter is composed of several interrelated themes. I began by analyzing in detail a classical Indian theory about the generation of new categories in the form of castes (*jati*) and occupational groups through the combination of the four *varnas* in socially approved and disapproved modes of mating. I then outlined the intellectual scheme in which the base *varna* categories and the ordered rules of combination generated castes which were automatically ranked and evaluated.

Although this theory is fictional and nonhistorical, it serves to illuminate certain theoretical and substantive issues. It is interesting as a classification system which, starting with a basic scheme of hierarchically arranged *varna* categories, then employs the *key* method to generate new categories by the overlapping or mixing of classes, a method of classification that is the opposite of the taxonomic hierarchy of discrete classes, which is implicitly the basis for the theories of taboo and pollution developed by Mary Douglas and Edmund Leach. I have supplemented their contribution by demonstrating that purity and pollution in the Indian caste system can be fruitfully viewed as being grounded in the *interrelation between castes* according to two principles of participation and interaction—namely, the "direct order" and the "inverse order" of castes. These principles are manifest in diverse spheres of caste life.

Although nonhistorical, the classical theory enshrines timeless truths about certain basic features of the Indian caste system. The differential privilege and dominance coded in the traditional theory in terms of the direct order of castes as regards sexual access to women of different *varna* status (*anuloma*) find their modified and transformed expression today in hypergamy and concubinage in different parts of India.

But, perhaps more unexpectedly, the rules of purity and pollution simultaneously reflect two overarching principles. The "direct order" of reckoning ensures the *dominance* of the higher *varna* and castes over the lower by declaring them naturally more endowed with the right to use the sanction of force and to be more immune from legal and ritual disabilities. In contrast, the "inverse order" of reckoning lays the burden of more stringent purification and vigilance on the superior in relation to the inferior when in a state of self-pollution and in case of improper contact with the lower castes. The very hierarchical ordering of *varna* and caste as a social system based on inequality requires us not to separate purity and pollution from the exercise of power and dominance, for both these are intertwined in the same single theory of society which the Brahman legal ideologists propounded for their glorification. It would be totally unrealistic to think that the *shastric* writers constructed a morality and a social theory of society based solely on the principle that pollution continually attacked purity, without securing for themselves and their fellows those primary privileges which first established the dominance of the pure over the impure.

APPENDIX 1

Occupations Accessible to the Varnas under Conditions of Stress

In the second half of Chapter X of Manu we are given the rules regarding the occupations of the *varnas* during normal times, followed by those that are permissible in times of stress. The following are rules that conform to the logic of the "direct order of castes":

1. The Brahman "unable to subsist by his peculiar occupation . . . may live according to the law applicable to Kshatriyas, *for the latter is next to him in rank*" (italics added). If the Brahman cannot maintain himself by the above, he may adopt a Vaisya's mode of life—but only the *purer aspects.* He must not practice agriculture, which causes injury to many beings; and he must avoid certain types of trade, such as selling condiments, cooked food, salt, cattle, human beings, dyed cloth, weapons, and meat (see Manu X, 83–94).

2. The Kshatriya who has fallen into distress may adopt a Vaisya's mode of life. Although he may not, like the Brahman, practice agriculture (which is sinful), he may practice those Vaisya trades and the sale of commodities (referred to above) which are forbidden to the Brahman.

3. A Vaisya may under similar conditions maintain himself by a Shudra's mode of life, while avoiding "acts forbidden to him."

4. A Shudra may, faced with hunger, practice handicrafts.

The opposite process which would constitute an upward status mobility is firmly denounced, for it attacks the privileges of "the direct order of castes." Thus, the Kshatriya, Vaisya, and Shudra may not arrogantly adopt the mode of life prescribed for their betters. "A man of low caste who through covetousness lives by the occupations of a higher one, the king shall deprive of his property and banish" (Manu X, 196). "It is better to discharge one's own appointed duty incompletely than to perform completely that of another; for he who lives according to the law of another caste is instantly excluded from his own" (Manu X, 97).

The same jural notions are applied to property rights. A Brahman may forcibly take from a Vaisya an article required for the completion of the sacrifice, and may take for the same reason two or three articles from a Shudra, "for a Shudra has no business with sacrifice." The reverse is heinous: stealing the property of a virtuous Brahman is like stealing the property of the gods and invites heavy penance and punishment; and that sinful man "feeds in another world on the leavings of the vultures" (Manu XI, 26). In fact, "stealing the gold of a Brahman" belongs to the class of mortal sins, or *mahapataka* (Manu XI, 55).

APPENDIX 2

Patidar Hypergamy

The overseas immigrants from Gujerat, Western India, to Uganda who belonged to such castes as the Patidar and Kanbi were found by Morris (1968) to have a lively idealized picture of a hypergamous scheme in their homeland to which they related their marriages. Following is his account (pp. 98, 195–196).

According to Patidars in East Africa the original marriage circle apparently included families in fourteen villages. It subsequently divided into two circles of six and five villages with a few families in the remaining three villages linked to both circles. The villages in these two circles were said to contain all the "men of family," but two other lower-ranking circles of twenty-seven and twenty-one smaller villages also existed . . .

In 1955 in Africa, marriages between boys and girls born and educated in Uganda were being contracted in terms of both marriage circles and prestige of lineages. Women of a circle of five villages in Gujerat still took high dowries with them when they married men in another circle of six, and their brothers were still forced to rely on finding wives among the girls in their own circle who did not marry up, or in villages outside the circle. Although in theory everybody thought the equality implicit in a marriage circle agreement most desirable, nobody was willing to forgo dowry or to consider that his family or lineage was equal to any other.

The following diagram was drawn with the assistance of an informant in Uganda to clarify the negotiations which were taking place for the marriage of his daughter.

High prestige

Circle of six villages

A.   Women of all six villages nominally married into all six villages;
B.   in practice women of village A tended not to marry men of vil-
C.   lage F or any below it.
D.
E.
F.

Villages linked with both circles

G.   Each village contained very few *kulia* (high-ranking) families,
H.   all of whom gave brides to the circle of six and took them from
I.   the circle of five. The *Kulia* families of villages G, H, and I did
      not usually marry their daughters into the circle of five.

Circle of five villages

J.   Women of all five villages nominally married into all five vil-
K.   lages; in practice women in village N married men of village J
L.   but not vice versa except into one or two "better" households.
M.   Women of all five villages married men from A to I, but the men
N.   did not get wives in exchange.

Low prestige

Villages outside the circles

Women from outside might marry into the circle of five but their brothers did not get wives in return.

The above diagram is, of course, a statement of ideal behavior but an indication of how far it guided real behavior can be obtained by examining marriages on genealogies and those celebrated in East Africa.

In the pedigree of a man belonging to village K in the circle of five were nine women born into his lineage whose marriages could be traced in detail. Five married up into the circle of six, four married within their own circle of five, and none married down. Of the fifteen men recorded, only one married a woman from the circle of six, eight married in the circle of five, and four brought in women from lower-ranking villages outside the circle. In this lineage at least, most marriages conformed to what the Patidars said was correct behavior.

In Kampala nineteen marriages of Patidars from the Charotar district were recorded. Eight were within the two highest circles (six and five) and all were hypergamous, though one man of the lowest-ranking village (N) of the circle of five had had to find a bride outside in a circle of twenty-seven villages. Of the two men in the circle of twenty-seven one married a bride from outside. No woman married down because, in the opinion of the Brahman priest who supplied the information, all families in Africa had sufficient means to make a hypergamous marriage for their sons in India, if not in Africa. But in all nineteen recorded marriages both bride and groom in fact lived in Africa.

7

The Galactic Polity
in Southeast Asia

I have coined the label *galactic polity* to represent the design of traditional Southeast Asian kingdoms, a design that coded in a composite way cosmological, topographical, and politico-economic features. The label itself is derived from the concept of *mandala*, which according to a common Indo-Tibetan tradition is composed of two elements—a core (*manda*) and a container or enclosing element (*la*). Mandala designs, both simple and complex of satellites arranged around a center, occur with such insistence at various levels of Hindu-Buddhist thought and practice that one is invited to probe their representational efficacy.

Mandala as Cosmological Topography

Cosmological schemes of various sorts in Tantric Hinduism and Buddhism have been referred to as mandala—for example, the cosmos as constituted of Mount Meru in the center surrounded by oceans and mountain ranges. At a philosophical and doctrinal level, the Buddhist Sarvastivadin school represented the relation between consciousness (*citta*) and its associated mental phenomena (*caitta*) in terms of the law of satellites, wherein consciousness placed in the center is surrounded by ten *caitta,* each of which again is surrounded by four *laksana,* or satellites (Stcherbatsky, 1923; Conze, 1970). The design and arrangement of the magnificent architectural monuments like Borobodur and Angkor Vat have been called mandala (Mus, 1935, 1936).

At quite a different level, Kautilya in his *Arthashastra* used mandala as a geopolitical concept to discuss the spatial configuration of friendly and enemy states from the perspective of a particular kingdom (Shamasastry, 1960). The human body is likened to a mandala (Tucci, 1971), a description that finds its resonances in ritual and medical practices. Finally, mandala designs are printed on textiles or are reproduced in the transitory designs drawn with powdered colors on numerous occasions.

My primary interest in this paper is the traditional Southeast Asian kingdoms that are described as conforming to the mandala scheme in their arrangement at various levels. Mandala as geometrical, topographical, cosmological, and societal blueprints are not a distinctive feature of complex kingdoms and polities only. The evidence is quite clear that simpler mandala designs appear in tribal lineage-based segmentary societies practicing slash-and-burn agriculture, and that the most elaborate designs are manifest in the more complex centralized polities of valley-based sedentary rice cultivators (for example, see Mus, 1935; Heine-Geldern, 1942; de Jong, 1952; Schrieke, 1955; Shorto, 1963; Moertono, 1968; Wheatley, 1971). But this is a simplification. There are indeed expressions both simple and complex found in phenomena standing between these poles—at the level of tribal polities and local communities. An excellent case in point are the Atoni of Timor. They have named patrilineal descent groups, live in villages, grow maize and rice by shifting agriculture on mountainous terrain, and at the same time belong to princedoms. Their village houses are made to a complex center-oriented design wherein concepts of inner and outer, right and left, four major mother posts, twelve peripheral chicken posts, and so on build up a scheme that simultaneously has cosmological, ritual, sexual, and practical ramifications (Cunningham, 1973). And, as may be expected, the wider encompassing polity as such is constituted according to an elaborate design of center and satellites and of successive bipartitions of various kinds (Nordholt, 1971).

Examples of the elementary geometric designs are the five-unit (quinary) and nine-unit samples. The first consists of four units deployed around a central one, and the second is composed of a center, four places in the major cardinal positions, and four more placed in between at the lesser cardinal points (Figures 7.1 and 7.2). In Indonesia, for example, the quinary formula called *mantjapat* ("five-four") had various usages: it denoted the arrangement of four village tracts around a fifth central one; it represented the rotational location of village markets in a five-day cycle; it made its appearance in the settle-

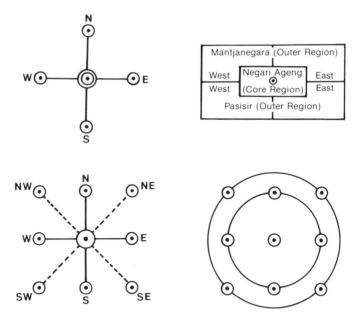

Figure 7.1. Upper left: The *mantjapat*. Upper right: The Mataram state—a five-unit system through successive bipartitions (after Schrieke, 1955). Lower left: Nine-unit system, showing a radial pattern. Lower right: The king's council, showing two concentric circles.

ment of Minangkabau land-ownership disputes in that the unanimous testimony of the heads of families owning the four surrounding plots was required (de Jong, 1952); it described the headman's council at the village level (in the same sense as that of the *panchayat* in village India); and it appears (Schrieke, 1955) to have been the underlying pattern of the Mataram kingdom during the second quarter of the eighteenth century, arrived at by successive bipartitions (Figure 7.1, upper right).

Similarly, the nine-unit design appears in stereotyped accounts of the king and his ministers arranged in two concentric circles. It also appears in the territorial design of the traditional Negrisembilan polity (Figure 7.2), with the domain of Sri Menanti in the center, immediately surrounded by four "verandah" (*serambi*) tracts and these again being flanked by four major districts (de Jong, 1952).

Here is the first problem posed by these facts: because these geometrical and radial constructs, traditionally conceived as cosmological designs, occur in slash-and-burn and wet-rice economies, occur at the

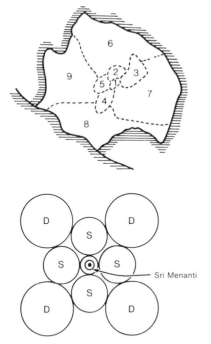

1 = Sri Menanti — capital
2 = Ulu Muar ⎤
3 = Djempol ⎥
4 = Gunnung ⎬ verandahs
   Pasir ⎥
5 = Teratji ⎦
6 = Djelebu ⎤
7 = Djohol ⎥
8 = Rembau ⎬ major
9 = Sungai- ⎥ districts
   Udjong ⎦
D = District
S = *Serambi* (verandah)

— Sri Menanti

Figure 7.2. Negrisembilan (after de Jong, 1952). Bottom: Schematic design of the Negrisembilan polity as a nine-unit system.

level of local community and the widest conception of polity, and occur in simpler and more complex societies, there are no *prima facie* grounds for explaining their manifestation as immediate and *direct* projections of ecological considerations or the logistical constraints of sociopolitical organization. The logic of their use cannot be reduced to a simple causal explanation.

It is clear that if we approached these center-oriented constructs or models as a form of classification, we could start with an initial pentadic or quinary system and progressively build up an expanding series of mandala circles comprising seventeen, thirty-three, and still larger clusters of units.

Perhaps the most famous of these complex schemes was realized in the Hindu-Buddhist polities of Southeast Asia that employed the thirty-three-unit scheme to express and organize cosmogonies and pantheons as well as religio-political groupings. In this scheme the king as wielder of *dharma* (the moral law), as the *chakravartin* (universal emperor) and *bodhisattva* (buddha-to-be), was seen as the pivot of the polity and as the mediating link between the upper regions of the cosmos, composed of the gods and their heavens, and the lower plane of humans and lesser beings.[1]

The best expression of this scheme is the thirty-two *myos* of the medieval Mon kingdom and the thirty-seven *nats* of the subsequent Burmese pantheon so well elucidated for us by Heine-Geldern (1942) and Shorto (1963); both these schemes derive from the paradigmatic heavenly scheme of the god Indra, flanked by the four guardians of the world (*lokapala*) and twenty-eight lesser *devatas* as retinue. For example, Thaton, the Mon kingdom overrun by Anawrahta in 1057, had thirty-two *myos* or provinces, each the seat of a subordinate prince, ringing the capital. All these political and territorial units were further linked together by the Buddhist *cetiya* cult of relic pagodas, also thirty-three in number. Similarly, the kingdom of Pegu in 1650 and the Mon kingdom of Rammanadesa of Lower Burma had their own permutations and variations of these schemes (Shorto, 1963). All these Buddhist courts also provided prolix examples of such mandala schemes as the king surrounded by thirty-three queens and thirty-three lineages into which they married, and the like.

Following is the second problem of interpretation. The classical descriptions of these Southeast Asian polities arranged in center-oriented galactic schemes were and are accompanied by a certain interpretation of their *raison d'être*, which I shall label as the *cosmological mode*. It is best exemplified by the writings of Eliade and Heine-Geldern (among others), and repeated by Shorto and Wheatley; surprisingly, it is also espoused by Riggs (1967) in his characterization of the traditional Siamese polity. Even Geertz's (1973) trinitarian formulation of the traditional Javanese and Balinese polities in terms of the doctrines of exemplary center, graded spirituality, and theater state resonates with a "cosmological" ontology, which provides the impulsion for the politics in these traditional kingdoms to be the enactment of ritual.

The doyen of contemporary cosmological interpreters is Eliade, who for instance in his *Cosmos and History: The Myth of the Eternal Return* (1959) argues that Archaic Man, as opposed to Modern Man, constantly enacted archetypes or exemplary models in his rituals (as well as other activities), of which the symbolism of the center as the *axis mundi* is the most celebrated. For Eliade, these center-oriented cosmologies are enacted and implemented by the archaic mentality, not because of any rational or practical considerations but because they constitute a prior ontology and therefore an absolute reality for the actors. In other words, the "sacred" orientation provides the impulsions and guidelines for the "profane" activities of traditional man. Thus, in Eliade's vision, archaic man's "reality is a function of the imitation of a celestial archetype [and this] reality is conferred through participation in the 'symbolism of the center': cities, temples, houses become real by the fact of being assimilated to the 'centre of the world.' "

Again, more recently, Wheatley, the author of a large work, *The Pivot of the Four Quarters* (1971), repeats in his inaugural lecture the same interpretive perspective: "In these religions which held that human order was brought into being at the creation of the world there was a pervasive tendency to dramatize the cosmogony by constructing on earth a reduced version of the cosmos, usually in the form of a state capital. In other words, Reality was achieved through the imitation of a celestial archetype by giving material expression to that parallelism between macrocosmos and microcosmos without which there could be no prosperity in the world of men" (1969: 10).

Let me be clear about what I am questioning in the received wisdom so persuasively purveyed by these eminent scholars. My own stand is far from a vulgar utilitarianism or pragmatism in terms of which the schemes in question ought to be explained. One must grant the validity of the galactic model as a collective representation. But what I question is seeing the rationale for this model in a cosmological mode of thought as an ontological priority, which is so interpreted as to constitute a sociological anteriority as well, such that for the imputed "traditional" or "archaic" mentality a notion of the "sacred" is alleged to engulf the "secular" and to serve as the ground of reality.

Apart from the limitation that such a cosmological mode of explanation is static and cannot account for either variations between the schemes employed by societies or polities or dynamic changes in the schemes over time, there is the major objection that in these examples of traditional thought and practice, the sacred as such cannot be persuasively distinguished from a profane domain, and that the cosmological, religious, political, economic dimensions cannot be disaggregated. What the Western analytical tradition separates and identifies as religion, economy, politics may have either been combined differently, or more likely constituted a single interpenetrating totality. If, as I believe, these entities under scrutiny were total social phenomena in the Maussian sense, then one has to employ a different analytical strategy from those already cited so as to recover something of their contours and relations.

My approach, which I shall call "totalization," aims to give an integrated account that is, as far as possible, a true representation of the traditional Southeast Asian kingdoms as extant actualities. But the task is not easy, least of all the problem of translation of indigenous concepts and their elucidation in terms of the analyst's concepts and vocabulary.

My thesis is that the kingdoms in question were arranged according to a galactic scheme, and that this scheme was conceptualized and actualized in ways that are best elucidated in terms of certain key indigenous concepts. The most central of these concepts is mandala (Thai: *monthon*), standing for an arrangement of a center and its surrounding satellites and employed in multiple contexts to describe, for example: the structure of a pantheon of gods; the deployment spatially of a capital region and its provinces; the arrangement socially of a ruler, princes, nobles, and their respective retinues; and the devolution of graduated power on a scale of decreasing autonomies. Other key concepts in the Thai language (which have their counterparts in other Southeast Asian languages as well) are: *muang*, which in a politico-territorial sense signifies kingdom/principality in terms of center-oriented space, and of central and satellite domains; and *krom*, which represents the radial mapping of an administrative system of departments and their subdivisions, as well as the constitution of successively expanding circles of leaders and followers or factions.

The range of meanings of these and other concepts will emerge in due course. Here I shall note certain features integral to the notion of totalization. First, there is a semantic overlap and a certain amount of redundancy in the meanings attributable to the Thai concepts cited, although they are not identical and do not occupy equal semantic space. Second, these (and other similar) concepts are polyvalent, and if their meanings are mapped onto a Western conceptual grid of "levels," they are revealed to be, in varying degrees of overlap, *at once* cosmological, territorial, politico-economic, administrative, and so on.

Thus, from the standpoint of the integrity of these traditional polities, it would be a mistake to disaggregate them into the above-mentioned Western conceptual levels and to treat them as analytically adequate and exegetically sufficient. Although not committing this error, I, as translator and analyst, can only give some idea of the totality by showing that the key concepts do resonate with the polyvalent implications that we attribute to these levels. Therefore, I shall adopt the descriptive strategy of showing that the galactic scheme was characterized by certain structured relations, which were reflected at various levels that I disaggregate or deal with in succession only so that later I can reconstitute the totality.

My descriptive strategy has two implications, which are paradoxically the two sides of the same coin. On the one hand, because the levels—cosmological, territorial, politico-economic, and so on—have no true analytical validity, it follows as a corollary that we cannot assign a deterministic and privileged role to any of them. On the other hand, because the key polyvalent concepts are totalistic and simultaneously carry those significances which we descriptively disaggregate (as cosmological, political, economic), we have to see the galactic scheme as encoding all the impulsions that we customarily attribute to each level. Thus, in requiring us not to assign priority to any one level or to ignore its impulsion—cosmological or logistical—the approach makes it possible to integrate the claims of a cosmological imperative with other imperatives without contradiction. Finally, the approach also makes it possible to relate the model of the galactic polity to certain parameters that define the outer limits of its existence and explain processual oscillations within those limits.

From Cosmology to Political Process

The so-called cosmological schemes can be seen dynamically as serving as frames for political processes and outcomes of a pulsating kind. Furthermore, and this is I hope a novel argument, the cosmological idiom together with its grandeur and imagery, if read correctly, can be shown to be a realistic reflection of the political pulls and pushes of these center-oriented but centrifugally fragmenting polities. In this instance myth and reality are closer than we think.

Before I enumerate its salient political and economic features, let me provide some factual illustrations of the galactic polity.

The Kingdom of Sukhothai

The kingdom of Sukhothai, which historically marked the first political emergence and realization of a Thai polity in the thirteenth century (in what is now Thailand), bore the unmistakable marks of a galactic polity (principal sources here are Wales, 1934; Griswold, 1967).

The concept of *muang* (the Mon parallel is *dun*) had a range of meanings signifying kingdom, country, province, town, capital, and region. The most relevant gloss for that concept is that it referred to "centered" or "center-oriented" space as opposed to "bounded" space, and typically stood for a capital, town, or settlement with the surrounding territory over which it exercised jursidiction. At the widest limit it was commonly the case that the name of a kingdom was synonymous with the name of the capital city (Sukhothai, Ayutthaya,

Pagan, Pegu, Majapahit). The Javanese analogy was that of a torch with its light radiating outward with decreasing intensity; the power of the center determined the range of its illumination (Moertono, 1968: 112).

This conception of territory as a variable space, control over which diminished as royal power radiated from a center, is integral to the schematic characterization of the traditional polity as a mandala composed of concentric circles, usually three in number. This concentric circle system, representing the center-periphery relations, was ordered thus: in the center was the king's capital and the region of its direct control, which was surrounded by a circle of "provinces" ruled by princes or "governors" appointed by the king, and these again were surrounded by tributary polities more or less independent. Note that the capital itself was an architectural representation of a mandala. Thus, the Sukhothai capital had in the inner core of the city the king's palace and the major temple and monastery (Wat Mahadhatu) standing side by side; this center was surrounded by three circles of earthern ramparts, with four gateways at the cardinal points (Griswold, 1967).

Prince Damrong is cited by Wales (1934) as giving this description of the territorial and administrative distribution of Sukhothai, after it had freed itself from Khmer control and had succeeded in bringing three neighboring *muang*—Sawankalok, Phitsanulok, and Kamphaengpet, all situated within a distance of two days' march—under its sway: 1) At the center was the capital province or region, ruled by the king, *muang luang* (great or chief *muang*). Within this royal domain, the king was situated in his capital "city" and within it again in his palace. 2) At the four cardinal points were the *muang*, each ruled by a son of the king (and their sons in turn often succeeded them). These regions, ruled by the princes as almost independent kingdoms, were regarded as having the status of "children" with respect to the capital province, as signified by the expression *muang luk luang*. The provinces were received from the king and governed on the same lines as the capital, the sons being sworn to cooperate with the father for mutual defense and on campaigns of conquest. 3) This principle of a decentralized constellation of units that replicate one another, in that they show minimal differentiation of function, finds expression also among those units recognized as the building blocks of the internal structure of a *muang*, whether capital or provincial. Examples of these lower-level components are the *pau ban*, "father" of the village settlement, and, following at the lowest level, the *pau krua*, the "father" of the hearth (head of commensal household/family). 4) The outer ring, the third concentric circle beyond the four provinces, was the region of independent kingdoms, which, wherever brought under sway, were in a tributary relation—that is, in a relation of overlordship rather than direct political control. When King Ram Kamheng claimed as part of his kingdom various Lao polities of the north and northeast, the old kingdom of Nagara Sri Dharmaraja in the south, and the kingdom of Pegu to the west, he was at best claiming this indirect overlordship.

King Ram Kamheng's inscriptions give evidence of the following social classification of the ruling stratum (and are reminiscent of the Mon concepts cited earlier):

1. *khun*, the ruling princes/nobles, especially of the relatively autonomous "provinces";
2. *pau khun*, the "father" of the khun, the appellation for the king, who was also called *chao muang;*
3. *luk khun*, literally "children" of the *khun*, who were lesser princes/nobles confined to the capital *muang* and who as "chiefs of the great body of retainers which formed the population of his capital and the land immediately surrounding, assisted the king in matters of administration" (Wales, 1934: 69).

Before taking up other examples of the galactic polity, I shall underline a fundamental duality concerning the constitution of the central or capital region of the king and its provinces, and the relations between them. On the one hand, there is a faithful reproduction on a reduced scale of the center in its outlying components; on the other, the satellites pose the constant threat of fission and incorporation in another sphere of influence. If we constantly keep in mind the expanding and shrinking character of the political constellations under scrutiny, we can grasp the central reality that although the constituent political units differed in size, each lesser unit was a reproduction and imitation of the larger. What emerges is a galactic picture of a central planet surrounded by differentiated satellites, which are more or less "autonomous" entities held in orbit and within the sphere of influence of the center. If we introduce at the margin other similar competing central principalities and their satellites, we shall be able to appreciate the logic of a system that as a hierarchy of central points is continually subject to the dynamics of pulsation and changing spheres of influence.

It is clear that the fortunes of the Sukhothai rulers waxed and waned with regard to territorial control. Although Ram Kamheng boasted of his vast area of control, Lu Thai (1347–1374), who succeeded a few generations later, ascended a throne that was on the verge of extinction. He had first to fight for his throne and then to regain as many of the lost vassal states as possible.[2] The problem of territorial control was related to the distribution of rival foci of power. To the north of Sukhothai was the kingdom of Lan Na, further to the northwest was Pagan, in the south was Ayutthaya, to the west Lan Chang, and far to the southeast Angkor. The interstitial provinces under governors and principalities under petty rulers were always disputed—for example, Prabang and Kamhaengpet frequently changed hands between Sukhothai and Ayutthaya in the middle of the fourteenth century. Furthermore, the exigencies of warfare and rebellions, and the overall fissiparous nature of the polities frequently dictated that the capital of the ruler shift its physical location. When Lu Thai began a campaign of pacification around 1362, he first went to Nan, from there eastward to Pra Sak, and finally for tactical reasons took up residence in Kong Swe and remained there for seven years before returning to Sukhothai. Thus, a measure of sober realism ought to teach us that we must match the doctrine of the capital as the exemplary center with the fact of a moving center of improvised bamboo palaces, and field camps of the warrior king on the march or on the run, whose area of control was hotly disputed and liable to shrink or expand with the fortunes of battle. The son of Lu Tai (Mahadharmaraja II) was reduced to a vassal of Ayutthaya in 1378, and by 1438 the Sukhothai provinces were decisively and irrevocably incorporated into the kingdom of Ayutthaya.

The Ayutthayan Polity Circa 1460–1590

I have in a previous work (1976) given a detailed description of the design of the kingdom of Ayutthaya and the pattern of its political process and administrative involution at certain points in its history. Here I shall briefly give a formal sketch of the Ayutthayan polity around the third quarter of the fifteenth century onward, so as to confirm the point that although more complexly ordered, the underlying principles of Ayutthaya's territorial and administrative organization conformed to the scheme of the galactic polity.

King Trailok is credited at this time with the reorganization of his kingdom. The emergent pattern was as follows (see Figure 7.3):

> 1. *Van rachathani:* This comprises the capital of Ayutthaya and its core region or royal domain, which was internally divided into small provinces (*muang noi,* later called

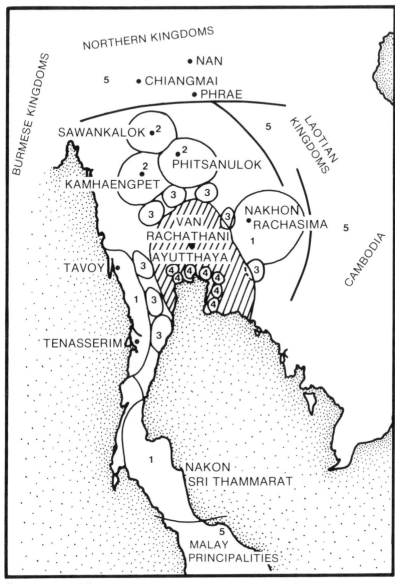

Figure 7.3. Schematic representation of the Ayutthayan polity (ca. 1460–1590). The shaded portion represents Van Rachathani (Van Rajadani), the royal domain of Ayutthaya. 1 = Brahyamahanagara (Phra Mahanakhon)—major provinces/principalities. 2 = Moaṅ Luk Hluaṅ (Muang Luk Luang)—provinces ruled by "sons" of the king. 3 = Moaṅ Hlan Hlvaṅ (Muang Lan Luang)—provinces ruled by grandsons/nephews of the king. 4 = Moaṅ Noi (Muang Noi)—small provinces making up the Van Rachathani. 5 = Moaṅ Pradhesa Raja—foreign (independent) kingdoms.

"fourth class" provinces). These lesser provinces were in
theory administered by officials directly responsible to the
ministers (*senapati*) resident in the capital.

2a.   *Muang luk luang:* In theory these were the provinces
ruled by the king's sons of *chao fa* status of the highest
class (born of mothers of royal status). (In a later classification they were called provinces of first-class status.)
The principalities that fitted this description were in fact
the three *muang* that previously composed the major portion of the now defunct kingdoms of Sukhothai-Phitsanu-
lok, Sawankalok, and Kahamphaengpet.

2b.   *Phra mahanakorn:* Roughly of the same category as
muang luk luang, but with a firmer history of local rulership and of more or less autonomy, were the principalities
of Nakhon Rachasima in the east, Tenasserim in the west,
and, most famous of all, Nakhon Srithammarat in the
south. These autonomous provinces provide the best historical evidence of reproducing the conceptions and arrangements prevailing in the capital domain.[3] All princely
governors and rulers of categories 2a and 2b maintained
their own armies.

3.   Between categories 1 and 2 were situated the *muang lan
luang* (literally, "provinces ruled by the grandsons/neph-
ews of the king"), administered by *chao fa* princes of the
second class; these were smaller, buffer provinces separating the central domain from the large provinces.

4.   At the perimeter were ranged the independent polities,
such as the northern kingdoms of Chiangmai, Chiang-
saen, Phrae, and Nan, and the peninsular Malay states of
Johore and Malacca: all these stood in a tributary relationship to Ayutthaya. Then there were the Cambodian and
Burmese polities; *vis-à-vis* the former, Ayutthaya exercised tributary privileges intermittently, while the latter
were unambiguously of enemy status and powerful foci of
galactic formation in their own right.

A still more complex mandala model representing the formal design
of the Ayutthaya kingdom was developed in the seventeenth century
in King Naresuan's time (Wales, 1934). Provinces were now classed
into four types: there were two of the first class, six of the second class,
seven of the third, and thirty-four of the fourth class directly under the
control of the capital. The first-, second-, and third-class provinces

also had minor provinces directly subordinate to them rather than to the capital. It was this classification that was written into the Palatine Law and the Law of Military Ranks and Ranks of Provinces, which was reproduced in the law code revised by Rama I in 1805. It is most apposite to note of this classification that, in theory, the first-class provinces were entitled to a full set of ministries and *damruot* officials duplicating those of the capital, second- and third-class provinces had the same number of ministries but fewer official positions, and all of these officials were appointed locally by the governor, except the *Yokrabat* sent from the capital. The fourth-class provinces lacked such local official ranks and in theory were controlled by the ministries in the capital, with governors appointed for three-year terms (Vickery, 1970: 865–866). Of course, reality deviated from the theory—but that leads us into the political dynamics of the galactic polity.

This center-oriented concentric circle view of the polity was pervasive in Southeast Asia. The Javanese text called *Nagarakertagama*, which documents various features of the Majapahit kingdom in the fourteenth century, gives most valuable evidence supporting my thesis of the galactic polity (Pigeaud, 1962). An analysis of the text read in relation to my concerns is presented as an appendix; here I shall note that the text's grand tapestry of the exemplary center and its "ring kingdoms," of the kings' royal progresses and the staging of court festivals, is systematically balanced by the countervailing scenario of dual powers within the capital and of dual (but complementary) religions within the kingdom, of the capital itself revolving into relatively self-contained compounds, just as the kingdom fragmented into the central domain and outer satellite province enjoying various degrees of autonomy.

It appears that Majapahit's successor, Mataram, also recognized three categories: *nagaragung* (the core region), *mantjanegara* and the *pasisir* (the outlying provinces), and the *tanah sabrang* (the lands across the sea). Moertono, having presented the above information, expounds a basic feature of these center-oriented pulsating polities (1968: 112): "What we have observed about the relative position of officials in the *nagaragung* and in the *mantjanegara* leads us to conclude that a territory was allocated to one of the three categories on the basis of the degree of influence that the center, that is, the king, exercised there. Consequently, territorial jurisdiction could not be strictly defined by permanent boundaries, but was characterized by a fluidity or flexibility of boundary dependent on the diminishing or increasing power of the center."

The Salient Political Features of the Traditional Kingdoms

At a surface level the cosmological account gives a magnificent picture of the exemplary center pulling together and holding in balance the surrounding polity. But we can properly appreciate in what manner the center attempted to hold the remainder—the centripetal role of the center—only after we have properly understood the decentralized locational propensity of the traditional polity and its replication of like entities on a decreasing scale; in other words, only after we have grasped the structure of the galactic constellation, which is a far cry from a bureaucratic hierarchy in the Weberian sense.

One of the principal implications of the cosmological model is that the center ideologically represents the totality and embodies the unity of the whole. The mechanisms that both express unity and that seek to achieve it are so well known that it will suffice to merely enumerate them:

The cosmology is realized in the architecture and layout of the palace and the capital; for example, the capital is the Mount Meru of the kingdom, and within the capital, the palace represents the same central pillar of the world ringed by concentric circles.

The capital is the starting point for the performance of annual cosmic rites—rites of regeneration and purification—and in a ripple effect the graduated provincial centers replicate in temporal succession the same rites on a diminishing scale (see Archaimbault 1971).

The royal harem and its forbidden women (*nang harng*)—forbidden in the double sense of the women's not being allowed, save on rare occasions, to leave the inner palace grounds, and of being inaccessible to men save the king himself—given to the king by princes, nobles, and officials, is a prime expression of the king as husband of the kingdom. In a sense, the king actively represented the subjects through obligatory and/or politically feasible marriage or concubinage alliances with women kinfolk of princes and officials and rulers of regional provinces and principalities. Once again, true to the galactic model, the princes, nobles, and officials in turn replicated the kingly model with courts and harems of their own.

In Thailand the biannual ceremony of drinking the water of allegiance to the king (there were of course similar ceremonies in other kingdoms) brought the officials and rulers of the outer periphery to the capital. Similarly, it was to the center that these same persons came to receive their titles and regalia of office.

Again in Thailand the institution of the royal corps of pages (*mahatlek*), whose members were sons of princes and nobles attached to the court, was a valued training in the arts of courtly life and royal administration, as well as a guarantee of the loyalty of the kings' agents and provincial rulers (*chao muang*) located outside the capital.

There were other administrative devices by which the center attempted to control or oversee directly the activities of the provincial rulers: for the Bangkok period we have evidence of the king posting his own agents, the *yokkrabat*, who, though formally invested with judicial tasks, were charged with the duty of spying on behalf of the king. Again, the king was strongly suspicious of the possible collusion between provincial governors and rulers against his own person and powers, and therefore treated unauthorized visiting among the latter as treason. In theory, the king was safe only when these rulers and officials had dyadic relations solely with him as the radial center of the network.

The Paradoxes of Kingship

The institution of kingship was shot through with many paradoxes.

The *dharma* of kingship—the very concept of *dharmaraja* itself— can hardly be interpreted as the king's capacity and warrant to innovate creatively and to initiate change in the field of legislation. As Mus (1964) put it, the king's role is better described as "inefficient causality," or an ordinating principle that represents and maintains an eternal order rather than initiating progressive change toward an ideal order in the future. Ideas of fixed regularity and noninterference inform this notion of *dharma* as order, and this sense instructively emerges in the Mon-Burmese-Thai juridical distinction between *dhammasatham/thamasat* as eternal order and *rajasatham* as the rules and orders issued by particular kings, which may or may not find their way into the *dharma* code (Lingat, 1950).

But the king's relatively passive and enduring aspect as maintainer of order is punctuated by his active heroic aspect in the conduct of warfare, which was an irregular activity, usually undertaken for the acquisition of booty and manpower (in the form of slaves). The campaigns themselves were brief, more in the form of raids than sustained battles, a feature that is also related to the fact that the soldiers were primarily the peasantry mobilized ad hoc from the immediate area or province in which or near which the war in question was being waged. The technology and weaponry of traditional warfare were of course primitive, and the peasantry brought their own weapons. Some kings may have had their own limited number of mercenaries, who would be more effective if the king's engagement in foreign trade gave him access to European guns.

Thus, warfare, in principle a quintessential royal activity, was in fact episodic and spasmodic, constrained by the prevalent mechanisms of manpower recruitment, technology of warfare, and its control. Warfare, then, is related to the larger questions of the institutional arrangements for manpower mobilization (normally called corvée in the literature), the pattern of extraction and distribution of agricultural surplus, and the volume of internal and overseas external trade directly entered upon or indirectly regulated and taxed by the political authorities.

As already mentioned, the objectives of warfare were really capture of booty, and, more importantly, prisoners for resettlement in the kingdom. "Loss of population by captivity was infinitely more serious than the comparatively small numbers of those killed in actual fighting" (Wales, 1934: 9). We should not for a moment lose sight of the manpower shortage and of the low demographic densities in all the traditional Southeast Asian mainland polities, and of the fact that control over men rather than over land was the dominant principle of their political organization.[4]

The foregoing is intimately connected with the major paradox of divine kingship and perennial rebellions that was the hallmark of the galactic polities. Any of the traditional chronicles such as the Sinhalese *Mahavamsa* or the Burmese, Thai, or Javanese counterparts will reveal the pattern of brief reigns, frequent rebellions, usurpations, and assassinations that characterize court politics. It is well known that there were no settled succession rules, and that the princes, procreated in profusion in the harems, formed a multitude of contestants, whose propensity for hatching intrigues was matched by the reigning king's own tendency to kill off his rivals. (In Burma, for instance, it appears that it was in part this goriness surrounding kingship that morally outraged the British of the nineteenth century and allegedly spurred them on to subdue the Burmese and deliver them from their savagery.)

It is precisely because there were perennial rebellions and usurpations and because legitimation through orderly succession was absent that the rituals of kingship, particularly the periodic *abhiseka*, which purified and replenished kings with sacred power, were so elaborate and considered so essential. Of course, usurpers frequently married royal women and fabricated royal genealogies retroactively in order to buttress their position. But equally important in such political systems was the charisma gained by special initiation or by ascetic practice or even by auspicious birth, all of which were recognized as signs of merit and power and capable of upstaging hereditary claims to kingship. A royal person was automatically conceived as possessing merit accumulated in previous lives. But it was the *dharma* of a king to act in the world, and therefore to expend his potency and to distribute his merit. He had, therefore, periodically to recoup his potency by withdrawal and engaging in ascetic practice, and by depending on transfer of power from the professional ascetic priest, whose vocation was to store up mystical powers by retreat from the world. But the king emerged from solitude or from ceremony charged with potency only to demonstrate his virility and to expend his potency in the harem or in war.

Just why and how divine kingship was dialectically conjoined with perennial rebellion can be better understood by studying the pattern of political relations that generated volatile factional struggles. I shall later describe the seedbed of factionalism for both Ayutthaya and early Bangkok periods under the label of *administrative involution*. Here I shall merely note that in a situation where power and wealth stemmed from the control of men, and where, as in the Thai kingdoms, the pool of subjects or commoners was divided between those who served the king (*phrai luang*) and those who served the princes (*phrai som*), and the king's men were at the same time allotted to administrative "departments" (*krom*) placed under the control of officials and nobles, the ground was laid for those kinds of factional struggles and aggrandizing exploits that produced an intermittent chain of usurpations and rebellions.

Parameters of the Galactic Polity: The Weaker and Stronger States

The lifecycles and trajectories of the traditional polities of Southeast Asia can be viewed as taking place within certain parameters that are the product of certain basic factors.

The polities can be said to have had a *weaker* form, which was perhaps the more usual state, and a *stronger* form, which was perhaps achieved during exceptional periods.

The weaker picture of the "origins" of the polity is as follows: Among certain decentralized "autonomous" petty principalities or chiefdoms (for example, *muang* ruled by *chao*, in Thai terminology) already existing on the ground, a dominant principality emerges that attempts to pull them together and hold them as a differentiated whole, but this centripetality is achieved not so much by real exercise of power and control but by the devices and mechanisms of a "ritual" kind which have, to use the English philosopher Austin's phrase, "performative validity."

Perhaps among contemporary studies, Gullick's *Political Systems of Western Malaya* (1958) is apt illustration of this weaker state of the traditional polities—in this case, in the period immediately preceding their coming under British control in 1874. The sultan at the apex of each Malay state "did not in most states of the nineteenth century embody any exceptional concentration of administrative authority. Powerful district chiefs could and sometimes did flout his wishes with impunity; some of them were wealthier than he was."[5] "A sultan was generally in control of a royal district which he governed after the fashion of a district chief. But his role in the political system of the state, as distinct from his additional and local role of district chief of the royal district, did not consist in the exercise of pre-eminent power" (1958: 44).[6]

The glue that held together the Western Malay polity was largely symbolic. The sultan's position of great dignity was related to his role as the apex of the political system of the state, as the symbol of its unity and *the titular source of rank and authority for the chiefs, among whom the real power was divided* (1958: 54). No doubt considerations such as threat of external attack, the need for a larger trade unit than the inland district, and even "sheer facts of geography" may have helped preserve the sultan and his satellite chiefs as a polity. But the collective representation of the polity, given the "replication" of the sultan by his chiefs, rested on exemplary enactments that took place at court.

The sultan was the source of aristocratic and chiefly titles, in that the impress of his seal was the concrete validation of titled position, and the regalia of office handed by the sultan to the chiefs and officials were again concrete "embodiments" of validation, and were "repositories" of efficacious "power." The regalia of office (*kebasaran*—"symbols of greatness") which the sultan distributed consisted of musical instruments (drums, pipes, flutes, and trumpets), insignia of office such as scepter, betel box, jewels, umbrella, seal of state, and secret verbal formulas, and weapons such as swords, lances, and long daggers of execution. There were also sumptuary privileges, such as kinds of clothing, domestic architecture and furnishings, rare meats and food, "anomalous" rare animals, and humans (albino elephants and buffaloes, dwarfs, and freak humans), which were associated with and considered the special possessions of titled offices and their objective signifiers. Finally, whatever the realities of power, formal obeisance ceremonies on the part of chiefs toward the sultan, and the enactment of a graded cosmos at the sultan's installation and mortuary rites, were indeed not merely an expression but the creation of the galactic polity in its usual form.

In Weber's discussion of "patrimonialism" (1968, vol. 3, ch. 12), the section entitled "Decentralized Patrimonial Domination: Satrapies and Divisional Principalities," which highlights the decentralized nature of the center's domination and the high degree of autonomy enjoyed by the dependent rulers, approximates in some respects my account of the galactic polity.[7] But much the greater part of Weber's discussion is devoted to the expansion of patrimonial domination over the "extrapatrimonial" areas.

To turn, then, to the stronger form of the polity. The processes by which this form of the polity was reached in Southeast Asia approximate some of those discussed by Weber in his classic treatment of patrimonial domination: how a patrimonial prince attempts to expand his direct control over the outlying extrapatrimonial areas by extending the relations and links of personal dependency, loyalty, and fidelity; by enlarging his control over the judicial institutions; by securing military control, by directly levying taxes and dues, and, more importantly, through forming an independent army which freed him from his dependence on his vassals; and by enforcing a monopolistic control over trade in luxury goods and weapons, and trade involving money. The dispatch of *ministeriales* and the incorporation of *honoratiores* were parallel processes.[8]

Returning to Southeast Asia, it can be confidently asserted that the stronger form of the polity was only rarely and temporarily achieved by strong rulers seizing the opportunities of favorable circumstances. I shall propose a hypothesis of transformation whereby the stronger form of the patrimonial polity is realized: Given a central domain and a surrounding field of satellite principalities, the process of cumulative strengthening of the center's hold over the satellites *goes hand in hand* with the cumulative strengthening of the hold of the satellite rulers and local authorities over their own subjects. There is, so to say, a "payoff" to all parties in this process by which a loose scattering of political aggregates is brought into a tighter relationship in a polity in which the central ruler exercises for a time decisive control. Schrieke (1955) imagines the process thus: "A change comes about in the character of the leaders of the primitive communities: henceforth they have not only to act as intermediaries for the will of the central authority ... but the support of the central authority opens a possibility for them to advance from *primi inter pares* to being ruling notables insofar as they are capable of this" (p. 172).

Schrieke, the Dutch historian of Indonesia (no doubt benefiting from Max Weber's discussion of patrimonial domination), enumerated certain means by which the increased authority of the central government was enforced in traditional Java, means which are exactly paralleled elsewhere. A well-worn method was the attempt to tighten dynastic links by marriage alliances, should the kingdom be composed of a number of smaller principalities in a state of loose coherence. But in more energetic and expansionary times, the king strove to neutralize the power of the princes by appointing *ministeriales* of humble origin as provincial rulers; but in the long run they too became hereditary and the *ministeriales* system did not escape the cleaving process of decentralization. Another strategy was for the ruler to form his own hired guard of praetors whose task would be to make the king independent of his vassals. Schrieke gives a historical illustration of this attempted change from "a loose coherence" to "state" system in the seventeenth-century Mataram Empire.[9] Comparing the policies of sultan Agung (1613–1646) and Mangkurat 1 (1646–1677), he points out the difference between the former's older policy of requiring autochthonous princes to remain at court and binding them to himself through marriage alliances, and Mangkurat's policy of destroying the princes, replacing them with closely supervised *ministeriales,* and introducing a more effective system of enriching his coffers by farming out revenue collection to them in exchange for fixed annual sums and by making trade with foreign lands a state monopoly.

Internal Limits of the Galactic Polity's Politico-Economic Basis

But this process of incremental centralization was abortive, because of certain parameters of the traditional polity that defined the internal limits of the agricultural base, the arrangements for revenue collection, the logistical and communication facilities, and so on.

I shall demarcate the parameters of the traditional polity by reference to twin motors in an engine room, one being the rice-plains economy with a particular relation of people to land and the patterns of mobilization of their services, and the other being the ruler's attempt to monopolize foreign trade, to tax riverine trade (and, in certain instances, to be a beneficiary of mining operations).

The first motor, which was concerned with the extraction of agricultural goods, peasant labor (corvée), and military service, was more unwieldy and ramshackle than the official theory would have us believe. In theory the king, raja, or sultan was the "lord of the land," "the lord of life," and so on. He distributed to his superior officials, both at the center and in the provinces, the rights over certain kinds of revenue collection and services in specified territories; the lesser officials in turn enjoyed from their superiors rights over smaller domains; and so on. In respect of these "rights" over land, in many a traditional polity a distinction was made between rights over territory and people attached to an office (that is, nonhereditary rights, unlike a "fief" in later European feudalism) and similar rights alienated by a king or ruler to a subject as a private estate in perpetuity (or until confiscation).[10]

The formal view of the traditional land tenure system is usually from the top: it sees the hierarchy of rights as radiating outward from the center and from the apex downward to the lower rungs of the king's functionaries. But the entire picture changes when we look at the process of extraction from the bottom upward as a process of collection and creaming off at each successive level of officers, until what trickles in to the king's treasury and warehouses is really a minuscule part of the gross produce and profits extracted at the ground level. To understand this process of how successive layers of political intermediaries slice off a portion of the revenue—a phenomenon that is remarkably like the small margins of profit successively appropriated by a chain of middlemen in contemporary peasant marketing structures (Mintz, 1960; Dewey, 1962; Geertz, 1963), also revealing a close fit between administrative involution and agricultural involution—we have to appreciate the mode of remuneration of officials and functionaries in the traditional polity. They appropriated a portion of the taxes they collected and the fees and fines they imposed, and commanded for their own use some of the corvée owed to the king. Thus, this process of collection and transmission of "revenue" upward made possible the support of a large number of functionaries, but scarcely put in the hands of the king a large capital that derived from *outside* his royal domain—that is, from his provinces and satellite principalities.[11] From these territories kings were able at the best of times to mobilize large-scale labor (corvée) for building palaces and religious monuments and as temporary armies to fight wars. But these were extraordinary projects, and the success of such mobilization was highly variable in these pulsating kingdoms.[12]

The rice-growing, land-based sector of the economy could support an administrative system of replicated courts and redundant retinues, and could at special times provide massive labor pools and armies for brief periods of time, but could not put directly in the hands of the center large economic resources which it could disburse and manipulate and thereby control the recipients. It is because of this insufficiency that the monopolistic control of certain items of foreign imports and exports, and the direct taxation of other kinds of trade goods, were crucial in the emergence and maintenance of the Southeast Asian kingdoms. It is primarily through this sector of the economy that in Thailand, the Ayutthaya-type polity (whose features persisted well into the early Bangkok period) achieved a transformation that in turn implicated the agricultural base.

A brief gloss on the role of trade in the traditional polity is relevant, especially because there was a complementary linkage between riverine rice-growing settlements on the one side and politically controlled and monopolized foreign trade on the other.

That the emergence of the ancient kingdoms, and their physical location on strategic coastal points or on river mouths in Southeast Asia was importantly related to the impact of an explosive expansion of trade at the beginning of the Christian era is well attested. The sea lanes of the great maritime trade route extending from the Red Sea to South China, and operated by Arabs, Indians, indigenous entrepreneurs of the Malayan waters, and Chinese, connected the emergent polities with riparian economies (producing exchangeable commodities, luxuries, and rare products) with one another. The earliest polities in existence by the third century A.D were located in the valleys and plains of the lower Mekong (the central Vietnam of today) and on the Isthmian tracts of the Thai-Malay peninsula (Briggs, 1951; Wheatley, 1961; Coedès, 1968). Later, by the sixth century, other polities had emerged in Sumatra and west Java, virtually all crystallizing along the maritime thoroughfare between India and China.[13] And in subsequent centuries "states predicated on similar principles came to occupy the Pyu country of central and upper Burma, the coastal plains of Arakan, the Mon lands around the lower courses of the Irawadi and Chao Phraya rivers, and other parts of Java and Sumatra. All, with significant exception of some of the Javanese kingdoms, were based in, and in most parts restricted to, the lowlands" (P. Wheatley, n.d.).

In their attempts to answer the riddle of the primary determinants of the emergence of these Southeast Asian polities, most writers have highlighted the impact of the activities of trading entrepreneurs and warrior adventurers, and of the consecratory and ideological roles of the Brahman priesthood that accompanied them. The resources, in the form of luxury goods for redistribution, of arms and weapons for strategic use of force, or of new ideas and concepts for representing new political horizons, which trade must have put in the hands of the newly emergent rulers and their satellites, are without question. But I also would like to insist that the riparian communities practicing rice agriculture, whose scale and density of settlement probably kept pace with the expansion of the trading sector, were an equally indispensable factor, in that they supported a stratum of rulers and officials and a network of ceremonial centers and religious foundations, provided labor for the projects of warfare and monument building, and, not to be minimized, collected and channeled to the center those forest products, spices, minerals (especially gold), and handicraft products that foreign traders avidly sought.

The vast distance from the early centuries of the Christian era to the late nineteenth century did not efface in Southeast Asia the importance of trade and rice cultivation in the petty chiefdoms and sultanates (which would soon be engulfed by colonial conquest). For example, Gullick (1958: 21) paints this general picture of the Malay polities of the last century: "The territory comprised in a State was related to the geographical structure of the peninsula and to the use of rivers as the main lines of communication and trade. A State was typically the basin of a large river or (less often) of a group of adjacent rivers, forming a block of land extending from the coast inland to the central watershed. The capital of the State was the point at which the main river ran into the sea. At this point the ruler of the State could control the movement of all persons who entered or left his State, he could defend it from external attack and he could levy taxes on its imports and exports."[14]

The importance of the river system for location of agricultural settlements, for transport and trade, in the Malay Sultanates, the Javanese kingdoms of Madjapahit and Mataram, the Thai kingdoms of Sukhodaya, and, even more significantly, Ayutthaya, needs no underlining. The increasing stabilization and cumulative centralization of the Thai kingdom in the Bangkok era were in large part both cause and result of the expansion of trade, and of the manner in which the agricultural sector articulated with it.

The Implications of Administrative Involution

Let me make a fuller comment now on the feature of administrative involution, which, as I said before, revealed a close fit with the agricultural involution so characteristic of Asian peasant societies.

It has already been suggested that the agricultural base of a developed traditional polity was capable of supporting not only the agriculturists themselves but also a heavy administrative overhead that skimmed off portions of the taxes and revenue as it was transmitted upward to the king's treasury and storehouses.

The arrangement of this administrative system itself is remarkable for its reflection of the *mandala* pattern. The principle of replication of the center on a progressively reduced scale by the satellites that were the major characteristic of the polity's territorial arrangement now finds its counterpart in the administrative system in the form of multiple palaces replicating the king's own palaces, and redundant retinues surrounding the individual princes, nobles, and officials. Structurally even more remarkable was the *duplication* of administrative, military, and judicial departments (*krom*) and subdepartments, and the fragmentation of administrative tasks not necessarily, or only remotely, dictated by considerations of functional specialization. I shall call this feature of administrative involution the principle of bipartition and duplication of similar units, so that not only are "departments" balanced against one another, duplicating functions, but also within departments there occurs bipartition into parallel, virtually redundant units. (See Wales, 1934; Riggs, 1967; and Rabibhadana, 1969 for ample evidence for these features of bipartition and replication during the late Ayutthaya and early Bangkok periods.)

Weber himself observed the occurrence of a similar feature in the patrimonial administrative structure which he called *typification* (in the sense, I think, of stereotypy), and which he said contrasted markedly with the principle of functional specialization in the rational bureaucratic system. Weber remarked that in the patrimonial system, office and person tend to become conflated; the king's power is regarded as a "personal possession," and this power is fragmented and allocated to princes and ministers of the royal house. "Since all powers economic as well as political are considered the ruler's personal property, hereditary division is a normal phenomenon" (Weber, 1968: 1052). Such subdivision on a hereditary basis on the one hand does not produce definitive division and on the other strives for equalization of revenues and seigneurial rights among the divisional rulers and claimants. Weber further argued that every prebendial decentralization and distribution of fee incomes among competitors and every appropriation of benefices signified typification rather than rationalization. As the appropriation of offices progresses, the ruler's political power "disintegrates into a bundle of powers separately appropriated by various individuals by virtue of special privileges" (p. 1040).

Weber's sociological explanation of administrative involution, bipartitioning, and replication—only partially satisfactory and capable of being taken further—nevertheless stands in stark contrast to that kind of explanation which (stemming from Heine-Geldern) attributes these features simply to the working of a cosmological (and therefore nonpragmatic) orientation (see, for example, Riggs, 1967).

I want to go beyond the Heine-Geldern-type explanation of attributing these features simply and solely to a cosmological orientation, and establish that the pattern of administrative involution faithfully mirrors the structure of political and social relations of a factional sort, and that these relations translated into space, so to say, represent the galactic polity in its territorial aspect.

Apart from meaning an administrative "department," the concept *krom* in Thailand additionally meant, as Rabibhadana (1969) tells us, a leader and his attached followers and retainers. A prince or *chao muang* (chief of a principality/province) had his own personal following, and a king assigned princes graduated *krom* privileges, primarily in the form of titles and retainers (*phrai som*). The most conspicuous examples were the princes who resided in the front and rear palaces (*van na* and *van lang*) and reproduced the king's own court and functionaries on a reduced scale. The *khunnang,* the nobility, who in the main ran the king's departments, similarly had control over the subjects owing service directly to the king (*phrai luang*) and who were allocated to the royal administrative divisions and units. In fact, groups of these freemen were registered under the name of individual leaders, *nai,* and the network of these *nai* from whom the nobility was recruited provided the grid for mobilization of subjects for royal tasks.

In short, the galactic structure is again reproduced in the domain of politico-social interpersonal relations, and can, in this context, be likened to an "emulsion" made of globules joined in (temporary) allegiance to leaders of the next-higher rank and so on until the entire political society is constituted of interlocking *nai-phrai* (leader-follower) circles or factions of varying size. The point of the emulsion metaphor is that these factions are impermanent, and that their constituent units can and do change their affiliations.

Such factionalism, for instance, resolved into a contest and strategy of divide and rule among three parties: the king and his following, the princes and their clients, and the nobility/officials and their circles. The death throes of the Ayutthaya kingdom were characterized by a suicidal conflict between the king and the princes; the early Bangkok period, including the reign of King Mongkut in the mid-nineteenth century, witnessed the corrective measure whereby the king curbed the power of the princes by seeking support among the nobility. This move, however, led in turn to the rise of powerful nobles such as the Bunnag family who successfully circumscribed the king's power. Thus, it comes as no surprise that the succeeding King Chulalongkorn managed to come into his own politically in the 1880s only by finding a way of superseding the nobles by means of an active reliance on and support from his princely half-brothers—such as Princes Damrong, Nares, Rabi, and Dewawong—who also spearheaded the program of modernization.

Reverting to a classical anthropological problem, I want also to suggest that the much misunderstood "debt bondage" or "debt slavery" which is reported to have been a common phenomenon in Southeast Asian polities—as also in "tribal" societies which were familiar with rank and political structures—is best understood in relation to the structure of patron-client relations and factionalism, and the premium placed on control of manpower.

As an illustration suggestive of a general paradigm, let me cite the debt bondage in the Malayan Sultanates, as described by Gullick (1958: 103): "*Contra* the prejudicial account of many British administrators, it is clear that debt-bondage was usually an asymmetrical relation of mutual advantage to the creditor-master and the debtor. Of particular relevance here are the bondsmen who were in actuality members of the household and the personal following of the creditor, usually the political chiefs. For the chiefs the bondsmen constituted followers who owed loyalty and service and were preferable to both mercenaries and free volunteers in the arena of political maneuvering. The bondsman in turn, especially if poor, wifeless and homeless, found his main wants satisfied by his master's 'bounty.' It was a recognized custom that a follower might ask his chief to give him a wife from among the women of his household."

Gullick (1958: 100) accounts for the institution of debt bondage in nineteenth-century Malaya thus: "A part of the population was mere flotsam and jetsam in a hostile world. In these circumstances, a homeless man might be tempted to attach himself in bondage to a chief. He thus got a living, the protection of a powerful patron, access to women and the ultimate prospect of obtaining a wife . . . The follower needed a patron, a living and a wife. But the chief on his side needed a private army. On balance it would appear that the bondsman's position, as Hugh Clifford put it, involved "no special hardship." And although the debtor's services did not count towards a reduction of the debt, he had a certain margin for manoeuvering as indicated by the rule that a debtor 'could demand to be transferred to any other creditor who would pay off his debt to the original creditor.' "

These features of debt slavery closely resemble accounts of the phenomenon reported in other Southeast Asian contexts—including the "tribal" societies of Upper Burma, which were familiar with rank and chiefly institutions. Examples are Leach's account of the Kachin *mayam* (Leach, 1954) and Stevenson's of the Chin *tefa* systems (1968). Leach, for example, has this to say about Kachin *mayam*, usually translated as "slavery" but in many respects similar to the serf system in England and the *boi* system among the Chins (p. 299):

> There were two types of *mayam*—the outside (*nong*) *mayam*, and the household (*tinung*) *mayam*, some grades of which may rightly be called slaves.
>
> The outside *mayam*, serf-like in many respects, owned their house and property and, when living in a *mayam* village, shared in the ownership of communal land. The dues they paid their master were heavy in goods, labour and half the marriage price, and although they had no rights in relation to their owner, few owners seemed to have been oppressive. Some of them even become slaves voluntarily and pay their dues in return for land and protection.
>
> The household *mayam* had no rights in relation to their master (paralleling unmarried children in relation to their fathers) and no rights of ownership. In practice, however, they are well cared for and hardly distinguishable from a child of the house. They are generally contented to receive their food, clothing, drink and opium. They are given wives and sacrifices are made on their behalf when they are sick. And although a socially inferior being, in practice there was very little difference between the life of a *mayam* and an ordinary member of the chief's household.
>
> Mayam were occasionally bought and sold. Nearly every unmarried household *mayam* woman was burdened with one or two children by fathers from the ruling class, and these children were known as *surawng*. It was customary for parents of chiefly status to give their daughter upon her marriage a slave as handmaiden.
>
> The large majority of *mayam* were inherited or born in that status, though some were bought, purchased as wives and obtained as handmaids to brides (and therefore sexually available to their husbands). Some *mayam* became so voluntarily, either in payment of debts or in order to get wives and food, forfeiting their liberty by taking on a *mayam* woman and thereby becoming themselves the property of her owner.

According to a 1931 census, the Triangle and adjacent areas in the Kachin hills had an estimated free population of 80,000; the total number of slaves was 3,989 (less than 4 percent), of whom 2,367 were born in bondage.

Conclusion

In this analysis of the traditional kingdoms of Southeast Asia as pulsating galactic polities, I hope I have escaped being impaled on the horns of a dilemma by not resorting to any of the following frameworks, to the exclusion of the others: 1) the "archaic" cosmological mentality, which entails the acceptance of the galactic structure as a given cultural system that serves as its own explanation without resort to historical or sociological factors—that is, an extreme form of priority attributed to the cultural order that verges on idealism; 2) a simpleminded determinism which believes it can directly and pragmatically generate the political and ideological superstructure of the galactic polity from a type of ecological and economic base; 3) a model of patrimonial domination that focuses on the imperatives of power and political control as the true arena for the emergence of the galactic structure; 4) a certain kind of laissez-faire utilitarianism as portrayed by the "central-place" theory which seeks to explain the location and hierarchy of central places (towns) in terms of their economic (and administrative) service functions.[15]

I have preferred to rely on a method of exposition that I have called totalization. I have tried to show that the geometry of the galactic polity is manifest as a recurring design at various levels that the analyst labeled cosmological, territorial, administrative, politico-economic, but of which the accurate exegesis is that this recurring design is the reflection of the multifaceted polyvalence built into the dominant indigenous concepts, and of the traditional idea of a simultaneous convergence of phenomena in a mandala pattern. A corollary of this demonstration is that the cultural model and the pragmatic parameters are in concordance and buttress one another, and cannot be disaggregated.

The galactic polity as a totalization is not, as I have indicated, a smooth and harmonious entity but one ridden with paradoxes and even contradictions. If it represents man's imposition of a conception upon the world, it is also a reflection of the contours of the politico-economic reality. The rhetoric and ritual display of the exemplary center and divine kingship is frequently deflated by perennial rebellions and sordid succession disputes at the capital, and defections and secessions at the periphery. A politico-economic system premised on the control of manpower as its chief resource, and whose building blocks are circles of leaders and followers that form and reform in highly unstable factions, frequently deteriorates into power struggles within and suffers continuous intrusions from without. These movements in political relations and groupings in turn disorient and redraw the boundaries of the polity's territorial space. Moreover, agricultural involution is matched by administrative involution. Just as at base the society has its mundane existence in a multitude of decentered rice-growing peasant communities, existing save for intermittent and spectacular intrusions from the theater state, in relative isolation from the capital's network of political exaction, so does the hierarchy of graduated power and merit fragment and shatter into the multitude of replicated, redundant, and competing administrative cells. The patterns for the mobilization of men, resources, and produce and the mechanisms of regulation and deployment of authority have their logistical limits. These are some of the paradoxes, restraints, and contradictions that motor the pulsations and oscillations of the traditional Southeast Asian polities within the parameters of their existence. They are also the features that match the cosmology and the actuality of the galactic polity in a closer fit than anyone has previously imagined.

A further implication, which I have not spelled out in this essay, is that these polities are not timeless entities but historically grounded, and that they can be subject to irreversible transformation—as, for example, happened with the impact of Western colonial powers during the nineteenth and twentieth centuries. In Thailand there was a change from a galactic to a more centralized "radial" polity that is by no means modern in the Western sense; in the ex-colonial new nations, galactic propensities still find their transformed expression in regionalism and communalism, despite the exaggerated hopes of an "integrative revolution."

APPENDIX
Some Galactic Features of the Majapahit Kingdom of Fourteenth-Century Java

What I propose to do in this brief account is begin with the conventional representation of a traditional Javanese polity—in this case Hayam Wuruk's Majapahit kingdom—as a mandala system allegedly expressing the cosmic symmetry of a graded ordering from an exemplary center outward to its periphery of "ring kingdoms," and then take the subversive step of revealing how this same account also contains other galactic features, such as asymmetrical bipartitioning (or dualism) and graded multicenteredness, which serve to explain why the substance of politics practiced by and allotted to the center was more ritualistic and exemplary than administrative and regulatory. (The principal source for this account is Pigeaud, 1962, vols. 1–5.)

My source for this illustration is the famous Javanese text called the *Nagara-Kertagama* (ca. A.D. 1365), attributed to a Buddhist court cleric; the title can be loosely translated as "a manual for the cosmic ordering of the capital and kingdom." The poet calls his poem *deshawarnana,* which is rendered as "topography" by Pigeaud (1962: vol. 4, 509). The text describes, among other things, the formal layout of the palace, capital, and kingdom, and treats at length the tribute-collecting and redistributive "royal progresses" (circuits) to parts of the kingdom, the staging of a court festival, and so on.

Majapahit was an inland rice-based agrarian kingdom and is to be contrasted with the harbor-focused mercantile coast (*pasisir*) principalities of the north coast of Java, which were the first to go Islamic in the fifteenth and sixteenth centuries. But we should be careful that in calling Majapahit an inland agrarian kingdom we do not obscure the fact that trade—overseas, interinsular, and internal—was a crucial arm of the royal economy. While the capital of Majapahit itself lay in the foothills of the East Java massif at some distance from the river Brantas, there was the important port of Bubat situated on the river, having as its inhabitants colonies of Chinese, Indian, and other merchants. (Another river port was Canggu.) Javanese rice was traded for Indian cloth and Chinese ceramics. The chief difference between the trade of Majapahit and the coastal mercantile principalities of North Java lay in this: in the latter, such as Tuban and Surabaya, the ruling aristocrats were directly involved as entrepreneurs in trading activities, while in the former the political rulers granted royal patents to traders for overseas trade, exacted tolls and duties on internal trade, and probably appointed port governors who regulated trade.[16] Majapahit's rulers administered trade rather than being merchant princes themselves. (See Pigeaud, 1962: vol. 4, pp. 37–38, 498, 502–504, 509.)

The mandala ordering of Majapahit is depicted in an exaggerated panegyric in keeping with the composer's court affiliation. The glorification of the king emphasizes three things: "Successively the King's works [especially public (*kirtis*) and religious (*dharmas*) foundations], the King's zenana, and the expanse of the King's dominions are praised." An example of the last is Canto 17, stanza 3, which states (Pigeaud, 1962):

1. The whole expanse of Yawa-land (Java) is to be compared with one town in the Prince's reign.
2. By thousands are (counted) the people's dwelling-places, to be compared with manors of Royal servants, surrounding the body of the Royal compound.
3. All kinds of foreign islands; to be compared with them are the cultivated lands' areas, made happy and quiet.
4. Of the aspect of the parks, then, are the forests and mountains, all of them set foot on by Him, without feeling anxiety.

The canto makes four comparisons and equivalences that derive from the mandala geometry which mirrors the outer in terms of the inner core:

The prince's town (capital) : the whole of Java;

The royal manors surrounding the royal compound : the multitude of common people's homesteads;

The cultivated lands : the other islands;

The parks : the forests and mountains.

Again, in Canto 12, stanza 6, the parts of the kingdom are correlated with the cosmic pattern of the heavenly bodies: the two central compounds of the capital with the sun and the moon, the groves surrounding the compounds and manors with the halos of light surrounding the sun and the moon, the towns and other islands (*nusantara*) of the kingdom with stars and planets. (The last circle—the ring kingdoms, or *mandalikarastra*—are described as dependent states.)

This is no doubt the imagery of an unrivaled exemplary center, a unified gradient of spirituality and cosmic symmetry—but let us look at the picture again and reconstitute it with additional details contained in the text. To begin with the poem is, not surprisingly, partial in suppressing any reference to the West Javanese kingdom of Sunda, Majapahit's immediate neighbor and rival, because the latter could not be included as either a friend or a tributary within the circle of dominion. Similarly, the prominent coastal mercantile harbor-principality of Tuban is ignored, for it too had cheekily defied Majapahit. Again, the expansive world ruler's claims have to be scaled down to the actuality: the Majapahit king's *effective domain of control was East Java*, the perimeters of which delineated area were made the "royal progresses." The king's effective power also possibly extended over the easterly islands of Bali and Madura, whose chiefs are described in the royal progress of 1359 as meeting with tribute the king's caravan when it arrived at the eastern coast of Java.[17]

Next, let us focus on those features that imply that the mandala is constituted by asymmetrical dualism and by a cluster of replicated entities, the net effect of which is to produce a centrifugality and a pointillist mosaic of the whole.

The previous reference to the sun and moon is a statement of the relation between the two central compounds within the capital complex, and of the two urban centers within the kingdom, standing in a dualistic though asymmetrical relation. The moon stands for the eastern *pura* of Wengker-Daha, the sun to the western royal compound of Majapahat-Singasari-Jiwana. Again, the town of Daha and the capital are lined up similarly. "Evidently the idea is that Daha is the chief of the lesser towns like the moon ruling over the stars and planets. Majapahit of course is the sun, spending [sic] light to all and sundry" (Pigeaud, 1962: vol. 4, p. 26).

The following excerpts from Pigeaud highlight a crosswise balancing of powers between the king of Majapahit and the Prince of Wengker, and their respective vizirs.

> Canto 12, stanza 3, 4. It is remarkable that the vizir of Daha had his manor north of the Royal compound and the vizir of Majapahit east of it, probably north of the Daha-Wengker compound. The four most important compounds and manors of the centre of the town appear to have been situated on the corners of a quadrangle. The holy crossroads of canto 8–2–4 probably was the point of intersection of the diagonals of that quadrangle and so it was considered as the centre of the town. The distances between the compounds and the manors are unknown and so the exact centre of the town can not be determined. Probably the Majapahit Javanese were perfectly satisfied with the notion that the holy centre of their town was situated somewhere north-east of the Royal compound.
>
> The crosswise relation between the compounds and the vizirs' manors is an instance of the importance attached to cross connections in Javanese thought. The idea of unity and cosmic interrelationship pervades Javanese social and religious organization to a very high degree. (Vol. 4, p. 24.)

According to the Nagara-Kertagama, Majapahit contained two main compounds and four main manors. Of the two compounds the western, the Royal compound, was inhabited by the family of Majapahit-Singasari-Jiwana, to which King Hayam Wuruk belonged; the eastern compound was the residence of the family of Wengker-Daha. Two of the manors were situated north of the compounds. The north-western manor was inhabited by the vizir of Daha, the north-eastern one by the vizir of Majapahit. The other two manors lay south of the compounds. The south-eastern one was the residence of the bishop of the Shiwaites, the south-western one was inhabited by the bishop of the Buddhists. Besides those six main compounds and manors there were many more manors of mandarins and noblemen along the edge of the great complex. (Vol. 4, p. 27).

Thus, the capital of Majapahit was more a complex of compounds than a single walled-in fortress town of the medieval European type. And the royal compound itself at the very center of the complex resolved into three areas of accessibility graded from public to private.

Topographically, then, the capital of Majapahit, the center of the mandala, was composed of a number of relatively self-contained and walled-in compounds; each of these was composed of the central residence of the patron, surrounded by the lesser residences of his personal following and retinue, and then again by the bondsmen's dwellings at the periphery. Open spaces intervened between compounds, whose gradation was indexed by their size and location. Finally, there was no city wall at the outer boundary of the town: "As neither any kind of fortification nor any city gate is mentioned at the boundary, Majapahit could not be defended as a town. Only the compounds and the manors had walls and gates. That state of things survived in all Javanese towns [and, one might add, Thai and Burmese and other Southeast Asian towns as well] up to modern times" (vol. 4, p. 157).

There are many other examples which can be adduced to support the thesis that the mandala unity is in good measure achieved through parallel structures and bipartitions. The glory and power of King Hayam Wuruk was rivaled not only by other princes but also by his grand-vizier, Gajah Mada,[18] as, for example, suggested by the poem's pointed mention in its account of the Royal Progress of 1359 (to eastern Java) that the Gajah Mada's caravan leading the procession (with the king's at the opposite end) contained some 400 carts.

At the level of religious cults and functionaries, parallelism and duality were manifested in the coexistence and mutual relations of

Shiwaism and Buddhism, the former apparently exoteric and associated with the "material element" and with "worldly rule," the latter
esoteric and expressive of the "immaterial" and the "inconceivable"
(vol. 4, p. 4). The two clergies collaborated and competed in the annual purification ceremonies (p. 14). The two sets of shrines were located side by side in the eastern part of the main public courtyard of
the palace compound, and the houses of the Shiwaite clergy were located on the eastern boundaries and those of the Buddhist on the
southern boundaries of the royal compound. The asymmetry between
the two systems was manifest in the fact that the Shiwaite cult and
clergy were accorded a slight superiority over the Buddhist, but their
common meeting in a single unity was achieved in the architecture of
the central building, the Jajawa temple, whose ornamentation of the
base and body was Shiwaite and of the top Buddhistic in design and
motif.

8

On Flying Witches and Flying Canoes: The Coding of Male and Female Values

The institution of *kula,* as Malinowski so vividly described it for us, had a conspicuous place in the Trobrianders'—especially the male Trobrianders'—scheme of aspirations and sense of achievement. It was, as is to be expected from Trobriand preoccupation with it, suffused with magical ideas and practices, including those which Malinowski identified as witchcraft and sorcery.

Although Malinowski did not always clearly separate "witchcraft" from "sorcery," his ethnography portrays a clear distinction between the *bwaga'u* (sorcerer), who is male, and the *yoyova* (witch), who is usually female, especially the *mulukwausi* (the flying witch).[1] There are several suggestive differences between their characterizations. Men learn the art of sorcery, transmit it through exchange relations, and practice it intentionally and externally, seeking to achieve effects on other persons or objects. Women's involvement in witchcraft is involuntary, it is transmitted on a hereditary basis, and its characteristic manifestation is as a "disembodied" internal entity which appropriately attacks the victim's insides.

The first problem is to seek the logic of this contrastive potency which is attributed differentially to male and female, and which ramifies with other features of the *kula* traffic. I shall here focus, as my second problem, on only one such ramification: the association between female flying witches and the flying canoe celebrated in *kula* myths and canoe magic. How in terms of Trobriand cosmology can one "explain" the extraordinary powers attributed to the flying witches, who are on the one hand believed to be deadly dangerous to the *kula* sailors, and on the other hand provide the positive model of imitation for the *kula* deepsea canoe (*masawa*)? Aside from the famous Kudayuri myth which treats of flying canoes and witches, canoes are addressed in spells as females and flying witches. Indeed, canoes are urged to bind their skirts and fly in imitation of flying witches, who in turn by a symmetrical transfer of attributes are described as wearing during their flight the fluttering pandanus streamers with which seagoing canoes are decorated. Furthermore, just as the flying witch attacks shipwrecked sailors in order to eat their insides, a wrecked canoe at sea turns cannibalistic at the moment the *wayugo* creeper lashings disintegrate.

My discovery procedure is not in "causal" terms, as these are conventionally understood, but in terms of revealing analogical structures that are embedded in the ethnographic accounts scrutinized—structures that are related to one another by parallelisms, inversions, oppositions, transpositions, and so on. I also intend to provide semantic maps of portions of the Trobriand cosmology that can be inferred from the ethnography examined, and also venture a hypothesis on how Trobriand classificatory thought generated "extraordinary" events and persons by "collapsing" already separated categories.

Male and Female Attributes in Production, Reproduction, and Exchange

The assembling of the Trobriand cultural code concerning male and female attributes and their distributional pattern is integral for the solution of the problems set out here. In attempting to do so, I shall use Annette Weiner's book *Women of Value, Men of Renown* (1976) both as a point of reference and a point of departure.

The Female in Trobriand thought is the reproducer of *dala* members, and the transmitter of *dala* identity or essence, which she carries *inside* her as part of her very constitution. This identity is inalienable, timeless, and unchanging, and manifest as the impersonal *baloma* entering her and becoming incarnated as children. But also note that the *baloma* permanent essences, in being cycled through women, are in continuous reincarnating *motion* as well. This double aspect has been labeled "matrilineal descent," shared by successive generations of brothers and sisters but transmitted only through females.

In contrast, the Male is the primary agent, who actively establishes and maintains a *network of interpersonal exchange relations*. The male—especially the representative of the localized *dala* as manager/senior male—is the holder and controller of *dala* land rights, names, decorations, and spells. With regard to such interpersonal relations, a Trobriand male faces a radical separation between, on the one hand, his subjection to the obligatory and invariant intra-*dala* rule of transmission of privileges and possessions to his younger brother and sister's son (note here the familiar *pokala* payment on the claimant's part, which seals the jural right), and, on the other hand, his freedom to engage in extra-*dala* voluntary, ambitious, affect-laden acts of aggrandizement and achievement. One instance in the latter domain is the Trobriand man's variable love for his (wife's) children, and his giving free gifts to them. (*Contra* Malinowski, who characterized it as extranormative instinctive behavior, I believe that this orientation of father to son is as much an ideological formulation as that of mother's brother to sister's son.) Another instance is the fact that *dala* possessions and rights are temporarily loanable in the interests of furthering exchange relations (and through them increasing his and his *dala*'s prestige or rank). But note that it is women who then reclaim on behalf of the *dala* these loaned-out possessions. My reading of the significance of the distribution of women's wealth in mortuary rites is that it is women of a man's *dala* (as well as his own and his brother's daughters who in this context stand with him) who after that man's death ceremonially sever his affinal ties and exchange relations (with principally his wife and her kin, and his father and his kin), and thereby reclaim the dead man back into his *dala* in his essential form (that is, without exchange connections with members of other *dala*). Women sever these quintessential extra-*dala* connections by concluding the mourning, especially through the distribution of banana bundles and colored skirts, thereby restoring to the deceased's affines their sexuality and enabling the widow to remarry.[2] Although the leeway given a man to forge voluntaristic networks is a central link in the larger switchboard of political and affinal relations, this manipulative possibility, if carried too far to the point of endangering the interests of other *dala* men and matrilineal heirs, results in counteraction by sorcery. Men who commit such excesses invite their murder and/or their supersession.[3]

According to the well-known Trobriand reproduction theory, it is women who "involuntarily" and "accidentally" (unless they deliberately expose themselves to the scum, leaves, branches, and seaweeds of the shallow waters and creeks) conceive by means of the penetration of *baloma* spirits, and it is the husband who transfers by periodic sexual activity and nurture his facial and bodily resemblance to the child in the womb, and after its birth leaves his imprint by means of

further nurturance and show of affection. The logic of this complementarity is *cross-referenced* in terms of the contrastive roles of father's sister (*tabu*) and mother's brother (*kada*) with regard to their
nephew (and niece). The father's sister, with whom joking and teasing with sexual overtones is allowed, is eminently desirable and appropriate as the person who beautifies her brother's son's appearance by
the performance of beauty magic and body decoration. Correspondingly, the mother's brother, who is normally rigidly separated from his
sister by the *suvasova* (incest) taboo, can however assist his sister in
conceiving a child by bringing her a baler of seawater in which the *baloma* spirit children are believed to be present, having journeyed from
Tuma (Malinowski, 1932: 150).

The Trobriand relation between brother and sister is both complex
and finely tuned on chords held in high tension. Although in the origin myths brothers and sisters emerge together (a situation which
provoked Malinowski to comment on the conspicuous absence of the
husband or wife in these myths), both myth and social practice insist
on the necessity for brothers and sisters to separate. Their emergence
together is dictated by their sharing of common *dala* identity, but their
continued coresidence is powerfully suggestive of incest. It is the sister's fate or mission then to be uprooted and to be *mobile*—to be given
away to go and live with her husband, to be "loaned" away by her
dala; her sons, however, are usually reclaimed (in Malinowski's classical description) by her mother's brothers, and they return (or have
the right to return) to live on *dala* land. Thus, men, in contrast to
women, once mature stay "anchored" on their own *dala* land, cultivate the gardens, and send the best part of the "children of their gardens," the *taitu* and *kuvi* yams, to their sisters as *urigubu*. Note that
the implication and meaning of "anchoring" is crucial in Trobriand
ritual: the growing yams are "anchored" in the belly of the garden so
that they can grow big and send out shoots (which aboveground can
branch out in free mobility). Again, the *urigubu* yams are "anchored"
in the storehouse by the ritual use of *binabina* stones with magical
words, so that the yams will endure and not be consumed quickly.

In line with this brother-sister differential is the *baloma-tabu* distinction within the category of ancestral spirits. Unlike the impersonal
cyclically reincarnating *baloma,* the *tabu* are marked, differentiated,
individuated, and often named ancestors, who emerged from holes in
the land (and other sites) and constitute the basis of *dala* land and
rank claims, and *dala*-linked garden and canoe magic, decorations,
and taboos. Though theoretically both brothers and sisters because of
coappearance qualify to be *tabu*, males are almost always the stereo-

type *tabu* personages by virtue of their residence on *dala* land and their control of *dala* possessions, while their sisters move away to reside with their husbands. Women, of course, carry their rank into marriage and observe taboos associated with their rank, and can "inherit" and learn certain kinds of *dala* magic. But they cannot practice this magic in their own right; they can only transmit it to their children, just as they transmit rank and descent to them.

What I am deliberately leading up to is the proposition that in Trobriand thought women and men have both stable and volatile capacities in their distinctive ways, that these capacities receive differential stress, and that the dualities of these sexes may be further coordinated in a pattern (as "the relations between the relations").

Women, the vehicles of cycling *dala* essence, are invested with the capacities of energy force and motion in their most potent, mobile, and natural (as an essential accompaniment of femaleness) forms. This stressed attribution has both positive and negative aspects, which I shall explore later.

The female who is on the move residentially (the mother separated from married daughters, married sisters from each other) finds her anchorage in the marriage relationship. She resides virilocally with her husband and receives the *urigubu* yams from her brother in recognition of her *dala* rights, the affinal relation between her husband and her brother, and the conjugal relation between her and her husband. This conjugal and affinal anchorage is in some ways so central a feature of Trobriand social relations that at least one tradition of analysis of kinship terminology, which claims to support and stem from Malinowski's "extensionist theory," actually flatly distorts a Malinowskian formulation, while quite correctly indicating the critical importance of the husband-wife solidarity unit.[4] From my perspective, the affinal anchorage is dependent on the marital relationship, which in Trobriand terms is effected as a *sexual relationship* between husband and wife—a voluntaristic exchange relationship (as exemplified by the "payment" to the woman for sexual favors granted) which separates the *sexuality* of a woman from her involuntary and inhering *procreative* capacity. Thus, if a woman disengages from her marital relationship, she is thought to reactivate her propensities for motion and (sexual) aggression, which is exactly what is symbolized, as we shall see later, in the notion of flying witch or the fantasies about sexual attacks by nymphomaniac females.[5] Furthermore, the characterization of the aggressive power of the detached flying witch as materializing inside her belly is an inversion of a woman's normal conception by *baloma* intrusion when she is attached in marriage.

Males, in contrast to females, are in a primary sense regarded as being "anchored" and stabilized on *dala* land together with the rights to use and manipulate *dala* possessions. But hinged to this is the correlated fact that it is men who are the prime political actors, who consciously and calculatedly go in search of *butura* (renown), which is a volatile, changing, and mercurial reward won and lost in the channels of exchange networks. And this volatility that carries with it suggestions of being unanchored reaches its pitch of uncertainty and fluidity on the *kula* seaways, *kula* exchange being for the Trobrianders a quintessential male activity. The physical state of the canoe on the sea, with fluttering pandanus streamers striving after maximum speed, is experienced by the men as the most liminal and "unanchored" state of physical and social existence.

Male Sorcerers, Female Witches, Flying Witches, and Nonhuman Malignant Spirits

We are now ready to grasp the logic of the characterizations of sorcerer and witch. Their modes of operation and their different capacities parallel—indeed, are "projected on"—the patterns discussed above.

Sorcerers

Sorcerers, who are always male, engage in concrete acts—they employ words, manipulate substances, have accomplices. According to one description of his technique (Malinowski, 1922: 74–76), the sorcerer makes his victim take to his bed by use of a spell; then, accompanied by accomplices such as "nightbirds, owls, and night-jars," he inserts through the thatch wall of the victim's hut at night a bunch of herbs impregnated with a charm and drops it into the fire. The victim inhales the fumes and is seized by a deadly disease. Should he be foiled in this attack, the sorcerer resorts to "a most fatal rite, that of the pointing bone": a sharp stingaree spine, impregnated with powerful spells and herbs boiled in coconut oil, is pointed at the victim and stabbed at him.

Feared as the black art is, yet the sorcerer produces by his spells and rites only ordinary ailments; he does not produce "very rapidly fulminating diseases and epidemics" (Malinowski, 1948: 105). Moreover, a sorcerer never eats his victim's flesh, and since he is responsible for lingering disease his work can be counteracted (Malinowski, 1932: 46).

Male sorcery is an "actual trade" and is transmitted through learning from practitioner to apprentice—who need not be a kinsman—accompanied by the proper gifts and payments. Malinowski reported that there were a number of sorcerers in the district, and in each village one or two men were known to practice. Spells are learned in return for high payment; as in other instances of transmission, a *pokala* payment by a sister's son ensures the transmission from a mother's brother, whereas a father may freely teach spells to a son. One of the striking features of sorcery is that it carries no negative evaluation. Every man may aspire to be a powerful sorcerer. True to Trobriand ascription, chiefs and aristocrats (*guyau*) have stronger sorcery and more sorcerers at their side than commoners, and a chief or headman can openly practice sorcery and may publicly boast of its effectiveness as evidence of his special powers. "Thus sorcery, which is one of the means of carrying on the established order, is in turn strengthened by it" (Malinowski, 1922: 76, and cf. 64).

How are we to understand the belief that a sorcerer must launch his career as a genuine practitioner by first committing the "matricidal act" of killing a mother or a sister (that is, a close female of his own *dala*) or "any of his maternal kindred"? This proposition carries at least two concordant meanings: a once and for all extreme act of violence on a (preferably close) female inside the *dala* ensures that the malevolence will be practiced thereafter outside the *dala* (that is, by those with whom he has exchange relations); or an extreme act of violence committed against a close kinswoman emancipates the sorcerer, so to say, from the realm of close affective kin-feelings and catapults him into "impersonal" violence against others. Either way, the sorcerer's look is "outward," not involuted or inward, after the primal "internal" act of violence.

The origin stories of sorcery reinforce the significance of its transmission among males in the present time. Sorcery, like all other malevolent phenomena, is believed to have come from the south, in this instance from the D'Entrecasteaux Archipelago. It entered Kiriwina at two points: at Vakuta Island in the south and in the low-status settlements of Ba'u and Bwoytalu. Here are two brief accounts of the first arrival from the south (Malinowski, 1948: 105–106).

1. A crab arrives in Bwoytalu "emerging out of a hole . . . or else traveling by the air and dropping from above." The crab, red in color, gives man his magic in return for a *pokala* payment; the man kills his benefactor and, according to rule, then kills "a near maternal relative." Crabs are black in color now because they have lost their powers of sorcery, and they are slow to die, for they once were "the masters of life and of death." Man thus receives sorcery from a nonhuman ani-

mal by means of an exchange relation; the crab, though nonhuman, emerges from under the ground and has a long life (near-immortality). In this sense, crabs are like the *baloma* ancestral spirits, who also live underground and emerge above and reincarnate themselves by shedding their skin.[6]

2. A malicious being of human shape (*tauva'u*) entered a piece of bamboo somewhere on the northern shore of Normanby Island; the bamboo drifted to a promontory on Vakuta, a man pried it open, and the demon taught him the sorcery. Once again there is a twofold idea: the demon this time travels like a *baloma* spirit from Tuma on water, and teaches man as an act of reciprocity and reward. I shall have more to say about the nonhuman malignant spirits (*tauva'u*) in comparison with witches.

Witches (Yoyova) and Flying Witches (Mulukwausi)

Witches move around at night by sending forth their invisible doubles, wreaking havoc by direct attack. The witch does not practice a trade compounded of spells and rites. The witch "can fly through the air and appears as a falling star; she assumes at will the shape of a firefly, of a night bird, or of a flying fox; she can hear and smell at enormous distances" (Malinowski, 1932: 39). The disease that witches cause is incurable and kills rapidly: "It is inflicted by the removal of the victim's insides, which the woman presently consumes" (ibid). Witches have sarcophagous propensities, and feed on corpses. They can also cause a number of minor ailments—such as toothache, certain kinds of tumors, swelling of the testicles, and genital discharge (venereal disease?). Witchcraft is involuntarily inherited by a daughter from her mother.

All these characteristics of a female witch that have been listed stand in stark comparison and opposition to the features that constitute a male sorcerer, on the following axes: visible / invisible; normal person / invisible double; external practice / internal transformation; ordinary, slowly killing diseases / sudden incurable diseases; voluntary transmission through exchange / involuntary transmission as heritage; noncannibalistic / cannibalistic; usually, male attack on male / frequently, female attack on male.

A few features from this array may be selected for special mention. The witch involuntarily transforms her "insides," a propensity so powerful that it is represented as flying (aerial motion) and virulent attack (malignant disease). Clearly the witch and her powers are projected from the procreative powers of women and the notion that *baloma* reincarnates and cycles through them. But together with parallels go systematic inversions. The involuntary passage of *baloma* "inside" a woman is matched by the involuntary hereditary transmission of witchcraft materializing inside her belly; but whereas the *baloma* is born as a child from the womb, the witch attacks and consumes the victim's insides. There is also a topographical displacement: whereas the *baloma* emerges from under the ground to become incarnate as humans on the ground, a witch already a human on the ground becomes disembodied and takes to the air. Thus, *baloma*, *human*, and *witch* belong to the three cosmological realms of under the ground, on the ground, and above the ground (sky).

The *mulukwausi*, the flying witches, are the most malignant agents of witchcraft and possess attributes that are magnifications of those of ordinary witches. They are actual living women, who have the power to make themselves invisible and to dispatch a double (*kakuluwala*), which can travel vast distances through the air. They are invisible maurauders who "perch on trees, house-tops, and other high places" and attack from above.[7] They carry their powers inside the "belly," which is the seat of emotions and understanding, the storehouse of magic, and the seat of memory (Tambiah, 1968), and appropriately attack the insides of their victims. They are associated with the smell of carrion, and on land they are feared when death takes place because they swarm and feed on the insides (*lopoulo* = lungs, also insides). At burial, magic is used to ward them off (Malinowski, 1948: 129).

The *mulukwausi* come always from the southern half of the island or from the east, from the islands of Kitawa, Iwa, Gawa, or Murua (1922: 76). The places of origin and the pathways of the flying witches thus follow closely the two *kula* routes that converge on Boyowa—they are associated with the easterners who come to Kiriwina (and to Vakuta and Sinaketa) from Kitava and more easterly places, and with the Dobuans and other southerners from the Amphlett Islands who come to Vakuta and Sinaketa. Within Boyowa itself it is the southern parts (including Wawela on the eastern shore) and certain degraded places that are the points of entry.

But whatever the mythic origins of this witchcraft (which, like sorcery, came from outside on the seaways), current Kiriwinan beliefs clearly portray their own women as capable of being witches. The most salient feature of these beliefs is that Kiriwinan women can gravely endanger the safety of their men at sea on *kula* voyages by transgressing certain taboos.

Thus, a critical theme for this essay is that the *mulukwausi* are especially dangerous at sea. They look for prey whenever there is a storm and a canoe is threatened. Men who have been exposed to such danger have affirmed that they became conscious of the smell of carrion, a sign of the presence of these evil women.

The *mulukwausi* conception intersects with the conception of the male sorcerer via the notions surrounding the *tauva'u*—the nonhuman malignant spirits which, as we have already seen, are the original transmitters of sorcery knowledge to men.

The flying witches and the *tauva'u* share the capacity to unleash sudden virulent disease. The flying witches cause sudden diseases, which show no perceptible symptoms and cause quick death (Malinowski, 1922: 76, 237–248). Epidemics are attributed to the direct action of *tauva'u* who likewise are invisible to human beings and "walk at night through the villages rattling their limegourds and clanking their wooden sword clubs." They strike humans with their wooden weapons and make them die of leria and other epidemic diseases, on a massive scale. During the severe dysentery that occurred in 1918 many Kiriwinans reported hearing the *tauva'u*.

This epidemic (probably influenza) was seen as the retribution for the killing of a giant lizard by a man of Wawela village—because the *tauva'u* sometimes change into reptiles and then become visible to human eyes. A reptile of this sort should be placed on a high platform and valuables placed in front of it, an injunction that is similar to that concerning how both chiefs and *baloma* (when visiting during the *milamala* festival) are to be treated on ceremonial occasions. A final piece of useful information is that "a number of witches are said to have had intercourse with *tauva'u* and of one living at present this is positively affirmed" (Malinowski, 1948: 109).

So, while *tauva'u* give their sorcery knowledge to men, they copulate with witches; and in their ability to emerge from the ground as reptiles or snakes they are like the *baloma*—underground creatures who shed skins are also immortal. But whereas *baloma* are incarnated through and in women, the *tauva'u* behave like human husbands toward malevolent women in having sexual intercourse with them.

Malinowski was correct when he observed that Trobriand beliefs toward disease and death "form an organic whole." My description and analysis show that notions surrounding disease, death, and danger form an interrelated set and involve an intricate set of contrasts and linkages among *four* conceptions: the male sorcerer, the female witch (and especially the flying witch), the nonhuman *tauva'u* malignant spirits, and the human *baloma* ancestral spirits. Their interrelations can be summarized in a single diagram (Figure 8.1).

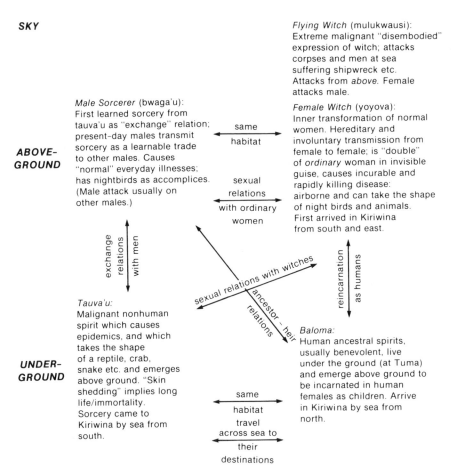

SKY

ABOVE-GROUND

UNDER-GROUND

Flying Witch (mulukwausi): Extreme malignant "disembodied" expression of witch; attacks corpses and men at sea suffering shipwreck etc. Attacks from *above*. Female attacks male.

Male Sorcerer (bwaga'u): First learned sorcery from tauva'u as "exchange" relation; present-day males transmit sorcery as a learnable trade to other males. Causes "normal" everyday illnesses; has nightbirds as accomplices. (Male attack usually on other males.)

Female Witch (yoyova): Inner transformation of normal women. Hereditary and involuntary transmission from female to female; is "double" of *ordinary* woman in invisible guise, causes incurable and rapidly killing disease: airborne and can take the shape of night birds and animals. First arrived in Kiriwina from south and east.

same habitat

sexual relations with ordinary women

exchange relations with men

sexual relations with witches

ancestor – heir relations

reincarnation as humans

Tauva'u: Malignant nonhuman spirit which causes epidemics, and which takes the shape of a reptile, crab, snake etc. and emerges above ground. "Skin shedding" implies long life/immortality. Sorcery came to Kiriwina by sea from south.

Baloma: Human ancestral spirits, usually benevolent, live under the ground (at Tuma) and emerge above ground to be incarnated in human females as children. Arrive in Kiriwina by sea from north.

same habitat travel across sea to their destinations

Figure 8.1 Interrelations among Trobriand beliefs about disease, death, and danger.

The Myth of the Flying Canoe of Kudayuri

Although Malinowski stated that he knew of three versions of the Kudayuri myth, he gave the full text of only one, and we for the most part do not know how the versions differed.

The myth text can be found in *Argonauts* (pp. 311–316). The main sequences of the story are as follows:

> Mokatuboda of the Lukuba clan and his younger brother Toweyre'i live in the village of Kudayuri in Kitava with their

three sisters (who are later described as *yoyova*). The whole group had emerged from underground, and are the first possessors of the *ligogu* (adze) and *wayugo* (creeper) canoe magic.

The men of Kitava plan an overseas *kula* expedition. (Kitava is a raised coral island. Its inland part is elevated to a height of about 500 feet. Cf. Scoditti, 1983.)

The ordinary Kitava people build their canoes on the beach.

Mokatuboda and his Kudayuri people build their canoe on the hill in the middle of the village.

The ordinary Kitava people launch their canoes in the ordinary way.

The Kudayuri canoe, through Mokatuboda's magic, is launched from the middle of the village and reaches its destination by flying; it starts late but arrives first at each destination.

Later there is a drought in Kitava. The gardens are burnt up and crops fail. Mokatuboda uses his magic to provide a private cloud and a private rainfall which fertilizes his garden exclusively.

Toweyre'i, thinking he has learned all Mokatuboda's magic, kills him, with the assistance of his subclan brothers and maternal nephews.

Next year another kula expedition is planned and the canoe building proceeds as before, with Toweyre'i in charge of the Kudayuri canoe builders. When he uses his magic, the canoe fails to fly. The dead Mokatuboda has not passed on the essential magic to Toweyre'i. The three sisters are then angry and fly away as witches, cutting through rocks, and following flight paths analogous to that of the magical canoe, and similar to those that would be taken today by *kula* fleets starting from Kitava. They eventually become named rocks in named locations.

I am here primarily concerned with certain implications of the myth integral to the theme of flying witches and flying canoes. The full value of a myth can be established only by relating its internal pattern to the patterns embedded in the other myths of the Trobriand corpus, but I cannot undertake such a structuralist analysis here.

My method of interpretation consists of comparing and contrasting the mythic events (the actions of the mythic heroes) with the *social norms* of everyday life incumbent on present-day Trobrianders, and with the patterns of the *canoe magic* that are also practiced today and alleged to stem from the Kudayuri myth. In other words, I will attempt to squeeze out meaning by dialectically relating this myth to two other domains: that of extant social norms and that of magical practices.

The first half of the myth is arranged as a repetitive contrastive enumeration of the activities of the Kudayuri group and the other villages of Kitava. These activities range from the sequential procedures of canoe building with emphasis on *parallel* tasks being done in *different* locations (*village* versus *beach*), followed by the *kula* exchanges at the *same* geographic sites but attended by *differential* success, this difference being dramatically described in terms of the *later departures* of the Kudayuri group but their *earlier arrival* at destinations. This repetitive and contrastive arrangement of the events explores the semantic implications of dislocation and displacement of the normal categorical ordering of space and time, and the normal synchronization of ceremonial activities. In the canoe building, both groups synchronize their activities, but the Kudayuri group enact them in the *wrong place*. Next, the usual custom in *kula* expeditions that the canoes depart and arrive as a fleet at the same time (with, no doubt, precedence in the procession given to chiefs or other leaders) is contravened by the dislocated timing of sailing and arriving.[8] Finally, the ordinary expectation that the late departer will also thereby arrive later is upset by the flying canoe—which represents a distortion of spatio-temporal, atmospheric, and gravitational realities. This method of generating and talking about extraordinary events and propensities through the distortion or dislocation of spatio-temporal order is formalized later in this chapter, where I discuss the mapping of the categories land, sea, and sky.

There are other ways in which the myth explores the implications of violence and excesses. Mokatuboda of the Lukuba clan and his brother and sisters, in being coresident in the same village, present a residential anomaly. The coresidence of mature brothers and sisters carries connotations of violating the norm of brother-sister social distance; indeed, it smacks of an "involuted" incestuous relationship between brothers and sisters. One could go so far as to say that the ratio of three sisters to two brothers in itself is motivated: it conveys powerfully the measure of the involution in which the sisters outnumber the men!

This involution of the Kudayuri group—associated with the *village* in contrast to the other villages associated with the open *beach*—is reinforced by the abnormal method of building a canoe. Normally the tree is scooped in the village center (*baku*), where also the component parts are made, and the canoe is assembled and lashed together at the beach, the latter being a public event with many helpers joining in. This two-phased procedure from village to beach where the canoe is assembled is all the more necessary on the island of Kitava, a raised atoll, with a sharp decline from the village on the "plateau" to the beach down below.

This extreme isolation of the Kudayuri sibling group is further marked by their pointed refraining from the obligatory ceremonial proceedings on the completion of the canoe, proceedings which emphasize exchange and reciprocity between villages (or settlements/canoe-building and -owning groups). These festivities are the *tasasoria*, or trial run, and the *kabigidoya*, or visit of ceremonial presentation (Malinowski, 1922: ch. 6). The launching is accompanied by the *sagali* distribution of food in payment to the canoe expert and helpers. Some days later the new canoe is displayed to friends and relatives, first in the neighboring villages and then in other districts; at this time, valuables and trade goods are collected for the *kula* expedition.

The myth conveys a strong impression that the "involuted" nonexchange relations of the Kudayuri group are the basis for its strong ("excessive") magical powers, and that the proper state of affairs is the *dispersion* and *differentiation* of this group (the separation of brothers and sisters), with the converse implication of its becoming open to relations with the outside world. This outcome necessarily also results in a *weakening* (a partial inheritance) of the original magic in its supranormal potent form.

Let us now face the logic of the fratricide. It seems to me that there can be two readings of this act and its consequences—readings which do not so much contradict each other as depict the two sides of the same coin.

One reading would be that the myth states in a fairly straightforward way that, if it had not been for the fratricide, not only would men still know how to build flying canoes but there would be no flying witches to haunt and ravage the real crews of ordinary real canoes. There has to be a younger brother so that he can inherit from his older brother, but he nevertheless inherits imperfectly what is known perfectly by the elder brother on account of his sin of fratricide. Moreover, since the three sisters also know the perfect magic (innately), the younger brother must cause them offense so that they also depart without revealing the secret. It is the offense of fratricide which converts the three sisters into flying witches, and removes them from being residents of Kudayuri village to the top of Botigalea hill.

The second reading tries to answer why the fratricide took place *in the gardens* and why the victim was killed "not by the Kitava men but by his kinsmen," a problem that puzzled Malinowski (1922: 319). The puzzle that must be interpreted is this: The Kudayuri group, with Mokatuboda as the *toliwaga* and his younger brother and "maternal nephews" (*kada*) as the crew, triumphantly return from the *kula* expedition having bested their rival villages by means of Mokatuboda's adze magic, which enables the Kudayuri boat to fly. But back in the village, when Mokatuboda practices evil magic (*bulubwalata*) by means of which rain falls only in his garden while drought destroys the gardens of the other men of Kitava, it is his own kin, his younger brother Toweyre'i and his maternal nephews (not the men of other villages), who kill him. In interpreting this event, one should first consider the different ethics associated with *kula* and with *gardening*. *Kula* activity is *competitive*, the rivals being the other canoe crews in the same expedition, sometimes individuals in the same canoe crew itself. Thus, invidious magic and sorcery are alleged to be practiced by rivals against each other: it is the order of the day. If you are beaten in a *kula* transaction you do not kill your successful rival; you practice sorcery against him. But gardening is surrounded by different canons of interpersonal behavior in the Trobriands (in contrast to Dobu). Gardening is informed by communal and cooperative norms. In theory, a whole garden with an enclosure around it (*buyagu*) is assigned to the care of a single garden magician and it is considered to "belong" to him; within this collective definition, an individual works his own plot (*baleko*). The magician right through the gardening cycle practices magic (not evil sorcery) on behalf of the community of gardeners, with individual gardeners subsequently doing their own supplementary rites (Malinowski, 1935: vol. 2, pp. 85, 291–292).[9] At the widest and highest level, the chief and his garden magician practice garden magic for the benefit of all in the district. As Malinowski records elsewhere, *waygigi*, the supreme magic of rain and sunshine, is the exclusive privilege of the paramount chiefs of Omarakana (1927: 130).

Hence, there is good reason why Mokatuboda, the headman, was killed for practicing evil rain magic. The fratricide itself is not so much a public delict as an internal affair of the subclan only, very much in the sense that the sin of Cain was adjudged (Schapera, 1955: 33–43). The Trobriand attitude is illustrated by Malinowski's account of a court case. A blind older brother killed a younger brother for taking his betelnut and was sentenced to twelve months' incarceration by the white resident magistrate. The natives regarded this sentence as an outrageous injustice because "the killing of one brother by another is a purely internal matter, certainly a dreadful crime and an awful tragedy, but one with which the outer world is in no way concerned, and it can only stand by and show its horror and pity."

The fratricide should also be considered in relation to the norms of succession of *dala* headship in Trobriand matrilineal society: a younger brother succeeds an older, and when the sibling group is exhausted the succession goes one generation down, starting with the oldest son of the oldest sister. Thus, the murderers in the myth are the immediate heir and potential heirs. In one sense, then, the younger brother succeeds his older brother legitimately, as succession rules go. And in fact this seems to be the implication in another version of the Kudayuri myth, fragmentarily reported by Malinowski: "Toweyre'i kills his elder brother in the garden. He then comes back to the village and instructs and admonishes Mokatuboda's children to take the body, to give it the mortuary attentions, and to prepare it for the burial. Then he himself arranges the sagali, the big mortuary distribution of food," as befits the new head (1922: 319; 1927: 119).

Both readings of the myth converge on the fact that the younger brother's inheritance of the older brother's magic was *incomplete*. Although Toweyre'i had thought he had received the magic of *ligogu* (adze), of *kunisaleli* (rain magic), of *wayugo* (lashing creeper), he was mistaken because his elder brother gave him *only part of the magic,* and this partial magic does not enable the canoe to take off from land and fly. "Thus humanity lost the flying magic forever" (1927: 119). There is no doubt that one of the messages of the myth is that the complete canoe magic of the fantastic kind possessed by the first elder, Mokatuboda, of the Kudayuri group, has been irretrievably lost, with a weakened (and more "realistic") version being actually transmitted to the next head, a younger brother.

At this point let me make a general proposition which is based on a prior analysis of other Trobriand myths. Trobriand myths appear to use the older brother–younger brother and the older sister–younger sister grids to code different messages. For example, like the Kudayuri myth, the Tudava-Gere'u myth also starts with the older brother as the first hero who in a sense has both very potent—and by that same token "excessive" and "unrestrained"—magical powers, and it is the younger brother who practices and transmits the more "restrained" and more "realistic" (more in accord with known human capacities) magic to the descendants. This is an exemplification of how the theme of "excess and restraint" runs like a thread through many Trobriand myths. The older-younger sister grid codes a quite different message. It is the older sister who is the more orthodox, keeps food taboos, and remains at the geographical center of the sub-clan, and the younger sister who departs to the periphery and breaks food taboos. The result is that an *absolute* distinction of rank is con-veyed to their respective descendants, a possibility that is in line with the rule of residence which disperses sisters. By comparison, the older-younger brother does not code permanent rank distinction, and *cannot do so*, because brothers ideally are coresident, and the younger brother can succeed the older.

We now come to the theme of the flying witches. The drama of the final section of the myth unfolds in this manner. The three sisters be-came very angry with Toweyre'i, for he killed the elder brother and did not learn in full his magic, particularly that which would make the canoe airborne. They themselves had learned the (complete) *ligogu* and *wayugo* magic, they had it in their belly (*lopoulo*), and in fact they were witches (*yoyova*) and could fly. I would claim that their re-fusal to share the magic with their younger brother is the counterpart of their own self-propelled takeoff. So from the top of Botigalea hill (an elevated aboveground position) they departed on their never-to-return flights.

The women's possession of the magic in their belly and of the power to fly is in line with the male and female propensities discussed above. While men learn magic and practice it externally upon the world, women inherit and carry sorcery-magic in their belly and internally transform themselves in the same way as they carry and transmit *dala* identity. This also accords with the ethnographic fact that if the males in a generation are about to die out, a woman could learn men's magic (even magic of gardening and canoe making), but she would not be allowed to practice it herself; her obligation is to teach it to a male heir when she bears him (1932: 48).

Finally, let us pay close attention to the flight of the sisters. Their piercing through rocks and creating sea passages is a vivid description of the magical potency contained within witches. A recurring Tro-briand theme is how these unattached witches (or, elsewhere, dy-namic *kula* heroes) representing fantastic speed and motion are finally stabilized as rocks. Rocks are a representation of immobility as well as of permanent *anchoring* (a positive Trobriand valuation). This stabilization of the witches, then, allows for their becoming agents for granting (restricted) benefits, and their locations appropriately be-come shrines for propitiation by *kula* sailors.

The first sister—Na'ukuwakula—flies west, piercing through and leaving a trail from Dikuwa'i to Simsim; the other two travel south, leaving the pierced seaway via Giribwa, Tewara, Kadimwatu, Dobu,

Saramwa, the Straits of Loma (Dawson Straits), and back to Tewara's vicinity. This detailed geographical indexing is actually a mapping of actual, currently used sea routes for *kula* and other expeditions (1922: maps on 50 and 82). The mythic routes then code knowledge of actual sailing routes, though the mythic voyages are much longer than those usually undertaken. A final detail is that one sister facing Dobu becomes thereby a cannibal (Dobuans are cannibals), and the other faces Boyowa and is therefore not a cannibal. This may be interpreted as representing the fact that the Dobuans and Boyowans, separated by the divide of cannibalism, are nevertheless in a reciprocal relationship (as represented by *kula* exchange), an idea nicely represented by two sisters sharing ties of kinship but standing back to back facing opposite directions and representing disjunctive orientations.

Since for the Trobrianders the eye or the tip (*dogina*) of the myth carries the pragmatic punch, what the myth finally leaves us with is the permanent loss of flying canoe magic, but the existence of flying witches as an experiential reality. What the younger brother had and present-day folk have today is a partial canoe magic, but these present-day humans know for a fact that their womenfolk can under certain circumstances turn into witches, flying with fantastic speed and wielding a potency for aggressive destruction.

The Making of a Canoe and Its Associated Magic

The *Argonauts* contains, together with the text of the myth of the flying canoe, a detailed account of the procedures of canoe construction which are followed through in real-life canoe building. Reciprocally, in real life canoe building there are significant cross-references to the myth. This section is concerned with this feedback relationship between mythical charter and magical performance.

Two important facts should be kept in mind when considering this relationship: canoe making is entirely a male activity, and canoes are male property. Moreover, the distancing of women from the artifact is powerfully expressed in the restriction that "women are not allowed to enter a new *waga* before it sails." Yet there is the contrapuntal theme that it is desirable that a canoe perform with the speed, aggressiveness, and lightness of a "flying witch," and in this sense the canoe is viewed as a "woman."

Although to the European the Trobriand canoe may look like "an abortive imperfect attempt to tackle the problem of sailing," "to the native his cumbersome sprawling canoe is a marvellous, almost miraculous achievement, a thing of beauty ... He has spun a tradition around it, and he adorns it with his best carvings, he colours and decorates it. It is to him a powerful contrivance for the mastery of Nature, which allows him to cross perilous seas to distant places" (1922: 106). On the lightness and buoyancy of the canoe, Malinowski wrote: "It skims the surface, gliding up and down the waves, now hidden by the crests, now riding on top of them. It is a precarious but delightful sensation to sit in the slender body, while the canoe darts on with the float raised, the platform steeply slanting, and water constantly breaking over" (1922: 107).

The reader of the ethnography gets a glimpse into why Trobriand canoe magic invokes the butterfly metaphor, and why crew members imagine themselves to be irresistibly attractive to the partners standing on the shore watching their approach: "When, on a trading expedition or as a visiting party, a fleet of native canoes appears in the offing with their triangular sails like butterfly wings scattered over the water, with the harmonious calls of conch shells blown in unison, the effect is unforgettable. When the canoes then approach, and you see them rocking in the blue water in all the splendour of their fresh white, red and black paint, with their finely designed prowboards, and clanking array of large, white cowrie shells—you understand well the admiring love which results in all this care bestowed by the native on the decoration of his canoe" (1922: 108).

There were three types of canoe in use in the Trobriands, and the *masawa* was the type used in deepsea sailing. Malinowski observed that up to the present not one single *masawa* had been constructed without the full observance of the magical rites. He went on to assert that for the Trobrianders both magical rites and technical craftsmanship were indispensable, and both acted "independently," the natives understanding "that magic, however efficient, will not make up for bad workmanship" (1922: 108). We may represent Malinowski as striving to say that the technical and magical operations formed an amalgam—one procedure could not work without being in tandem with the other—and in this sense magic "regulated," "completed," and lent a creative and anticipatory dimension to the entire activity of canoe making, which was the first link in the chain of *kula* performances. Indeed, the launching of the canoe and especially the formal presentation visit (*Kabigidoya*) are in one sense the final acts of canoe building and in another sense the preliminaries to the *kula* voyage.

The construction of the canoe goes through two main phases. The first phase consists in the lengthy and leisurely process (spanning months of work punctuated by intervals) of preparing the components of the canoe, usually in the village center (*baku*); this is the business of the canoe builder (expert) and his few helpers. The canoe expert also performs the appropriate magic. The second phase, by contrast, is brief (a week or two), characterized by intensive work done on a large-scale communal basis. Its principal operations are the transport of the dug-out hull of the canoe and its components to the beach, the piecing together of planks and prowboards, the lashing of the outrigger, and the caulking and painting of the canoe. During this second phase are performed certain kinds of *kula* (*mwasila*) magic and rites of exorcism, all performed by the canoe's owner (*toliwaga*) or his representative.

Examples of Magic of the First Phase: Ethnographic Details

1. The *kaygagabili* spell, which is uttered to make the log lighter for pulling and also to impart to it great speed, employs these words: "the tree flies; the tree becomes like a breath of wind, the tree becomes like a butterfly" (1922: 130).

2. The canoe expert, when performing the adze magic, makes several recitations which make explicit references to the flying witches of the Kudayuri myth:

a. The *kapitunena duku* spell, after emphatically stating that other canoes will be "waved back" so as not to overtake, invokes the "women of Tokuna, on the top of Si'a Hill," and ends with the onomatopoetic word *saydididi*, in imitation of the sound made by flying witches (1922: 130–131).

b. The next, even more important magic performed before the special *ligogu* adze is used for scooping out the felled log "stands in close connection to the myth of the flying canoe." Here are three excerpts from the spells (1922: 132):

b.1. "We shall fly like butterflies, like wind; . . . You will pierce the straits of Kadimwatu (between the islands of Tewara and Umama), you will break the promontory of Saramwa (near Dobu), pierce the passage of Loma (in Dawson Straits)."[10]

b.2. "Break through your seaweeds. Put on your wreath (of seaweeds), make your bed in the sand."[11]

b.3. "Bind your grass skirt together, O canoe (personal name) fly."

Examples of Magic of the Second Phase: Ethnographic Details

The scene now shifts to "the clean snow-white sand of a coral beach" where the dug-out canoe and its accessories are being assembled, watched in the case of a big chief's canoe by hundreds of natives.

a. The rite of *katuliliva tabuyo* belongs to the *kula mwasila* magic directed at influencing the mind of the *kula* partner, and is here connected with the inserting of the ornamental prowboards into their grooves at both ends of the canoe. The canoe owner inserts sprigs of mint plant under the board and while hammering them recites a formula which we may interpret as an act by which the owner "charms" and "coaxes" the canoe "as if it were a woman." We note in this context that the mint plant (*sulumwoya*) plays an important part in the *kula mwasila* magic as well as in the magic of beauty and in the recitation of love spells. In contexts of "charming, seducing, or persuading as a rule *sulumwoya* is used" (1922: 135).

b. The body of the canoe, brightened by its three-colored prowboards, is pushed into the water: "A handful of leaves, of a shrub called *bobi'u*, was charmed by the owner or by the builder, and the body of the canoe is washed in sea water with the leaves. All the men participate in the washing, and this rite is intended to make the canoe fast, by removing the traces of evil influence."[12]

c. After washing, the canoe is pulled ashore again for what is considered the most important technical and magical operation in canoe construction—namely, the lashing with the *wayugo* creeper of the internal framework of twelve to twenty pairs of ribs, which help to keep in position the gunwale planks that are attached to the sides of the dugout so as to form the deep and wide walls of the canoe. Of the *wayugo* creeper, Malinowski wrote these significant words (1922: 135): "It is this alone that maintains the cohesion of the various parts, and in rough weather, very much depends on how the lashings will stand the strain . . . Thus the element of danger and uncertainty in a canoe is due mainly to the creeper."

The *wayugo* spell clearly contains numerous references to the flying sisters of the Kudayuri myth. Here are two examples:

1. After suggesting the "flutter" of pandanus streamers and the "foaming" of stormy seas, the spell continues: "Before you lies the sea arm of Pilolu. Today, they kindle the festive fire of the Kudayuri, thou, O my boat . . . bind thy skirts together and fly." Malinowski notes that this allusion to binding the skirt during flying is to Na'ukuwakula, the oldest of the Kudayuri sisters, and that the main part of the spell then goes on to say that "Na'ukuwakula flew from Kitava through Sinaketa and Kayleula to Simsim, where she settled down and transmitted the magic to her progeny."[13] The leading words of this *tapwana* part of the spell are *three places* which in sequence are flown to in an aura of mist and smoke and with the force of a wind eddy: Kuyawa (a creek or hillock near Sinaketa), Dikutuwa (a rock near Kayleula), and La'u (a cleft in the sea near Simsim).

2. In the *dogina,* the last part of the spell, the magician again urges the canoe to "fly, break through your sea passage of Kadimwatu, cleave through the promontory of Saramwa, pass through Loma; die away, disappear . . . cut through seaweed, go, put on your wreath of aromatic herbs" (1922: 139). The *dogina* actually refers to the flight details of the younger two sisters, especially their journey in a southernly direction toward Dobu.

Relations between the Kudayuri Myth and the Canoe Magic

An unexpected and previously unseen significance (from the analysis of the myth per se) reveals itself in the details of the *ligogu* and *wayugo* spells.

No mention at all is made in the magic to Mokatuboda, the oldest brother and original headman of Kudayuri village, who knew how to make the canoe fly by reciting spells, and whose murder led to the actual loss of that potent magic. In contrast, the spells *explicitly invoke the three sisters,* and the details of their flight and the places they pierced are meticulously recounted. In addition, the canoe is addressed as a woman.

One must infer from these facts that it is paradoxically the sisters, transforming themselves without divulging the magic, as if the very withholding fuels their self-transformation into flying agents, who have *become the basis of the speed magic,* which men attempt to imitate and impart to the canoes that they make.

Thus, we get a new perspective on the myth itself if we apply to it the tripartite division of *u'ula, tapwana,* and *dogina.* The *u'ula,* the foundation of the canoe magic via Mokatuboda, is irretrievably lost; the *tapwana* is the main story of the myth; and the *dogina* which Malinowski translated as the "end" as well as the "eye" of the spell or myth, is I believe the "point" of the text, the part that is historically relevant and that is "pragmatically" alive today. It concerns the transformation of the sisters into flying witches, and the *continued capacity of women to do so,* while men really cannot make canoes fly. By this route we arrive at the phenomenological truth, which I have suggested in different words before: that the Trobrianders at some level of experience and knowledge are aware not only that canoes cannot fly but also that their magic is a culturally constructed technique that attempts to convey to canoes "performatively" and "analogously" an innate capacity attributed to women.

A few insights into the manner in which a myth should be read in Trobriand terms are provided by the magic. The concluding portion of the myth deals with the exploits of the *two younger* sisters; it is the flight of the two younger sisters that covers the longest distance, touches the most number of places, and is recorded in greatest detail. It is no accident that the *wayugo* and *ligogu* spells are concerned with the exploits of the sisters, and that they again pay most attention to the doings of the two younger sisters. This magical emphasis tells us what part of a Trobriand myth is to be seen as having the greatest relevance *as charter for current practice*. The concluding part is metonymically and indexically closest to the present. If valid, this proposal gives us a new insight into Malinowski's pragmatic charter theory—an insight which escaped him.

Let me next raise a problem (without resolving it) concerning the relation between the Kudayuri myth and related canoe magic. The myth (in the only full version that we have) states that the original flying canoe magic practiced by the older brother is irretrievably lost, and that the three sisters refused to impart the *ligogu* and *wayugo* magic to their surviving brother. This, strictly speaking, implies that their magical potency was also lost.[14] But the magical practice, which attempts to recapture the transformed flying propensities of the sisters turned witches, is based on the premise that males can recapture the potency which is peculiarly female (and was not gifted to them). Thus, myth and rite stand in a dialectical relation: one states that the original power was lost and only a weakened form now exists; the other consists of an invocatory formulaic technique combined with manipulation of substances devised by males to activate a potency which is peculiarly female and inaccessible to them.

A Semantic Mapping of Some Trobriand Categories

Following is a recapitulation of the facts already considered in terms of a tripartite scheme consisting of the categories land, sea, and sky.

Land. In certain contexts, land signifies the value of "anchoring" and stability; the depths of the land (beneath the surface, the underneath) are the place of habitation of *baloma* and *tabu* (as well as of the nonhuman spirits and various forms of reptiles which shed their skin) who are all long-lived and virtually "immortal." The *yams* are also anchored in the garden land, which is considered the "belly." *Yams, baloma,* and reptiles all emerge from below onto land surface to manifest themselves. Although land is also the point of origin of spirits that can cause havoc, in an overall sense land is positively valued by the Trobrianders as the resource for gardening and as the place of emergence of *tabu* ancestors and the traditions and possessions they brought with them.

Sea. In this scheme the sea represents motion, turbulence, speed, upward and downward motion, the state of being "unanchored" as when traveling in a moving canoe. The association of sea with upward motion (1922: 107) is aided by the buoyancy of the craft and the paraphernalia of sailing: pandanus streamers and prowboards. Stability on the sea in the sense of being anchored, or lack of motion for lack of wind, is not a desirable condition. But at the same time, turbulence of the sea is connected with shipwreck and disaster. Finally, overseas is where the *kula* valuables and specialized goods and items, not locally available, are acquired—and a *kula* journey on sea therefore carries all the positive (and negative) associations of speed, competition, renown, failure, and disaster. In the tripartite scheme as a whole, the sea is the intermediate and liminal zone. It is concordant, therefore, that the *baloma* ancestral spirits travel from Tuma to Boyowa on the sea in a journey from the other world to this world.

Sky. The sky and aerial space represent an even more intensified form of the values associated with the sea—as speed, motion, buoyancy, expanse of vision, and so forth. Trobrianders, especially the garden magicians, watch (aside from the sun and moon) the location and movement of certain constellations of stars which are particularly relevant for the calendrical calculations of lunar months and gardening schedules (1922: 68, 221; Austen, 1939). Shooting stars dramatically represent motion in the sky. Of course, the flying of birds represents for the Trobriander aerial motion at its best: hence the vast symbolism associated with reef herons (which skim over the surface of the sea at great speed), parrots and parakeets, and various other birds that are carved on the prowboards of Trobriand canoes (1922: chs. 4, 5; Seligmann, 1910) and that are also invoked in canoe magic and in myths. (Interestingly, the night birds—owl, night-jar, and so on—are considered accomplices of sorcerers, while of course flying witches can also sometimes turn themselves into night birds of prey.)

Let me at this point briefly bring into focus 1) the theme of *flying canoes* and *flying witches* and their *necessary* interconnection in Trobriand thought, and 2) the theme of *shipwreck* in *kula* expeditions. I would like to propose a hypothesis as to how both themes represent a certain kind of conjunction in the sea-sky-land categories already outlined.

In Trobriand thought, the witch who "peels off her skin" (*inini wowola*) and transforms herself into a disembodied "inside" is the epitome of uncanny speed. Trobrianders fantasize their own *kula* canoes as flying through the air like flying witches.

The *mulukwausi*, as we have seen, are "black" in color, and can take the form of flying foxes, night birds, and falling stars (1922: 320, 412–420).

The canoe urged to fly is actually painted in three colors with black dominant; and black substances, together with materials light in weight, are used for special effect in the three magical rites of exorcism staged when a canoe is built. Also, as noted earlier, the adze (*li-gogu*) and creeper (*wayugo*) magic, which attempt to impart the speed of a flying witch to the canoe, explicitly refer to the Kudayuri myth of the flying canoe and the flying witches.

But there is a certain inversion in the comparison between flying witch and flying canoe. Being women, the flying witches cannot build canoes or sail them; but they transform themselves and fly through the air, which men cannot do. Thus, the men's canoe magic is an exteriorized activity performed on a manufactured object, and this cultural action, so to say, corresponds to the fact that a flying canoe, difficult to create, is a much valued productive enterprise, while a flying witch, not difficult to become in actual life, is a highly feared and disapproved manifestation.

However, by another twist in the logic, shipwreck is a point of conjunction where the flying witch in her most malevolent and potent form attacks a "flying canoe" at its weakest and most exposed state of falling apart, its own component parts breaking loose from the lashing creeper which integrates them and themselves turning cannibalistic.

It is clear that, if we study in particular Malinowski's account of shipwreck (1922: ch. 10), and place it side by side with his other scattered accounts of sailing and attitudes toward the sea, we could draw a chart representing the different realms spanning sky and sea, the positive and negative features associated with each realm, and the magical "substances" (and associated spells) used to counter the dangers experienced at sea.

Table 8.1 plots the dangers and positive features associated with the sky, surface of the sea, and underneath the sea (in a vertical gradient), and the magical operations, especially the substances, used in countering sailing dangers. *All* three levels on a vertical gradient from above to below—above the sea (sky), surface of the sea, and underneath the sea—are, by the very nature of the sea as an unstable domain, associated in general with motion and speed, and, in their negative aspects, with turbulence, instability, danger, violence, and disintegration. Of the three levels, the turbulence of the sky is taken to be the most dangerous and violent during a storm.

The time of sailing on overseas expeditions is relevant to the actual

Table 8.1. *Spatial levels of sea and sky and their attributes.*

Spatial levels	Negative/dangerous features	Magical substances to counter danger	Positive/helpful features
Sky (above the sea)	Flying witches, flying foxes, night birds, balls of fire, fireflies, shooting stars. Storms, rain, strong winds. (The dangers of the above are worse than the dangers below.) (1922: 246)	Various systems of "mist magic" (*kayga'u*): bespelled lime from gourd thrown into the air to blind flying witches and to make sailors invisible (*giyoro-kaywa*).	Moon and constellations such as Orion and Pleiades useful for calendrical calculations; also moon's qualities of whiteness, light, roundness, of positive symbolic value. Small and light seabirds—e.g., *manuderi, kidikidi*—invoked in spells. (1922: 253)
Surface of sea	The falling apart of the mast, ribs, and other parts of the canoe, and their becoming eaters of humans.	Wild gingers (*leyya*) charmed, chewed, and spat to keep danger at bay.	The outriggers lost in shipwreck as floats to hold on to; seaweed as floating substance (associated with *baloma*).
Underneath the sea	Attackers/eaters of drowning sailors: sharks, poisonous fish (*soka*), stringaree, spiky fish (*baibai*), crabs, seaworms; "jumping stones" (*vineylida* or *nu'akekepaki*. (1922: 246) The giant octopus (*kwita*) "traps" a canoe and holds it fast from moving.	Charmed *binabina* stones to sink/hold down sharks and sea animals; also mist magic to make the shipwrecked sailors invisible (*giyotanava*). (The "mist magic of the underneath" is associated with the dog of the Lukuba clan.)	*Iraviyaka* fish (also called *suyu-sayu*) invoked in *kaytaria* spell to carry the shipwrecked on its back to the shore.

occurrence of storms. The Trobrianders preferred to do their sailings in the calm periods between the seasons—especially November and December or March and April, or in the time *when the monsoon blows* from the northwest or southwest (usually in the hot summer months from December till March). On the one hand, Malinowski correctly noted that much of this sailing was safe: "Taking the bearing by sight, and helped by the uniformity of winds, the natives have no need of even the most elementary knowledge of navigation" (1922: 225). But on the other hand, the very lightness of the *masawa* canoes and their general fragility combined with poor navigational skills constituted a real danger when unexpected storms were met with at sea during the monsoon period: a rough sea or a strong wind may drive the canoe into a quarter where there is no landfall to be made. "Or in stormy weather, it may be smashed on sandbanks, or even be unable to withstand the impact of waves . . . In rough weather, a waterlogged canoe loses its buoyancy and gets broken up" (1922: 228). In actual fact, accidents were comparatively rare.

A shipwreck in semantic terms is the *unwanted conjunction* of sea and sky at their most turbulent—the meeting point of cosmological and spatial categories previously kept apart. When sky and sea meet, so to say, there is also generated in this collapsed space storm, rain, wind, mist, and so on. Similarly, the flying witches also represent the meeting of sky and sea: the flying witches descend from above onto their helpless victims bobbing on the sea, accompanied by shrieks which are the howling winds. The canoe, on the other hand, is the victim of the conjunction—when turbulent sea lifts it up to jam it against the collapsing sky, crushing it by that conjunction.

There is yet another important conjunction (and paradox). According to both myths and local beliefs, a large number of the sea passages, straits between land masses, cleavages in rocky promontories—all important points on the actual *kula* routes of today—were forced open by flying witches, so powerful and speedy was their motion. Interestingly, these same stories also recount that witches end their flying careers by becoming the opposite of speed and motion: petrified humans (that is, immobile rock outcrops). These rocks represent, then, the frozen residue of the preceding violent contact between sky (aerial beings), sea, and land.

I should like to use the notion of *conjunction* between semantic spaces or categories that are usually kept separate to add a point or two to the theory of liminal space as developed by Edmund Leach, Claude Lévi-Strauss, and Mary Douglas. The structuralist view is that since the world out there is in flux and a continuous process, man in his cultural garb imposed on this flux a classificatory grid which introduces discontinuities; the intervals or spaces that divide the categories then become ambiguous, sacred, and tabooed.

I wish to suggest a classificatory perspective that accords with Trobriand mental dispositions and proclivities; it gives the structuralist formulation a new twist.

It is my sense that Trobriand thought actually operates on and manipulates the classificatory system in such a way that categories already separated are then collapsed or brought into conjunction, so that these meeting points are viewed in themselves as, or as sites for, heightened manifestations, extraordinary events, and highly charged "excessive" acts. In support of this proposition, let me briefly allude to two examples relating to the grid land-sea-sky. The sea is a "middle" domain between land surface (on which humans live and move) and the sky (in which they do not normally move). Humans sail on the sea, but sailing is an "unanchored" and buoyant experience of upward and downward movement, capable of variant expression between the poles of windless calm and fearful storm.

Although land, sea, and sky are, in ordinary Trobriand experience, separate categories and phenomena, they clearly also meet:

a. The meeting point between land and sea is the beach and shallows (and creeks). In ordinary life it is significant that this is the place where women become impregnated by *baloma* spirits who have come floating from Tuma; this event of procreation is normal and desirable (for married women) and expected as an everyday fact.

It is no surprise, then, that the same site is chosen for the emotionally charged, violent, and tabooed copulation of brother and sister described in the Trobriand incest myth (1932: ch. 14). Three successive copulations take place in shallow sea, beach, and in the grotto located on the coral outcrop between beach and village. Out of this union was produced the most potent form of love magic.

b. The meeting point between sea and sky in everyday Trobriand experience is either the horizon or the much reduced shapes of the not too distant island of Kitava (seen from the eastern shore of Boyowa) and of some of the Amphlett Islands (seen from Vakuta). In normal times these islands are points reached on *kula* and other journeys where exchange of valuables and goods is effected. But the shipwreck is the violent and catastrophic conjunction that may occur on a *kula* voyage. At this junction is released the full force of the elements, and the cannibalistic attack of flying witches from "above" and of creatures from "below" the sea. It is the site at which men sailors are drowned, dismembered, and sucked down by the undercurrents of the sea, and where also the victims (and heroes wielding excessive magical powers) become petrified as solid immobile rocks, landmarks for the *kula* voyagers.

The Trobriand classificatory operations could perhaps be cast in Saussurean language, especially in terms of the distinction between the arbitrary or conventional nature of "signs" and the motivated nature of "symbols." For Saussure, the notion of the *value* (*valeur*) of a sign is a function of its position in an associative network, of paradigmatic and contrastive relations existing between all the signs in a set: "Language is a system of interdependent terms in which the value of each term results solely from the simultaneous presence of the others" (1966: 114). A *symbol*, by contrast, was motivated, in that its signifier-signified relation was deliberately intended to represent what Saussure called a "natural" (that is, appropriate in terms of "content") relation—as, for example, when a pair of scales is chosen to represent justice. The Trobriand mode of thought employs the motivated "symbolic" operations of collapsing and bringing into conjunction, colliding and conflating, differentiated terms or "signs" in an associative network so as to generate heightened meanings that are considered excessive in terms of the social norms of everyday conduct and/or extra-ordinary in terms of achievements possible in everyday life. This is a Trobriand way of thinking about moral issues, the limits and boundaries of conduct, the circumstances leading to excessive conduct, and the qualities of "heroic" achievements—together with their nemesis of death or abandonment.

9

A Reformulation of Geertz's Conception of the Theater State

Although Clifford Geertz in his remarkable book *Negara* (1980) cautions that the Balinese state of the nineteenth century he describes cannot be taken to be the same as the Balinese state of preceding times (an argument against the assumption of statis), and although he warns that in size, scale, and internal features of economic organization, as in irrigation, the Balinese polity was different from the classical Javanese (and some other Southeast Asian kingdoms), he makes a general claim for his profile of the Balinese *negara,* a claim I would like to take as my point of reference and departure.[1]

Geertz's general claim is that his decidedly nonannalistic account, which avoids a narrative of kings and their achievements, has pertinence for "an understanding of the Indicized state in Indonesia and beyond": "This is true because, no matter what alterations the Balinese state had suffered by 1906, no matter how special its environmental setting or divergent its cultural context, it was still but one example of a system of government once very much more widespread. On the basis of the Balinese material, one can construct, therefore, a model of the *negara* as a distinct variety of political order, a model which can then be used generally to extend our understanding of the developmental history of Indic Indonesia (Cambodia, Thailand, Burma)" (1980: 9). Such a model, conceptual and abstract, is offered by Geertz as a guide for the representation "of a whole set of relatively less well-known but presumptively similar institutions: the classical Southeast Asian Indic states of the fifth to the fifteenth centuries."

Geertz has with considerable artistry created a vision of the Balinese polity as a "theater state." The words "theatrical performance" in ordinary Western parlance imply a "make-believe" presentation on a "stage" that by artifices, rhetoric, and other props creates an "illusion." The theatrical performance mimics "reality," seduces the audience into thinking that the enactments on stage are "realistic" or that they reflect or illuminate "real life," and thereby induces a catharsis in the audience or teaches it a moral through the process of empathy.

The cosmic rituals of kingship, court, and state in traditional Southeast Asia were only in small part theatrical diversions of this sort. They were, as Geertz says, meant "to image" the cosmological truths of the society in question. The Balinese rituals were predicated on the supposition that "to mirror a reality is to become it" (1980: 116). They "were not mere aesthetic embellishments, celebrations of domination independently existing: they were the thing itself" (1980: 120). Bali demonstrates "the ordering force of display, regard, and drama," such that kingship, the master image of Bali, was thereby constructed: "If a state was constructed by constructing a king, a king was constructed by constructing a god" (1980: 124).

I think this capacity of court and other cosmic rituals to construct and image a reality was as true for Burma and Thailand as it was true for Bali. Adapting a term coined by the linguistic philosopher Austin, I shall label these ritual acts *performative* acts. Austin's notion of the performative utterance is that the saying of an illocutionary speech act is "the doing of an action" which, "conforming to a convention" in "appropriate circumstances," is subjected to normative judgments of felicity or legitimacy and not to rational tests of truth and falsity.[2]

In his last chapter, "Bali and Political Theory," Geertz says that "the divine king cult" amounted "in practical terms" to three concrete exemplifications of royal authority: "the relations of kings to priests, of kings to the material world, and of kings to themselves" (1980: 125).

The first of these axes, the relation between priest and king, Brahman and raja, inevitably raises the question of how Balinese ideas about this paired relation compared with the classical Indian (Vedic-Brahmanical-Hindu) conceptions. In line with most interpreters, Geertz remarks that the original Indian conceptions probably suffered a sea change in their passage to Bali (and Java), such that kingship became the dominant component and priesthood a subordinate vehicle for constructing king and state. While this assertion is not wrong—and because this transformation per se is not central to Geertz's conception of the theater state, and because to do full justice to the issue of transformation of Indian ideology when it traveled to

Southeast Asia, one would have to make a long journey through the halls of Indological, Buddhological, Southeast Asian (and other) scholarship, and salute a galaxy of scholars on the way (Dumézil, Hocart, Lingat, Kane, Heesterman, Dumont, Gonda, Heine-Geldern, Mus, Coedes, Luce, Bosch, Berg, van Leur, Pigeaud, Friedrich, Schrieke, Moertono, and several others)—I would prefer not to undertake the task here of assessing how Bali agrees with or differs from other Southeast Asian instances, and they from the Indian conception(s). It is my impression that a more complex statement can be made about the priest-king relation in Bali than has been done by Geertz, and that Geertz has also missed the opportunity of saying something about the significance of the priest-king relation for political theory in general. I shall try to expand on this programmatic statement at another time.

The second axis which Geertz deals with, and which is central to his conception of the theater state, is the relation of the king to his polity—alternatively, the relation between *negara* (as capital) and *desa* (as realm). This dialectic invokes the classical master conception of the *cakravartin* as universal ruler, his relation to lesser kings and rulers and chiefs, and the nature of the distribution of powers between them in a mandala formation. This issue once again resonates with classical Buddhist and Hindu conceptions widely shared in South and Southeast Asia.

The third axis, the relation of ruler to himself, is, as far as I am concerned, subsumed under the second and will be discussed as such. In sum, then, the ruler-realm relation is the subject of my detailed reconsideration, in which I shall try to show that Geertz's lacquered rhetoric does not successfully glaze over the deep rupture he creates between expressive action, which he assigns to the still center, and instrumental action, which he aligns with the base and periphery. I shall engage in a critical reading of Geertz's own text to expose certain insufficiencies and shall simultaneously interweave some features and processes historically prevalent in some of the mainland Southeast Asian states, particularly Thailand and Burma. When I do so, I am not simply engaging in the alleged stereotypical ploy of the anthropologist that "my society is different from yours" but am claiming a privilege which Geertz claimed for himself. He suggests that Balinese facts can be used "to suggest possibilities for which Javanese (or Cambodian, Thai, Burmese) evidence can then be sought" (1980: 8). I hope that my hypotheses will in turn stimulate a reexamination of his Balinese data.

Geertz's *Negara* is hobbled by a certain polarity, which makes its most marked appearance in the opposition between the character of activities at the level of the *negara* (as capital and state) and the character of activities at the level of *desa* (as countryside and region). Particularly in Chapter 3, entitled "Political Anatomy: The Village and the State," Geertz, driven by a dichotomous logic, asserts that the activities of the realm and court—that is, the *negara*—are "expressive" in nature whereas the activities of the local society—that is, the *desa*—as transacted through the hamlet (*banjar*), the irrigation society (*subak*), and the temple congregation (*premaksan*), are "instrumental" in nature. He repeatedly tells us that "the political centre of gravity sat very low" in the Balinese polity, that "culture came from the top down . . . while power welled from the bottom" (1980: 85). Wealth, social status, personal power, and other such "familiar realities," Geertz tells us, "played their role in the *subak* and inter*subak* legal-political system, not in the state apparatus" which, beyond such activities as taxation, ritual, and occasional mediation, "was not officially concerned with these matters" (1980: 84).[3]

Pushing the emphasis on the two poles of Balinese society too far, Geertz proposes that the king, court, and *negara* were primarily engaged in ritual action (imaging the cosmic truth), whereas the lower orders in the countryside were engaged in "practical" politics (and economics). The former action portrays a "symbology of power" deemphasized in, and separated from, modern notions of rational (instrumental) politics. Geertz suggests that perhaps it ought to be restored as an integral component of politics enacted everywhere, not merely in Bali.

The Geertzian exegesis poses an awesome challenge to conventional Marxist and neo-Marxist paradigms. Geertz is proposing that in Bali (and elsewhere in Southeast Asia, at least) one cannot generate or derive from the local peasant agricultural sector of the society the mode of domination, the semiotics of the ritual action of the rulers, or their passion for status and display. But this same stance leaves Geertz himself in a peculiar "disconnected" situation. If there is such a divide between the "symbology" of ritual and other action at the level of the court and realm, and the pragmatics of political and economic conduct at the level of the village and region, then how indeed do we understand their existential basis and the manner of their fit and conjunction? If Geertz ignores or fails to convincingly address this problem, he exposes himself to the Marxist riposte that the Balinese *negara* is truly a "mystification," an illusory representation of the unity of the village communities (as Marx put it in his sketch of "oriental despotism"), and that the ceremonies of state are nothing but the spiritualizing of material interests and the covering up of material conflicts.

The Geertzian disjunction furthermore leaves us with some awkward puzzles and inconvenient facts. First, what interpretation are we to put upon the ritual enactments and cosmic preoccupations of the *sudra* farmers and villagers, who, besides performing agricultural rites to ensure adequate water and rice yields (rites that are interlaced with technical activities to constitute an amalgam), also stage tooth fillings and cremations in emulation of their more refined and highly ranked lords?

Second (and this problem emerges directly from Geertz's ethnography), what are we to make of the members and segments of the *dadia*? These are largely endogamous and differentiated patrilineal descent groups, in part reminiscent of "conical clans," whose calculated jockeyings internally and externally with other *dadia*, both vertically up and down mountain slopes and laterally across mountain ridges and valleys, are described by Geertz as drenched with the motivations and techniques associated with the pursuit of "power." Geertz treats us to some pithy evaluations of this power game of the gentry as "institutionalized perfidy," "Hobbesian discord," "Florentine closet politics"—labels quite different from his previous urgings, to the effect that we should see the preoccupations and activities of the multicentric courts in terms of imaging cosmic truths regarding status. Or, to put the question slightly differently, how do we conjoin and reconcile the cosmological axioms at the heart of kingship and realm—that status/power be seen as a gradation of excellence scattering down from a divine unity and as a radiation of it dispersing from a divine core to the king, his kinsmen, his lords, their henchmen, and finally the peasantry—with the cutthroat politics of these same segments linked by graded status, and competing for advantage at one another's cost?

The nineteenth century, Geertz tells us, "was rent by virtually continuous intrigue, dispute, violence and an enormous amount of micro-upheaval" (1980: 133) among the small kingdoms (although the overall pattern of repute and precedence in the entire arena was largely the same at its end as it was at the beginning). For example, between 1800 and 1840 there were major interregional conflicts. In 1800 the royal *dadia* of Klungkung and Gianyar, together with their clients, allied against Bangli, while Karengasem attacked Lombok and Buleleng. Then Buleleng fought Jembrana in 1804 and reattacked Karengasem a little later. After 1820 "the would-be potentates of Gianyar fought wars not only with Badung, but with Klungkung, Mengwi, and Bangli as well. In Bangli one of three rivalrous brothers seized power and allied first with Karengasem to attack Klungkung and then with Klungkung to attack Buleleng. Tabanan fought with Badung around 1808; and Menwi, allied with Klungkung, attacked Badung in 1813" (1980: 44).

Curiously, despite the flair with which Geertz presents this turmoil of invasions and retreats and this cycle of expanding and contracting domains, the actors are reduced to paper tigers and flat shadowplay figures, and their battles to mock heroics, because Geertz fails to tell us what these battles were all about. In the Southeast Asia I know, these periodic campaigns and changing zones of control had to do with the capture of booty and of manpower to resettle as "slaves" or "serfs" nearer one's centers of control. Moreover, since (as Geertz himself documents for Bali) taxes in kind (rice) were extracted from the commoners, as was their labor power for conducting wars and staging rituals, the expansion and contraction of the warring kingdoms must have had a direct relation to the control of these resources, and these in turn to the symbology of status competition and display, which were the overwhelming passion of Balinese aristocrats.

Finally, Geertz, unable to curb the temptation to dazzle by exaggerating and to typify by sharp-line etching, allows himself to paint all kings at the summits of exemplary centers as still points, immobilized into passivity and reflective trances. The higher their position and the greater their kingdom's glory and prosperity, the more they were reduced to "mere signs among signs." That such a tendency and process was there in all Southeast Asian polities is undeniable. But one's account must embrace as well the dynamic, radiant, charismatic monarchs who periodically emerged to sponsor revivals and renascences and to implement imperial ambitions. In Thailand, Ramkhamhaeng and Lithai of Sukhothai, or Rama I and Mongkut of the Bangkok period, represent such vital radiating centers that affected the peripheries of their expanding realms. Burma, Cambodia, and Sri Lanka can boast of such heroes as well. Were all Balinese kings closeted in their divine cages, mere birds of paradise?

In short, Geertz's brilliant and dazzling sketches do not transcend the classical disjunctions between expressive and instrumental action, between ideology and practice, between power as pomp and power as control of resources and people—disjunctions which he tends to distribute to different segments of the body politic. Since papering over cracks does not do away with the cracks, it is relevant to ask whether certain shifts in exegesis might show that ideology and practice in Southeast Asian polities were closer and more homologous than we are led to think. This is what I propose to do in this chapter, where I shall set out my model of the galactic polity based on my own work in Southeast Asia. Naturally there are overlaps between portions of my portrait and portions of Geertz's. I shall, however, endeavor to suggest that the rituals of state, the historical myths enshrined in the chronicles, and the pattern of politics in these realms were all of a piece. My intention is to dissolve the frequently unproven gap between ideology and practice by showing that what are often identified by the outsider as "practices" in fact exemplify the "ideological constructs," and vice versa. I hope that such a demonstration will be a plausible reply to the Marxist critique of ideology whenever it is employed as a blanket formula.

The Galactic Polity as Conception and Manifestation

The cosmological schemes, both Hindu and Buddhist, that are best-developed in the tantric traditions hold that creation spreads from a still center outward, and from a refined summit downward, each outer entity or circle being progressively a weaker representation of the preceding. The same schemes hold that the outlying and lower levels (for example, demons *vis-à-vis* gods) are progressively grosser in constitution as well as more involved and imprisoned in the pursuits and motivations of sensory worldly desires. It is therefore logical that this doctrine, translated in terms of a society or polity, would attribute the most intense passions and activities to the lower orders—that is, to use Geertz's words, that the center of political and economic gravity would be located low in the system. At the same time, this blueprint of graded qualities as a hierarchy holds (and this is missed in Geertz's exegesis) that the higher always encompasses the lower, and that although it is more refined it can, when the situation demands, take on a more potent manifestation than the lower in order to vanquish it. In the opposite direction, the lower attempts to raise itself by emulation of and contact with the immediately superior. This "theology" is in accord with the facts of the political economy: the higher orders do not determine, or participate in, the production arrangements and activities of the peasantry, but by virtue of corvée and taxation rights they are in a position to extract goods and services and to mobilize the commoners for spasmodic and short-lived public activities, whether these be wars or aristocratic cremations or monument building. Given these principles, it is implausible to hold that "culture came from the top down . . . while power welled from the bottom" (1980: 85).

I have coined the label "galactic polity" to represent the design of traditional Southeast Asian kingdoms, a design that coded in a composite way cosmological, topographical, and politico-economic features. (The full characterization is found in Tambiah, 1976, chs. 7, 8; and in Chapter 7, above.) The term "galactic polity" is a translation of the concept mandala, which is indigenous to Southeast Asia and which is employed in many contexts ranging from Hindu and Buddhist philosophy and meditational practice, through art, architecture, court ritual, and theater, to geopolitics and administrative organization. In many parts of Southeast Asia—for example, in Burma and Thailand—the mandala pattern is pervasively employed in many contexts to describe the structure of a pantheon of gods and demons, the deployment spatially of a capital region and its provinces, the arrangement socially of a ruler, princes, nobles, and their respective retinues, and the devolution of power on a scale of decreasing autonomies. In the Thai instance, other key concepts that order the polity are *muang*, which signifies principality in terms of center-oriented space, and of central and surrounding satellite domains; and *krom*, which represents the radial mapping of an administrative system of departments and their subdivisions, as well as the constitution of successively expanding circles of leaders and followers or factions. These concepts thus are polyvalent and are at once cosmological, territorial, politico-economic, and administrative.

In the Thai or Burmese instances, the galactic polity, seen from a static perspective, was best conceptualized in terms of the imperium of the *cakravartin*, or universal king. (This conception is also known to the classical polities of Java and Bali.) The *cakravartin*'s rule was not absolute; it was best expressed in the formula "king of kings," a term which implies the existence of lesser kings over whom the *cakravartin* presided. The lesser kings, once they recognized the supremacy of the center, were allowed to remain as heads of virtually autonomous vassal states. Hence, the polity could be represented as a center-oriented arrangement wherein satellite principalities or provinces of various magnitudes revolved around the central domain. The satellites reproduced the features of the center on a decreasing scale in a system of graduated autonomies.

Within any single multicentric polity such as Ayutthaya in Thailand, or Pagan in Burma, cosmic rites of basically two sorts imaged these principles. Rites such as the First Ploughing would be staged in the main capital by the king or his representative to initiate the agricultural year, and subsequently the rite would be successively staged in provincial capitals and so on until the ripple finally terminated in the rice fields of the villagers themselves. An analogue of this in Bali was the Water-Opening ritual, described by Geertz as he observed it in Tabanan: the cycle for the whole region was set in motion with the "Opening of Openings" performed at the "all-Bali" temple of the region, Batu Kau by name (Geertz, 1980: 81).

These rites of dispersion were balanced by the periodic rites of aggregation, such as the annual Oath of Allegiance ceremony in Bangkok, attended by the provincial and satellite governors and rulers. At another level the king's harem, composed of women given by various subordinates to the central king, was an institution of an aggregative nature that made him the husband of the realm.

A conspicuous dynamic principle of the galactic polity seen in the regional arena was that it was of a pulsating nature, in the sense that it was part of a large field of coexisting galaxies which mutually inflected one another, and thus expanded or shrank their outer frontiers according to their success in attracting, and then keeping, the outermost satellites within their orbits. Thus, in mainland Southeast Asia, the kingdoms of Pagan, Pegu, Chiangmai, Sukhothai, Ayutthaya, Laos, and Cambodia were located on one continuous landscape in which there were several core domains and satellite regions that continually changed their affiliation according to the fortunes of war and diplomacy. These multiple centers all claimed to be the seats of *cakravartins*, and all bigger universal monarchs sat on the backs of lesser ones for a while. Bali, on a much smaller arena, manifested the same pulsations. The various realms—Den Pasar, Tabanan, Badung, Karengasem, Klungkung, and so on—were, as Geertz puts it, an acrobat's pyramid of "kingdoms of varying degrees of substantial autonomy and effective power" (Geertz, 1980: 16).[4] Their perennial warfare, interregional conflicts, and litigious treaties attest to the fact that the Balinese polity could not be statically viewed as "a set of seven or eight bounded, more or less equally powerful states led by a *primus inter pares* Klungkung raj." "These alliances involved an encounter of whole collections of separate, semi-independent, intensely rivalrous political figures joined at best in unstable blocs by ties of kinship and clientship" (1980: 43).

Divine Kingship, Perennial Rebellions, and Personal Charisma

In the light of the above observations, one may say that in the Southeast Asian realms—among which I would include the Balinese *negara*—"divine kingship" was dialectically conjoined with perennial rebellions and succession disputes, which were exacerbated by the multiple ranked marriages and concubinages, and the rules of "descending" or "sinking status,"[5] and that this dynamic was a function of the pattern of political relations that linked central and peripheral domains. The center's ideology of devolution of control over territory and men was matched by the volatile factional and centrifugal struggles mounted by the periphery against the center, which itself harbored competing interests at its heart, the capital.

I submit that one corollary of such political instability was that there were no stable dynasties of rulers who succeeded one another according to defined and implementable rules of heredity. If there were "divine kings," they were continually dethroned by palace rebellions and wars of succession and secession. Divinity, or claims to universal and righteous kingship, was based on personal charisma as much as or even more than on institutionalized rules pertaining to the tenure of office. Dynasties when founded were short-lived. Factional coalitions and oppositions, rather than constitutional blueprints and strict considerations of division of labor, dictated the galactic distribution of power and administrative organization in terms of replication, duplication, and parallelism. The cosmologized state had to be continually reimaged and reincarnated.

If these propositions might plausibly apply for the late Ayutthaya period in Thailand (seventeenth and eighteenth centuries), can they possibly be true of Bali in the nineteenth century? Geertz has put much emphasis on the formal, ascriptive rules of "sinking status" by which "cadet lines" become separated from the "core line" and progressively lose status. Consequently, within a *dadia* as a whole, sub-*dadia* are differentiated and ranked according to the rules of genealogical distance which underlie the phenomenon of sinking status. If these rules were strictly observed, then Balinese succession rules would rigidly confine rulership to predictably few candidates. But Geertz gives us in *Negara* no account of dynasties and the pattern of succession over time for any Balinese realm. And in places he suggests that there was plenty of space for satisfying political ambitions through competition within the ranks of the gentry (*satrias* and *wesias*). These sentences celebrate mobility: "Nevertheless to be a *triwangsa* [the three upper orders], a *wong jero* [insider], meant one was at least a potential *rajah;* and every upper-caste man, no matter how politically insignificant, worked to find some place in the state from which he could, by intrigue, flattery, useful service, or just plain luck, achieve the authority for which his patrician heritage rendered him theoretically eligible" (1980: 26–27).

Thus, because in fact the politics within and between realms were "intensely competitive" in a context of enormous "institutional dispersion," it is reasonable to hypothesize that the doctrine of a "still center" was compatible with volatile changes in the men who were kings, by virtue of their show of personal prowess and charisma. In the same way, the claims of universal rulership were compatible with the

fact that the entire set of Balinese realms was at any one time an un-
steady house of cards.

Charisma and Legitimacy

In Thailand, Burma, and Sri Lanka, individuals of personal charisma
who assumed kingship found, among other things, two more or less
enduring bases for claiming legitimacy and through it stability of
power. One was the claim to being a *cakkavatti* or a *dharmaraja* on
the basis of personal achievement and commitment to Buddhist
norms of kingship. These positions, according to Buddhists, are not so
much inherited as proven by individual *karma* and meritorious conduct. Though they cannot be inherited, those attaining them can
claim to be incarnations and avatars of archetypal heroes. The various
"historical" chronicles of the kingdoms of these countries—the *Mahavamsa, Dipavamsa, Culavamsa, Jinakalamali, Sasanavamsa,* and
so on—rarely, if ever, systematically record a line or dynasty of kings
on the basis of descent. Rather, the list of the reigns of kings records
their kingly acts—in particular, donations to the *sangha* and conspicuous works of public welfare (such as construction of hydraulic
works)—and includes comments explicitly or implicitly on the rise
and fall of particular kings as a consequence of their different *karmic*
attainments. It seems to me that the claims of Buddhist kings to be
cakkavatti, dharmaraja, kammaraja, or *bodhisattva* are concordant
with this emphasis on individual merit rather than genealogical descent. This point is underscored by the Buddhist canonical notion,
highlighted by the *Cakkavatti Sihanada Sutta,* that the *cakra* (wheel
of righteous dominion) of the universal king cannot be inherited but
must be won anew by each king by his own virtuous acts.

The classical Buddhist notion of the reincarnation of the *cakkavatti*
(the Buddha himself allegedly claimed that he had many times previously been born a *cakkavatti*),[6] and the tradition that developed in
later times by which *bodhisattva* status is attributed to the great lamas
of Tibet or claimed by many kings of Burma and Sri Lanka can be said
to be the opposite of the claims of status through descent, which emphasize connection through procreation, filiation, and membership in
a lineage.[7]

The dogma that one identifiable being is repeatedly reincarnated
allows unrelated (or distantly related) persons to mount the throne on
the basis of individual attainment. Mendelson has aptly commented
about Burma that the Setkyamin (*cakkavatti*) is above all the king of

Burma, and that the Burmese texts profusely claim "the reincarnation of Burmese kings into the Burmese kingship at different times." For a king to state that he had been a king before in the same land "probably strengthened his claim to the throne in a situation where personal charisma was all-important and the royal *kamma* was an important factor in the king's power" (Mendelson, 1961: 579).

Thus, it can be said that the reincarnation of the "same personage" as the Bodhisattva Avalokitesvara (in the case of the Dalai Lama) or as a *cakravartin* (in the case of many a Southeast Asian Buddhist king) ties in with the Buddhist (and Hindu-Buddhist) theory of transmigration and with indigenous regional or local evaluation of personal charisma of an achieved nature. Once such charisma becomes manifest as political success, its possessor seeks retrospective legitimation in terms of reincarnation of famous predecessors.

Sacra and Legitimacy

The second basis for claiming royal legitimacy, which is intimately linked with the foregoing, is the possession of palladia, regalia, and other sacra which are enduring sedimentations of power and virtue. They are believed to remain with their possessors for as long as these rulers are deserving.

It is clear that in Bali various sacra were closely associated with the capacities and legitimacy of kingship (the following account is based on Geertz's discussion, 1980: 114–116). For example, the most sacred spot in the palace complex was the *ukiran* ("world pillar and axis"),[8] which contained inside it the *giri suci* ("holy mountain"), which in turn protected the heirlooms (*wari*)—the sacred weapons such as the *kris* and the spear which ensured and "incorporated the dynasty's power." Geertz describes these heirlooms as "the charismatic inheritance of the house to which they belong, and most particularly of its head." These heirlooms had "transordinary force" and were associated "with elaborate legends of divine origin" and "with military miracles rescuing the dynasty from its enemies." "They are the king's *potentia*, without which . . . he would be incapable." Once a year these weapons were brought out by the king to be blessed by the high priest.

Geertz's brief discussion of them suggests that these sacra, credited with powers and transmitting *potentia* to their royal holders, were exclusive possessions that remained within dynasties as their heirlooms. We do not know what happened to them when dynasties changed—

whether they circulated, whether a conquering king carried away the loser's *sacra,* or whether new "heirlooms" or duplicates of old ones were manufactured and consecrated. Be that as it may, I would like to highlight how famous sacra of Southeast Asian Buddhist realms—sacra credited with charismatic powers, such as those possessed by the Balinese *wari*—had a marvelous history of passing from hand to hand between diverse kings and realms, and in this process spawning "copies" of the "original" which helped disperse the radiant powers of the sacra to satellite realms and the outer regions. In doing so, they paradoxically expressed and created a continuity and an identity in mainland Buddhist Southeast Asia that are in accord with my exegesis of the galactic polity.

Various prominent Buddha statues have served as the sacra of Thai realms—notably the Emerald Buddha Jewel, which is the primary palladium of the Kingdom of Thailand today; the Phra Sihing, or Sinhala Buddha, which played an illustrious role in the past; and the Phra Jinasiha (the Victorious Lion) and Phra Jinaraja (the Victorious King), which were also held in high veneration and to which were attributed great virtues and powers. (In Sri Lanka the tooth relic of the Buddha has played a similar political role.) [9]

The Thai Buddha images are credited with "radiance," "fiery energy," and various potencies to bless and fecundate the world. These powers derive from a number of bases. First, the attribution of radiance ultimately goes back to the experience of enlightenment of the Buddha, during which he underwent four *jhanic* meditative trances, and attained various cognitions and mystical powers. The canonical account of this (as for example related in the *Vinaya Pitaka*) has been embellished in later traditions. Thus, the fourteenth-century Thai cosmological treatise *Traiphum* has an account of the miracle of the Buddha's six rays. These rays are emitted from the Buddha's body, and owe their origins to various of the Buddha's great deeds (see Reynolds and Reynolds, 1982: 263–269).

Second, the power of the images stem from their alleged authentic likeness to the historical Buddha. This likeness was vouched for by the fact that the images were made by divine sculptors, or that they were copies of visions of the Buddha seen by holy men, and so on. Subsequently a sacred iconography of the Buddha's dimensions and features was established, and was followed by artists over the ages.

Third, the images once constructed were—and are, even in the present day—subject to elaborate rites of consecration, installation, and activation (such as the "opening of the eyes"). The new images are linked by a cord to earlier historic images which transmit their virtue to them, thereby enabling them to become the lineal descendants or reincarnations of those earlier images. Moreover, at these same rites of consecration, famous monks recite sacred chants and "open the eyes" of the images in the presence of kings, ministers, and other lay patrons (who likewise may participate in the eye-opening rite). Thus, the images also embody the energies and charisma of the living, who are in turn their worshippers.

Finally, the myths of origin of the statues and their "travels"—that is, the line of diverse kings in diverse polities into whose possession the statues came—are celebrated in famous chronicles.[10] Thus, the chronicle of the Sinhala Buddha relates that the Sinhala Buddha image traveled in this fashion from the earliest Thai polity of Sukhothai, to Ayutthaya and Kamphaengpet, and then to Chiangmai.

For anthropologists and historians, the travels of Buddha statues, such as those of the Sinhala Buddha, provide a chain or genealogy of kingdoms and polities that these statues have legitimated. They also provide a map of a vast political arena in Southeast Asia, made up of a number of principalities, changing boundaries, and varying affiliations and possessing an identity by virtue of commitment to a religio-political ideology, on the one hand, and of sharing similar economic, demographic, and logistical features, on the other.

A second significance is that since in the traditional polities dynasties were shallow and unstable, the galactic polities being characterized by divine kingship accompanied by perennial rebellions and secessions, sacred objects like Buddha images (and regalia and "heirlooms") had a special place. Recognized as permanent embodiments of virtue and power, they helped provide their temporary possessors with legitimation, and at the same time embodied a genealogy of kingship by serving as the common thread that joined a succession of kings and polities with separate identities.

The Sinhala Buddha chronicle also informs us that King Mahabrahma of Chiangmai placed the image in a *wat* situated in the inner city of his capital—that is, it was housed in a shrine in the palace grounds, and was propitiated as the royal palladium. These facts pertain to a Thai royal cult which continues to this day.

Let us now turn to the Emerald Buddha Jewel, which became the primary palladium of the Kingdom of Thailand when the founder of the Chakkri dynasty, Rama I, removed it from Laos after a successful military campaign, and later, on becoming king, placed it in his own royal chapel (Wat Phra Kaeo) within the compound of the Grand Palace in Bangkok. The history and religio-political significance of this statue have already been richly documented (some major references are Lingat, 1934; Notton, 1933a; Reynolds, in Smith, 1978; and Tambiah, 1976, ch. 6), and at least two traditional Thai chronicles relate its myth of origin and the story of its travels and miraculous powers.[11] There are two implications to the alleged travels of the Emerald Buddha, from Pataliputta in India (its place of divine origin), to Sri Lanka, then to Angkor, and finally to Chiangmai (where it was united with the Pali scriptures which became separated from it, and went from Sri Lanka to Pagan). The statement being made (whatever the "true" facts) is that the Chiangmai polity was the meeting point and coalescence of the two socio-religious traditions of Pagan and Angkor; and it is the destiny of this Thai polity to become the bearer and protector of the pure and complete religion previously splintered. In its last phase, the Emerald Buddha was taken from Chiangmai to Laos, whence it was brought to Bangkok.

It is fitting that since I alluded at the beginning of this chapter to rituals of state as performative acts that imaged the cosmology of the Southeast Asian polity, I should draw attention to a preeminent Thai cult of state associated with the Emerald Buddha and practiced to this day. At the highest level in the Buddhist realms of Southeast Asia, the coupling of political sovereignty with the sponsorship of Buddhism, and the fusion of kingship with *bodhisattva*-ship, made the king himself, in certain contexts, a ritual officiant of central importance. Not only were the Buddha's tooth relic in Sri Lanka and the Emerald Buddha in Thailand placed in shrines within the palace complex, but the Sinhalese kings of Kandy officiated at the daily offerings to the relic just as in Thailand even today the changing of the ornaments and the clothes of the Emerald Buddha three times a year according to the seasons is performed by the Thai king in person. The parallelism is strengthened when we realize that both palladia were associated with rainmaking and fertility. Especially in the Thai case, the clothing of the statue in a sparse monk's robe in the wet season (the period of the rainy season retreat of the monks) and in full regal costume in the succeeding cool season[12] is an apt representation of the oscillatory and complementary relation between the Buddha as renouncer and the *cakravartin* as world ruler, between the season of rain (and the planting of crops) and the season of harvest and plenty, between the phases of intensified piety in lay life and the phase of life-affirming revelry.[13]

The rite of changing the Emerald Buddha's clothes is one of the numerous ways in which the sanctity and creative potency of the Thai monarch is celebrated and performatively imaged in contemporary Thailand. That a "constitutional monarchy" and a "modernizing" country of the late twentieth century should continue with a cosmic ritual, to which a fervent efficacy is attributed by many Thai, merits an ethnographic report (see appendix).

Returning to Bali, I would like to apply there the lessons learned from Burma and Thailand. I have, among other things, drawn attention to divine kingship and perennial (but short-lived) civil strife; to the fact that "personal" charismatic claims of kingship are as important as, or even more important than, succession through strict lineal counting;[14] to dynastic shallowness; to sacra, regalia, and palladia as independent repositories of power whose possession itself is a conferral of legitimacy to the royal claimant; to these same sacra as changing hands, their "travels" serving as the genealogy of kingdoms; and to the overall fact that the ideology of *cakravartin* and of rebirth and reincarnation, properly viewed, imply all these volatile and punctuated imagings of the galactic polity.

That Bali is no stranger to these truths is attested by the *Babad Bulelen* (see Worsley, 1972), one of the few indigenous Balinese texts that Geertz cites among an embarrassment of colonial Dutch reportage and commentarial riches.

Worsley, the translator and commentator of this chronicle, calls it "a Balinese dynastic genealogy"; it is a relatively recent document, composed in all probability after 1872, a good guess being around 1890. In any case, the kingdom of Den Bukit was subject to the direct rule of the Dutch by the mid-1850s. As a tendentious document (like other Javanese and Balinese chronicles of the same genre), it upholds the claims of the ruling clan of Den Bukit and relates those claims to certain presuppositions and axioms of a cosmological nature to which the Balinese subscribed. That a post-conquest, late nineteenth-century document should invoke canons and claims of a traditional kind is especially interesting for us. If we concentrate on what the text itself communicates by virtue of its preoccupations we see these themes foregrounded.

The *Babad* opens with, and devotes more than half its space to, the story of the founding hero, Panji Sakti. We learn that his ancestry is problematic, and that in him two lines of descent meet. He is on the one hand the son of Dalem Sagenin, the ruler of the royal house of Gelgel in South Bali, *but by a wife of low birth*, who came from North Bali. Panji is adopted by an official called Jarantik, who belongs to another clan. It is a branch of this adoptive clan that Panji himself will in turn procreate. Moreover, it is because his own royal father sees Panji as a threat to the direct heir of Gelgel that he is sent north, to his mother's land, to establish a kingdom at Den Bukit. In order to do so, Panji murders the incumbent (and rightful) king with the help of his miraculous sword (*kris*).

Equally noteworthy, and underscored, is Panji's personal charisma: at his birth the child's fontanel emits a shining flame which the text describes as "a sign of his strength and valour, his heroism and might (*sakti*) as a conqueror in battle in the future" (Worsley, 1972: 131). His radiance and fiery energy is further fortified by the fact that his mother, though low born, herself possessed *sakti* (as signified by her hot urine). Panji's destiny was to be a great monarch because of his sweet eloquence and good character matched by his valor (*virya-guna*) and heroic strength (*kasuradiran*). The *babad* regards the bellicose and terrifying aspects of Panji as contributing to his maintaining political order and his protection of his subjects.

Moreover, Panji's royal power is at the same time identified with—indeed, embodied in—various sacra, the foremost of which is his *kris*, of mysterious origin, which often acts on his behalf and takes responsibility for some of his questionable deeds. It becomes the preeminent emblem of the state of Den Bukit (*kris kaprabon*) and the royal clan's heirloom (*kaliliran*). The *kris*, which is named Ki Seman, is described by the text as containing a *pasupati-astra* (flaming arrow) by which Panji becomes the ruler of the world (*cakravartinin sarat*). This same *kris* of conquest also brings wealth (*rajabarana*) to the hero, wealth being an essential component of legitimate kingship, because it bestows blessings and ensures prosperity (*mangala*). Truly echoing the classical Buddhist and Hindu visions of the universal ruler, the "jewels" of this king are his club, called Ki Pankajatatwa; his orchestra, whose different-sounding instruments were each carriers of his energetic force; and, above all, the Brahman *purohita*, the first of the *padanda* (priests). The chronicle celebrates the complementary relationship and permanent friendship over generations between the line of Panji and his descendants and the line of his *purohita* (named Kumenuh) and his descendants.[15]

The chronicle, after a full sketch of Panji's virtues and career, "surprisingly" makes only brief and perfunctory references to Panji's *next three successors*, two of whom, his son and grandson, are recognized as his direct lineal heirs. If this was orderly succession, it was also uneventful. The chronicle becomes voluble and alive at the next round of succession when two brothers—Nurah Panji and Nurah Jlantik—engage in fratricidal warfare, thereby ending the reign of the Panji Sakti dynasty and allowing the rulers of a neighboring realm, Karanasem, to take over and rule Den Bukit for several generations as usurpers, from the point of view of the chronicler.

The war of the two brothers is interesting also because the heirloom of the dynasty—the potent *kris*, Ki Seman—figures critically. The laying down of the *kris* by one brother enables the other to kill him, and the *kris* changes hands.

The chronicle next mentions a string of three Karanasem rulers, before the occurrence of the disastrous mudflow of 1815. Then follows an account of the terrible acts and nemesis of the prototypical evil king, Ki Gusti Agun; mentioned are his incestuous relations with his sister, an abortive rebellion by the displaced descendants of Panji and their death in a gory massacre, and his final removal by his own courtiers. Agun's replacement, another Karanasem ruler, did not last long.

After this hiatus, members of the seventh generation of Panji's descendants see one of their own installed as ruler of Den Bukit, with the help of the Dutch, whose action is described as righteous. But the return of the clan of Panji only lasts the short reigns of two rulers—who were either dissolute or weak—before the Dutch finally abolish the throne and rule directly. The chronicle sees the royal clan of Den Bukit as having reached the end of its cycle and its *yuga*.

In sum, then, the *Babad Bulelen* amply ratifies my suggestion: that the dynasties that ruled in *direct succession* were shallow in Bali; that succession to the throne was fraught with competition, strife, and discontinuities; that simple claims of lineal descent to the throne were not efficacious without the valor and personal charisma of a king whose conduct in approaching the norms of the ideal *cakravartin* ruler was seen as ensuring the prosperity of his realm; that various sacra, regalia, and heirlooms were viewed as repositories and missiles of power, whose possession ratified kingship and whose potency ensured their change of hands; and that not a single realm but clutches of realms constituted the political arena whose centers of gravity and whose territorial control shifted and changed, as the fortunes, ambitions, and resources of the rulers waxed and waned.

When I consulted *Kinship in Bali* by Hildred Geertz and Clifford Geertz (1975), I encountered to my pleasant surprise, in a revealing chapter entitled "Kinship in the Public Domain: The Gentry Dadia," a "history" that the Geertzes pieced together from informants of the rise of the royal *dadia* of the realm of Gianyar. This account—an oral history perhaps—is in remarkable accord with the structure of the *Babad Bulelen* (with expectable variations on and inversions of the dynastic themes), and confirms my general hunches about political processes in Bali.

The lifecycle of the *dadia* of Gianyar stretches over some seven generations. The founding hero, the first Dewa Manggis, was of questionable origins. One version has it that he was the illegitimate son of the Klungkung Raja, a rival house: "such stories of obscure origins, illegitimacy, foster parenthood, and so on, are often found in gentry *dadia* histories" (Geertz and Geertz, 1975: 120). The founder's son moves up in the world by marriage to a gentry family of Beng, and becomes a client of the royal house of Sukawati which ruled Gianyar. This mobility upward continues until the fourth Dewa Manggis can claim the title of prince. And taking advantage of a fratricidal war between two Sukawati princes for the throne, he intervenes as an ally of one of them and eventually takes over the throne of Gianyar as the first raja of this line.

But interestingly the royal house of Dewa Manggis had, in all, *only three successive rajas:* the first, who died in 1820; the second, his brother's son; the third, his son, who died in 1867. The third ruler was the most expansionist territorially, reducing some adjacent royal houses to dependency, and he was "the first paramount lord in the region to be able to institute a direct tax on rice land, payable in kind at every harvest, a tax which was not mediated or shared by his stewards and underlings" (Geertz and Geertz, 1957: 121). But his downfall at the hands of the king of Klungkung happened soon after, and the house of Gianyar never recovered. In 1899 the son of this deposed king requested the Dutch army to intervene. This was the end of a classic Balinese state.

The shallow Gianyar dynasty is the *only* empirical case for which the Geertzes can provide (in *Kinship in Bali*) a reasonably reliable "historical" record, and, as we have seen, it bears a remarkable resemblance to the dynastic history of the house of Den Bukit (as related by the *Babad Bulelen*). But the Geertzes suggest that there are other, more long-lived royal *dadia*, such as the house of Tabanan, which is alleged to have a "six-hundred-year history." This history is even sketched as a "genealogy" of the royal subhouses. But as the Geertzes' sensitive and shrewd commentary points out, only a record of the core line of kings is possible; and since this core line has to be viewed as "a title line, not as a sequence of individuals"—this is what Audrey Richards has aptly labeled "positional succession"—the line of kings provides no evidence on orderly succession according to descent rules. The Geertzes' commentary speaks for itself: "Only [a] small cluster of houses in the royal sub*dadia* maintains fully documented genealogies which connect them to the core line. The gentry house of lower status, usually, can supply concrete genealogical information back only a few generations . . . There is considerable room in this sort of system for fictional manipulations, and at least some of the Tabanan gentry houses were . . . not actually related to the core line at all but were migrants from elsewhere" (Geertz and Geertz, 1957: 127).

Indeed, "The core line itself is not immune to manipulations of various sorts. While the form of the diagram suggests a straight line of fathers and sons succeeding one another, in reality there were considerable variations, with brothers succeeding brothers (peaceably or by fraternal murder), and it is possible that outsiders too may have wormed their way into the throne by a *sentana* marriage [incoming son-in-law], or by more devious means. The line, thus, represents the sequence of incumbents of the position however they in fact got there, and the crux of the claim of gentry houses to high status is that they are descendent from a former holder of the royal title" (Geertz and Geertz, 1957: 127–128).

There is, again, much in the Geertzes' chapter "The Politics of Marriage" which reveals sources of flexibility in the whole system of gentry *dadia*, in the whole arithmetic of sinking status, and in the cumulative implications of multiple marriages by royals which *necessarily combine* close endogamous marriage with women of the same status, with hypergamous marriages with lower gentry, and, even more importantly, with a number of very low village-gentry and commoner families, whose far-flung location and whose resources of manpower and agricultural production are of great strategic importance. Thus, if we follow through the implications of these inquiries we shall find that the allegedly "still center" was, whenever a dynasty was in a robust muscle-flexing phase, in addition to its other expansionist activities, also extending its tentacles high and low in the social system. (In the 1870s in Tabanan, the origins of the royal wives who bore children were as follows: the paramount wife came from the royal house of Mengwi, a nearby kingdom later conquered by Tabanan; another royal wife came from the Krambitan royal house; "two others came from very low village-gentry families; and four others were commoners. In the following generation, the sons of the king brought in at least eight village women and one low gentry woman." Geertz and Geertz, 1957: 136.)

Under the label "the spatialization of kingship" the Geertzes provide information which is perfectly in accord with my own "galactic model." The nearest collaterals of a ruler, those of highest status, are usually located within the central capital settlement itself—that is, in the core domain. The lesser noble houses are scattered around the countryside. And significantly, the Geertzes note that there could in a realm exist "very high noble houses at some distance from the court as *secondary rulers*" (emphasis added); this is a clear confirmation of the fact that any realm is multicentric and in its interior has satellite rulers, who have claims more or less independent of the core line in the core domain.

I have made a somewhat extensive appeal to *Kinship in Bali* as a counterfoil to *Negara*, for it contains critical facts and insights that have not been incorporated in the latter. More than one reader has suspected that *Negara*'s overly flat, static, immobile, and "ritualized" view of the Balinese ruler and his court might have been derived either from aged Balinese informants who had had no experience of a Javanese realm in unimpeded existence, or from "dated" but engrossing Dutch accounts of royal cosmic rites divorced from the nitty gritty of native politics. Certainly "the theater state" as now sketched does not square with or blend with the Geertzes' lively documentation of the push and pull of Balinese perfidious manipulations, consensual harmonies, multiplex entanglements, and orchestrations of diffused energies at all levels—not merely at the level of lower gentry and ordinary peasantry in village communities. It remains a mystery why Clifford Geertz has not incorporated these facts and trends into his model of the *negara*. If his two orders of information (polarized as expressive pertaining to *negara* and instrumental as pertaining to *desa*) are granted a realistic coexistence, the only plausible time that coexistence might have occurred is the time of the Dutch conquest of the Balinese polities and afterward. If that is the case, a more appropriate title for Geertz's *Negara* is *The Twilight of the Balinese State*.

APPENDIX

Changing the Clothes of the Emerald Buddha in Contemporary Thailand

Nowadays in Thailand, at the rite of the changing of the Emerald Buddha's clothes, the king as chief officiant is assisted by the chief court Brahman (*rajaguru*) and his assistants, and by various officials of the royal household and the government. No monks are present during this rite,[16] which is exclusive in that the public is not admitted. But the rite is not esoteric,[17] and the day on which the rite is performed is public knowledge. Indeed, hundreds of pious laymen surround the temple, while the rite is performed behind closed doors.

In 1971 I was among these crowds, orderly and expectant, massed in the compound of Wat Phra Kaeo. The following account is drawn from my notes.

In that year, *khaw phansa* (when monks enter Lent, at the beginning of the rainy season) and the changing of the clothes of the Emerald Buddha fell on the same day. There were several hundred people present—of all ages, classes, and shades, including *farang* tourists. I was impressed by the fact that I could detect in the crowd affluent and sophisticated urbanites, ordinary city laborers, and rural folk.

The public was not allowed entry into the temple, but I was told that the king was inside decking the statue in its wet-season clothes. A bystander told me: "The wet-season clothes are the monk's robe; in the hot season the statue is clothed in sparse [that is, cool] but rich clothes; and in the cool season, it is clothed in full regal costume."

I saw moving about Brahman priests, wearing traditional-style white clothes and long hair knotted at the back, and impeccably groomed and uniformed royal officials. The ceremony was punctuated at various times by the dramatic beat of drums, the blowing of conches, and the wailing of flutes.

It started to rain fairly heavily, but the crowd did not seek shelter and sat down or stood in rows, four to five deep because the king was about to emerge. The king emerged at the left door, a large parasol held above his head, with officials surrounding him, and he sprinkled lustral water on the people, all now on their knees, hands joined in respectful worship and receiving the auspicious water of life with an intensity and eagerness that has to be seen to be believed.

Some months later I had the good fortune to meet and to have several conversations with the *rajaguru*, and he gave me this account of the rite. Three features are especially noteworthy. First, the essence of the life-affirming holy water is that it is the water with which the statue is washed. (This is in accord with the ideas of fertility and auspiciousness associated with the bath water and food leavings of eminent Hindu deities.) Second, the king who begins by acting as the chief officiant is at the end of the rite identified with the Emerald Buddha himself.[18] Finally, the king, having first sprinkled the water on his head, lustrates his courtiers and the people of his kingdom.

According to the *rajaguru*, he and his assistant Brahmans and the king's officials prepare the ritual articles and await the king's arrival. Before his arrival, a senior official will have already climbed up the steps and removed the clothes on the statue and dusted it. But the statue's crown is left in place.

The king climbs up and removes the crown. Then he pours water on its body (not on its head) from a conch shell, and wipes it with a small towel. He then places the wet towel in a golden bowl and hands it to an official. Then the king puts on the statue's head the new crown appropriate for the season, and descends. A senior officer climbs up and puts the new season's clothes on the statue.

Next the king squeezes the water from the towel into the bowl, and this water is mixed with a larger quantity of ordinary water. An officer pours some of the holy water into a conch shell and takes it to the king, who sprinkles his own head with it, and thereafter sprinkles water first on the heads of the royal family present, in order of rank, and then on the heads of all the officers present.

The next sequence is the candle ceremony (*wian thian*). The king sits on a chair placed on the right of the Emerald Buddha. All the Brahmans and the officers surround them in a circle. Three Brahmans, led by the *rajaguru*, light in turn fifteen candles, which are passed from hand to hand in a clockwise direction. Each person waves the candle and wafts the smoke toward the Buddha and the king. The Brahmans then put out the candles.

Now the *rajaguru* ascends and marks with powder the back of the Emerald Buddha with a sacred sign (*unalom*). Finally, the king emerges from the temple and sprinkles holy water on the people, and in doing so he circumambulates the temple once in a clockwise direction.

During the rite, four Brahman priests blow the conch shell loudly during the following critical sequences: first, throughout the time when the king removes the crown of the Emerald Buddha, bathes it, and puts on it a new crown; second, during each of the three rounds when the candles are lit by each of the three Brahmans, then passed around and waved before the Buddha and the king; finally, when the Brahmans put out the candles.

Conclusion

An Anthropologist's Creed

There are in the United States today some scholars—hardly homogeneous in terms of skills and interests, which range from systems theory to the return of the sacred into a secularized world—who call themselves "futurologists." I cannot claim to be one of them. I have in the course of fieldwork in Southeast Asia dabbled in astrology, but that uncertain knowledge is of no use here because the date and time of birth of Anthropology are unknown. For these and other reasons I shall not presume to look down from a lofty eminence and claim a special competence to comment on the present state of the discipline and its future prospects. What I have to say represents the attitudes and values of one practicing anthropologist concerning the question of the "relevance" of anthropology as an agent of positive change and reform in the modern world.

Since the forties and the fifties, after the termination of the Second World War, the vast majority of those who have gone from the metropolitan centers of wealth, knowledge, and power in the West to the countries of the Third World with a mission to change and better them have not been anthropologists but other social scientists such as economists and political scientists, and professionals such as educationists, doctors, engineers, and agronomists. The economists coined the label "underdeveloped country," and they saw as the objective indices of underdevelopment such features as the vicious circle of poverty, underemployment (and disguised employment), and undercapitalization, and prescribed as the cures for these the stimulation of economic growth, the increase of gross national product, and the securing of basic needs (food, health care) through such seemingly practical remedies as the creation of import substitution industries, injection of foreign aid supplemented by forced domestic savings, the building of infrastructures, the creation of markets, and so on. The political scientists had a similar view of Third World countries as being "backward," and saw their mission as the "modernization" of these societies through political development—that is, through the adoption of democratic institutions and procedures such as universal suffrage and voting, the party system, parliamentary assemblies, and rational bureaucracies built on universalistic criteria of recruitment. The securing of political legitimacy by governments on these terms would, it was claimed, enable their stability and growth. Both these reforming postures, informed by Neo-Keynesian and Neo-Weberian (and other) principles, implied two things. One was a shared problem orientation—namely, the necessary transformation and reshaping of the Third World. The other was the effecting of that transformation in the image of Western conceptions of the good industrial, bourgeois, liberal society in whose institutions and rationality the reforming experts had explicit faith. Of a third infirmity these reformers were largely unaware: their naïve optimism and innocent assurance of smoothly and quickly changing continents other than theirs were strangely at variance with the history of Europe, and the West in general, in the eighteenth and nineteenth (and even twentieth) centuries—a history which showed that the path of Western industrial development and progress had been signposted with upheavals, class conflicts, revolutions, and malignant growths, of which the Nazi era was the most proximate.

In this brave new epoch in which "experts" confidently took their missions to the ends of the world, the social and cultural anthropologists, who at least from the beginnings of this century had persistently visited, lived in, and studied "other" cultures, seemed to have no such clear reforming and messianic missions toward the objects of their vocation. Though they showed the adventurousness of the explorer, they lacked the sense of purpose of the Christian missionary. Though they showed qualities of fortitude by enduring strange diseases and exotic realities, they seemed to lack a settled attitude toward that experience.

In this postwar epoch, Anthropology, committed to studying the "natives" and the "pagans," seemed ill-fitted for positive action on three counts. First, it seemed to be tainted by its past; it was taunted as a child of colonialism and imperialism, and if not their actual accomplice it had at least functioned comfortably and unmolested within the imperial context.[1] Second, documentation and deep knowledge of their archaic customs and arcane knowledge seemed demeaning and uncomplimentary to the new "nationalistic" ruling elites of the Third World, who were waving the flag of modernization. Third, that same knowledge made anthropologists look conservative, ambiguous, equivocal, and muddled to the eyes of modernizing Western developers. Anthropology was a Western discipline, yet it was committed to the deep appreciative study of other cultures and their ideas. Anthropology endlessly debated the relation between universals and relativities without bringing the debate to a close. Anthropology might on the one hand affirm the psychic unity of mankind and a single universal rationality for it, and on the other insist on the historicity and diversity of cultures and societies, claiming that they are all meaningful and rational as human creations. A series of unhappy euphemisms, such as the shifting names for the sinister left hand of dual classification, exposed the anthropologists' predicament in labeling their object of study: "primitive societies," "traditional societies," "preliterate societies," "cold societies," "precapitalist social formations," and (finally) "posttraditional societies." Nothing so clean and frank and gothic as the economist's "underdeveloped societies."

It is no accident, then, that those of us who felt impelled to and agreed to participate as "applied" anthropologists in programs of development usually did so under conditions that were not of our own choosing. And it is no accident that the planning experts and implementers of development programs viewed anthropology not as the queen of the social sciences but as the mother of low-status servants and handmaids fitted for the labor-intensive job of pitching their tents in the outbacks and wildernesses in order to collect information on wasteful feasting, vexatious land tenure systems, aggravating factional politics, and mystifying notions of purity and danger—information that hopefully could then be processed and converted to variables such as "the cultural factor" or "the psychic components of income and consumption" in macromodels. At the same time, these "rationalists" tended to view the concern of anthropologists to document "backward" peoples' customs and practices as an odd preoccupation with weird irrationalities that could not promise "hard" knowledge. We the producers of the most concrete information were also the least abstract; the producers of the most contextual information, the least predictive; the "thickest" describers of the local scene, the least assured on policy matters.

There were other "characterological" reasons which seemed to confirm the views of development economists and UNESCO's spreaders of literacy, and to justly condemn anthropologists to a Popperian nonfalsifiable hell and to the bottom of the social science heap. Because of their search for an authentic knowledge of the other, which requires a relatively long period of residence in the field as participant and witness, anthropologists readily consented to employment as field consultants while other professionals landed the contracts with the Agency for International Development and the International Monetary Fund, and cooked up the designs and the budgets, seasoned with surveys, censuses, and cost-benefit equations.

At the beginning of the eighties things have changed, as may be judged by the title of a recent essay by the eminent nonconformist economist Albert Hirschman: "The Rise and Decline of Development Economists" (1981). Hirschman laments that the discipline of economics has become progressively narrower at precisely the moment when the problems it addresses demand more political and social insight. The story is equally bleak in cognate fields. The band of neo-Weberian political scientists and sociologists centered at the University of Chicago, who foretold the onset of the "integrative revolution" and the decline of "primordial" loyalties in Third World countries, disbanded some years ago, since the routinization of rationality as a world historical process had not occurred.[2] The disillusionment of the eighties is not merely that the economists or the agronomists or some other professionals cannot do it alone. It is, more importantly, the disconcerting realization that although there have been successes and conquests in the field of development and modernization, development programs have stimulated and generated in the Third World— whether by collusion or reaction, doubtless in good faith and poor anticipation—massive civil war, gruesome interracial and interethnic bloodshed, repressive authoritarianism by military coteries fortified by Western weaponry, flagrant misuse of mass media, and fundamentalist religious bigotry. More often than not, development has produced sharper differences in wealth, income distribution, and education than were ever known before—especially between, on the one side, the city-based comprador agents of international corporations and the local military elites feeding off them, and, on the other, the rural poor, whose subsistence agriculture has increasingly become irrelevant to world trade. Countries in Latin America, Africa, and Asia, in this respect showing no discrimination, have experienced social and political upheavals unforeseen by neoclassical or liberal or communist models of linear change. And it is not merely the radical Marxists, but also many other commentators of a less polemical persuasion, who have begun to see the encounters between West and East, North and South, in the last three decades in terms of "unequal development," "dependent economies," "unequal terms of exchange," "multinational corporations," the "military-industrial complex," "comprador and bureaucratic capitalism," and the like. A sober account has yet to be written as to why and how in Southeast Asia radical groups, bred in deprived border provinces and in the mountains, have risen in massive hatred and unimaginable fury against the elite populations of primate cities like Pnom Penh and Saigon, whom they have denounced as flabby, undesirable, deracinated creatures and pawns of Western imperialism. (That same account must also tell us why imperialist communist powers and dogmas that at first inspired the periphery later spawned internecine warfare that has wrought further havoc in the same arena.)

It is in the face of an academic crisis in the West, combined with derailment of the West's development efforts to do well by doing good to the backward countries, that the time is propitious for the discipline of anthropology to rethink the opportunities and possibilities and hazards of a more activist engagement with the world. There are essentially three formidable reasons for anthropologists to address this question.

First, those who previously dominated and steered aid programs realize more than ever before the need for interdisciplinary cooperation where anthropologists are an integral component in both the planning and implementation of schemes urgently requested by the countries of the Third World. (A modest example is that the Harvard Institute for International Development, predominantly staffed by economists, is now seeking to invite anthropologists to join them as equal Fellows.)

The second reason is a bread and butter question for anthropologists. With a decline in the number of academic positions, and in research funding for "pure" as opposed to "applied" research, younger anthropologists, if they are to make a living (and indeed if they are to do any research at all) find it increasingly necessary to seek employment as consultants, extension agents, welfare workers, therapeutic agents, field staff of agencies, and the like. Moreover, departments of anthropology at established universities, to ensure that graduate students will enroll in the future in the face of declining financial support for students, as well as to ensure that federal agencies such as the National Science Foundation and the National Institutes of Health will give training and research grants, are thinking of initiating vocationally disposed programs of study consistent with upholding high academic standards.[3]

The third reason, all too often ignored as not romantic or exotic enough, is that virtually all Third World countries, however persistent and entrenched many of their valuations and social institutions may be, are today self-consciously sponsoring "modernization" projects, and the visiting anthropologist cannot fail to witness uncontrolled accelerated urbanization, massive long-distance migrations, the spread of literacy, the fateful impact of modern mass media, the diffusion of Western medicine and its coexistence with traditional forms, changing patterns of land tenure and agricultural cropping, expansion of industrial employment, the intensification and transformation of traditional cults and religious movements, and the inflation of political rhetoric and theater, both old and new. Anthropologists cannot resist being placed in the midst of these streams of events, and even being swept along by them, and when they characterize them as processes of continuity and transformation, or as manifestations of the modernity of tradition, or as change without development, they are in some sense evaluating them.

In line with these considerations is the inescapable realization that anthropology and anthropologists are not merely concerned with non-Western societies or the depressed societies on the fringes of the Western world, but have an integral role to play in their own countries right in the core regions of Europe and North America.

What is it that anthropology can tell the world at large today about its relevance and its qualifications to be consulted?

Let me approach this question obliquely. In recent historical studies, particularly in the domain of political economy, the center-periphery grid has been used to arrange facts in space and time and to describe the dialectics of transforming influences. This scheme is, of course, not new. David Quinn in *Raleigh and the British Empire* (1947) and *The Elizabethans and the Irish* (1966) used it to describe the expansion of the English world from its core in southeastern England into successive alien peripheries: Wales and the North Country in the sixteenth century, Scotland, Ireland, and North America in the seventeenth. Franco Venturi's works—for example, *Utopia and Reform in the Enlightenment* (1971)—consist of an illuminating mapping of the radiation of the Enlightenment from its center in Paris to the near peripheries in western Europe and then to the outer margins in eastern Europe, Russia, and North America.[4] From quite another quarter, Edward Shils (1975) and other sociologists have employed the center-periphery paradigm to explicate the way in which values that are central to a society are diffused into the society at large. But in recent years it is Immanuel Wallerstein's *The Modern World-System: Capitalist Agriculture and the Origins of the European World*

Economy in the Sixteenth Century (1974) that has stated in elaborate and climactic fashion a radical Marxist perspective (also associated with such scholars as Gundar Frank) on the dynamics of capitalism as a world historical process.[5] And there have since then appeared different versions of this basic theme—whether it be construed as a single monolithic process or as creating in the periphery a different breed of capitalism best called "unequal development."[6]

All in all, however, these powerful analyses have emphasized the steamroller effect of global capitalism, and the inevitable subservience and decline of village populations as a result of the onslaught of a capitalist world economy and centralizing, extractive state systems. Claude Meillassoux captures this mood, which is meant to apply to regions other than just West Africa, when he asserts that when precapitalist forms are affected by world capitalism they are "undermined and perpetuated at the same time."[7] The ironic underside of this imagined omnipotence is the reflex that Washington and London and Moscow must and can monitor the world's political processes—a dangerous doctrine that motivates exasperated military interventions in Vietnam or El Salvador or the Falkland Islands or Afghanistan that result in ignominious retreats, costly stalemates, or pyrrhic victories.

It seems to me that many anthropologists are in a position to say something about this regnant paradigm, and to insert a deflationary corrective and counterpoint to it, precisely because we have pitched our tents on the peripheries of societies, both territorially in distant provinces and socially among the common people at the bottom of the hierarchy.

The truth of contemporary world processes lies not simply in the rolling of a juggernaut in a single direction but in the dialectic, the push and pull, between the center's impetus and the periphery's not infrequent sturdy adaptation and resistance to it and appropriation of some of its prizes. Anthropologists who have worked in rural communities, small towns, and city slums and bazaars have a different story to tell: of local dominant groups and hierarchies, local entrepreneurs and politicians, who have met the encroaching central state's foreign-funded development and welfare programs and ingeniously and creatively captured positions and resources in the administrative networks; of how these same local interest groups have seriously muted land reform measures and have simultaneously expanded the scope and transformed the meanings of traditional social forms to implement new tasks and launch new enterprises; of how their folk ballads and popular theater caricature the gullibilities and pomposities of foreign developers and native bureaucrats; and of how wherever feasible, they have mobilized peasant mobs and coolie insurrections to foil alien intrusions.[8]

It seems that in the mid-1980s we have already begun to forget the rich studies by a generation of anthropologists who are still among us—studies which documented these encounters, structures, and networks as they appeared from the vantage point of the periphery. Following is some of the past literature in areas familiar to me: concerning India, the classical studies of F. G. Bailey, Adrian Mayer, Kathleen Gough, Scarlett Epstein, Louis Dumont, M. N. Srinivas, Milton Singer, Bernard Cohn, Owen Lynch, Jonathan Parry, and McKim Marriott; concerning Sri Lanka, the works of Edmund Leach, Nur Yalman, and Gananath Obeyesekere. No doubt similar bodies of literature exist and are even now being written with regard to West Africa, East Africa, Melanesia, and so on.

It seems to me that one task for the eighties is to collate and consolidate these materials with two objects in mind. One is to tell a measured story of the give and take between, on the one side, the initiatives, demands, and impulsions originating within the metropolitan centers of the world system and their satellite capitals, and, on the other, the reactions of the ensemble of social institutions, systems of land tenure, forms of labor, and patterns of leadership typical of the local zones. This, in brief, would be a discussion of the varying interactions and modes of "integration of local segments of the periphery with the world economy and, on the local level itself, of one subsegment with another" (Mintz, 1977: 266).

But the discussion must go beyond the dialectics of these interactions. It must vigorously argue and demonstrate—because this matter is fundamental to the role of the anthropologist who engages in development activities—that the future contours and trajectories of Third World countries do not depend merely, or even decisively, on the ways in which the ruling elites and privileged minorities in their Third World primate cities mesh with and collaborate with multinational corporations, or with United Nations agencies, or with foreign powers with global interests. The ruling indigenous brokers and mediators may in the short run enrich themselves and deepen their power bases; they may in the short run warp democratic institutions into authoritarian regimes, and put their faith in military power acquired through control of foreign guns. But the anthropologist's rhetoric ought to be that the final outcome of the alleged world historical process depends as much or more on the way in which the social base of urban poor and rural peasants adapts with creative resilience and resistance to the moves from metropolitan and satellite centers.

It is with this identity and slogan nailed to his mast—a charter born of a cumulative anthropological knowledge and sympathetic field-work—that the development anthropologist should embark upon his activist tasks. And this charter is more positive than the somewhat weak-kneed position that the question today cannot be whether or not development efforts should be undertaken at all but rather how to soften the contact and how to regulate the changes so that their consequences for Third World societies are minimally harmful.[9]

Moreover, as a challenge to the thesis that the rest of the world's fate is to react to the monopolistic propensities of Western capitalism, we ought to propose the positive thesis that just as modern Japan and China, and perhaps India, are following their own destinies to construct social formations different from those the West has ever known, so in due course might various other regions in Southeast Asia, Melanesia, and elsewhere. I do not think that it is time yet for the classical anthropological phoenix, the diversity of social formations, to be released from its chain of rebirths by a capitalist conflagration of alleged world proportions.

Development anthropologists, usually of Western origins and in almost all cases salaried by Western agencies, must forge their orientations by squarely facing up to the fact that they—whether white, black, yellow, or brown—travel to other lands in the wake of metropolitan capitalism and a tendentious modernization. They will also not amount to much if they do not entertain the nagging doubt, voiced by Edmund Leach (1982: 50) that development anthropology might be a form of neocolonialism. There are two kinds of anthropologist activists who might not sympathize with my views. One is the self-assured Westerner who feels that history is automatically and inevitably on his or her side; who is an unreconstructed believer in neoclassical economics, in society as a mere adjunct of the market system, and in formal democracy as prevails in the West; and who unreflectively wants to change circumstances "out there" in seeming ignorance of the fact that the modes and terms of collaboration of the indigenous elites with foreign interests influence importantly the shape of the resulting political economy. The other is the anthropologist-revolutionary who is convinced that the world capitalist system in place will permanently enslave and exploit and cripple his or her native or adopted country, and that the only self-defense possible is to refuse all forms of aid programs and to work toward a socialist revolution from within.

Most anthropologists (and I count myself among them) fall in the middle, suffering from a deep sense of ambiguity, tension, and agnosticism about the ethics and activity of development, which is financed by one side and vociferously demanded by the other. Most anthropologists who have lived and worked with the common people know how much distress and poverty and ill health they endure. And most anthropologists are also realistic enough to know that he who pays the piper tries to call the tune.

My conception of the responsible and committed development anthropologist incorporates at least three minimal features. His (or her) task is that of a "journeyman-clinician"; his role is that of a "double agent"; and his intervention is as an "actor in history." By "journeyman" I have in mind the person described by Meyer Fortes—the anthropologist who has learned a craft and a discipline, who has a stock of plausible ideas and hunches which he can bring to bear on his work. By "clinician" I mean an anthropologist who treats each community, each task within that community, as a case in its own right whose history and trajectory he will track and monitor, and who remains at his field post throughout the lifecycle of his task. The journeyman-clinician-anthropologist must be open to the suggestion (even if it is not always true) that each society or each community may present him with a development problematic which is in large measure unique.

By "double agent" I mean not that the development anthropologist should be a double-crosser but that he should be fully conscious and thoughtful of the mediations he has to achieve. There is, first of all, the translation of cultures to negotiate. If he believes there is a message of change and reform that the subjects must adopt, he must make them understand the alleged validity of this message. And in receiving their response and in understanding their conceptions of their present and their future, he needs to consider how they may affect and transform his own message and his own view of the world. And so the dialogue must go on recursively, frequently in a triangular contest. The development anthropologist not only must serve and interpret for his Western donor and patron, who has his own preconceptions; he must negotiate with the Third World ruling elites and intelligentsia, who have their own interests and even misconceptions; and he must serve, fortify, and protect his third master—namely, the ordinary people, who, though not immaculate in their conceptions, shall always claim his primary loyalty, and who are both beneficiaries and victims of the outsiders. Not least among the anthropologist's labors on behalf of these people is the exercise of vigilance and craft so that the institutions and circumstances of engagement and encounter between government and people do not become grossly unequal.

By "historical actor" I mean that the development anthropologist must inevitably experience contemporary history in "narrative form." As actor, agent, decision maker, dispute settler, he will have in the field a lively sense of how individual decisions, and even accidents, help shape the sequence of events. He will witness day by day how the various participants taking a hand in their fates and fortunes pull at the story in the direction in which they want to carry it, such that one can never quite guess at any moment what will happen next.

This action context requires of the anthropologist the awareness that he is consciously implicated in encounters with certain others in the field with whom he transacts and negotiates the terms of participation, information gathering, and project implementation. To give a twist to a current trend that insists that the anthropologist in the field is a party to privileged and tendentious encounters which color the information he elicits,[10] I submit that it is precisely the relatively short-term consultant and policy adviser, wheeling and dealing with high politicians, middle-level brokers, and quizzical peasants, who needs to be most mindful of the contingent nature of his role. The phenomenological perspective, which brings the observer, analyst, or reformer actively into a single picture as integrally implicated in the "reality" produced, has in certain quarters been seen as the enemy of structural-functional or structuralist or Marxist (or some other) claims of providing accounts of an objective reality, confirmable by method and by verification, and little distorted by the circumstantial particularities of the observer-participant. In mitigation of this charge, it is still worth saying that the long-term anthropologist in the field, who has a better chance of engaging a cross-section of the society, and of gaining a deeper knowledge of the collective past and the dynamics of the present, is less prone to the shortcomings of the phenomenological critique of partial and short-lived encounters.[11]

There is, I would emphasize, a critical difference between the applied anthropologist and the development economist or political scientist in their field orientations. The latter usually conceive of their task as a transfer of a valid technology they already possess to the field site, wherever it may be. All that is necessary is to make a few adjustments to interfering local impediments and bottlenecks. The anthropologist, by contrast, while asserting that his previous knowledge is an aid, and that he too carries with him a set of anticipations, is prone to insist that the most relevant and decisive knowledge is constructed anew in the field. And it is this openness to the context demanding intensive study that shall be his entitlement to being a regional specialist.

In recent years, certain philosophical and moral misgivings have been aired about the problematic role of the anthropologist—misgivings which ought then to attach to development anthropologists with even greater force. They principally revolve around the question of whether it is possible to study other people without asserting a power over them, whether too many anthropologists take knowledge away to advance their careers abroad rather than share their skills with those they study, whether this appropriated knowledge and heritage when deposited and concretized in museums and authoritative texts become enduring emblems and repositories of "looting" without reciprocity. I think we are all more conscious now of the fact that the research process itself—let alone the reforming and ameliorative activities of aid programs—reflects dialectics of differential power, privilege, and leverage between the outsider and the locals, and in this sense the "colonial" and "colonizing" connotations will always be present to tempt and haunt us. We also know full well that the information we collect can be put to evil use by both local and foreign interests. But we cannot agonize too much over these issues, or else paralysis will overtake those who want to make anthropology relevant to the world in more responsible ways than has been done before.[12] There are some comforting thoughts to tide us over these dark moments: that aid is frequently solicited by the needy; that outside anthropologists, archaeologists, linguists, and historians have recovered for Third World countries traditions and treasures they have lost or neglected; that such scholars have rescued customs and myths and tales from uncertain oral transmission and secured them in written texts for Third World cultures, thereby raising their consciousness, increasing their pride in their past, and contributing to their identity as a people.

I think there is still another task that awaits the development anthropologist. This is stated in a timely Rockefeller Foundation document, "Reflections on Development: A Program of Fellowship Awards" (May 1983), which says that the foundation has been seeking to enable scholars from Southeast Asia and English-speaking Africa to undertake social and historical studies which can contribute to a deeper understanding of the processes and content of development as it relates to their individual societies: "The program was developed in part out of a concern that much of social science at present consists of short-term consultations and evaluation tasks inspired by immediate practical problems and requested by national and international agencies. While this work is essential, it tends to distract scholars from the pursuit of broader subjects that might shed light on the complexities and contradictions inherent in the overall development process."

There is no doubt that there is a crying need for anthropological assessments, backed by scholarship, field experience, and reflection, of the assumptions underlying alternative development policies, practices, and actions, and of the larger moral and cultural dimensions of rapid economic and technological change. This is supremely a task for the pontiffs of anthropology, who standing back can transcend narrative in favor of structure and system, with this proviso: that he who has not been a good journeyman cannot succeed as a pontiff.

The commitment to an authentic engagement with the Other ought to make anthropologists sensitive, self-reflective commentators on development experts in general as professionals. My tentative script for a sociology of that profession is as follows. Because most development experts view their task in terms of "project implementation" (and this again in terms of a transfer to a field site of prevalidated policies and techniques), they comfortably begin to think of themselves as a worldwide transferable service, similar to diplomats or traveling salesmen. Moreover, since approved projects have budgets and voted monies tied to specified times and places, the development experts are encouraged to act in the belief that time is of the essence in their vocation. This serves as a protectionist perspective in which the interests of the donor, the aid receiver, and the deliverer converge. The other side of the coin of this nonphilosophy of action is that development experts and agencies are not disposed to build an institutional memory or to consult it. Evaluations are undertaken after projects have been implemented; they are sometimes sensitive and incisive, but the project is done and its designers have moved on, usually to higher office. When a new project is hatched the men of action repeat the same pattern, not because they are lazy or ignorant but because to consult and study their own archives in the manner of historians is antithetical to them: they have the dispositions of delivery men rather than of carpenters who fashion furniture on the spot. These are the reasons why prospective feasibility reports will take precedence over postmortem evaluation reports, and why the historian-anthropologist might write the best sociology of development.

If the applied anthropologist, usually a Westerner working in an alien country, has to pick his way carefully through a minefield, the task of the same anthropologist working in his own country is less vexatious, because the country in question is his own: he can more forthrightly and openly admit and state his ideological commitments, and his vision of the better society he wishes to help build. The applied anthropologist in England or France must necessarily contemplate and agonize, as Emile Durkheim did, about the grounds on which sociology (and anthropology) can make a claim to be a "moral science."[13] Is it possible to breathe new meaning into Edward Tylor's Victorian motto "The science of culture is essentially a reformer's science"? In doing so, the distinctive accomplishment of anthropology, its "totalizing" perspective, must be invoked as having a timely relevance for the state of Western society today.

Once again, let me argue this proposition obliquely. The splitting of man into a parade of Latinized men, *homo economicus, homo politicus, homo religiosus,* and so on, and the fragmentation of knowledge into ever more specialized domains and subdomains of economics, politics, the physical sciences—this "atomization of information" as one of the hallmarks of positive science—has no doubt aided the advance of knowledge. A second orientation that has aided the physical sciences has been the separation of moral valuation from the understanding of the "order of nature," in contrast to the Platonic yoking of knowledge with goodness and wisdom, understanding with attunement (see Taylor, in Hollis and Lukes, 1982). Or, as Marc Bloch puts it: "The lesson of the intellectual development of mankind is clear: the sciences have shown themselves ever more fruitful and, hence, in the long run more practical, in proportion as they deliberately abandon the old anthropomorphism of good and evil. Today we should laugh at a chemist who separated the bad gases, like chlorine, from the good ones like oxygen. But, had chemistry adopted this classification in its infancy, it would have run the grave risk of getting stuck there, to the great detriment of the knowledge of matter" (1953: 142).

A third orientation of the scientific method was the abandonment by the physical sciences of the observer in order to understand better the thing observed. Because the connections which our minds weave between things appear arbitrary and subjective, the physical sciences deliberately break them in order to reestablish a diversity which is more authentic.

These orientations, whatever their payoffs, have wreaked two kinds of havoc on the human sciences which emulated them. The tendency to create special domains with their own logics by the process of atomization of information has simultaneously and paradoxically produced more gaps and holes in knowledge, even while it grew. As science has advanced, the more bereft we have become of synthesizing conceptual systems and overarching norms to constrain its alleged neutral knowledge and its pragmatic successes. Moreover, in the human sciences, the pretense that the observer is divorced from the thing observed does not accord with the fact that human consciousness and social representations are their ultimate subject matter, and the realities they deal with are the products of intersubjective interactions and conventions created in an open-ended historical process.

The extreme pursuit of the amoral splitting strategy of knowledge making has tended to rob each scientific discipline of any assured normative basis, and has upheld "instrumentation" and "instrumental action" as the essence of "hard science," and technological success as the critical measure of its validity as knowledge.

These developments have brought modern medicine in the United States and the technologically advanced countries of the North to a crisis point. The "biomedical" paradigm of disease and cure reigns supreme in the West's prestigious medical schools and leading hospitals. Because physiological and anatomical processes of the human body are amenable to rigorous experimental study, knowledge and techniques of certain kinds have made remarkable advances and hit the headlines: conspicuous examples are gene splicing and cloning, coronary bypass surgery, the transplant of organs, and chemotherapy to contain cancer. The triumphs of biochemical knowledge are mighty indeed, and the investment of medicine in high technology is necessary and warranted.

But the more the biomedical paradigm of disease and cure reigns supreme the more human beings are reduced to material entities, and correspondingly the more insignificant and unsupported becomes the study of all those social and psychological aspects of humanity that have a direct and immediate influence on the etiology and treatment of many of the very same diseases of the head, heart, liver, and stomach that biomedicine treats.

It is precisely in New York, Chicago, London, and other metropolitan citadels of Western civilization that we see the most heightened manifestations of social and individual ill-health and stress: massive divorce rates, the breakup of families, increasing numbers of children from broken homes and one-parent families, widespread theft and homicide—all violent actions reflecting, among other things, relative deprivation in an atmosphere of affluence; frequent rapes which betray intense isolation in the midst of teeming humanity, racial antagonism, and an aggression against women in a time of feminist advancement; spasmodic orgiastic rioting in a milieu of ethnic diversity, intolerance, and discrimination; pervasive drug abuse and alcoholism not only among adults but also among a frightening number of teenagers, who take the generational gap and conflict to be a fact of life. The high incidence of mental depression, stomach ulcers, coronary attacks, and liver ailments cannot be divorced from the strains and pressures of the larger social context.

Recently a popular magazine dramatically titled its cover story "Stress! Seeking Cures for Modern Anxieties" and carried a picture of what looked like a college student yelling his midnight primal scream to assuage the demands of his academic prison. Here are some excerpts from this report:

> According to the American Academy of Family Physicians, two-thirds of office visits to family doctors are prompted by stress-related symptoms. At the same time, leaders of industry have become alarmed by the huge cost of such symptoms in absenteeism, company medical expenses and lost productivity. Based on national samples, these costs have been estimated at $50 billion to $75 billion a year, more than $750 for every U.S. worker. Stress is now known to be a major contributor, either directly or indirectly, to coronary heart disease, cancer, lung ailments, accidental injuries, cirrhosis of the liver and suicide—six of the leading causes of death in the U.S. Stress also plays a role in aggravating such diverse conditions as multiple sclerosis, diabetes, genital herpes and even trench mouth. It is a sorry sign of the times that the three bestselling drugs in the country are an ulcer medication (Tagamet), a hypertension drug (Inderal) and a tranquilizer (Valium) . . .
>
> The relentless stresses of poverty and ghetto life have also been associated with higher health risks. Studies of poor black neighborhoods in Detroit and Boston have correlated hypertension, which is twice as common among American blacks as among whites, with overcrowded housing and high levels of unemployment and crime. Research conducted by Epidemiologist David Jenkins . . . showed that the two areas with the highest mortality rates in [Massachusetts] were the Boston black ghetto of Roxbury and the working-class white enclave of South Boston, which had been locked in a bitter feud over school busing. (*Time*, June 6, 1983)

The study of stress as an aggravating factor in the disease process has now been launched in the United States: old fields such as psychosomatic medicine have revived, and new fields such as behavioral medicine, psychoendocrinology, and psychoneuroimmunology have come into being. New jargon is being coined. And numerous "stress management" enterprises are offering their services to hospitals and clinics, advocating such techniques as biofeedback, self-hypnosis, rhythmic breathing, muscle relaxation, and the like.

Certain excesses in recent medical history attest to the possible counterproductive, dysfunctional, "magical" role of science as a "belief system"—not merely among us, the lay public, but in the world of professional medicine, in hospitals, in pharmaceutical companies, and among physicians and surgeons who practice both in prestigious hospitals and a multitude of private clinics. This issue is the subject of a growing body of critical literature.[14]

There are several examples in our time of disastrous informal experimentation in medical therapy, and of faddism and quick resort to incompletely tested treatments—tendencies which are the outcome of a variety of causes: the sensational journalism of newspapers, the self-serving advertising of firms which publicize "wonder drugs" and "miracle cures," the reliance of ordinary physicians on the premature pronouncements of acclaimed "experts" in prestigious schools and hospitals, the social pressures on the part of patients and their families on the one side and competing medical institutions on the other for speedy and widely applicable clinical cures, and finally the boomerang effects of American affluence which readily invests in, and puts its trust in, expensive machinery and gadgetry. In all this, one cannot dismiss the existence of a "medical-industrial complex" in which altruistic physicians and surgeons exist in mutual symbiosis with profit-oriented manufacturing companies.[15] Worthy of contemplation is this apocryphal saying in factories that manufacture fireworks: "It is better to curse in darkness than to light the wrong candle."

Now, then, might be the proper time for anthropologists—for whom a "totalized" account of how the various levels and domains of man's life intersect and hang together is a necessary entailment of their disciplinary perspective—to infiltrate health care, the legal system, and other domains, and to maintain strenuously that the physical and the mental in man, his sense of person and self and of his rights and obligations, are embedded in his social relations, and these again in the collectivities of family, occupation, class, community, and nation. The times are appropriate to reiterate and demonstrate that the pursuit of social sanity and prosperity requires the broadening of the frontiers of knowledge into areas which, because they are difficult to quantify or to atomize and reduce to the models of molecular biology and genetics, should not therefore be abandoned as worthless or subversive to orthodoxy.

A distinguished biologist, Stephen Jay Gould, whose "potentialist" perspective I much prefer to E. O. Wilson's "reductionism," has recently said from the other side what most anthropologists of my kind have always said: that it is history, collective understandings, and current uses rather than biology that will explain cultural diversity, and that the same reductionist strategy that worked for molecular biology will not work for human culture.[16]

In a recent study of patients in China suffering from "major depressive disorder," Arthur Kleinman, psychiatrist and anthropologist, discovered (1982: 163) that while the majority reported symptomatic relief when treated with antidepressant drugs, they experienced no change in their social impairment associated with their work, political, and marital circumstances. Despite symptomatic improvement, the patients maintained their sick role paradoxically even as their sicknesses diminished.

Silverman's warnings against abuses stemming from a blind faith in the efficacy of biomedical "science," Gould's strictures against an inappropriate reductionism in the study of human evolution and cultural diversity, and Kleinman's finding that symptomatic improvement in patients cannot be ordinarily equated with healing could all serve as parables to the issue of illness and health as a sociopsychosomatic phenomenon, and a prologue to the issue of the role of the anthropologist as a totalizing and synthesizing theorist in a world in which specialisms spawn rapidly to fragment and differentiate knowledge into realms, which are incapable of being interrelated in a coherent overarching cosmology.

I previously dubbed the applied anthropologist's role in the Third World as being that of a journeyman-clinician. This figure of speech has been appositely employed in the United States by an avant-garde group of psychiatrists and social scientists (Kleinman, Eisenberg, and Good, 1978: 251–258), who, placing their faith in medical anthropology, have proposed "the idea of a clinical social science" with regard to primary health care. They have suggested "that social science be developed as a clinical discipline in medical schools and teaching hospitals. A department of clinical social science would be staffed by physicians with training in anthropology or sociology, and by anthropologists or sociologists with training in a medical setting."

The theses of a clinical social science are these. Traditional biomedical understanding and cure of *disease,* while unassailable within its own terms, does not effectively exhaust what is implied by the healing of *illness.* Since there is often a disjunction between disease (understood in the Western medical paradigm as the malfunctioning of biological and psychophysiological processes in the individual) and illness (which is the patient's experience of sickness, strongly inflected by culturally and socially defined meanings and expectations), the existing clinical encounter is frequently abortive. Patient dissatis-

faction, patient abandonment or improper observance of the prescribed treatment, and patient resort to other forms of healing and advice are evidence of this disjunction. At the level of clinical health care,
therefore, patient and doctor must negotiate a mutually meaningful
clinical reality and understanding that enables cure. The anthropological perspective and approach is eminently suited to constructing this
clinical reality and the mapping of the larger social and psychological
context which impinges on illness and disease.

Today in the United States there are several medical schools and
hospitals[17] where the need to develop an encompassing and totalizing
biopsychosocial framework for effective primary clinical and epide-
miological health care is being realized, and steps are being taken to
integrate medical anthropology into the training of clinician-social scientists. These are some of the relevant issues for whose investigation
anthropological skills are appropriate: the interrelationship between
stress and social involvements in the onset of illness; the role of the
family in inducing illness, or in providing supports for health maintenance and in influencing illness outcome (these concerns are
eminently relevant to what is labeled "family medicine"); the manifestation of somatization (that is, the presentation of somatic com-
plaints which exceed the biomedical assessment of pathology) and its
sociocultural meanings and social uses by patients as manipulative,
coping, or help-seeking behavior; the linguistic, communicational, and
differential-power aspects of the patient-doctor discourse and their
implications for the construction of the clinical reality; the semantics
and pragmatics of the language of emotions and affective states (see
Kleinman, 1983). If we cross-factor these issues by social class, education, occupation, ethnic application, sex, lifecycle stage, we shall
find ourselves even more fully into the domains of anthropology and
sociology as traditionally defined.

I do not think it is the mission of anthropologists to follow *pukka*
economists into the construction of econometric models, *pukka* sociologists into mathematical modeling, or *pukka* psychologists into computer simulation of mental processes. The more these disciplines are
enticed into the narrow corridors of mechanistic prediction, the
greater the obligation of anthropology to hold fast to its totalizing aspirations. The anthropology of the eighties must engage more ven-
turously in the areas of its strengths: the social construction of the
person, the dynamics of interpersonal relations and intersubjective
understandings, the structure of small-scale communities and social
forms; the integration of all these into regional complexes through
grids of descent and the networks of marriage alliance, through the

transmission of property over generations, the exchanges of gifts between partners, the vertical hierarchies of power, debt, and patronage; and the conflicts and harmonies within and between collectivities. It is this melding of concrete particularities and meaning clusters with expanding ranges of relationships and systems of ideas in both space and time that has enabled anthropologists to constitute large social formations by means of their totalizing perspective. If for this task "the hermeneutics of tradition" and "the critique of ideology," quantification and archival historical research, semiotics and linguistic philosophy, and other skills are germane, we must master them, grapple with their antinomies, and incorporate them. And finally, let us bear in mind the general law that the more efficacious applications in science, whether physical or social, derive from theoretical endeavors into the larger questions of life, unfettered by the need to produce immediate practical results.

References
Notes
Sources
Index

References

Introduction

Berlin, Brent, and Paul Kay. 1969. *Basic color terms.* Berkeley: University of California Press.

Bulmer, Ralph N. H., and M. J. Tyler. 1968. Karam classification of frogs. *The Journal of the Polynesian Society* 77, no. 4: 333–385.

Bulmer, Ralph N. H., and J. I. Menzies. 1972. Karam classifications of marsupials and rodents. *The Journal of the Polynesian Society* 81, no. 4: 472–499.

Bulmer, Ralph N. H.; J. I. Menzies; and E. Parker. 1975. Kalam classification of reptiles and fishes. *The Journal of the Polynesian Society* 84, no. 3: 267–308.

Kuhn, Thomas. 1968. *The structure of scientific revolutions.* Chicago: University of Chicago Press.

Popper, Karl R. 1968. *The logic of scientific discovery.* New York: Harper Torchbooks.

Sahlins, Marshall. 1976. Colors and cultures. *Semiotica* 16, no. 1: 1–22.

1. The Magical Power of Words

Andris Appuhamy, W. D. 1927. *Maha mantra pota.* 2nd ed. Velitara, Ceylon: W. D. Andris Appuhamy.

Cassirer, Ernst. 1953. *Language and myth.* New York: Dover.

——— 1966. *The philosophy of symbolic forms.* Vol. 1: *Language.* New Haven: Yale University Press.

Cherry, Colin. 1961. *On human communication.* New York: Science Editions.

Evans-Pritchard, Edward E. 1937. *Witchcraft, oracles and magic among the Azande.* Oxford: Clarendon.

Firth, J. R. 1957. Ethnographic analysis and language with reference to Malinowski's views. In *Man and culture*, ed. R. Firth. London: Routledge & Kegan Paul.

Firth, Raymond. 1967. *Tikopia ritual and belief.* London: Allen & Unwin.

Fortune, Reo F. 1963. *Sorcerers of Dobu.* New York: Dutton.

Frazer, James. 1922. *The golden bough: A study in magic and religion.* Abridged ed. London: Macmillan.

Freedman, Maurice. 1967. *Rites and duties, or Chinese marriage.* London: G. Bell.

Gellner, Ernest. 1959. *Words and things.* London: Gollancz.

Gluckman, Max. 1954. *Rituals of rebellion in south-east Africa.* Manchester: Manchester University Press.

Goody, Jack. 1962. *Death, property and the ancestors.* London: Tavistock.

Izutsu, T. 1956. *Language and magic.* Tokyo: Keio Institute of Philological Studies.

Jakobson, Roman. 1956. Two aspects of language and two types of aphasic disturbance. In R. Jakobson and M. Halle, *Fundamentals of Language.* The Hague: Mouton.

Kuper, Hilda. 1961. *An African aristocracy.* London: Oxford University Press.

Leach, Edmund. 1964. Anthropological aspects of language: Animal categories and verbal abuse. In *New directions in the study of language*, ed. E. H. Lenneberg. Cambridge, Mass.: MIT Press.

———— 1966. Ritualization in man in relation to conceptual and social development. *Philosophical Transactions of the Royal Society of London*, series B, vol. 251, no. 722: 403–408.

Lévi-Strauss, Claude. 1963. *Structural anthropology.* New York: Basic Books.

———— 1966. *The savage mind.* London: Weidenfeld & Nicolson.

Malinowski, Bronislaw. 1929. *The sexual life of savages in northwestern Melanesia.* London: Routledge.

———— 1948. *Magic, science and religion and other essays.* Boston: Beacon Press.

———— 1960. *Argonauts of the western Pacific.* New York: Dutton.

———— 1965a. *Coral gardens and their magic.* Vol. 1. Bloomington: Indiana University Press.

———— 1965b. *Coral gardens and their magic.* Vol. 2. Bloomington: Indiana University Press.

Mauss, Marcel, and Henri Hubert. 1902–3. Esquisse d'une théorie générale de la magie. *Année Sociologique* 7: 1–146.

Middleton, John. 1960. *Lugbara religion.* London: Oxford University Press.

Ogden, C. K., and I. A. Richards. 1923. *The meaning of meaning.* London: Kegan Paul, Trench, Trübner.

Richards, Audrey. 1956. *Chisungu.* London: Faber & Faber.

Richards, I. A. 1938. *Principles of literary criticism.* 2nd ed. London: International Library of Psychology, Philosophy and Scientific Method.

Sapir, Edward. 1921. *Language.* New York: Harcourt, Brace.

Skeat, Walter William. 1900. *Malay magic.* London: Macmillan.

Spencer, Paul. 1965. *The Samburu: A study in gerontocracy in a nomadic tribe.* London: Routledge & Kegan Paul.

Strathern, Andrew, and Marilyn Strathern. 1968. Marsupials and magic: A study of spell symbolism among the Mbowamb. In *Dialectic in practical religion,* ed. Edmund Leach. Cambridge Papers in Social Anthropology, 5. Cambridge: Cambridge University Press.

Tambiah, Stanley J. 1968. The ideology of merit and the social correlates of Buddhism in a Thai village. In *Dialectic in practical religion,* ed. Edmund Leach. Cambridge Papers in Social Anthropology, 5. Cambridge: Cambridge University Press.

Turner, Victor W. 1961. Ndembu divination: Its symbolism and techniques. Rhodes-Livingstone Papers, 31. Manchester: Manchester University Press.

——— 1962. Three symbols of passage in Ndembu circumcision ritual: An interpretation. In *Essays in the ritual of social relations,* ed. Max Gluckman. Manchester: Manchester University Press.

——— 1964. An Ndembu doctor in practice. In *Magic, faith and healing,* ed. Ari Kiev. Glencoe, Ill.: Free Press.

——— 1966. Colour classification in Ndembu ritual. In *Anthropological approaches to the study of religion,* ed. M. Banton. Association of Social Anthropology Monographs, 3. London: Tavistock.

Ullman, Stephen. 1957. *The principles of semantics.* Oxford: Blackwell.

Urban, Wilbur Marshall. 1939. *Language and reality.* London: Library of Philosophy.

Vansina, Jan. 1965. *Oral tradition.* London: Routledge & Kegan Paul.

Wirz, Paul. 1954. *Exorcism and the art of healing in Ceylon.* Leiden: Brill.

Wittgenstein, Ludwig. 1953. *Philosophical investigations.* Oxford: Blackwell.

2. Form and Meaning of Magical Acts

Austin, John L. 1962. *How to do things with words.* Oxford: Clarendon.

Evans-Pritchard, Edward E. 1929. The morphology and function of magic: A comparative study of Trobriand and Zande ritual and spells. *American Anthropologist* 31: 619–641.

——— 1937. *Witchcraft, oracles and magic among the Azande.* Oxford: Clarendon.

Filliozat, Jean. 1964. *The classical doctrine in Indian medicine: Its origin and Greek parallels.* Delhi: Munshiram Manoharlal.

Finnegan, Ruth. 1969. How to do things with words: Performative utterances among the Limba of Sierra Leone. *Man,* n.s., 4: 537–552.

Fortune, Reo F. 1932. *Sorcerers of Dobu.* London: Routledge & Kegan Paul.

Hesse, Mary B. 1961. *Forces and fields: The concept of action at a distance in the history of physics.* London: Nelson.

——— 1963. *Models and analogies in science.* Newman History and Philosophy and Science Series, 14. London: Sheed and Ward.

Horton, Robin. 1967. African traditional thought and Western science. *Africa* 37: 50–71.

Lloyd, Geoffrey E. R. 1966. *Polarity and analogy: Two types of argumentation in early Greek thought.* Cambridge: Cambridge University Press.

Malinowski, Bronislaw. 1965. *Coral gardens and their magic.* Vol. 1. Bloomington: Indiana University Press.

Searle, John R. 1969. *Speech acts: An essay in the philosophy of language.* Cambridge: Cambridge University Press.

Turner, Victor W. 1968. *The drums of affliction: A study of religious processes among the Ndembu of Zambia.* Oxford: Clarendon.

3. A Thai Cult of Healing through Meditation

Conze, E. 1970. *Buddhist thought in India.* Ann Arbor: Ann Arbor Paperbacks.

Dimock, Edward, et al. 1974. *The literature of India: An introduction.* Chicago: University of Chicago Press.

Eliade, Mircea. 1958. *Yoga.* Bollingen Series, 56. New York: Pantheon.

Evans-Wentz, Walter Y., trans. 1960. *The Tibetan book of the dead.* London: Oxford University Press.

Gooneratne, Dandris de Silva. 1865. On demonology and witchcraft in Ceylon. *Journal of the Ceylon Branch of the Royal Asiatic Society* 4: 1–117.

Kleinman, Arthur; Leon Eisenberg; and Byron Good. 1978. Culture, illness and care: Clinical lessons from anthropological and cross-cultural research. *Annals of Internal Medicine* 88, no. 2: 251–258.

Nash, Manning. 1965. *The golden road to modernity: Village life in contemporary Burma.* London: Wiley.

O'Flaherty, Wendy D. 1973. *Asceticism and eroticism in the mythology of Siva.* London: Oxford University Press.

Pertold, O. 1930. The ceremonial dances of the Sinhalese: An inquiry into the Sinhalese folk-religion. *Archiv Orientalni* 2. Rpt. as *Ceremonial dances of the Sinhalese.* Colombo: Tisara Prakasakayo, 1973.

Sarathchandra, Edwin R. 1953. *The Sinhalese folk play and the modern stage.* Colombo: Ceylon University Press.

Spiro, Melford E. 1967. *Burmese supernaturalism.* Englewood Cliffs: Prentice-Hall.

Stcherbatsky, Theodore. 1923. *The central conception of Buddhism and the meaning of the word "dharma."* London: Royal Asiatic Society.

Tambiah, Stanley J. 1970. *Buddhism and the spirit cults in northeast Thailand.* Cambridge: Cambridge University Press.

Wadley, Sue S. 1975. *Shakti: Power in the conceptual universe of Karimpur religion.* Chicago: University of Chicago Press.

Wirz, Paul. 1954. *Exorcism and the art of healing in Ceylon.* Leiden: Brill.

Yalman, Nur. 1964. The structure of Sinhalese healing rituals. In *Religion in South Asia,* ed. E. B. Harper. Seattle: University of Washington Press.

4. A Performative Approach to Ritual

Austin, John. 1962. *How to do things with words.* London: Oxford University Press.

Barth, Frederik. 1975. *Ritual and knowledge among the Baktaman of New Guinea.* New Haven: Yale University Press.

Bateson, Gregory. 1972. *Steps to an ecology of mind.* London: Intertext Books.

Bateson, Mary Catherine. 1974. Ritualization: A study in texture and texture change. In *Religious movements in contemporary America,* ed.

Irving I. Zaretsky and Mark P. Leone. Princeton: Princeton University Press.

Birdwhistell, Ray L. 1970. *Kinesics and context: Essays on body motion and communication.* Philadelphia: University of Pennsylvania Press.

Bloch, Maurice. 1974. Symbols, song, dance and features of articulation. *European Journal of Sociology* 15: 55–81.

————— ed. 1975. *Political language and oratory in traditional society.* New York: Academic Press.

Brown, Roger, and Albert Gilman. 1960. The pronouns of power and solidarity. In *Style in language,* ed. Thomas A. Sebeok. Cambridge, Mass.: MIT Press.

Burks, Arthur W. 1949. Icon, index, and symbol. In *Philosophy and Phenomenological Research* 9, no. 4: 673–689.

Cherry, Colin. 1961. *On human communication.* New York: Science Editions.

Corcoran, D. W. J. 1971. *Pattern recognition.* Harmondsworth: Penguin.

Eco, Umberto. 1979. *A theory of semiotics.* Bloomington: Indiana University Press.

Egan, Michael J. (n.d.) A configurational analysis of a Sinhalese healing ritual. Unpublished manuscript, based on diss., University of Cambridge, 1970.

Eliade, Mircea. 1958. *Yoga.* Bollingen Series, 56. New York: Pantheon.

————— 1959. *Cosmos and history: The myth of the eternal return.* New York: Harper & Row.

Ervin-Tripp, Susan. 1972. On sociolinguistic rules: Alternation and co-occurrence. In *Directions in sociolinguistics: The ethnography of communication,* ed. John J. Gumperz and Dell Hymes. New York: Holt, Rinehart & Winston.

Fox, James J. 1971. Semantic parallelism in Rotinese ritual language. *Bijdragen tot de Taal-, Land-, en Volkenkunde* 127: 215–255. The Hague: Nijhoff.

————— 1975. On binary categories and primary symbols. In *The interpretation of symbolism,* ed. Roy Willis. New York: Wiley.

————— 1977. Roman Jakobson and the comparative study of parallelism. In James J. Fox, *Roman Jakobson: Echoes of his scholarship.* Lisse: Peter de Redder.

Geertz, Clifford. 1960. *The religion of Java.* Glencoe, Ill.: Free Press.

————— 1966. Religion as a cultural system. In *Anthropological approaches to the study of religion,* ed. Michael Banton. ASA Monographs, 3. London: Tavistock.

Gerini, G. E. 1976. *Chulakantamangala: The tonsure ceremony as performed in Siam.* Orig. pub. 1895. Bangkok: Siam Society.

Goody, Jack. 1962. *Death, property and the ancestors: A study of the mortuary customs of the Lodagaa of West Africa.* London: Tavistock.

Gooneratne, Dandris de Silva. 1865. On demonology and witchcraft in Ceylon. *Journal of the Ceylon Branch of the Royal Asiatic Society* 4: 1–117.

Gossen, Gary H. 1974. To speak with a heated heart: Chamula canons of style and good performance. In *Explorations in the ethnography of speaking,* ed. R. Bauman and J. Sherzer. London: Cambridge University Press.

—— 1976. Language as ritual substance. In *Language in religious practice,* ed. William J. Samarin. Rowley, Mass.: Newbury House.

Grice, H. P. 1957. Meaning. *Philosophical Review* 66 (July): 377–388.

—— 1967. Logic and conversation. William James Lectures, Harvard University. Unpublished manuscript.

Habermas, Jürgen. 1976. Some distinctions in universal pragmatics. *Theory and Society* 3: 155–167.

Jakobson, Roman. 1960. Concluding statement: Linguistics and poetics. In *Style in language,* ed. Thomas A. Sebeok. Cambridge, Mass.: MIT Press.

—— 1966. Grammatical parallelism and its Russian facet. *Language* 42: 398–429.

—— 1971. *Selected writings.* Vol. 2: *Word and language.* The Hague: Mouton.

Kapferer, Bruce. 1977. First class to Maradana: Secular drama in Sinhalese healing rites. In *Secular ritual,* ed. Sally Falk Moore and Barbara Myerhoff. Assen, The Netherlands: Van Gorcum.

Labov, William. 1972. *Language in the inner city: Studies in the black English vernacular.* Philadelphia: University of Pennsylvania Press.

—— and David Fanshel. 1977. *Therapeutic discourse.* New York: Academic Press.

Langer, Susanne K. 1951. *Philosophy in a new key.* New York: New American Library.

—— 1953. *Feeling and form: A theory of art.* New York: Scribners.

Leach, Edmund. 1966. Ritualization in man. In *Philosophical Transactions of the Royal Society of London,* series B, vol. 251, no. 722: 403–408.

—— 1976. *Culture and communication.* Cambridge: Cambridge University Press.

Lévi-Strauss, Claude. 1966. *The savage mind.* London: Weidenfeld & Nicolson.

—— 1970. *The raw and the cooked.* London: Jonathan Cape.

Lord, Albert. 1958. *The singer of tales.* Cambridge, Mass.: Harvard University Press.

Lyons, John. 1963. *Structural semantics.* Publications of the Philosophical Society, 20. Oxford: Blackwell.

Maha Boowa, Phra Acharn. 1976. *The venerable Phra Acharn Mun Bhuridatta Thera, meditation master.* Trans. Siri Buddhasukh. Bangkok: Mahamakut Press.

Malinowski, Bronislaw. 1935. *Coral gardens and their magic.* Vol. 2. London: Allen & Unwin.

McLuhan, Marshall. 1964. *Understanding media: The extensions of man.* New York: McGraw-Hill.

Miller, George A. 1951. *Language and communication.* New York: McGraw-Hill.

Moore, Sally Falk, and Barbara G. Myerhoff, eds. 1977. *Secular ritual.* Assen, The Netherlands: Van Gorcum.

Munn, Nancy D. 1973. *Walbiri iconography.* Ithaca: Cornell University Press.

———— (n.d.) The symbolism of perceptual qualities: A study of Trobriand ritual aesthetics. Unpublished manuscript.

Needham, Rodney. 1967. Percussion and transition. *Man,* n.s., 2, no. 4: 606–614.

Obeyesekere, Gananath. 1969. The ritual drama of the Sanni demons: Collective representations of disease in Ceylon. *Comparative Studies in Society and History* 12: 174–216.

———— (n.d.) Social change and the deities. Unpublished manuscript.

Peacock, James L. 1968. *Rites of modernization.* Chicago: University of Chicago Press.

Pertold, O. 1930. The ceremonial dances of the Sinhalese: An inquiry into the Sinhalese folk-religion. *Archiv Orientalni* 2. Rpt. as *Ceremonial dances of the Sinhalese.* Colombo: Tisara Prakasakayo, 1973.

Radcliffe-Brown, A. R. 1952. *Structure and function in primitive society.* London: Cohen and West.

———— 1964. *The Andaman Islanders.* New York: Free Press. Orig. pub. Cambridge: Cambridge University Press, 1922.

Rappaport, Roy A. 1971. Ritual sanctity and cybernetics. *American Anthropologist* 73, no. 1: 59–76.

———— 1974. Obvious aspects of ritual. *Cambridge Anthropology* 2, no. 1.

Richards, Audrey I. 1956. *Chisungu.* London: Faber & Faber.

Rosaldo, Michelle Zimbalist. 1975. It's all uphill: The creative metaphors of Ilongot magical spells. In *Sociocultural dimensions of language use,* ed. Mary Sanches and B. G. Blount. New York: Academic Press.

Sacks, H.; E. Schegloff; and G. Jefferson. 1974. A simplest systematics for the organization of turn-taking for conversation. *Language,* 50, no. 4: 696–735.

Sahlins, Marshall. 1976. *Culture and practical reason.* Chicago: University of Chicago Press.

Sapir, J. David, and J. C. Crocker. 1977. *The social use of metaphor: Essays in the anthropology of rhetoric.* Philadelphia: University of Pennsylvania Press.

Schegloff, Emanuel A. 1972. Sequencing in conversational openings. In *Directions in sociolinguistics: The ethnography of communication,* ed. John J. Gumperz and Dell Hymes. New York: Holt, Rinehart & Winston.

Searle, John R. 1969. *Speech acts: An essay in the philosophy of language.* Cambridge: Cambridge University Press.

Silverstein, Michael. 1976. Shifters, linguistic categories and cultural description. In *Meaning in anthropology,* ed. Keith H. Basso and Henry A. Selby. Albuquerque: University of New Mexico Press.

Singer, Milton. 1972. *When a great tradition modernizes: An anthropological approach to Indian civilization.* London: Pall Mall Press.

Skorupski, John. 1976. *Symbol and theory: A philosophical study of theories of religion in social anthropology.* Cambridge: Cambridge University Press.

Staal, Frits. 1975. *Exploring mysticism: A methodological essay.* Berkeley: University of California Press.

Stanner, W. E. H. 1958–9. On the interpretation of cargo cults. *Oceania* 29: 1–25.

Strathern, Andrew, and Marilyn Strathern. 1968. Marsupials and magic: A study of spell symbolism among the Mbowamb. In *Dialectic in practical religion*, ed. E. R. Leach. Cambridge Papers in Social Anthropology, 5. Cambridge: Cambridge University Press.

Suzuki, D. T. 1970. *Essays in Zen Buddhism*. London: Rider.

Tambiah, Stanley J. 1970. *Buddhism and the spirit cults in northeast Thailand*. Cambridge: Cambridge University Press.

—— 1977. The cosmological and performative significance of a Thai cult of healing through meditation. *Culture, Medicine and Psychiatry* 1: 97–132.

Turner, Terence. (n.d.) Narrative structure and mythopoesis: A critique and reformulation of structuralist concepts of myth, narrative and poetics. Unpublished manuscript.

Wales, Quaritch H. G. 1931. *Siamese state ceremonies*. London: B. Quaritch.

Wallace, Anthony F. C. 1966. *Religion: An anthropological view*. New York: Random House.

Wirz, Paul. 1954. *Exorcism and the art of healing in Ceylon*. Leiden: Brill.

Yalman, Nur. 1966. Dual organization in central Ceylon. In *Anthropological studies in Theravada Buddhism*, ed. Manning Nash et al. Cultural Report Series, 13. New Haven: Yale University Press.

5. Animals Are Good to Think and Good to Prohibit

Bulmer, Ralph. 1967. Why is the Cassowary not a bird? A problem of zoological taxonomy among the Karam of the New Guinea highlands. *Man*, n.s., 2: 5–25.

Douglas, Mary. 1957. Animals in Lele religious symbolism. *Africa* 27: 46–57.

—— 1966. *Purity and danger*. London: Praeger.

Fortes, Meyer. 1967. Totem and taboo. In *Proceedings of the Royal Anthropological Institute of Great Britain and Ireland for 1966*. London: Royal Anthropological Institute.

Haas, Mary. 1951. Interlingual word taboos. *American Anthropologist* 53: 338–344.

—— 1964. *Thai-English student's dictionary*. Stanford: Stanford University Press.

Leach, Edmund. 1964. Anthropological aspects of language: Animal categories and verbal abuse. In *New directions in the study of language*, ed. E. H. Lenneberg. Cambridge, Mass.: MIT Press.

Lévi-Strauss, Claude. 1962. *Totemism*. Trans. R. Needham. London: Merlin Press.

—— 1966. *The savage mind*. London: Weidenfeld & Nicolson.

Mayer, Adrian C. 1960. *Caste and kinship in central India*. London: Routledge & Kegan Paul.

McFarland, G. B. 1944. *Thai-English dictionary*. Stanford: Stanford University Press.

Meggitt, Mervin J. 1965. *The lineage system of the Mae-Enga of New Guinea.* New York: Barnes and Noble.

Middleton, John L., and D. Tait. 1958. *Tribes without rulers.* London: Routledge & Kegan Paul.

Radcliffe-Brown, A. R. 1922. *The Andaman Islanders.* Cambridge: Cambridge University Press.

——— 1952. *Structure and function in primitive society.* London: Cohen and West.

Rajadhon, Phya Anuman. 1958. *Five papers on Thai custom.* Southeast Asia Program Data Papers, 28. Ithaca: Cornell University Press.

Tambiah, Stanley J. 1970. *Buddhism and the spirit cults of northeast Thailand.* Cambridge: Cambridge University Press.

Wijewardene, Gehan. 1968. Address, abuse and animal categories in northern Thailand. *Man,* n.s., 3: 76–93.

6. From Varna to Caste through Mixed Unions

Berreman, Gerald D. 1963. *Hindus of the Himalayas.* Berkeley: University of California Press.

Blunt, E. A. H. 1931. *The caste system of northern India.* London: Oxford University Press.

Bühler, G. 1879. The sacred laws of the Aryas. Part 1: Apastamba and Gautama. In *The sacred books of the East,* ed. F. M. Muller. Oxford: Clarendon.

——— 1882. The sacred laws of the Aryas. Part 2: Vasishtha, Baudhayana. In *The sacred books of the East,* ed. F. M. Muller. Oxford: Clarendon.

——— 1886. The laws of Manu. In *The sacred books of the East,* ed. F. M. Muller. Oxford: Clarendon.

Conklin, Harold C. 1964. Ethnogenealogical method. In *Explorations in cultural anthropology: Essays in honor of George Peter Murdock.* New York: McGraw-Hill.

Douglas, Mary. 1966. *Purity and danger.* London: Routledge & Kegan Paul.

Dumont, Louis. 1957. Hierarchy and marriage alliance in South Indian kinship. Royal Anthropological Institute of Great Britain and Ireland Occasional Papers, 12.

——— 1961. Les marriages Nayar comme faits indiens. *L'Homme* 1: 11–36.

——— 1970. *Homo hierarchicus: The caste system and its implications.* London: Weidenfeld & Nicolson.

Harper, Edward B. 1968. A comparative analysis of caste: The United States and India. In *Structure and change in Indian society,* ed. M. Singer and B. S. Cohn. Chicago: Aldine.

Hutton, J. H. 1951. *Caste in India.* 2nd ed. London: Oxford University Press.

Kane, P. V. 1941. *History of Dharmasastra.* Vol. 2. Poona: Bhandarkar Oriental Research Institute.

Karve, Indrawati. 1961. *Hindu society: An interpretation.* Poona: Deccan College.

Leach, Edmund R. 1964. Anthropological aspects of language: Animal categories and verbal abuse. In *New directions in the study of language,* ed. E. H. Lenneberg. Cambridge, Mass.: MIT Press.

Marriott, McKim H. 1968. Caste ranking and food transactions: A matrix analysis. In *Structure and change in Indian society,* ed. M. Singer and B. S. Cohn. Chicago: Aldine.

Morris, H. S. 1968. *The Indians in Uganda: Caste and sect in a plural society.* Chicago: Chicago University Press.

Orenstein, H. 1965. The structure of Hindu caste values: A preliminary study of hierarchy and ritual defilement. *Ethnology* 4: 1–15.

———— 1968. Toward a grammar of defilement in Hindu sacred law. In *Structure and change in Indian society,* ed. M. Singer and B. S. Cohn. Chicago: Aldine.

———— 1970. Logical congruence in Hindu sacred law: Another interpretation. *Contributions to Indian Sociology,* n.s., 4: 22–35.

Parry, Jonathan. (n.d.) Hypergamy in the hills of northwest India. Unpublished manuscript.

Pocock, David. 1972. *Kanbi and Patidar: A study of the Patidar community of Gujerat.* London: Oxford University Press.

Schneider, David M., and Kathleen Gough, eds. *Matrilineal kinship.* Berkeley: University of California Press.

Simpson, George G. 1961. *Principles of animal taxonomy.* New York: Columbia University Press.

Srinivas, M. N. 1952. *Religion and society among the Coorgs of south India.* Oxford: Clarendon.

Tod, J. 1832. *The annals of antiquities of Rajasthan or the central and western Rajpoot states of India.* Vols. 1 and 2. London: Smith, Elder.

7.   The Galactic Polity in Southeast Asia

Archaimbault, Charles. 1971. The new year ceremony at Basak (south Laos). Southeast Asia Program Data Papers, 78. Ithaca: Cornell University Press.

Berry, Brian J. L., and Allen Pred. 1961. Central place studies: A bibliography of theory and application. Regional Science Research Institute Bibliography Series, 1. Philadelphia: Regional Science Research Institute.

Briggs, Lawrence P. 1951. The ancient Khmer empire. *Transactions of the American Philosophical Society,* n.s., 41, pt. 1: 1–295.

Christaller, W. 1966. *Central places in southern Germany.* Trans. C. W. Baskin. Englewood Cliffs: Prentice-Hall.

Coedès, G. 1968. *The Indianized states of Southeast Asia.* Honolulu: East-West Center Press.

Conze, Edward. 1970. *Buddhist thought in India.* Ann Arbor: Ann Arbor Paperbacks.

Cunningham, Clark. 1973. Order in the Atoni house. In *Right and left: Essays on dual symbolic classification,* ed. R. Needham. Chicago: University of Chicago Press.

De Jong, P. E. 1952. *Minangkabau and Negri Sembilan: Sociopolitical structure in Indonesia.* The Hague: Nijhoff.

Dewey, Alice J. 1962. *Peasant marketing in Java.* New York: Free Press.

Eliade, Mircea. 1959. *Cosmos and history: The myth of the eternal return.* New York: Harper & Row.

Geertz, Clifford. 1963. *Pedlars and princes: Social change and economic modernization in two Indonesian towns.* Chicago: University of Chicago Press.

———— 1973. *Islam observed: Religious development in Moroccco and Indonesia.* Chicago: University of Chicago Press.

Griswold, A. B. 1967. *Towards a history of Sukhodaya art.* Bangkok: Fine Arts Department of the Government of Thailand.

Gullick, J. M. 1958. *Indigenous political systems of western Malaya.* London: Athlone Press.

Heine-Geldern, Robert. 1942. Conceptions of state and kingship in Southeast Asia. *Far Eastern Quarterly* 2: 15–30.

Holt, Claire, et al., eds. 1970. *Culture and politics in Indonesia.* Ithaca: Cornell University Press.

Kessler, Clive. 1974. Islam and politics in Malay society: Kelantan 1886–1969. Diss., University of London.

Leach, Edmund R. 1954. *Political systems of highland Burma.* London: London School of Economics.

Lingat, R. 1950. Evolution of the concept of law in Burma and Siam. *Journal of the Siam Society* 38: 9–31.

Lösch, August. 1954. *The economics of location.* Trans. W. H. Woglom and W. F. Stolper. New Haven: Yale University Press.

Mintz, Sidney W. 1960. A tentative typology of eight Haitian market places. *Revista de Ciencias Sociales* (Puerto Rico) 4: 15–57.

Moertono, S. 1968. *State and statecraft in Old Java: A study of the later Mataram period, sixteenth to nineteenth century.* Ithaca: Cornell University Press.

Mus, Paul. 1935. *Barabadur: Esquisse d'une Histoire du Bouddhisme fondée sur la critique archéologique des textes.* Hanoi: Imprimerie d'Extrême-Orient.

———— 1936. Symbolisme à Ankor-Thom. Académie des Inscriptions et Belles-Lettres. Comptes rendus des séances.

———— 1964. Thousand-armed Kannon: A mystery or a problem. *Journal of Indian Buddhist Studies* (Tokyo): 1–33.

Nordholt, H. G. S. 1971. *The political system of the Atoni of Timor.* The Hague: Nijhoff.

Pigeaud, T. 1962. *Java in the fourteenth century: A study in cultural history.* 5 vols. The Hague: Nijhoff.

Rabibhadana, A. 1969. The organization of Thai society in the early Bangkok period, 1782–1873. Southeast Asia Program Data Papers, 74. Ithaca: Cornell University Press.

Riggs, F. W. 1967. *The modernization of a bureaucratic polity.* Honolulu: East-West Center Press.

Schrieke, B. 1955. *Indonesian sociological studies: Selected writings.* The Hague: W. van Hoeve.

Shamasastry, R., trans. 1960. Kautilya's *Arthashastra.* Mysore (India): Mysore Printing and Publishing House.

Shorto, Harry L. 1963. The thirty-two Myos in the medieval Mon kingdom. *Bulletin of the School of Oriental and African Studies* 26, no. 3: 572–591.

Soetjatmoko, et al., eds. 1965. *An introduction to Indonesian historiography.* Ithaca: Cornell University Press.

Stcherbatsky, Theodore. 1923. *The central conception of Buddhism and the meaning of the word "dharma."* London: Royal Asiatic Society.

Stevenson, H. N. C. 1968. *The economics of the central Chin tribes.* Orig. pub. 1943. Farnborough Hants, England: Gregg Press.

Tambiah, Stanley J. 1976. *World conqueror and world renouncer: A study of religion and polity in Thailand against a historical background.* Cambridge: Cambridge University Press.

Tucci, Giuseppe. 1971. *The theory and practice of the mandala.* London: Rider.

Vickery, Michael. 1970. Thai regional elites and the reforms of King Chulalongkorn. *Journal of Asian Studies* 24, no. 4: 863–881.

Wales, Quaritch H. G. 1934. *Ancient Siamese government and administration.* London: B. Quaritch.

Weber, Max. 1968. *Economy and society.* Vol. 3. Ed. G. Roth and C. Wittich. New York: Bedminster Press.

Wenk, Klaus. 1968. *The restoration of Thailand under Rama I, 1782–1809.* Tucson: University of Arizona Press.

Wheatley, Paul. 1961. *The golden Khersonese.* Kuala Lumpur: University of Malaya Press.

———— 1969. *City as symbol.* Text of lecture delivered at University College, London, 1967. London: H. K. Lewis.

———— 1971. *The pivot of the four quarters.* Chicago: Aldine.

———— (n.d.) Satyantra in Suvarnadvipa: From reciprocity to redistribution in ancient Southeast Asia. Unpublished manuscript.

Wolters, O. W. 1967. *Early Indonesian commerce: A study on the origins of Sri Vijaya.* Ithaca: Cornell University Press.

8. On Flying Witches and Flying Canoes

Austen, L. 1939. The seasonal calendar of Kiriwina, Trobriand Islands. *Oceania* 9, no. 3: 237–253.

Leach, Edmund. 1958. Concerning Trobriand clans and the kinship category "tabu." In *The developmental cycle in domestic groups,* ed. J. Goody. Cambridge: Cambridge University Press.

Lounsbury, Floyd G. 1965. Another view of the Trobriand kinship categories. *American Anthropologist* 67, no. 5, pt. 2: 142–185.

Malinowski, Bronislaw. 1922. *Argonauts of the western Pacific.* London: Routledge & Kegan Paul. Rpt. London: Dutton, 1961; and London: Routledge & Kegan Paul, 1978.

————— 1927. *Sex and repression in savage society.* London: Routledge & Kegan Paul.

————— 1929. *Sexual life of savages.* London: Routledge & Kegan Paul. 3rd ed. entitled *Sexual life of savages in northwestern Melanesia.* London: Routledge & Kegan Paul, 1932; rpt. 1968.

————— 1935. *Coral gardens and their magic.* Vols. 1 and 2. London: Allen & Unwin. Rpt. Bloomington: Indiana University Press, 1965.

————— 1948. Myth in primitive psychology. Baloma: The spirits of the dead in the Trobriand Islands. Both in *Magic, science and religion, and other essays.* Glencoe, Ill.: Free Press. Rpt. New York: Doubleday Anchor, 1954.

Saussure, Ferdinand de. 1966. *Course in general linguistics.* New York: McGraw-Hill.

Schapera, I. 1955. The sin of Cain. *Journal of the Royal Anthropological Institute* 85: 33–43.

Scoditti, Giancarlo M. G. Kula on Kitava. In *New Perspectives on the Kula,* ed. Edmund Leach and Jerry Leach. Cambridge: Cambridge University Press, 1983.

Seligmann, C. 1910. *Melanesians of British New Guinea.* Cambridge: Cambridge University Press.

Weiner, Annette. 1976. *Women of value, men of renown: New perspectives in Trobriand exchange.* Austin: University of Texas Press.

9. The Theater State in Southeast Asia

Dalada Sirita: A fourteenth-century Sinhalese prose work dealing with the history of the Dalada. 1955. Pandita Valvitiye Sorata Edition. Colombo: M. D. Gunasena.

Geertz, Clifford. 1980. *Negara: The Theater State in Nineteenth-Century Bali.* Princeton: Princeton University Press.

————— and Hildred Geertz. 1975. *Kinship in Bali.* Chicago: University of Chicago Press.

Hocart, A. M. 1931. *The temple of the tooth in Kandy: Memoirs of the archaeological survey of Ceylon.* Vol. 4. Written for the government of Ceylon. London: Luzac.

Jayawickrama, N. A. 1968. *The sheaf of garlands of the epoch of the conqueror.* London: Pali Text Society.

Lingat, Robert. 1934. Le culte du Bouddha d'Emeraude. *Journal of the Siam Society* 27, no. 1: 9–38.

Marglin, Frederique. 1981. Wives of the God King. Diss., Brandeis University.

Mendelson, E. M. 1961. A messianic Buddhist association in upper Burma. *Bulletin of the School of Oriental and African Studies* 24: 560–580.

Notton, Camille, trans. 1933a. *The chronicle of the Emerald Buddha.* Bangkok: Bangkok Times Press.

————— trans. 1933b. *P'ra Buddha Sihing.* Bangkok: Bangkok Times Press.

Reynolds, Frank E. 1978. The holy Emerald Jewel. In *Religion and the legitimation of power in Thailand, Laos, and Burma,* ed. Bardwell Smith. Chambersburg, Pa.: Conococheague Associates.

―――― and Mani B. Reynolds, trans. 1982. *Three worlds according to King Ruang: A Thai Buddhist cosmology.* Berkeley Buddhist Studies Series, 4. Berkeley: Berkeley University Press.

Seneviratne, H. L. 1978. *Rituals of the Kandyan state.* Cambridge: Cambridge University Press.

Tambiah, Stanley J. 1976. *World Conqueror and World Renouncer.* Cambridge: Cambridge University Press.

―――― 1982. Famous Buddha images and the legitimation of kings: The case of the Sinhala Buddha (Phra Sihing) in Thailand. *Res* 4 (Autumn): 5–19.

Worsley, Peter J. 1972. *Babad Bulelen: A Balinese dynastic genealogy.* Biblioteca Indonesica. Koninklijk Instituut Voor Taal-, Land-, en Volkenkunde, 8. The Hague: Nijhoff.

Conclusion

Adas, Michael. 1980. "Moral economy" or "contest state"? Elite demands and the origins of peasant protest in Southeast Asia. *Journal of Social History* 13, no. 4: 521–545.

―――― 1981. From avoidance to confrontation: Peasant protest in precolonial and colonial Southeast Asia. *Comparative Studies in History and Society* 23, no. 3: 325–349.

Amin, Samir. 1976. *Unequal development: An essay on the social formations of peripheral capitalism.* Trans. Brian Pearce. Sussex: Harvester Press.

Bailyn, Bernard. 1982. The challenge of modern historiography. *American Historical Review* 87, no. 1: 1–24.

Bloch, Marc. 1953. *The historian's craft.* New York: Vintage.

Chrisman, Noel, and Thomas Maretylsi, eds. 1982. *Clinically applied anthropology: Anthropologists in health science settings.* Dordrecht, The Netherlands: D. Reidel.

Clifford, James. 1982. *Person and myth: Maurice Leenhardt in the Melanesian world.* Berkeley: University of California Press.

Crapanzano, Vincent. 1980. *Tuhami: A portrait of a Moroccan.* Chicago: University of Chicago Press.

Geertz, Clifford, ed. 1963. *Old societies and new states.* New York: Free Press.

Gottmann, Jean, ed. 1980. *Center and periphery: Spatial variations in politics.* Beverly Hills: Sage Publications.

Gould, Stephen Jay. 1983. Sociobiology, goodbye. *New York Review of Books* (June 30): 5–10.

Grillo, Ralph D. 1980. Introduction. In *Nation and state in Europe: Anthropological perspectives,* ed. R. D. Grillo. New York: Academic Press.

Hirschman, Albert O. 1981. *Essays in trespassing: Economics to politics and beyond.* Cambridge: Cambridge University Press.

Hollis, Martin, and Steven Lukes, eds. 1982. *Rationality and relativism.* Oxford: Blackwell.

Irschick, Eugene F. 1982. Peasant survival strategies and rehearsals for rebellions in eighteenth-century South India. *Peasant Studies* 9, no. 4: 216–241.

Kleinman, Arthur. 1982. Neurasthenia and depression: A study of somatization and culture in China. *Culture, Medicine and Psychiatry* 6, no. 2: 117–190.

———— 1983. The cultural meanings and social uses of illness. *Journal of Family Practice* 16, no. 3: 539–545.

————; Leon Eisenberg; and Byron Good. 1978. Culture, illness, and care: Clinical lessons from anthropologic and cross-cultural research. *Annals of Internal Medicine* (February): 251–258.

Leach, Sir Edmund. 1982. *Social anthropology.* London: Fontana Paperbacks.

Lévi-Strauss, Claude. 1964. Anthropology: Its achievement and future. *Current Anthropology* 5: 432–437.

Lukes, Steven. 1973. *Emile Durkheim, his life and work: A historical and critical study.* Harmondsworth: Penguin.

Meillassoux, Claude. 1981. *Maidens, meal and money: Capitalism and the domestic community.* Cambridge: Cambridge University Press.

Mintz, Sidney. 1977. The so-called world system: Local initiative and local response. *Dialectical Anthropology* 2: 253–270.

Nash, June. 1981. Ethnographic aspects of the world capitalist system. *Annual Reviews in Anthropology* 10: 393–423.

Parry, J. H. 1963. *The age of renaissance.* London: Weidenfeld & Nicolson.

Popkin, Samuel. 1979. *The rational peasant: The political economy of rural society in Vietnam.* Berkeley: University of California Press.

Quinn, David. 1947. *Raleigh and the British Empire.* London: Hodder and Stoughton.

———— 1966. *The Elizabethans and the Irish.* Ithaca: Cornell University Press.

Scott, James C. 1976. *The moral economy of the peasant.* New Haven: Yale University Press.

Shils, Edward. 1975. *Centre and periphery: Essays in macrosociology.* Chicago: University of Chicago Press.

Silverman, William A. 1980. *Retrolental fibroplasia: A modern parable.* New York: Grune and Stratton.

Trimberger, E. K. 1979. World systems analysis: The problem of unequal development. *Theory and Society* 8: 101–106.

Venturi, Franco. 1971. *Utopia and reform in the Enlightenment.* Cambridge: Cambridge University Press.

———— 1972. *Italy and the Enlightenment.* Ed. Stuart Woolf. London: Longman.

Williams, E. 1944. *Capitalism and slavery.* Chapel Hill: University of North Carolina Press.

Notes

Introduction

1. The comparativists, on the other hand, view these conceptions of "nature" as well as the "classifications" as conventional phenomena and as constructed toward some (teleological) purpose. They are to that extent relativizers and historicizers.

2. I am referring here to Brent Berlin and Paul Kay, 1969.

3. Also see the continuations: R. N. H. Bulmer, J. I. Menzies, and E. Parker, 1975; R. N. H. Bulmer and M. J. Tyler, 1968.

4. I am referring only to animals here. Objects of all kinds are of course manipulated in ritual in this way.

1. The Magical Power of Words

1. Malinowski's theoretical concern with language probably started after his first trip to Kiriwina in 1916. In *Argonauts of the Western Pacific* he had begun to state the ideas which were formalized in the classic supplement to Ogden and Richards (1923). Since magic was so pervasive in the Trobriands, all his other works (1929, for example) contained further elaborations of his views on language. He attempted his most complex statement in the two volumes of *Coral Gardens and Their Magic*, which he considered his best work.

2. Recent literature in one way or another has been sensitive to the role of words in ritual. Freedman (1967) referred to the didactic nature of the songs sung when a Chinese bride leaves her home, and the significance of bawdy songs before she is deflowered. Goody (1962) reported Lodaga funeral speeches and chants (which, interestingly, are largely impromptu though they always use phrases of a proverbial kind). Middleton's analysis (1960) of the cult of the dead among the Lugbara alludes to the ritual addresses (*adi*) made by elders. In the rites of sacrifice and purification, which legitimize changes in

the alignment of lineage segments, the addresses recount traditional lore, genealogical history, the animosities and quarrels of the participants, and the motive and identity of the agent responsible for the illness. More dramatic is Spencer's description (1965) of the "brainwashing" of Samburu brides by inquisitorial elders. Turner (1961) described the cybernetic function of Ndembu divination as a form of social analysis and a mechanism of social redress. But even this supreme exponent concentrates on major symbols (Turner, 1962, 1964, 1966) to the exclusion of words said. It is precisely because Turner seeks the meanings of symbols in the verbal explanation (exegesis) of his informants that he has successfully pushed our understanding of ritual away from sympathetic magic to expressive symbolism. Would not then an analysis of the words used directly in the ritual advance this kind of interpretation further? In a way, it is A. I. Richards's *Chisungu* (1956) which shines more brilliantly in this galaxy: for in her description of the initiation ceremony for girls among the Bemba, a ceremony which was explicitly a teaching device, Richards highlights the complex interrelation of songs, mimes, ritual objects, and actions which make up a system of knowledge and a mnemonic of the roles to be assumed. She concludes that the mumbo-jumbo was one of the prized items of information in the society. I throw in for good measure Kuper's description (1961) of the Royal Incwala ceremony, if only to indicate that Gluckman's theory (1954) of the rituals of rebellion, rightly or wrongly conceived, turns crucially on the interpretation of songs sung during the installation.

3. There is also a fourth use of words which I will not discuss here—namely, comic dialogues in prose which are interludes in the ritual.

4. My account owes much to information provided by M. Egan and W. Dissanayake. Egan's study of Sinhalese ritual will, when it is published, give a more correct and revealing analysis of the use of words and the kinds of verbal form that build up the ceremony.

5. A book written in Sinhalese (Andris Appuhamy, 1927) makes a cogent case for the comprehensibility and intellectual structure of *mantra*. *Mantra* are usually recorded and memorized, though some of them may be transmitted orally.

6. Although the Buddhist situation shows a disjunction between the sacred language and the language of ordinary discourse, we should be careful in drawing conclusions about the lack of understanding of Pali chants by the congregation. Villagers can recognize chants, know which are appropriate for which occasion, and understand some of the key words, for they have some measure of moral instruction through sermons which are in full or in part rendered in the local language. Furthermore a number of the villagers have themselves been monks in the past, although this is countered by the quick obsolescence of liturgical learning that has no direct relevance or frequent use in lay life. Thus, the disjunction is nevertheless there.

7. With respect to the first conclusion, some readers may feel that I have cheated by ignoring the case of the use of "mystical sounds" and "unintelligible" phonemes in the *mantra* and *dhāranī* of tantric Hinduism and Buddhism (and the Muslim technique of *dhikr* in mystical Sufism, about which I am altogether uninformed except to say that it appears to resemble the tantric tech-

nique). The theory of the *dhāraṇī* is that the phonemes are "supports" for concentration and meditation. The sounds as such are not "meaningless"; they will reveal their meaning to the initiated only during meditation accompanied by yogic exercises. Thus, the sounds are secret to the initiated and unintelligible to the uninitiated. Furthermore the *dhāraṇī* are different from ordinary secular language only because the latter is considered inadequate to communicate the mystical experience; they represent a language that discovers the primordial consciousness. This theory then squarely places the language of *dhāraṇī* within the confines and conventions of normal language as a system of communication. The phonemes and "distorted" words are taken from the secular language and put to special use by the sects. They hardly constitute a full-blown language as such. My argument in any case relates to mass religions.

8. There are thus about six functional relations to be analyzed relating to the four levels: 1) the relation of myth to what is enacted in the ritual; 2) the relation of the persona of myth to the ritual practitioners (pedigree, recruitment, and so forth); 3) the relation of mythical time to present-day reality; 4) the relation between ritual (as a symbolic form) and the officiants who enact it (this includes the mode of training of the officiant and the taboos and special rules that apply to him); 5) the relation between ritual and the social or practical activities which it is supposed to influence; 6) the relation between ritual practitioners and nonritual activities and occupations.

9. There appears to be a resemblance between Malinowski's pragmatic formulation and Wittgenstein's oft-quoted operational view that "the meaning of words lies in their use" (1953:80, 109). But this resemblance is superficial, for although Wittgenstein placed emphasis on context in the determination of meaning, he went on to argue that meanings are best established by substituting words for each other, and that language is like a game of chess. This argument brings his functional theory in line with structuralist views (Ullman, 1957).

10. Malinowski distinguished rites of impregnation, in which the mediating object was an essential component of the final object of magic (either as an implement in the making of it, or as a constituent part of it), from rites of transference, in which the object chanted over and then used as the medium of transfer of magical virtue had no intrinsic connection with the final object of magic (for example, a pregnancy cloak or a stone). But there is no real distinction between the rites, and in my view they have the same arrangement. The rite of impregnation also involves a transfer.

11. The naming of the parts and the transfer of attributes which are both evident in Trobriand spells appear in identical form in Dobuan magic (Fortune, 1963), in some of the spells cited by Skeat (1900), and in Sinhalese *mantra* (Wirz, 1954). One can see two ways in which the verbal technique can be exploited. The recipient of the transfer may be described in terms of his body parts (that is, metonymically) and the required attribute present in the desirable symbol or metaphor transferred to it. The converse is where an "unknown" disease or evil is given objective definition and form by describing its parts in terms of the characteristics of known concrete objects or persons—for example, the description of a demon. By thus describing it metaphorically and metonymically one is able to control it, or, by thus representing it to a patient,

enables the patient to expel or reject the demon and by implication the disease as well.

12. The native commentary indicates that many of the words used in the spells are polyvalent in meaning and have ranges of meaning, as is the case with Western poetic language and indeed with Western ordinary discourse. Malinowski's startling commentary on these phenomena, which linguists discuss under the labels of synonymy, polyvalence, and homonymy, is as follows: "It is important to realise that the native commentaries are not to be regarded as correct translations, but rather as free associations suggested to the native by the word mentioned to them. We must remember that the very character of magical words makes it futile to attribute to them a precise and definite lexical meaning" (1965b:261). He misses the native point of view when he reports, "It is the multifarious associations, the emotional fringe of the word, which is believed by them to influence the course of nature, and which through this really influences their own psychology and the organisation of their work" (1965b:261).

13. Evans-Pritchard in his classic contribution (1937), while analyzing Zande witchcraft and magic as a coherent system in their own right, felt it necessary to ask what their relation was to Zande empirical activity, and also how magic, which was oriented to achieving effects, compared with Western empiricism based on canons of proof and experimentation. This brilliant book thus faced intellectual problems, some of which were the creation of a European mentality. Like Malinowski, Evans-Pritchard (1937:81) states that "Azande undoubtedly perceive a difference between what we consider the workings of nature on the one hand and the workings of magic and witchcraft on the other, though in the absence of a formulated doctrine of natural law they do not, and cannot, express the difference as we express it" (see also 1937:463). Again (1937:73 and passim) he argues that belief in witchcraft in no way contradicts empirical knowledge of cause and effect, because what witchcraft focuses on is "the socially relevant cause, since it is the only one which allows intervention and determines social behaviour"; in other words, it is on a different wavelength from empirical action altogether.

Certain of my conclusions concerning Trobriand magic are confirmed by Evans-Pritchard with respect to Zande prospective magic: "The results which magic is supposed to produce actually happen after rites are performed"; "Magic is only made to produce events which are likely to happen in any case . . . Magic is not asked to achieve what is unlikely to occur"; "Magic is seldom asked to produce a result by itself, but is associated with empirical action that does in fact produce it" (1937:475, 476, 477).

There are thus important convergences in the ideas of Malinowski and Evans-Pritchard, whatever their other differences. Evans-Pritchard's critique of Lévy-Bruhl is Malinowskian: Why do primitives in some situations behave "ritually" or "mystically" while in others they behave "empirically," and why do the same objects evoke different attitudes in ritual and nonritual contexts?

2. Form and Meaning of Magical Acts

1. *Ima-*, the prefix literally meaning "bringing misfortune," is translated as "disease"; the suffix is the name of the natural object or animal which re-

sembles the disease—for example, *imanzingini* (*ima* = sickness; *nzingini* = porcupine).

2. For me, magic is embedded in ritual.

3. It is for this reason that J. R. Searle (1969: ch. 2) prefers a different classification in terms of the elements of speech acts, although, and this is what is important here, he too preserves the essential distinction between an *assertion*, which is a very special kind of commitment to the *truth* of a proposition (usually in terms of empirical verification), and the *illocutionary* act, which contains Austin's performative verbs and which in contrast is appropriately subject to judgments of success, defectiveness, and felicity of performance.

4. I cannot go into this question here, but, in brief, the relation between the media may be 1) equal and "redundant"; 2) "unequal," one medium being dominant and the other subsidiary; 3) "complementary" and "linked"—for example, the words being "metaphorical," and action "metonymic"; and 4) separate and discontinuous. These kinds of relation are not necessarily exclusive, and any complex rite may express all relations not only between these two media but between them and others as well, such as music, dancing, use of diagrams, food prestations, and so forth.

3.   A Thai Cult of Healing through Meditation

1. Renunciation of sex in the *achan*'s case also has direct implications for his conservation of "energy" and his thereby having "power" within him.

2. This tasting of the food brought by the deities is supposed to cure patients and give sustenance to disciples. As my discussion of the cosmological scheme and the meditation technology will show, the water and fruits have "subtle" bodies which are the appropriate form of representation of objects in the higher worlds.

3. This is possible because patients have to practice "meditation."

4. We were unable to observe the proceedings there, but at the next session we attended we gained entry inside. I shall give additional details in my description of Curing Session 2.

5. The Thais consider north an auspicious direction.

6. First *namo tassa* was recited three times, followed by an excerpt from *Jet Tamnan*, usually recited to pay respect to monks (*tawai phra*).

7. The list of deities may be incompletely recorded.

8. If the patients are too sick or unable to come they can send representatives, who can "meditate" on their behalf and transfer to them the *achan*'s potency.

9. The location of the *achan* himself will be described in the second description of a healing session, as it has important symbolic meaning. At this first session, we could not see him (until he emerged later to mingle with the group).

10. These are objects embedded in the body that cause illness and have to be extracted.

11. The Emerald Buddha is the palladium of the kingdom and is located in a temple standing in the old palace complex. The Luang Phau Sauthaun is likewise a "powerful" Buddha statue located in Chachaengsao province.

12. This is a reference to the *samphraphoom,* the spirit house, that is found in the compounds of many Thai houses, and in which offerings are made to the guardian spirits of the land and house.

13. As is the case with the Sinhalese example I cite later in my interpretation of the cosmology.

14. The audience is like a *darshan* which a god gives his devotees or a king his subjects.

15. I spotted in the congregation a Thai bank manager (and his American wife), a bank executive, a naval officer, a police major and his family, and three university or teachers' college faculty members. The first four were old *luksit* and acted as the leader's assistants.

16. In the curing sessions previously described the women did not outnumber the men.

17. An informant, the wife of a major in the Thai navy, clarified this incident for me. A young boy who was "possessed" by a spirit was brought for cure. The spirit actually grabbed the *achan* and became violent, but the *achan* was able to quiet it. The informant then commented: "Had you been present on that occasion you could have witnessed the power [*rit*] of the *achan.* It is from that day onward that I came to believe in the *achan* very much."

18. See Tambiah, 1970: ch. 3, for a fuller account and for references. Thailand's great cosmological treatise *Traibhumikatha* was composed in 1345 and has been reproduced since then in several versions.

19. This point is also made with regard to Hinduism by S. S. Wadley (1975). For example, she states: "There is no bounded supernatural spatial domain . . . Hindu deities exist in any or all three worlds of the universe . . . Good and bad deities exist in all three worlds, and movement back and forth among them is considered plausible and natural" (p. 54).

20. It is also, of course, a Hindu concept (Sanskrit: *siddhi*).

21. There are additional nuances and refractions which I can barely suggest here. For one thing, the exorcist and his assistants, in enacting the excesses that please the demons, themselves become like the demons temporarily; this may have cathartic value for them, but it also depresses their position in the hierarchy of officiants. For the audience, too, the enactment is a context for ribaldry, drinking, gambling, and a loosening of restraints, just as their witnessing of the gross behavior of the demons and their final expulsion terminates the period of license.

22. The strongest expression of this idea is the *paritta* chants which monks recite and which are supposed to have the potency to ward off and protect humans from misfortune.

23. The *varam* formulation fits in with and supports the *karma* theory that the position and propensities of each entity in the hierarchy are concordant with the consequences of actions in previous lives.

24. But there may be a difference in the staging of the encounter between superior and virtuous deities and gross uncontrolled spirits in India and Sri Lanka on the one hand, and in Southeast Asia—for example, Thailand and Java—on the other. In the South Indian Hindu festivals concluding with the god slaying the demon, the god at first moves in the procession smoothly and in majesty, but later becomes frenzied and demonic and makes jagged movements immediately before slaying the demon. In contrast, in Javanese repre-

sentation—as, for example, in the *wayang* (puppet shows)—a hero such as Ardjuna is characterized by *alus* refinement and control, as opposed to the *madju* crudity and grossness of the demon, who moves frenziedly. The refined hero's slaying is done with coolness, detachment, and deadly effect powered by inner strength. In Thai dancing, such as *lakon* and *kon*, there is a similar marked contrast between the heroic Rama and his brothers, who are regal and refined in their movements, and the bestiality of Thosakan's (Ravana's) agents.

It may well be that in Southeast Asia control, refinement, and inner strength (which are associated not only with godly or regal status but also with the practice of meditation) become an encompassing code which is dialectically contrasted with its opposite. The mediating and victorious hero then transcends the dichotomy of refined passive control and effective action by combining refinement with an inner spiritual strength, which enables him to disregard outward forms of respect and morals.

25. If this is so, then there is a correspondence between the ritual categories of this cult and the classical Indian aesthetic categories of *rasa* which inform the ideals of a "work of art"—for example, theater (see Gerow, in Dimock et al., 1974: ch. 6).

26. I was informed that a Western-trained doctor had in the past attended the *achan*'s curing and meditation sessions and had confirmed and authenticated the reality of the curing effects his procedures produced.

27. See my earlier reference to the Sinhalese exorcism act which invokes the lower half of the cosmological scheme, and the "symbolic logic" of the words, acts, and offerings in that context.

4. A Performative Approach to Ritual

1. Lévi-Strauss (1970) surmises how music affects the listener by referring to two dimensions—the "visceral" (physiological) time of the listener and the cultural grid consisting of the scale of musical sounds.

2. In his Henry Myers Lecture of 1945, entitled "Religion and Society," Radcliffe-Brown drew attention to Confucian philosophy, which considers music and ritual as means for the establishment and preservation of the social order, and offered this advice: "I suggest that an anthropological study of the relations between music (and dancing) and religious rituals would provide some interesting results" (1952:158).

3. The reference is to play especially in its manifestation as contemporary competitive sports.

4. To give another example that fits the Lévi-Strauss scheme: the outcome of the *An Keliya* ritual performed as a contest in Sri Lanka is open in that either team may win, but the preferred and usual winner is the team representing the Pattini goddess. The final contest in a series is always won by her, and the ritual concludes as a conjunction between the two teams (see Nur Yalman, 1966).

5. McLuhan (1964), who has some relevance for my topic, has argued that the "message" of any medium or technology is "the change of scale or pace or pattern that it introduces into human affairs," and that it is a mistake

to think that a medium's message lies in its contents. Rather, the message is to be found in the character of the medium itself. This view errs on the side of formalism.

6. Thus, while I agree with Moore and Myerhoff (1977) that the term "sacred" need not be coterminous with "religious," I do not share with them the desire to carve out a category of "secular ritual" when the analytic objective is to inquire into the features of ritual as a medium of communication.

7. These categories are of course not "equivalent" or the same in different cosmologies. They are stated here for illustrative purposes.

8. To give concrete ethnographic examples: The rituals of the Walbiri of Australia (Munn, 1973) cannot be understood outside their cosmological ideas of how dream time and phenomenal time are related. Similarly, the Thai rites, whether Buddhist or pertaining to the spirits, derive their fullest meaning only when placed in relation to the cosmological scheme of three *lokas*, of a hierarchy of heavens, hells, and human habitat, and of the bodily, material, mental, and sensory values attached to the Buddha, to gods, to humans, and to demonic spirits (Tambiah, 1970, 1977). A person alien to Christianity cannot feel moved or spiritually strengthened by the spectacle of wine and bread being transformed into the blood and flesh of Christ in the Roman Catholic Mass. The special reverence in which Americans hold their constitution cannot be understood without a feel for their special historical experience, which includes the American Revolution and the Civil War.

9. Leach in his pioneering essay (1966) and Wallace (1966), and of course Malinowski before them, should be considered our immediate predecessors who highlighted various implications of ritual's stereotyped form.

10. Let me make clear, so as to remove misunderstanding, that the "conventional-intentional" and "ordinary behavior–conventional behavior" distinctions are *relative* ones. All social conduct is colored by convention and subject to cultural understanding and codification. My distinction is between *degrees* of formalization and stereotyping in what I label conventional and ordinary behavior, as modes of conduct that stand in a contrast of relative distinction.

11. And once again such elaborations into stereotyped forms may in certain extreme circumstances—as we shall see—reduce the ritual of social interaction to mere *phatic* communication, or to a mere buttressing of status differentials, allowing ritual to take on only pragmatic or indexical functions and to lose its referential and semantic meanings. I discuss this development toward the end of this essay.

12. Of the peace-making ceremony, he wrote that the rite compels participants "to act as though they felt certain emotions, and therefore does, to some extent, produce these emotions in them" (1964: 241).

13. Skorupski (1976: ch. 6) is making the same point when he says that as "interaction code behavior" gets increasingly elaborated into "convention-dependent communication," socially shared and socially on record, "the allusion made to the original base of appropriate feeling may be increasingly indirect, increasingly mediated by a more indirect allusion" (pp. 90–91). Thus, as norms become ceremonialized, "what occupies the foreground is neither the feeling nor the expression of feeling, but the propriety of the expression of feeling" (p. 91).

14. Geertz in a well-known essay (1966) on religion as a cultural system also makes this Langerian point.

15. A good example is the *alus* (refined) etiquette as opposed to *kasar* (vulgar) manners, as recognized in Javanese culture and explicitly coded in Javanese popular theater (*ludruk*). See, for example, Peacock's *Rites of Modernization* (1968) and Geertz's *The Religion of Java* (1960).

16. My reference here is to H. P. Grice, "Meaning," in *Philosophical Review* (1957) and to subsequent modifications by Searle, Strawson, and others. According to this formulation, communication is essentially the expression of an attitude, such as a belief (in the case of statements) or a desire (in the case of requests). To express an attitude, one intends the recipient to regard what one is doing (for example, saying something) as reason to believe one has that attitude. Communication succeeds only if the recipient recognizes this intention, and genuine communication can take place only between beings who not only have intentions and beliefs but can have and recognize intentions of this complex sort. And this is possible only if each communicant is not only aware of the other's intentions but also aware that the other is aware of his own intentions, and so on.

17. If we still want to use the concept of "intentionality" we can say that a large part of the intentions of the actors as regards the purpose and results of the ritual are already *culturally defined, presupposed, and conventionalized*. Of course, there may be other personal intentions and purposes shared by the participants which may additionally motivate them to engage in a ritual, but these motivations do not affect the validity and performative efficacy of the rite per se. For example, the intention to get married implies the cultural requirement, say, of undergoing the marriage rite. The fact that the bride and groom want to get married in order to attain respectability is immaterial to the rite's validity and efficacy.

18. Searle's revisions of Austin are noteworthy: he rejects Austin's distinction between locutionary and illocutionary acts (preferring to embed the propositional features within the illocutionary acts), but accepts the Austinian notion of perlocutionary effects or consequences as being separate from the conventional efficacy of the illocutionary or performative act per se.

19. It is interesting that Malinowski asserted that Trobrianders distinguished between "the road of magic" (*megwa la keda*) and "the road of garden work" (*bagula la keda*), while also maintaining that gardening rituals and cultivation made up one totality.

20. Of course drastic changes in technology introduced in traditional societies by modernization and development programs may or may not affect the practice of the regulative rites. The evidence is uncertain and goes both ways; the same is true for the evidence on adaptive changes in ritual. See Milton Singer (1972) for rituals addressed to modern machinery by Indian factory workers; they are transposed from a previous traditional milieu of crafts and handicrafts.

21. In simpler terms, this implies many things for the communication engineer. The more alternative units or signs there are in a code that may occur in a message, the less likely is each unit to occur, and therefore the more information it will carry when it occurs; conversely the fewer the alternative units that can occur in a message, the more probable is the occurrence of each

unit, and the lower, therefore, is each unit's information content. In a message, the items that appear more frequently carry less information than those items that appear less frequently, and can also be more easily guessed at by the receiver if some of them are left out or distorted. For these reasons, those items which occur frequently in a message can be transmitted in a shorter time by economical use of symbols or digits of a code.

22. Also, if the communication system is made entirely free of redundancy, the information lost could prove to be irrecoverable.

23. The latter procedure is usually preferred because by the time the entire message is relayed and then repeated, there is the risk of the recipient losing sight of the first message, and because it is easier for the recipient to catch mistakes caused by unexpected interruptions if sections of a message are repeated in turn.

24. Bloch (1974) commits this mistake of conflating stereotypy in ritual with lack of propositional force. See my analyses of Trobriand and Azande magic (chapters 1 and 2) for examples of referential and analogical devices by which the performative transfer is made. An illuminating work on the various dimensions of metaphorical usage is Sapir and Crocker (1977).

25. In this connection, see the interpretation of John Lyons (1963). Starting with the proposition, closely related to information theory, that "meaning implies choice," Lyons asserts that any linguistic item whose occurrence in a given context is completely determined *has no meaning* in that context: "Having meaning, as the notion is here defined, is a matter of *how much* meaning items have in context . . . not what meaning they have." Insofar as Lyons is equating "meaning" with "information" in the technical sense, his is a narrow or limited conception of "meaning." Second, insofar as there are modes of meaning and functional uses of speech acts other than purely informational defined in terms of probability of occurrence, Lyons's "how much" criterion becomes irrelevant as a criterion for judging the meaning of those modes and uses. As a matter of fact, Lyons in this work advances two notions of meaning—one in terms of information theory (probability of occurrence in context) and the other in the structuralist sense of paradigmatic relations between units (Saussure's *valuer*). In this latter sense—which is Lyons's more important conception—he discusses synonymy, antonymy, hyponymy, incompatibility, and so on. It is clear that redundancey subject to the second kind of analysis will deliver meaning in terms of "patterns" of various kinds, which is outside the view of meaning treated in the informational sense.

26. What is stereotyped, predictable knowledge for the already initiated is *new information* for the initiates, for supposedly they hear it for the first time. In this context, ritual speech is informational for the initiates.

27. Restraint in cybernetic terms, says Bateson, consists of "factors which determine inequality of probability." Elsewhere he writes: "The essence and *raison d'être* of communication is the creation of redundancy, meaning, pattern, predictability, information, and/or the reduction of the random by restraint" (1972: 131–132). As Aram Yengoyan has commented (personal communication), Bateson does not explore the different implications of externally imposed restraints, and internal restraints in which the cosmological axioms set a range in which meaning can operate.

28. The authors state at one point: "The framework that we have provided

so far indicates that conversations to be studied will form a complex matrix of utterances, propositions and actions. The matrix shows two kinds of relations: the vertical relations between surface utterances and deeper actions, which are united by rules of interpretation and production; the horizontal relations of sequencing between actions and utterances, which are united by sequencing rules" (see Labov and Fanshel, 1977: 37).

29. The "great sentences" (*mahāvākaya*) of the Upanishads ("you are that" [brahman]) or the *koāns* of Zen Buddhism ("What is the sound of one hand clapping?") are held to be meaningful and capable of much interpretive commentary. On the other hand, many of the Tantric *mantras* are literally meaningless (though of course always open to symbolic interpretations), and their main function is as aids in meditation (Staal, 1975). On Zen formulas see Suzuki (1970).

30. In all the examples of mediumship and spirit possession I have seen, the entry into the trance or possession state is a "conventional" act of passage marked by enacting a culturally defined ritual sequence; but of course once a supranormal or dissociative state is reached, the medium or the patient can manifest convulsive behavior and talk in tongues. This behavior, which is the opposite of "normal" behavior, is also inflected by cultural expectations of how the invasion of the other world manifests itself in the human vessel.

31. I mean this section to be a tribute to the late M. J. Egan. Egan's Ph.D. dissertation, submitted to the University of Cambridge in 1970, is the most detailed and most meticulous documentation of a Sinhalese exorcism rite hitherto accomplished. Before his unfortunate death, he completed in 1975 a manuscript with the title *A Configurational Analysis of a Sinhalese Healing Ritual,* which is yet to be published. The ethnographic information for my analysis is largely taken from the dissertation. Some years ago Egan kindly gave me permission to make use of his data for whatever purposes I had in mind. I take responsibility for the analysis presented here.

32. The exorcist and his troupe are not only the creators of the demonic reality but also its means. The performers manipulate the media for expressive purposes while they themselves become the vehicles of the media and are possessed by them. The specialist (the *edura*) normally has a troupe of two assistants and a couple of drummers. At crucial stages various roles can be assigned to different actors; at the time the assistants represent the demons, the specialist impersonates the patient; and the same performer may change his roles throughout the ceremony (as, for example, when the specialist is the corpse in one sequence, and in the next one becomes the demon). The whole spectacular performance, from sunset of one day to dawn of the next, entrances and wears out both performers and spectators.

33. Except for certain distinctive sequences associated with particular demons, most Sinhalese exorcistic ceremonies of this region employ the same or similar sequences or subsequences and are recognizable as having similar syntagmatic strings. The rites may be lengthened or shortened by including or deleting or abbreviating certain sequences. The mode of putting together such lengthy performances is similar to that described by Peacock (1968) for Javanese folk plays.

34. The three watches are dramatically described in Kapferer (1977).

35. The structure and ordering is the same, though of course the origin myth recounted for each demon is different and the spells differently worded.

36. Habermas (1976), also building on the same ideas, talks of "the double structure of every speech act"—the illocutionary component supplemented by a propositional one. He notes, as does Searle, that the same propositional content can be held invariant over changing types of speech acts.

37. For one thing such a grouping of formal speech, song, dance, and (I would imagine) music under one rubric contradicts Bloch's initial methodological claim that while other interpreters of ritual language have used linguistic theory analogously, he was performing a direct linguistic analysis on ritual language. It is inconsistent, then, for Bloch to assimilate to his linguistic model, as if they were extensions of language, such modalities as song, dance, and material symbols by resorting to the same analogy condemned in others. See, for instance, the distinctions drawn between these art forms by Langer (1953). Bloch also fails to note the important point that in complex rituals there is a combined use of these modalities and media both concurrently and serially, and he fails to investigate how they act to produce a total effect.

38. In an overall sense, the difference between Bloch's perspective and mine lies in the "readings" we make of linguistic and information theory. In my view a maximum choice in linguistic expression, a wholly creative unpredictable natural speech, would produce such opacities and ambiguities as to lead to a virtual breakdown of communication.

A generative view of language holds only that an infinite number of utterances can be generated from base and transformational rules or that there are ascertainable rules by which surface forms relate to deep structures. The same creative freedom within constraints is the hallmark of dance, song, and music. Therefore what makes art possible at all is controlled modulations and combinations, the elaboration from rules, the creation of patterns.

39. Certain neo-Marxists and adaption ecologists use the epithet "mystification" too facilely as an excuse or coverup for either not seriously investigating or not comprehending ritual symbolism and ritual patterning; they merely see functional and utilitarian uses for ritual action.

40. Silverstein (1976) labels the same phenomena *referential indexes* in contrast to *nonreferential indexes*.

41. Jakobson (1971: 131–132) computed a four-fold typology of "duplex structures" by the interplay of message (M) and code (C) as vehicles of communication, and identified shifters or indexical symbols as a C/M duplex structure of an overlapping sort in that shifters "cannot be defined without reference to a message"; indeed, they have a "compulsory reference to the given message."

42. Grice separates conventional implicature from nonconventional implicature. In the former, the implication is *normally* carried by the proposition made. Both kinds of implicature require that certain contextual features be present and certain maxims be followed. Grice's examples of contextual features are the identity of the thing or person being talked about, the time of utterance, and the exact conventional meaning of the phrase in question on the particular occasion of utterance. He also proposes certain maxims that compose the "cooperative principle" which parties to talk-exchanges are expected

to observe. Nonconventional conversational implicature arises when a man by (in, when) saying something has *implicated* something, provided that he is presumed to be observing the cooperative principle in an overall sense (although he may be exploiting or violating particular maxims), that the implication is deemed by him as necessary to make his point, that he thinks the hearer can work out the implication. Grice emphasizes that a criterion of nonconventional implicature is that it must be capable of being "worked-out"; if it is grasped without further inferential work, it is a conventional implicature. Examples of nonconventional conversational implicatures are irony, meiosis, certain kinds of metaphor, hyperbole, ambiguity; in these examples there should be no room "for the idea that an implicature of this sort is *normally* carried by that proposition."

43. The implications of *paritta* recitation by monks, and of the rite of calling the *khwan*, are dealt with in many publications (see Tambiah, 1970).

44. Commoners (*phrai*) and nobility (*khun nang*) were of course differentiated socially, but not apparently for the rite in question.

45. Gerini gives the gloss that "Chulakantamangala . . . is the Pali form of the term, and the generic, and at the same time classic, name by which the tonsure ceremony is known in Siam" (1976: 22), but states that the vocabulary of actual usage was different.

46. To be precise: the eve of tonsure (*wan suk dip* = "half-ripe day") and the day of the tonsure itself.

47. In the early period of the Chakkri dynasty, it was clear that a council of ministers and princes with *krom* (administrative) titles actually chose the new king, though it was agreed that under normal circumstances the eldest son by a senior queen would be the first choice. But as is well known, Mongkut's accession was passed over on behalf of a less eligible half-brother when Rama III died, because Mongkut was too young and his brother was experienced in administration. Mongkut later succeeded his brother.

48. King Mongkut set a similar precedent with regard to the Swing Ceremony: he personally attended the ceremony and added a Buddhist sequence to it, but did not personally play the role of Shiva (see Wales, 1931).

49. It is not surprising, then, that King Chulalongkorn did not bother to appoint a successor to the *Uparat*—the resident of the Front Palace (*Wang Na*) and usually referred to as "second king" in translations—when the incumbent died during the king's reign.

Wales gives the following description of Prince Vajiravudh's tonsure rite: "The King, dressed in full state; wearing the Great Crown of Victory, and holding in his hand the Sword of Victory, impersonated Siva, and . . . ascended to his palace on the top of Kailasa. [Two celestial assistants] led [the prince] up the mountain by the Western approach to where, at the top of the stairs, Siva was waiting. *The latter presented him to the public*, who offered homage, and the two then proceeded to the central pavilion on the top of the hill. There the prince amid the congratulations of all present, received from the King's hand a jewelled coronet larger than the one he had formerly worn and other insignias of high station" (1931: 130, emphasis added). See also Gerini (1976: 88) for details of the king's presenting "the tonsurate to the public who offered homage," and of the proceedings at the central pavilion on the hill's summit:

"Then the prince, amid the congratulations of all present, received from the King's hands the jewelled coronet and other insignia of high station."

50. In the brief essay on an American prayer group speaking in tongues, Catherine Bateson says that what are usually taken to be separate segments and vocalizations (such as prayers, prophecies, speaking in tongues, and conversational commentaries) were, from the point of view of the participants, fused into larger single events, which in turn made up the evening as a single event. What is lacking in this interesting essay is a *demonstration* of the processes by which fusion and intensity of experience are created.

51. C. Bateson writes: "When words are set to music, spoken in unison or both danced and sung, only the high-level boundaries are likely to match perfectly, and therefore the structure is only fully intelligible at the highest levels with lower-level segmentation destroyed" (1974: 161).

52. Jakobson (1960: 358) offered this memorable definition of the "poetic function" which is one of the various functions embedded in speech acts, and which is the dominant function of "verbal art": "The poetic function projects the principle of equivalence from the axis of selection to the axis of combination": in poetry "similarity is superimposed on contiguity and equivalence becomes the constitutive device of the sequence—syllables are equalized, prosodic features are matched, word stress and unstress balanced, and various other phonemic effects and verse structures exploited."

5. *Animals Are Good to Think and Good to Prohibit*

1. Phya Anuman Rajadhon (1958) confirms this interpretation. He describes the role of the cat in "the ceremony for preparing the bridal bed" and in other rites such as "the assumption of the Royal Residence" and "house warming." Among other things, the cat signifies coolness, permanence, and fertility.

2. *Tua* is also a classifier for some inanimate objects, such as tables, chairs, trousers, and coats, and it could perhaps be argued that this usage represents an extension from the primary meaning to things that have characteristics analogous to those of living beings—for example, arms and legs. However, *tua* is also a classifier for such other things as numeral digits and letters of the alphabet, and to these the same logic cannot be applied. The classifier for people in general is *khon*, but there are certain exceptions where differences in status or rank are involved. Thus, the classifier for royal personages and monks is *ong*, and degraded noun usages for human beings—for example, *man* (an inferior person)—have the classifier *tua*, indicating clearly that such a term reduces them to animal status.

3. Examples of *maeng* are: *maeng saab* (cockroach), *maeng mum* (black spider), *maeng pueng* (honeybee), *maeng thau* or *thaan* (wasp), *maeng mot* (ant, further differentiated into red, white, and black ants), *maeng wan* (fly, housefly), *maeng haw* (louse), *maeng yung* (mosquito), *maeng ngam* (crab), *maeng phii sya* or *ka bya* (butterfly), *maeng bong kue* (millipede), and *maeng kee kep* (centipede). The grasshopper (*tak taen*), which is edible, interestingly does not take the prefix *maeng*. In general, *maeng* may be said to comprise insects and a few aquatic invertebrates, of which a good example is the

crab. The crab, which is eminently edible, has another appellation, *puu naa,* which virtually removes it from the class *maeng,* most but not all of whose members are inedible.

4. Examples of *nog* are: *nog kaew* (parrot), *nog caug* (sparrow), *nog khiilab* (pigeon), *nog yaang* (crane), *nog khaukaag* (stork), *nog khaw* (dove), *nog kiano* (flamingo), *nog huug* or *nog khaw maew* (owl). The class *nog* may be said to consist of all feathered bipeds with the exception of domesticated fowl, their wild counterparts, and those whose names have the prefix *ii*—for example, crow (*ii kaa*) and vulture (*ii haeng*). Most but not all *nog* are edible.

5. Central Thai vocabulary, as used in the northeastern villages, has an elaborate set of words for describing special features of the members of the *sad* class. Haas (1964) and McFarland (1944), for example, list such usages as *sad kinnom* (mammal), *sad kinnya* (carnivore), *sad lyajkhlaan* (reptile), *sad saungthaaw* (biped), and *sad siithaaw* (quadruped). It is possible that many of these expressions are not traditional but have been devised in recent times under the influence of Western biological concepts. The subdivisions of *sad* that I list, also given in the dictionaries, are the important operative ones in Phraan Muan village as well as the major classes traditional to Thailand: *sad nam* (water animals), *sad bog* (land animals), *sad baan* (domesticated animals), and *sad paa* (forest animals). In any case, the welter of intermediate distinctions, which are largely absent for *nog* and *maeng,* indicate a focus on *sad* as the animals of greatest interest to the Thai.

6. Examples of water animals are: *plaa* (fish, subdivided into various species), *gung* (shrimp), *haui* (oyster), *kop, kiad,* and *huag* (kinds of frogs), *puu naa* (field crab), *lan* (eel), *taw* (tortoise or turtle), *kee* (crocodile), *naag* (otter), *ping* (water leech). Most are *sad naam,* but the crocodile, otter, and water leech are exceptions.

7. This was pointed out to me by Brent Berlin in a personal communication.

8. Mary Haas (1964) elucidates the following usages of the prefix *ii,* presumably in central Thailand. 1) It is a bound element in names of birds and animals—for example, crow, barking deer, vulture, palm civet, oyster, and swallow. 2) It is a derogatory title used with the first names of women; formerly used for female slaves, it is now applied as an insult to women criminals and prostitutes. (As an exclamation, *ii* expresses dislike, revulsion, and aversion.) 3) It is also apparently a colloquial term freely used in reference to objects and persons, regardless of sex and without special connotation.

The use of the prefixes *ai* and *ii* in northern Thailand is the subject of an interesting analysis by Wijewardene (1968). Some of the points he makes have relevance for my theme. *Ii* is used as a prefix for a number of animals which are intermediate between (foolish) domestic and (wise) remote wild forest animals—for example, the monkey, gibbon, squirrel, iguana, and civet cat. *Ai* and *ii* are legitimate terms of address for younger relatives (male and female respectively) and younger members of Ego's circle of familiar social relations. The terms are insulting if used outside this field, for they imply low social status. One of the puzzles probed by Wijewardene is why parents are addressed as *ii-pau* and *ii-mae.* Finally, the prefixes *ai* and *ii* appear as strong terms of abuse in conjunction with dog and monkey (*ai-maa* or *ii-maa; ai-wauk* or *ii-wauk*).

It is perhaps premature to generalize for Thailand as a whole because there appear to be regional and local variations in linguistic usage. In Phraan Muan village the prefix *ii* is used, as far as I know, only in conjunction with the vulture and crow. It appears to be used more widely for animals in northern Thailand, but it is interesting that the majority of animals listed by Wijewardene and Haas are also "intermediate" or "anomalous" animals in the northeast. It is in central Thailand that the prefix has the widest range of application, which apparently includes a number of birds. It is not a distortion to say that there, too, the prefix, when used in relation to human beings, implies abuse, insult, low social status, and also understandably familiarity between equals. It is possible that the logic by which the prefix is used for some animals and birds may be similar to the one I have expounded.

6. *From Varna to Caste through Mixed Unions*

1. These analytically separate procedures can be and sometimes are combined to produce classifications. The key technique can produce a hierarchical arrangement, and hierarchical schemes such as the Linnaean may in turn exploit the key form as a result of applying multiple differentia at different levels to generate new classes.

2. Conklin goes on to say about the key: "The selection and arrangement of dichotomous exclusions may result in a branching structure resembling a taxonomy, but the geometrical similarity is illusory" (1964: 40). The other methods of classification Conklin identifies are *index* (which in its simplest form is a sequence of entities arranged in accordance with one arbitrary dimension such as an alphabetical order (for example, a dictionary or a telephone directory), *paradigm*, and *typology* (both of which are multidimensional forms of arrangement by class intersection and cannot be transformed into taxonomy, as is largely the case with key, but which show internal differences in the manner in which they partition "attribute space"). Overall, Conklin agrees with Simpson in admitting that the basic contrast is between type as *taxon* or kind and type as *attribute combination.*

3. Consider these examples: "Dirt is the by-product of a systematic ordering and classification of matter, in so far as ordering involves rejecting inappropriate elements" (1966: 35); "an anomaly is an element which does not fit a given set of series" (p. 37); "any given system of classification must give rise to anomalies" (p. 39). And at one point in her exposition she exclaims: "Surely now it would be difficult to maintain that 'Be ye Holy' means no more than 'Be ye separate.' " When Mary Douglas does deal with the "union of opposites which is a source of power for good" (p. 119) she has in mind *exceptional* phenomena such as the pangolin's acting as a mediator for the Lele (p. 170) and similar cases.

4. Mary Douglas manages to make a good deal of sense of the food taboos by showing that there is an underlying three-fold division of creatures into those that belong to the Earth, Water, and Firmament. The "normal" members of the Earth category are four-legged animals which hop, jump, or walk; of

the Water are those with fins and scales. Thus, creatures which mix the attributes of the major classes are taboo—for example, four-footed creatures which fly; also taboo are creatures which are imperfect members of their class, such as animals with two "legs" and "hands" which crawl, and animals which creep, crawl, or swarm or adopt a mode of propulsion not proper to any particular element (eels, worms, reptiles). What Douglas entirely misses is that the Leviticus rules derive the edible animals of the earth—the most important class—by a key-type derivation. The rules posit two initial classes: animals that chew the cud and animals that have cloven hooves. The edible animals are those which have both features (such as the ox, sheep, and goat); the inedible animals are animals that chew the cud but do not have cloven hooves (camel, hare) and animals that have cloven hooves but do not chew the cud (swine).

5. Leach's theory of taboo is based on two propositions. First, the environment (which is a continuum) is perceived "as composed of separate things by suppressing our recognition of the nonthings which fill the interstices" (1964: 37). Second, these interstitial things are "the ambiguous categories that attract the maximum interest and the most intense feelings of taboo. The general theory is that taboo applies to categories which are anomalous with respect to clearcut category oppositions" (p. 39).

6. The Indian classification of *varna* and castes as embodied in Manu (and other writers) shows a combination of procedures of both *hierarchy* and *key* forms (see Figure 6.1).

7. Dumont does not, however, ignore the theory of "mixed castes" in the classical texts. He says that the texts "described in terms of *varna* what must surely have been at that time a caste system in embryo" (1970: 71). Pointing out that "the word *jati* does occur, but it is generally confused with *varna* . . . and, according to Kane, the emphasis is on birth rather than function," Dumont sees an additional inadequacy in the classical account in that no fifth *varna* is allowed for. Nevertheless, Dumont makes a comment which I shall take up in detail here: "The normative Hindu texts mostly present the groups [despised castes and inferior occupations] they name as if they were products of crossing between *varnas* . . . It is generally admitted that this theory was used to refer real *jati* to the *varnas*" (p. 71).

8. Kane (1941: vol. 2, pt. 2, ch. 2) has a full and authoritative account of the differences in interpretations, the contradictions, and the inconsistencies. See also Bühler's introduction to *The Laws of Manu* (1886).

9. As I previously mentioned, in this scheme the groups generated are recognizable as primarily castes (*jati*) and occupational groups, and less frequently as tribes and ethnic groups. The juxaposition of castes and occupations is understandable, since the distinctive features of many low-level castes are their occupations.

10. Note that what is under discussion here is union between a superior male and an inferior female.

11. Referring to the lack of unanimity among the sages as to the progeny of such unions, Kane says that they expressed three different views: "The first view is that if a male of one *varna* married a female of the *varna* immediately after it, the progeny belonged to the *varna* of the father" (for example, Baudhayana I,8,6, and I,9,3; also Narada, Kautiliya, and Anusasanaparva). "The second view is that the progeny of *anuloma* unions is in status lower than the

father, but higher than the mother" (for example, Manu X, 6). "The third view (and this is the common view) is that the progeny . . . is of the same *varna* as regards its privileges and obligations as the mother's" (for example, Visnu, Mitaksara commentary on Yajnavalkya and Aparaka). Kane misinterprets Manu, for he fails to consider Manu X, 14.

12. The greatest dishonor is naturally attached to the union of a Brahman with a Shudra female. Vasishtha, for example, describes the condition of the son thus born—the Parasava—as "that of one who living is as impure as a corpse" (XVIII, 9,10).

13. According to Vasishtha, the son by a Brahman wife shall receive three shares; by a Kshatriya wife, two shares and the "other sons shall inherit equal shares" (presumably one each).

14. Similar principles of caste mobility are propounded by other shastric writers such as Gautama and Yajnavalkya. The differences in interpretation relate to the number of generations to be counted before increment or loss of status is achieved. See Kane, 1941: 62ff.

15. The process of downward mobility is the inverse of that represented in Figure 6.2 (left)—for example, a Brahman uniting with a Shudra female produces a Parasava son, and if he and his male descendants unite repeatedly with Shudra females, the male descendant of the seventh generation (counting from the first Brahman ancestor) is judged a fallen Shudra.

16. The names of the issue from these unions differ in some cases in Vasishtha, whose list in corresponding order is Suta, Ramaka, Pulkasa, Antyavasayin, Vaina, and Kandala.

17. See the same page for other calculations.

18. The Antyavasayin is the perfect example of the fusion of two symmetrically reversed, despised unions between Brahman and Sudra. No wonder the Antyavasayins are described as being despised even by those already excluded from the Aryan community.

19. The most frequent appearance is by the Shudra *varna*, since it is the most available, especially for *anuloma*-type unions.

20. Berreman (1963), for instance, notes how in the sub-Himalayan Pahari villages he studied, low castes claimed respectable ancestors and explained the decline of their caste status in terms of unfortunate circumstances. He writes: "Atkinson notes that in Kumaon 'the Doms like all the others, claim an exalted origin and say that they are the descendants of a Brahman named Gorakhnath and were turned out of caste for eating forbidden food' . . . The blacksmiths and Bajgis of Sirkanda lay claim to relatively recent but unrecognized Rajput and Brahmin ancestry, respectively" (p. 222). Similarly, he cites Cohn as reporting that the Chamars of Senapur trace their ancestry to Rajputs or Brahmins.

21. Orenstein in his 1968 essay classifies pollution rules into 1) *relational pollution* (in 1965 called intransitive pollution) and 2) *act pollution* (previously labeled transitive pollution), which again he subdivides into *internal pollution* and *external pollution*. In the 1970 essay he deals with *self-pollution* as a subcategory of external pollution.

I find these labels misleading because in my framework all these forms of pollution are "relational"—that is, they all imply contact between persons and things. Orenstein fails to undertand fully the underlying design of the rules because he does not place them against the framework of *varna* and caste hierarchy and interrelations as the classical writers saw them—for example, the direct and inverse order of castes and the principles of dominance and compounded degradation they imply.

Furthermore, Orenstein has missed seeing the linkage between the base categories of *varna* and the derived *jati* categories as part of the thought structure of the law codes, as is attested by these words: "The Dharmashastras speak both of caste and of *varna,* more frequently of the latter. The rules, however, are applied in the same way to both. As our concern is with ways of thinking, not the definition of social groups, we may ignore the difference."

Orenstein clearly sees the important fact that the *shastric* writers, although they vary in details and although their treatment of subjects is not identical, yet legislated in accordance with a shared set of principles. But he fails to use the discrepancies to advantage: these contradictions and differences in interpretation and emphasis may be indicators of ambiguities inevitably generated by systems of classification.

22. This answers a question that puzzles Orenstein: Why are the theorists less interested in "clean" women (those not in a condition of self-pollution) having contacts with lower castes, and only concerned with women already self-polluted?

23. Marriott aptly stated in an unpublished essay: "What unifies Indian transactional thought is assumption as to 1) the divisible or particulate nature of substance and 2) the constant circulation of divisible substance and 3) the inevitable transformation of substance by mixtures and separations."

24. I document below the privileges in the realm of occupations granted by Manu to the *varna* according to the principle of the direct order of *varna* (see Appendix 1).

25. *Hypergamy* is not a Hindu but an anthropological concept. The *dharmashastras* speak only of *anuloma* and *pratiloma,* of "direct" and "inverse" order of castes, whose implications are as I have described them.

7. The Galactic Polity in Southeast Asia

1. The cosmological scheme contains three *lokas:* the *kama loka* (world of sense and form), the *rupa loka* (world of form), and the *arupa loka* (world of no sense and no form). In this context I am primarily referring to the *kama loka,* which is divided into eleven levels—six inhabited by gods (including the second heaven of Indra, and the fourth Tusita heaven which is the abode of the next Buddha, Maitreya), and the remaining five divided among the four lower worlds of men, animals, *asuras* (demons), and ghosts (*preta*), and the last world which consists of various abominable hells.

2. See Griswold (1967: 33–34) for inscriptional evidence of the *muang* that had broken away before Lu Thai's ascension and returned to his suzerainty between 1347 and 1357.

3. For instance, see Wenk's description (1968: 29) of the administrative arrangements prevailing in the southern province of Phattalung at a much later time, at the beginning of the Bangkok era. The traditional divisions (*krom*) of the capital's administration into the treasury (*khlang*), city (*muang*), palace (*wang*), and fields (*na*) were reproduced in the province.

4. The same point is cogently argued for Ayutthaya and early Bangkok by Rabibhadana (1969: 16). It is clear that similar considerations applied in traditional Java, where control of populations was more important than control of territory, and rulers also attempted wholesale deportations of prisoners (Anderson, in Holt, 1970: 30).

5. This discrepancy was partly, at least, an accident of the economic activities, especially tin mining, of Western and Chinese entrepreneurs. These activities made chiefs in whose territory the mines were located wealthier than others.

6. Clive Kessler (personal communication) informs me that in comparison with the Western Malay Sultanates, those on the east coast were even more weakly centralized and larger in scale. He has kindly made available to me chapter 2 of his dissertation (1974), in which he states: "The basic riverine state did not fail to emerge in Kelantan, but it developed in the midst of an expanding area of independent districts and chiefdoms" (p. 47); "Prior to the nineteenth century Kelantan constituted a mosaic of coastal baronies and principalities arranged about a politically turbulent core" (p. 51).

7. With regard to the light Weber may throw on the understanding of the "galactic polity," Weber's presentation has two inadequacies. First, he was curiously "unmusical" toward the cosmological and ritual aspects of the galactic polity; second, he envisaged "patrimonial domination" as grounded in the ruler's control of land on which he settled dependents or which he distributed to them. To cite his own words: "Patrimonial domination is thus a special case of patriarchal domination—domestic authority decentralized through assignment of land and sometimes of equipment to the sons of the house or other dependents" (1968: 1011). The nuclear idea that patrimonial domination is the "patriarchal household" writ large, or that it was basically realized in a manoral-type system, does not correspond to the politico-economic facts of the traditional polity in Thailand (and elsewhere), in which it is the leader's control over men (that is, a leader surrounded by his followers) and not his control over land per se that is the nuclear cell.

8. Patrimonial domination historically adopted two strategies. In the first instance, the king's own agents, and officials directly dependent on him—the *ministeriales*—managed to exercise administrative power both at the center and in the provinces. This was achieved in Egypt and China and in the Ottoman Empire (via the famous Janissaries). In the second instance, the local landed interests and the gentry—the *honoratiores*—were coopted through compromise and concessions, and made to serve the interests of the ruling power. Cases in point were the nobility of Tsarist Russia, and the gentry of seventeenth- and eighteenth-century England (who were made justices of the peace).

9. Schrieke defined the "state" as a type of political organization "in which the state prevents the disruption of component parts of the kingdom and makes the local notables more effective in its service" (1955: 173). Wertheim (in Soetajatmoko, 1965: 346–347) compares this description to Weber's "Patrimonial bureaucratic state."

10. Regarding Java of the later Mataram period, scholars have distinguished between "appanage" (*lungguh*) and "salary field" (*bengkok* or *tjatu*). An appanage has been defined as an assigned region where one has the

right to gain from the land and from the inhabitants a profit, from which the king himself can draw a portion, but which gives no rights over the land itself. Taxes, fees, services, and incomes from domains are examples of the profit accruing. A "salary field," by contrast, is a piece of arable land that is part of the lands of the king and is assigned to an official, kinsman, or favored person. It is tilled by levy-service to the benefit of the person granted (Moertono, 1968: 117).

11. Wenk (1968: 34–35) gives an account of taxes collected and the distribution of income in the early Bangkok period that provides additional supporting evidence for our thesis.

12. In my view, Polanyi's concept of "redistribution" as operating in such traditional "centric" polities tends to be applied indiscriminately. In the polities that I am discussing, redistribution of the consumable-agricultural surplus extracted appears less sumptuous and elaborate than is commonly assumed.

13. For example, Wolters says this of the maritime empire of Srivijaya, based in southeastern Sumatra: "Srivijaya, sometimes in control of territory on the Malay peninsula, has been ascribed a career from the seventh to the fourteenth century, spanning much of the history of Asian maritime trade and responsible in no small measure for its expansion by providing efficient harbour facilities for merchants making the long voyage between Middle East and China" (1967: 1).

14. Perhaps the most historic of the Malay Sultanates, the Malacca Sultanate, was a compact centralized polity which lived on the foreign trade of its port; it perhaps approaches Polanyi's conception of "the port of trade" which mediated between service- and agriculture-based kingdoms. Gullick leaves us in no doubt as to the importance of tin mining for the maintenance of the Malay polities in the nineteenth century: "Malay chiefs taxed tin mines in various ways and thus diverted into their own hands from a fifth to a third of the value of the output. Revenue from tin was the mainstay of the Malay political system" (1958: 6).

15. The possible contribution of central-place theory to my subject can be fully treated only in a separate paper. The theory is primarily concerned with the principles that order the distribution and hierarchy of cities and towns in their role as service centers; it is a theory of location of tertiary activity. It is not this major aspect of the theory, but another that was relatively marginal to it—namely, the system of central places according to the sociopolitical principle (rather than according to the marketing and traffic principles)—that is germane to my discussion of the traditional Southeast Asian kingdoms. For example, Christaller's application of the "separation principle" based on political and administrative considerations produces a distinct system of central places reminiscent of my galactic pattern: "The ideal of such a spatial community has the nucleus as the capital (a central place of higher rank), around it, a wreath of satellite places of lesser importance, and toward the edge of the region a thinning population density" (1966: 77). While we may remark on the convergence of design at a general level, we can truthfully say that Christaller's fragmentary discussion of the pattern deduced from sociopolitical and administrative considerations neither profitably adds to or subtracts from my fuller

account of the galactic polity as it is inflected by several factors—cosmological, territorial, administrative, and political. It, however, helps support my view that in a comprehensive understanding of the galactic polity, what we customarily see as political and administrative orientations and considerations cannot be ignored.

16.   A comparison with Ayutthaya, an inland capital but built on the main river artery of Chaophraya, is interesting. In Ayutthaya (as well as in early Bangkok), trade with foreigners was conducted via royal monopolies (controlled directly in the king's interest or farmed out to ruling princes and nobles), and there was an important administrative division called the *Khlang* which administered the coastal ports in the gulf, supervised overseas trade, and collected the revenue accruing from it.

17.   In other words, as in Ayutthaya, the central royal domain is the area of direct control, the outer provinces being satellites enjoying varying degrees of autonomy.

18.   "The grand-vizier Gajah Mada, the mediator (of wealth) was considered as chthonic in opposition to the Royal Family" (Pigeaud, 1962: vol. 4, p. 54).

8.   *On Flying Witches and Flying Canoes*

1.   Although Annette Weiner (1976) mentions that men, too, can be considered to be witches, it is clear that witches are predominantly—indeed, almost always—female.

2.   *Contra* Annette Weiner (1976), I prefer to see women's wealth as associated with female "sexuality," particularly the colored skirts (festively worn by young women) and the banana leaf bundles out of which skirts are made. The plain natural-colored skirts worn on soot-blackened bodies in the mourning period appropriately signal the depression of sex during that time. So it is appropriate that women's wealth is distributed to the mourners, thus releasing them from further affinal ties and obligations of mourning and restoring them to an active sexual life.

3.   This is one of the concerns of many Trobriand myths—for example, the myths which relate to Kudayuri, Kasabwaybwayreta, Tokosikuna, and Tudava.

4.   For Malinowski, *tama* was in Trobriand terms "husband of my mother" (1932: 6); he was "not regarded as of the same bodily substance" but nevertheless stood in a "close emotional, legal, and economic relation to the child" (1932: 518). Lounsbury's componential analysis (1965) of Trobriand terms gives "father" in the genealogical sense as the "primary meaning" of *tama*.

E. Leach, in line with Malinowski, glosses *tama* as "a domiciled male of my father's sub-clan hamlet" (1958). It is interesting that despite distorting Malinowski at the very beginning of his analysis, Lounsbury makes this sociological assertion as stemming from his linguistic analysis: "What emerges in the Trobriand case is the clear priority of the husband-wife solidarity unit over that between brother and brother, or between sister and sister, or between mother's brother and sister's son."

5. I refer here to that description of the flying witch as a woman who leaves her bed by shedding her grass skirt and taking to the air, and the correlated belief that the way to frustrate her is to cover her pubes with her grass skirt.

6. Insofar as the crab is described as flying through the air and dropping down, it is being assimilated to the description of a malevolent flying witch, or, more accurately, of a *baloma*-like underground creature who then has the extraordinary power to fly as well, like a flying witch.

7. Malinowski was not very consistent in his accounts of the relationship between *yoyova* and *mulukwausi*, though variant accounts never resulted in flat contradictions. In one place, for instance (1922: 236), he gave the following gloss: The most dreaded danger for the Trobrianders on an expedition was "the flying witches, the *yoyova* or *mulukwausi*. The former name means a woman endowed with such powers, whereas *mulukwausi* describes the second self of the woman, as it flies disembodied through the air." Moreover, in moments of great fear, "the deprecating euphemism '*vivila*' (woman) would be used"—for fear of attracting the flying witches by sounding their real name.

Although the canonical account says that the *mulukwausi* sends a double, Malinowski reports that there are other beliefs which state that the flying witch sometimes "travels bodily," and sometimes takes the shape of black night-birds and other creatures.

8. I mean, for example, that the first canoe to touch shore is that of the *toliuvalaku*, who receives his ceremonial gift from the partner; thereafter the other canoes can transact with their partners, the *toliwaga* having precedence over his crew.

9. Rain magic is *dala* property and is not competitively practiced so as to ruin others; and one of the bases of chiefship is that a chief practices rain magic on everyone's behalf. In contrast, canoe magic (as opposed to *kula mwasila* magic, which is public property and widely accessible), though also *dala* property, can be competitively practiced to outdistance or undo a rival.

10. This is a reference to the actual path traveled by the two younger Kudayuri sisters when they transformed themselves into flying witches.

11. Malinowski's exegesis of this portion of the spell can be improved, by referring to his own ethnography documented in *Argonauts* (1922: 150–151) on human decoration. The natives decorate themselves with large red hibiscus blossoms stuck in their hair and "wreaths of the white, wonderfully scented *butia* flowers crowned the dense black mops." The canoe is described similarly as wearing wreaths of seaweed when it is beached.

In both the *ligogu* and *wayugo* spells the canoe is told to "break through seaweeds, put on wreath and make bed in sand." The erotic uses of the *butia* wreath are documented in *Sexual Life of Savages* (1932: 254–255). The *butia kayasa* ("competitive activity") occurs at the flowering of the *butia* tree which coincides with the *milamala* festival; this occasion evokes erotic activities and provides opportunities for courtship (1932: 255). Interestingly, *butia* wreaths are exchanged ceremonially with the blowing of conch shells and these exchanges are called *kula;* indeed, Malinowski reports that the terminology of *kula* is used in these exchanges. Here, definitely, *kula* exchange between male partners is brought into juxtaposition with courtship and erotic exchange among male and female youth, and the same attribute of beauty and irresistibility is transferred to the *kula* canoe.

12. The following allusions will, I think, help us further understand the symbolism of washing the canoe.

First, the washing of the canoe reminds us of the importance of body washing and rubbing with leaves in the sea when performing love magic (1932: 365n), or in freshwater when performing beauty magic (1932: 351n); also to be remembered is the final beautification of the *kula* sailors by washing in seawater with leaves (*silasila*) and by painting themselves at the final halt before meeting their partners (1922: 335). These associations convey the idea that the canoe is being "beautified" by washing.

Second, we are reminded of the rites of birth. A newborn baby is bathed regularly in warm (fresh) water, with which the mother also washes her own skin, in order to "keep the skin of the mother and child white." And, most interestingly, a witch is believed to wash its newborn child *in seawater,* and then to show it to other witches. Thus, these associations convey the idea that the canoe is also viewed as being a "newborn infant" and is washed in seawater just as a witch washes her infant, and is ceremonially presented to the relevant community.

13. There is a discrepancy here: according to the myth itself she turned into a stone (1922: 315), but in this exegesis Malinowski gives the variant report (1922: 138) that she settled down and transmitted the magic to her descendants.

14. Though the myth states that the flying witches were turned to stone, we know that flying witches are believed to exist in the present, and that witches transmit their potency to their daughters on a hereditary basis. Hence the conclusion that the male canoe magic is an attempt to convey to their canoes attributes which they believe are possessed by females.

9. The Theater State in Southeast Asia

1. In an at times alarming oscillation between particularistic modesty and generalizing ambition, Geertz has this to say about Bali's special features which push it out of alignment with other Southeast Asian polities: "The scale of the Balinese states crowded into the narrow southern piedmont . . . was almost certainly always smaller than those of somewhat more spacious Java, with obvious effects on their organization. Further, the island's natural orientation toward the south and the treacherous Indian Ocean rather than toward the north and the tranquil Java Sea caused it to be almost wholly marginal to the elaborate international trade economy which played so crucial a role in the Indic-period economy generally. The superb drainage pattern in Bali, and its climate—perhaps the most ideal for traditional *sawah* cultivation in all of Indonesia—made irrigation both less technically problematic and less seasonally uncertain than almost everywhere in Java" (1980: 8).

There is a lack of fit in scale and organization between, say, Thai and Burmese kingdoms of the sixteenth to early nineteenth centuries and Bali in the nineteenth century in the following features. The major Thai and Burmese kingdoms were much larger in territory. They participated in a lively network of foreign trade extending from East Africa via India and Ceylon to the Far East. As Geertz remarks elsewhere, confirming my earlier point, Bali "in large part . . . looked away from this trade. It faced south toward the Indian Ocean, where, given poor harbors and rough seas, there was hardly any traffic, rather than north toward the Java Sea, the Asian Mediterranean around which Chinese, Indian, Arabic, Javanese, Buginese, Malay, and European merchants shuttled like so many itinerant street peddlers" (1980: 87–88).

While the Balinese ruler leased trading rights to Chinese trade lords (*subandar*) who operated in their trade realms (*kebandaran*), the Thai rulers of the Bangkok period (and even earlier in Ayutthaya) had more elaborate systems of "administered trade"—officials ran departments (*krom*) which administered maritime trade, collected dues, and even acted as sole monopolies for the sale of certain local goods to foreign merchants. Moreover, rulers sought to control the import of guns and of certain luxury goods: the first ensured that the royal troops centered in the capital were well armed, and the second, redistributed down toward courtiers and officials, served as rewards of office and as prestige goods.

Another important difference between Bali on the one hand and the Buddhist kingdoms of Burma, Thailand, Laos (and Cambodia of later times) on the other was the existence in the latter of the *sangha* (monastic communities and the order of monks as a whole) in an ideologically recognized and institutionally structured complementary relationship with the ruler and his state. In Burma, Thailand, and Laos the Brahmans were not a stratum in the population at large, as in Bali, but were court functionaries performing the cosmic rites of states, while the *sangha* and ruler constituted the major paired components. The Balinese realms on the one hand lacked the counterpart of the Buddhist *sangha*, and on the other showed a more salient and structured Brahmana-ruler complementarity.

It is possible that another comparativist might reject the Geertzian project on the grounds that the Balinese realms and the polities of mainland Southeast Asia (and even of Java and Sumatra as instanced by Majapahit) were in scale and structure too dissimilar. I, however, feel that the differences in territorial and administrative scale are less important than the fact of certain shared basic similarities. I therefore accept Geertz's project and will engage with him on his chosen ground.

2. I developed the Austinian notion of performative acts with regard to the explication of ritual in Chapters 2 and 4.

3. Again we are told on p. 134 that "because the actual control over men and resources (the political center of gravity, so to speak) sat very low in the system, and because concrete attachments were multiple, fragile, overlapping and personal, a complex and changeful system of alliances and oppositions emerged as the lords tried to immobilize their immediate upward rivals (make them dependent) and maintain the support of their immediate downward ones (keep them deferential)."

4. However, Geertz may mislead by interpreting the rhetorical claims of universal monarchs over lesser rulers as being "pronouncements of overlordship" that were "total in their claims" (1980: 125).

5.   Like those of Bali, Thai and Burmese royal circles and ruling strata engaged in polygyny and observed much the same rules regarding the ranking of queens, wives, and concubines, and their children, and regarding the decline in status of these children every generation. According to Thai rules, the fifth-generation descendants of a blue-blooded prince (*chaofa*) became commoners.

6.   For example, see the *Mahaparinibbana Sutta.* Of course, the *Jataka* stories recount the chain of rebirths of the Buddha, frequently in the status of king.

7.   The Tibetan notion of the reincarnation of the Dalai Lama, and the procedures for "discovering" the new Dalai Lama born to an unknown family after the death of the previous one, illustrate this point. Also noteworthy is the belief that a "great man" (*mahapurusha*) can be recognized at his birth by various markings on his body.

8.   "It is in the *ukiran,* even more than the [royal] core-line temple, that the *sekti* of the *puri,* its truth-imaging mimetic force, is concentrated" (1980: 114).

9.   See *Dalada Sirita* (Pandita Valvitiye Sorata Edition, 1955). This is a fourteenth-century prose work dealing with the history of the tooth relic, including its travels. The classic description of the cult is *The Temple of the Tooth in Kandy: Memoirs of the Archaeological Survey of Ceylon* (Hocart, 1931). By far the most comprehensive and illuminating study of the cult of the tooth relic in past and contemporary times is *Rituals of the Kandyan State* (Seneviratne, 1978).

10.   For a detailed analysis of the myths of origin, the travels, and the religio-political significance of the Sinhala Buddha, see Tambiah, 1982. For the chronicle about the image, see Notton, 1933b.

11.   The chronicles are the *Amarakatabuddharupinidana* (see Notton, 1933a) and the *Jinakalamali* (see Jayawickrama, 1968). Both chronicles were composed in the sixteenth century, the *Jinakalamali* preceding the other.

12.   Rama III, who ruled in the first half of the nineteenth century, introduced a third royal outfit for the dry season, to be in conformity with the idea of three seasons.

13.   The oscillation in the existence of the Emerald Buddha between renunciation and rulership is further attested by the fact that the *Vessantara Jataka,* called in Thailand the *Mahachad* (Great Story), is recited at the end of the rains retreat, actually at the time of the changing of the Emerald Buddha's clothes from a monk's robes to the full regalia of kingship. The *Vessantara Jataka* itself relates that the Buddha, as king in his life immediately before the penultimate one, gave away his raingiving elephant and children, was banished to the forest, and was finally restored to full and prosperous kingship.

14.   I mean by this that succession according to some strict rule of lineal or genealogical counting—say, from older brother to younger brother, or father to oldest/youngest son—did not occur over any length of time. In fact, the king's multiple queens and concubines, and the claims of collateral branches even in the face of sinking status (which, too, obtained in Thailand), ensured rivalrous claims, which the court officials maneuvered to adjudicate in the context of factional politics. Moreover, especially in times of near collapse of

existing regimes (which happened quite a few times in the destructive warfare between Pagan and Ayutthaya), entirely new and charismatic generals and usurpers made their moves.

15.   As stated earlier, the priest-king relationship in Bali is in itself interesting to analyze in relation to other Southeast Asian examples—and all of them, in turn, in relation to the initial classical Indian conception. I shall not undertake such an analysis here.

16.   In Sri Lanka the monks assisted the king in the past, and are the chief officiants of the cult today.

17.   Those allowed to attend the rite are not barred from describing the proceedings to others.

18.   This is reminiscent of the fact that in the cult of Jagannath staged at Orissa, the king is both the god's principal "servant" (who sweeps the chariot in which the god is taken in procession) and a lesser "incarnation" of the deity (see Marglin, 1981).

Conclusion

1.   The following is not the rhetoric of a revolutionary but of a master of the field: "[Anthropology] is the outcome of an historical process, which has made the larger part of mankind subservient to the other . . . Anthropology is the daughter to this era of violence. Its capacity to assess more objectively the facts pertaining to the human condition reflects, on the epistemological level, a state of affairs in which one part of mankind treats the other as an object" (Lévi-Strauss, 1964).

2.   The concepts, aspirations, and perplexities of these scholars of modernization are embodied in Geertz (1963).

3.   At Harvard, for instance, the Department of Anthropology has begun to design M.A. programs that will enable candidates to specialize in the fields of medical anthropology, anthropology of development, and legal anthropology—fields that have clearly both practical and social relevance in the "real world" outside campus limits.

4.   See Bailyn (1982) for a discussion of these and other historical works of this genre; also Gottmann (1980) and Venturi (1972).

5.   Nash (1981), whose essay I came upon after I had completed this address, mentions Parry (1963) and Williams (1944) as some precursors of Wallerstein who discussed the operation of the world system in the sixteenth century.

6.   There are internal disputes between Gundar Frank (and his followers) and Samir Amin (1976), who proposes the second thesis. A work that has caught the eye of Southeast Asian scholars—James C. Scott's *The Moral Economy of the Peasant* (1976)—combines a Wallersteinian approach with an alleged "phenomenological" account of the morality of landlord-tenant, patron-client relations as seen from the subsistence-oriented peasants' point of view. For a critique of this book, see Michael Adas (1980, 1981). For a counterthesis, see Samuel Popkin (1979).

7.   See Meillassoux (1981) for his thesis on how the precapitalist sector continually produces and reproduces cheap labor for the capitalist sector; in-

deed, he claims, imperialism is a "means of reproducing cheap labour power."

8.   Although I am primarily concerned with anthropological contributions here, I should mention as supporting literature Eugene F. Irschick (1982). Irschick, a historian of South India, influenced by anthropological contributions, documents how certain dominant agrarian groups (the Vellala *mirāsidars*) successfully battled against the revenue demands of the British colonial government on two fronts: by mobilizing their low-caste farm servants for withdrawal from agricultural activities and for violent contest, and by exploiting their connections with their literate representatives (the *dubashes*) in the Company's employ who were aware of British administrative vulnerabilities. Irschick documents how the local groups effectively manipulated the British perceptions of Indian society to their own advantage.

9.   This protectionist and cushioning role may well be appropriate for small tribal groups on the point of being wiped out and robbed of their lands by rapacious developers from the dominant community. But these are certainly not the typical contact situations in the world at large today.

June Nash (1981) mentions certain works that accord with the views I am expressing. For example, Trimberger (1979) objects to treating the periphery as a passive victim universally giving way to the capitalist invasion, and counters that although precapitalist relations of production may be subordinated and distorted by the impact of capitalism, they too have their own dynamic which has an impact on capitalist development and may serve as the base for the genesis of resistance to capitalism. See also the views expressed by Grillo (1980) regarding the complex interactions between centers and peripheries in Europe—interactions that cannot be reduced to simple unilateral schemes in which centers economically dominate and swallow peripheries.

10.   These views are discussed in Crapanzano (1980) and Clifford (1982).

11.   It is also pertinent to remark that Crapanzano alternates his lively encounters and dialogues with Tuhami with "objective" accounts of Moroccan rites, institutions, and customs in the usual ethnographic mode. This shows that an ethnography solely in terms of negotiated encounters might not be self-sufficient, and that an anthropologist with a long and deep familiarity with another society could write worthwhile "objective" accounts in an impersonal mode.

12.   A number of measures have been devised over the years to remedy the inequities of one-way traffic. Besides training local scientists as counterparts, local museums and documentation centers have been established where copies of recordings, field notes, and films are deposited and where the finds from archaeological digs are stored, with arrangements for loans to foreign scholars.

13.   Steven Lukes (1973) offers relevant information on Durkheim's position on this matter. The French defeat in the Franco-Prussian War caused in Durkheim a desire to contribute to the regeneration of France. He appreciated Renouvier, one of his teachers at the Ecole Normale Supérieure, for his uncompromising rationalism, his central concern with morality, and his determination to study it scientifically. As Davy put it, Durkheim aspired to see sociology as the "philosophy which would contribute to giving the Republic a basis and inspiring in it rational reforms while giving the nation a principle of

order and a moral doctrine" (Lukes, 1973: 46). Durkheim's concern with the centrality of morality is manifest in *The Theory and Practice of Education.*

While he of course appreciated the expressive and moral role of traditional religion and its indispensability, Durkheim had aspired to substitute for it in modern France some kind of secular religion of humanity based on science and reason. In the cognitive sphere, at least, scientific thought was a more perfect form of religious thought, and sociology was its successor. Secular religion should be subject to the criticism and control of science. Durkheim's optimism contrasts with Max Weber's more sober and pessimistic assessment of the possibility of an objective rationality of values that can be distilled from positive science.

14. An insightful, though chilling, discussion of such medical excesses is provided by William A. Silverman (1980). Dr. Silverman provides case studies of medical disasters such as the following. a) Retrolental fibroplasia (RLF) literally means "scar tissue behind the lens of the eye." In the forties and early fifties, an epidemic of RLF blindness, especially in prematurely born infants, rose to alarming proportions in the Western world, particularly in the United States. This was probably associated with the unregulated oversupply of oxygen through "airlocks" and other devices into incubators in which prematurely born infants were placed. Another associated abuse was the injection of nebulized detergent mist into incubators for the relief of respiratory difficulties in infants. b) Antibacterial drugs, especially the sulfonamide drugs, were widely administered to babies, which resulted in high mortality due to the onset of the "gray syndrome" (distension of the abdomen, vomiting, and other complications such as the entry into the brain of yellow pigment, bilirubin, released in the blood of jaundiced infants).

15. If the blind belief in the efficacy of biomedical doings and gadgets is rife in the West, it is an even more malignant curse in Third World countries, where pharmaceutical companies dump drugs that have expired or are banned in the West, local dispensaries peddle them unrestrained by any regulation, and the man in the street ingests them, preferably through injections, irrespective of the appropriateness for the ailment in question. The locals, however, say that although these drugs act quickly, they do not ensure long-term health and peace of mind.

16. See Stephen Jay Gould, "Sociobiology, Goodbye" (1983). Gould bemoans the current valuation that is obstructive to the open-ended potentialist direction suited to the social sciences: "A hierarchy of sciences runs from hard to soft, quantitative to qualitative, firm to squishy, from physics through biology to the loose domain of social sciences. Any time we can jack an explanation up from the realm of a soft science to a harder one, this is intrinsically a good thing. Genetics really is better than history as a scientific explanation" (p. 8).

17. Examples are Case Western Reserve, the University of California at San Francisco, the University of California at Los Angeles, Michigan State University, the University of Connecticut, Southern Methodist University, and Harvard University.

Sources

The introduction appears for the first time in this volume. Sources for the other chapters are as follows:

Chapter 1. Originally published in *Man* 3, no. 2 (1968): 175–208. Reprinted by permission of the Royal Anthropological Institute of Great Britain and Ireland.

Chapter 2. Originally published in *Modes of Thought*, ed. Robin Horton and Ruth Finnegan (London: Faber and Faber, 1973), pp. 199–229. Reprinted by permission of Faber and Faber Ltd.

Chapter 3. Originally published as "The Cosmological and Performative Significance of a Thai Cult of Healing through Meditation," in *Culture, Medicine and Psychiatry* 1 (1977): 97–132. Copyright © by D. Reidel Publishing Company, Dordrecht, Holland.

Chapter 4. Originally published in *Proceedings of the British Academy, 1979* 65 (1981): 113–169. Reprinted by permission of the British Academy.

Chapter 5. Originally published in *Ethnology* 8, no. 4 (1969): 423–459. Copyright © 1969 Stanley J. Tambiah.

Chapter 6. Originally published in *The Character of Kinship*, ed. Jack Goody (Cambridge: Cambridge University Press, 1973), pp. 191–229. Reprinted by permission of Cambridge University Press.

Chapter 7. Originally published as "The Galactic Polity: The Structure of Traditional Kingdoms in Southeast Asia," in *Anthropology and the Climate of Opinion*, ed. Stanley Freed (New York: New York Academy of Sciences, 1977), pp. 69–97. Reprinted by permission of the New York Academy of Sciences.

Chapter 8. Originally published in *New Perspectives on the Kula*, ed. Edmund Leach and Jerry Leach (Cambridge: Cambridge University Press, 1983), pp. 171–200. Reprinted by permission of Cambridge University Press.

Chapter 9. Originally presented, in shorter form, as an address at the Thirty-first International Congress of the Human Sciences in Asia and North Africa, held at Tokyo and Kyoto in 1983.

Conclusion. Originally presented as a keynote address at the Third Decennial Conference of the Association of Social Anthropologists, held in Cambridge, England, in 1983.

Index